Also by Hiroko Shimbo

The Japanese Kitchen

The Sushi Experience

The Sushi Experience

HIROKO SHIMBO

PHOTOGRAPHS BY JIM SMITH

Alfred A. Knopf　New York　2006

THIS IS A BORZOI BOOK PUBLISHED BY ALFRED A. KNOPF

Published in the United States by Alfred A. Knopf, New York, and in Canada by
Random House of Canada Limited, Toronto.

www.aaknopf.com

Knopf, Borzoi Books, and the colophon are registered trademarks of Random House, Inc.

Photographs by Jim Smith

Library of Congress Cataloging-in-Publication Data
Shimbo, Hiroko.
The sushi experience / Hiroko Shimbo.
p. cm.
Includes bibliographical references and index.
ISBN 1-4000-4208-9
1. Cookery (Fish)   2. Sushi.   I. Title.
TX747.S528 2006
641.6'92—dc22   2006041028

Manufactured in Singapore

FIRST EDITION

To all sushi lovers

Contents

Acknowledgments

My wish to research all aspects of the sushi story compelled me to travel to many parts of Japan and the United States. During my investigations, I was privileged to meet with so many professionals—chefs, food and equipment producers, fishermen, fishmongers, distributors, and professors—who all contributed their precious time and enormous knowledge to this book.

My deepest thanks go to those both in Japan and the U.S. who shared with me their knowledge of the fascinating history and culture of sushi: Shingo and Ayako Nakajima, Noritoshi Kanai, Michael Cardenas, Nobu Matsuhisa, Minoru Yokoshima, Kikuzo Shiraishi, Makoto Fukue, Takafumi Shiroi, Yosuke Imada, and Professors Henry Smith and Kiyoshi Asahina.

For details about food products and equipment that are essential to the sushi kitchen I am grateful to Tatsu Yamasaki, Junro Aoki, Kenjiro Doi, Yukinori Oda, Yui Yamamoto, Toshiyuki Kiuchi, Noboru Kubo, Hiroyuki Yamanashi, Yoshihiko Shiratori, Chris Pearce, Keiko Sato, Noboru Ogata, Guy Gomes, and Robin Kohda. Special thanks to Ryoichi Matsushita of the Mizkan company, who donated a historical company-owned woodblock illustration (page 62).

The fresh, wholesome, and delicious seafood used for sushi is the responsibility of a special community. Those who helped me in this area are Nozue Makoto, Seiji Nojiri, Masahiro Nakata, Yoshimori Tomei, Masamitsu Furuta, Glenn Sakata, Nobu Ishida, and Hidehiko Fukura.

My greatest respect and thanks go to sushi chefs both in Japan and the U.S., from whom I received information and guidance. I am particularly grateful for the unstinting assistance of Koji Sekiya, Hiroaki Sasaki, Hiroshi Tajima, Hiroshi Shima, Hideo Kuribara, Ken Tominaga, Noboru Kubo, Zhong Zhen Seki, Noboru and Tokio Endo, Shigenori Tanaka, and Andrew Semler.

My heartfelt thanks to Suehiko Shimizu, the devoted and charming sushi instructor who, during a period of intensive work, taught me not only the techniques of sushi making, but the true meaning of sushi. His lucid and precise instructions became the basis of the information on fish and *nigiri-zushi* preparation in this book. I extend the same gratitude to Linda Ziedrich, who assisted me by polishing my stories.

This extensive work could not have been assembled without Judith Jones, my editor. Her enormous interest in the subject, professionalism, and deep insight helped make this book what it is. Judith's support was invaluable.

I thank my publisher, Alfred A. Knopf, for their confidence and their attentive professional support in all areas in producing *The Sushi Experience*. Their recognition of the value of this book is very gratifying to me. Special thanks to Iris Weinstein for the design of the book, and to Ken Schneider, Judith's assistant.

My agent, Janis Donnaud, from our first meeting expressed her deep understanding and confidence in my project and found the best home, Alfred A. Knopf, for the book.

The skills of Jim Smith, photographer, and his assistant, Ryan Basten, bring this book to life. Jim's artistic and appealing shots of prepared dishes add many colors to the book and help readers to understand and appreciate that the visual aspects of sushi are as important as the flavors.

Special thanks go to my young friend Odessa Ernst; my stepson, David Beitchman; my sister, Keiko Arakawa; and my nephew, Takahiro Arakawa, for their contributions.

And finally, I thank and acknowledge two people who are very important in my life. I owe so much to my mother, a wonderful woman who has taught and inspired me since my youngest days. I am in New York and she is in Tokyo, but whenever there is a question or something I don't understand, she is always there to help. My great love and heartfelt thanks to Buzz, my husband, who wears many hats as a husband, a best friend, a charming lover, and an unpaid in-house editor—and all he asks in return is delicious meals each day. It is my great pleasure to honor his request.

Certainly this book is a child of all these many fine people.

Introduction

Sushi:
A Star to Stay

Food trends come and go. Few suddenly fashionable foods survive long in a world of fickle tastes. Sushi, though, is so healthy, delicious, attractive, and adaptable that its popularity only continues to expand. Sushi restaurants have mushroomed in cities all over the United States and around the world. Supermarkets as well as gourmet shops sell ready-made sushi in plastic containers. High-end restaurants have added sushi to formerly all-Western menus, and some of these establishments have even built in sushi bars and hired sushi chefs. At the beginning of the twenty-first century, sushi is no longer exclusively Japanese. Rather, it is an established element of world cuisine.

How this international favorite was born and grew up in Japan and became adopted in America is a fascinating story that reflects the shrinking world in which we live. So I'll start by telling you this story. Then, in chapters 2 and 3, we'll explore the world of sushi restaurants. Throughout the rest of the book, you'll learn all about making and enjoying sushi at home.

The Sushi Bar: A Unique
Dining Experience

When I was growing up in Japan, eating at our neighborhood sushi restaurant was a rare, awe-inspiring treat. To walk into the impeccably clean restaurant was like entering a shrine. After my family was seated at a table, my attention was always drawn to the sushi bar nearby. Seated in front of the polished wood counter was a coterie of elderly regulars, nearly always all men, eating piece after piece of sushi while drinking glasses of beer or small cups of *sake.* Behind the bar, a man in a crisp, clean white chef's jacket moved swiftly and deliberately. He listened attentively to a cascade of orders from the diners all along the counter. Although he seemed to concentrate intensely as he prepared the sushi, from time to time he exchanged light-hearted conversation with his customers, about the seasonal fish before him, about politics, or about the arts. He delivered the beautiful sushi calmly and confidently, with a small bow to each customer. From a child's point of view, his finesse seemed miraculous. I longed for the day when I could sit in front of such a fabulous chef and eat sushi as only adults did.

Later I learned that the job of the sushi chef was even more complicated than I'd imagined. He had to remember the preferences of each of his regulars—lightly cured fish for one, oily fish for another. He had to prepare every order according to particular specifications, spoken or remembered.

When you eat in a sushi restaurant, you are the guest and the audience, and the chef is the host and the performer. The sushi meal is a collaboration between you and your host, especially when you sit at the counter. Just as a waiter can make or break your evening at the finest French restaurant, your communication with the sushi chef can make the difference between a dull or a wonderful experience. Sushi dining, though, is more about rapport than service. Talking with the chef guarantees you'll get sushi you like and a meal that's much more fun. In chapter 3, I'll tell all you need to know to uphold your end of the sushi bar experience.

From Tools to Dolls

It is important that you have the right basic equipment for sushi making, so before you begin, consult chapter 6, which explains everything you need, from a wooden rice tub to proper knives and how to maintain them. I want sushi to become part of your everyday kitchen, and you'll find many dishes such as tossed sushi that can be put together for an easy meal. I encourage you to get your family involved, too: put together a good sushi lunch box to take to school or the office or make sushi dolls with the children in your life (see pages 155 and 158).

Sushi Seafood: Absolutely Fresh

It may come as a surprise to you that sushi isn't always made with raw seafood. There is a world of sushi beyond raw fish, and you'll find many recipes here that call for preserved or cooked fish as well as various vegetables for fillings. In part 5, I have also included more than fifty recipes for dishes to accompany your sushi.

Preparing sushi is a lot like putting together a sandwich and not much more difficult. But if you want to use raw fish or shellfish, you'll need to know how to shop for it—which species to look for in which season and how to judge freshness. You'll need to know how to store your fresh seafood safely and how to prepare it in ways that best capture the flavor and texture of each variety. In chapter 10, you'll learn when fish for sushi should be frozen before use, and whether fish sold at an ordinary fishmonger's may be safe to use raw. Once you understand the necessary precautions for handling raw seafood, you'll be able to enjoy all kinds of sushi without concern for your health.

In chapter 11, you will find step-by-step instructions for how to prepare and expertly slice the most commonly used fish and shellfish for your sushi or *sashimi,* as well as some more exotic seasonal varieties now being flown in from Japanese waters. These instructions are geared both for home cooks who are now ready to take the next step and put into practice all they have learned and for professional chefs who may welcome a refresher course or would benefit from trying a different sushi teacher's techniques.

Sushi: A Child of the World

Before I began my research for this book, my ideas about sushi were traditional and rather rigid. I focused on classical *nigiri-zushi,* a well-behaved culinary princess whom I associated with formal Japanese manners and refinement. But when this princess traveled to America, she did as I did: she entered the embrace of a new, easygoing culture. Transforming herself into a robust but charming commoner, she appeared as the now ubiquitous California roll and eventually as an almost-anything roll.

But just as any cultural revolution is apt to spark a countertrend, American diners are now turning from liberated sushi to more traditional types. So in this book, I'll introduce you to the sushi princess in all her guises, from modern and playful to very refined and Japanese.

Throughout I have also tried to give you a view of the inside world of sushi by introducing you to people who make up that world: a producer of ancient sushi, a knife maker, fish wholesalers and distributors, a tea grower, a *nori* maker, a *wasabi* farmer, a *sake* brewer, restaurant owners, and above all, some of the dedicated sushi chefs of Japan and America. Through their voices, you will get the inside story of sushi.

I hope that now you will be inspired to try sushi in all her varied forms and to adopt this culinary child as your own.

Part One
The World of Sushi

Chapter 1
The History of Sushi

Ancient Sushi

The tale of sushi begins centuries ago. Sushi originated not from a desire for novelty but from economic need—the need to preserve fish, an important source of protein. The first sushi—freshwater fish salted and pickled in fermenting rice—originated not in Japan but in the rice-growing region of northern Southeast Asia, where the method is still used. That primordial sushi making soon spread to China but disappeared there during the thirteenth century, when the Mongolian nomads who subjugated the country introduced a very different food culture. Before the Chinese abandoned this method of fish pickling, though, their frequent contact with the Japanese brought the practice to my country. No one can say with certainty when sushi crossed the Sea of Japan, but the earliest written references to it appeared in the eighth century AD. Over subsequent centuries, this ancient form of sushi evolved into today's world-famous sushi cuisine.

In ancient times, the most common way to preserve fish was to salt it, and this method is still used throughout much of the world. But fish that is salted and dried gets hard as a board, such as bacalao, the salt cod of Europe and America. Using rice as well as salt in hot, humid areas of Asia created a product markedly different in flavor, aroma, and texture. The cooked rice fermented, producing lactic acid, which both aided preservation and imparted a pleasant sharp, tart flavor. (Some scholars believe that the word *sushi* comes from an older Japanese word meaning "tart" or "acid.") At the same time, the plump, moist rice grains kept the fish tender and moist.

But there were drawbacks to this early preservation method. The pickling took at least a year, and when the process was through, the rice was too pasty to eat. It was wiped off the fish and thrown away. This wasted the always valuable rice crop.

Primitive sushi making is still practiced in some rural areas of Japan. In Shiga Prefecture, *funa-zushi* is made from local *funa,* freshwater carp, which is pickled in rice and salt for a year. Proud locals enjoy watching the reactions of outsiders who taste this delicacy for the first time. Most tourists—and I mean Japanese tourists, not foreigners—are so repelled by the smell of *funa-zushi* that they shun it without taking a bite.

I find that owners of *funa-zushi* souvenir shops, who sell gift-wrapped boxes of the delicacy to curious out-of-towners, like to exchange stories about their experiences. Some have received angry phone calls from customers: "The sushi was spoiled when I opened it; I had to throw it away! Send me back my money."

Locals lament that the world doesn't appreciate the strong smell and distinctive taste of *funa-zushi,* which they compare to mature Roquefort cheese. One 8-inch *funa-zushi,* however, can cost eighty dollars, much more than a generous slice of Roquefort cheese. Alas, these die-hard traditionalists are unlikely to succeed in bringing *funa-zushi* to the world.

The Evolution of Sushi

By the fourteenth century, sushi began to change. Although agricultural improvements had greatly increased Japanese rice production, rice was still an expensive food, and the Japanese had come to believe that it shouldn't be wasted in preserving fish. So a new sushi evolved, *nama nare-zushi,* or short-pickled sushi. With the shorter fermentation time, the fish grew only mildly tart, and because the rice didn't disintegrate, it was good to eat along with the fish.

By the seventeenth century, the Japanese were producing rice vinegar, and this new product inspired the development of an even faster sushi. Rice vinegar and *sake,* rice wine, now served as preserving agents in place of lactic-acid fermentation. By the nineteenth century, *haya-zushi,* quick sushi, had nearly replaced the ancient, slow method of preserving fish in fermenting rice.

But soon even *haya-zushi* was found too slow. It was the beginning of the mercantile age in Japan, and busy artisans and merchants needed a fast lunch; travelers wanted a tasty snack. Inevitably a quickly produced item such as *oshi-zushi,* pressed sushi, would become the vogue. It was called *hako-zushi,* boxed sushi, because of the way it was made. Vinegar-flavored rice was laid in a round or square wooden mold about one foot across. Sliced fish was laid over the rice, and a lid that fit inside the mold was pressed on top of the fish and rice. The mold was removed, the sushi was cut into bite-sized pieces, and presto—there was the world's first fast food. As boxed sushi became popular, eggs and vegetables joined fish as toppings for the rice. In the Kansai region around Osaka and Kyoto, this sushi is still popular today.

But in Edo—the city now known as Tokyo—even boxed sushi was soon considered too slow. With more than a million residents, Edo was Japan's political and business center and the capital of the powerful Tokugawa shogunate, whose regimes spanned the interval from 1600 to 1868. During this feudal era, when Japan was closed to nearly all foreign trade and influence, the domestic economy flourished, peace reigned, and Japanese culture and arts, including the culinary arts, reached their zenith.

Imagine that you had a sushi stand in Edo, then the largest city in the world. You would have served *nigiri-zushi* or even invented it. You would have cooked the rice, tossed it with salt and *sake* lee vinegar (page 25), and waited for a customer to approach. Upon receiving his order, you would have formed a small rice ball in your hand, carefully laid a slice of fish on top, and immediately

(continued on page 7)

The Craft of *Funa-zushi*

I learned about *funa-zushi* in the town of Katata, on the shore of beautiful Lake Biwa in Shiga Prefecture, where the Nakajima family has been preserving fish in this ancient style since the beginning of the eighteenth century.

Shingo Nakajima and his wife, Ayako, are the sole workers in this family business. Each February, local fishermen deliver to the Nakajimas live locally caught carp, *nigoro-buna.* The Nakajimas use only female carp, because the eggs add texture, flavor, and color to the pickled fish. After slaughtering and cleaning the fish, the Nakajimas layer the fish, with their egg sacs intact, with salt in barrels. In May, they remove the carp from the barrels and clean each fish well with cold water and a hard brush. It is this laborious, time-consuming cleaning, according to Mr. Nakajima, that makes their *funa-zushi* the best in Japan. The Nakajimas then arrange the cleaned fish in bamboo baskets and place the baskets on a stone floor outdoors for drying. For a day, the fish glisten in the early summer sun like platinum ornaments.

Early the next morning, Mrs. Nakajima cooks rice and tosses it with salt. She scoops the rice into shallow, square wooden boxes, where it cools for three hours. Her husband, meanwhile, sets out well-used but very clean wooden pickling barrels, each about 20 inches across and 22 inches high. Made of pine staves bound by knitted bamboo ropes, the barrels are almost one hundred years old. Worn staves are replaced from time to time, but Mr. Nakajima has no intention of ordering new barrels. The old ones are the breeding ground for the bacteria that have for so many years produced the region's best-tasting *funa-zushi.*

When the barrels are ready, Mrs. Nakajima packs the cooled cooked rice into the

mouths and stomachs of the dried fish. It took her many years, she says, to learn to do this without damaging the egg sacs. She then layers the stuffed fish with more rice in the barrels. When the barrels are full,

with thirty to fifty fish each, the rice is topped with the husks of bamboo shoots and a wooden lid. The final operation requires enormous strength: Mr. Nakajima has to heave two 100-pound boulders onto the top of each barrel.

As I watched him do this, Mrs. Nakajima whispered a story to me. "In the heat of summer, when the fermentation is at its peak, the trapped carbon dioxide sometimes pushes off a lid. There is a small explosion, and then the crash of the boulders as they hit the floor. When he hears that noise, even in the dead of night, my husband jumps from his bed and runs to the barrels to put back the stones."

Mr. Nakajima overheard. "The rebellious nature of the fermentation," he said, "is very amusing to me. It's the part of *funa-zushi* production that I cherish the most."

During the hot, humid summer, the bacteria produce abundant lactic acid. The pH of the brew drops to 4.0. This strong acidity ensures the quality—fragrance, texture, and flavor—of the *funa-zushi* as well as its safety. Harmful bacteria cannot survive in this environment. After fifteen months of patience and anticipation, the pickled carp are ready to be eaten.

I tasted *funa-zushi* for the first time in my life in the Nakajimas' pickling house. With a razor-sharp knife, Mrs. Nakajima cut the pickled fish very thin and laid a few slices, along with the bright orange roe, beside some of the snow-white pickled rice on a small plate. The arrangement looked beautiful, and without bending my head to the plate, I smelled an aroma both tart and sweet. With one bite of the *funa-zushi,* a sharp, yogurtlike flavor exploded in my mouth, and it was instantly mellowed by the rich, sweet flavor of the pickled eggs. The eggs reminded me of bottarga, the preserved roe of Mediterranean countries.

Relieved at my obvious pleasure, Mrs. Nakajima made me a *funa-zushi* soup. In a lacquerware bowl, she placed a teaspoon of pickled rice and three slices of the fish. She added a few drops of *shoyu* (soy sauce) and some boiling water and covered the bowl. A minute or two later, the fish oil had turned the water to a savory broth, and the slightly cooked fish and eggs were more tender and mild. As I happily sipped the soup, the Nakajimas told me about Shingo's father, Jiro, who has been drinking *funa-zushi* soup all his life and at ninety-two remains very fit. By this time, I was convinced that *funa-zushi* could become a world-famous sushi in its own right. But perhaps it wouldn't be to everyone's taste!

Actually, *funa-zushi* production has an

uncertain future, as Mr. Nakajima explained. Because of pollution and the introduction of a foreign bass ten years ago, the native carp, *nigoro-buna,* is declining in numbers and may soon face extinction. Other *funa-zushi* producers have begun using cultured carp or other species, as well as plastic barrels and shortcut production methods.

It's pointless to try to maintain the *funa-zushi* tradition using fake ingredients and modified methods, Mr. Nakajima told me. "As long as *nigoro-buna* is available, we will continue to make the best *funa-zushi*." He doesn't know whether the family business will last beyond his lifetime, though. The Nakajimas' two sons live in other prefectures, and Mr. Nakajima is not pressing them to keep up the family tradition. "They will decide what they want to do."

(continued from page 4)

handed the ball to the impatient customer standing in front of you. No pressing in a box, no cutting, no waiting. Such a morsel was *nigiri-zushi,* the ultimate fast food. It was an instant success, and its popularity was contagious. Sushi stands, sushi caterers, and sushi restaurants sprang up like mushrooms on every corner of this busy city. The demand for sushi grew so great and the sellers so greedy that the embarrassed shogun government arrested two hundred sushi chefs for drastically overcharging their customers.

In those early days, *nigiri-zushi* was always topped with cooked or cured fish or shellfish, such as *kohada* (gizzard shad), *maguro* (tuna), *aji* (horse mackerel), *miru-gai* (gaper clam), *anago* (conger eel), *awabi* (abalone), *kuruma-ebi* (*kuruma* prawn), or *ika* (squid). The use of raw fish, the essence of today's sushi, began only after World War II, when the development of high-speed transportation and modern refrigeration and freezing equipment made it possible to transport and store raw fish safely.

Early *nigiri-zushi* was different from today's in another way: it was almost three times as large. There is a curious bit of history behind the shrinking of sushi. At the end of World War II, Japan faced a severe rice shortage. The American occupational forces set up a rice-rationing system and decreed that all sushi restaurants must close. Kataro Kurata, a well-known chef at Sushi-ei (a restaurant still operating in the Ginza district of Tokyo), appealed to the staff at general headquarters: "Sushi plays as important a role in Japan's culinary culture," he said, "as the sandwich does in America's." When the appeal reached the highest levels, sushi restaurants were allowed to reopen—on the condition that the chefs use only rationed rice brought in by their customers. And so a standard was set: each cup of raw rice made ten pieces of sushi, including seven *nigiri-zushi* and three pieces of a traditional thin roll. Although a few heretical restaurants are now supersizing sushi to satisfy the American craving for larger food portions, the postwar prescription is still nearly universally followed. General of the Army Douglas MacArthur himself may have set the size of modern sushi.

More Sushi!

In the nineteenth century, other kinds of sushi developed: thick and thin rolls (*maki-zushi* and *nori-maki*), stuffed tofu pockets (*inari-zushi*), and sushi rice served in a bowl (*chirashi-zushi*).

Nori-maki *and* Maki-zushi. Both the thin sushi roll, *nori-maki* (*nori* roll), and the thick roll, *maki-zushi* (sushi roll), first appeared late in the Edo period. The thin roll arose in Edo (now Tokyo) and the thick roll in the Kansai region (Osaka and Kyoto prefectures). Both rolls are made with *nori,* a sea vegetable known as laver in England and Wales. In Japan, *nori* is harvested from bays, formed into thin, dark green sheets by a process similar to papermaking, and dried. For *nori-maki* and *maki-zushi, nori* is rolled around sushi rice and a filling, and then the roll is sliced into white rounds with a green perimeter and colorful center. Both thin and thick sushi rolls are frequently prepared at home as lunch box fare.

The Kansai thick roll, *futo-maki,* uses a whole sheet of *nori* plus an added quarter-sheet for strength; traditional fillings include simmered *kanpyo* gourd, *shiitake* mushrooms, omelet, and sweet fish flakes. Today's thick rolls may have other ingredients, such as raw fish and *tempura* shrimp.

The Tokyo thin roll, *hoso-maki,* uses only a half sheet of *nori,* and in the early days, *kanpyo* gourd was the only filling used. Today's thin rolls come in many varieties, including *kappa-maki* (with cucumber), *tekka-maki* (with tuna), and *oshinko-maki* (with pickled *daikon*).

Inari-zushi. This sushi arose near the end of the Edo period as an inexpensive vegetarian snack. Thin sheets of tofu were deep-fried, simmered in a sweet broth, slit open to form a bag, and then packed with a mixture of sushi rice, cooked *kanpyo* gourd, and *kikurage* (tree fungus). *Inari-zushi* was peddled not at *nigiri-zushi* stands, which occupied the busiest street corners, but at plain stands set up on quiet streets at dusk and marked by flags bearing the image of a fox. In Japanese folk religion, foxes are the mediators between the people and the god of the harvest, *o-inari-san,* who ensures good business. Foxes were believed to love *abura-age* (fried tofu), which forms the bag that holds the sushi rice. So *inari-zushi* was a favorite food of all foxes. (How did foxes come to love fried tofu? Please don't ask.)

Modern *inari-zushi* is a little bigger than a matchbox but still only a third to a fourth as large as the old version, which was cut into pieces and eaten with *shoyu* (soy sauce) laced with *wasabi.* Today *inari-zushi* is often prepared by home cooks for lunch or snacks.

Chirashi-zushi. Another invention of the late Edo period, this sushi is the easiest to make. The word *chirashi,* meaning "to scatter" or "to sprinkle," describes the way to make this delightful dish. It requires no special ingredients, just sushi rice and whatever colorful, delicious additions you have on hand.

There are two basic styles of *chirashi-zushi.* The first is said to have originated in boxed sushi. The story goes like this: A customer went to a stand and ordered boxed sushi. The vendor asked the customer to wait while he removed the sushi from the mold and cut it into bite-sized pieces. Impatient, the customer asked the vendor to stir the sushi in the mold, spoon it out, and serve it immediately.

Today this style of *chirashi-zushi* is made by tossing sushi rice with many chopped or sliced ingredients—*nori*, cooked vegetables such as *shiitake* mushrooms or *kikurage* (tree fungus), seasonal herbs, and julienned omelet. Extra bits of omelet or other ingredients are scattered over the top as a garnish.

Edo-mae chirashi-zushi is the Edo, or Tokyo, version of the dish. Instead of tossing the sushi rice with other ingredients, the Edo sushi maker would pack the rice into an individual serving bowl

and decorate the top with bits of fish or shellfish, usually cured or cooked. After World War II, the use of raw fish became widespread in this dish.

Today both styles of *chirashi-zushi* remain very popular in Japan, where home cooks make them frequently. Since this sushi is so easy to prepare and so adaptable, it is a natural for American home cooks, too.

Today's Sushi in Japan

After conveyor-belt restaurants made sushi dining affordable to ordinary people, sushi entrepreneurs found other ways to cut costs. They formed franchises to improve purchasing power. They hired corporate managers, who used company manuals to train young employees in the least labor-intensive ways to produce reasonably good sushi. They brought inexpensive sushi to an even larger public, and in so doing, they threatened the long tradition of owner-operated restaurants staffed by chefs who have completed fifteen-year apprenticeships.

The new sushi chains even threatened *kaiten-sushi* operators, who reacted by throwing off the "cheap sushi" image and upgrading their operations with chic, modern interiors. *Kaiten-zushi* restaurants brought better-trained chefs back to the sushi bar, so that customers willing to pay more could have freshly made sushi to order and could watch as the chef prepared it. Half-*kaiten,* half-traditional sushi restaurants are popular in Japan today.

Disappearing in Japan, however, is the moderately priced sushi restaurant that catered to neighborhood people

Sushi Styles in Brief

Funa-zushi	Carp fermented in rice
Oshi-zushi, or *hako-zushi*	Sushi pressed in a box
Nigiri-zushi	Rice ball topped with (usually raw) seafood
Maki-zushi, or *futo-maki*	Kansai-style thick sushi roll
Nori-maki, or *hoso-maki*	Tokyo-style thin sushi roll
Inari-zushi	Fried tofu pocket stuffed with sushi rice
Chirashi-zushi	Sushi rice tossed with other ingredients in a bowl
Edo-mae chirashi-zushi	Sushi rice in a bowl topped with seafood
California roll	Sushi roll with crab and avocado
Inside-out roll	Sushi roll with *nori* on the inside, not the outside

and provided home delivery service. When I was a child, my mother would on special occasions phone in a sushi order. The sushi was delivered not in a disposable plastic package but in a red and black lacquered wooden box. Inside was a colorful assortment of *nigiri-zushi* and thin rolls, so beautifully arranged that we could proudly set the box in front of the most distinguished guest at a formal dinner. There was no need for a serving plate. The next day, someone from the restaurant would come by to retrieve the lacquerware box. Until I was old enough to accompany my parents to a sushi restaurant, this take-out sushi was the only sushi I knew.

Now Japanese families have other, cheaper ways to buy sushi to eat at home. Freshly made, restaurant-quality sushi packed in plastic containers is available in the food section of every department store, supermarket, and specialty food store in Japan.

Sushi itself has been changing. New, foreign-born styles—California rolls, *tempura* rolls, caterpillar rolls, rainbow rolls, and so on—are mingling with the traditional varieties. One hundred and fifty years after the arrival of Admiral Perry's fleet, our country is facing another invasion. Sushi chefs at venerable establishments laugh scornfully at the innovations and deny that they are

sushi at all. But younger restaurateurs and chefs, who feel less bound by the old rules, are adopting new sushi creations to please their fashion-conscious customers. And these customers are cheering.

Sushi continues to evolve in Japan. Tradition, training, technology, and a welcome breeze of new creativity are together guiding this evolution.

Sushi by Conveyor Belt

Yoshiaki Shiraishi, a sushi chef in Osaka in the 1950s, wished passionately to revolutionize sushi dining. Because of the handwork involved in producing and serving *nigiri-zushi,* it was a dining experience reserved for affluent and expense account customers. Mr. Shiraishi wanted to introduce inexpensive, casual sushi dining to the masses—ordinary businesspeople, students, and families with children.

On a visit to a beer factory, Mr. Shiraishi watched in fascination as the bottles moved continuously on a conveyor belt. They were filled, capped, labeled, checked, and boxed in a smooth, rapid process with almost no human intervention. Mr. Shiraishi immediately decided to apply this kind of operation to a sushi counter.

His first conveyor-belt sushi shop, Genroku Sushi, opened in 1958 in Higashi Osaka, in western Japan. After a machine formed the sushi rice blocks, quickly trained young workers flipped prepared toppings onto the blocks, one after the other, without waiting for orders from customers. The sushi was placed on color-coded plates for price identification and sent on a journey around the counter on the belt, in a continuous parade before the seated diners. Thus was *kaiten-zushi* born. By drastically cutting costs and thereby lowering prices, the operation exploded the notion that sushi dining was expensive, formal, and ostentatious. The informality, low cost, and instant price tallying had immediate appeal for many people who had never before experienced sushi dining.

During the heyday of his business, Mr. Shiraishi owned about 240 *kaiten-zushi* restaurants across Japan. He is now deceased, and only eleven or so of his restaurants survive, all of them in or near his native Osaka. Mr. Shiraishi's influence, however, has spread to more than a dozen countries, including the United States, Britain, France, and the Netherlands, all of which now have *kaiten-zushi* restaurants. On every continent, *kaiten-zushi* continues to convert hungry people into sushi lovers.

Sushi Comes to America

The first American sushi bar was initiated in the early 1960s by Noritoshi Kanai, a Japanese native who ran a food import business in Los Angeles. Craving the *nigiri-zushi* he had known in his youth, he persuaded the owner of Kawafuku, a popular restaurant in Little Tokyo, to build a traditional sushi bar. Mr. Kanai imported everything needed for the new venture—the wooden counter, the countertop refrigerated case, the fish and shellfish to go in it, and even the professional sushi chefs. Since the venture coincided with a steady increase in the numbers of Japanese businesspeople visiting Los Angeles, the sushi bar clientele grew quickly. Soon other Los Angeles restaurants began to install their own sushi bars and sushi chefs, and more and more non-Japanese Americans joined the clientele.

The first American-born sushi—the California roll—originated early in this period. According to Minoru Yokoshima, the vice-chairman of the import company Eiwa International, it occurred at his company's Los Angeles restaurant, Tokyo Kaikan, the third genuine sushi bar established in the city. The management asked the chefs to devise a new roll to please American customers. Noting that Californians loved crab and avocado, the chefs combined these with mayonnaise and some cucumber for crunchiness in a new sushi roll.

Today the California roll is also known as the inside-out roll, but this wasn't the case in the beginning. At first, this sushi was made in the traditional way, with a green-black sheet of *nori* on the outside and the rice and other ingredients on the inside. At some point, the rice and *nori* were flipped, so the white rice was on the outside. How did this roll turn inside out? Many chefs claim credit, but so far this bit of history remains clouded in the mists of the past.

By the mid-1970s, Los Angeles residents of all backgrounds were flocking to sushi bar restaurants. One of the most popular was Osho, on Pico Boulevard. The owner, Sadao Kubo, a retired Japanese gardener, started his restaurant by snatching skilled chefs from other sushi bars. Hollywood actors and wealthy residents of Beverly Hills visited Osho regularly. In Southern California, eating at a sushi restaurant became a status symbol.

Also particularly successful was Hiro Sushi. The first white-owned sushi restaurant in Los Angeles, it opened in 1977. Two years later, the owners sold it and opened Teru-zushi, which has been a local favorite for twenty-five years now. Hiro Sushi and Teru-zushi, like Osho, became haunts of the Hollywood elite. It may be no exaggeration to say that the crowd mentality of Hollywood celebrities and their followers fueled the popularization of sushi in America.

Sushi bars came later to New York, which had a much smaller Japanese immigrant population than California. The founder of New York's first sushi restaurant was Hirotaka Matsumoto, a graduate of Tokyo University (known as the Harvard of Japan). As a young employee at the Sapporo Beer Company, he watched the *Apollo 11* moon landing on a TV in the company cafeteria. "This is one small step for a man," Neil Armstrong said as he descended from the lunar module, "one giant leap for mankind." The historic words so moved Mr. Matsumoto that he soon quit his job and got on a plane to the United States, where he took his first step in the country that nurtured such great achievements as moon landings. This was 1969. After working for some time as a fish distributor in New York, Mr. Matsumoto met an unhappy sushi chef. The chef wanted to leave his job at a big, generic Japanese restaurant to work at a small sushi bar restaurant. Mr. Matsumoto leaped at the opportunity: in 1975, he opened Takezushi, the first New York sushi bar restaurant to attract non-Japanese. Thanks to the brisk Japanese economy and the concurrent local interest in Japanese film, food, and culture, the New York sushi boom quickly gathered momentum. New York's second popular sushi restaurant, Hatsuhana, opened in 1976, and thirty years later, it still thrives.

During the 1980s and 1990s, sushi became established in American cities as healthful, fashionable fare. Nobu Matsuhisa, a sushi chef who started his signature restaurant, Matsuhisa, in Los Angeles in 1987, went on to open "Nobu" restaurants in New York, London, and even Tokyo. Michael Cardenas, after working as manager at Matsuhisa, created a chain of sushi restaurants in Los Angeles. Two New York sushi restaurants, Sushi Samba and Haru Sushi, sprouted branches across the city. Independent, chef-owned sushi bar restaurants opened in other cities all over the country.

Today new sushi restaurants are popping up everywhere in America, even hundreds or a thousand miles from the ocean. Because of advanced systems of refrigeration, freezing, storage, and transportation, these restaurants can prepare excellent raw-fish sushi. And in cities where sushi has been popular for twenty to thirty years, the locals have a thorough understanding of and appreciation for the sushi dining tradition. This is a welcome change for sushi chefs, according to Hiroshi Shima of Katana, a sushi restaurant in Los Angeles. "In the beginning, we made many Americanized sushi to please our diners. These were not foods that we liked to prepare, because they were not at the heart of our traditional cuisine. But this actually turned out to be good for us. The process allowed us to free ourselves from our strict ideas, and we began to see sushi from a different point of view. Now, contrary to our expectations, our knowledgeable clientele are asking for real, well-made, traditional sushi. Our business is more challenging than ever."

Sushi continues to evolve in its adopted country. While American-born inside-out rolls in ever more novel forms keep growing in popularity, old-style sushi is finding a dedicated following. Before long, sushi will surely attain full U.S. citizenship.

Chapter 2
Sushi Chefs

Among the world's professional cooks, sushi chefs must travel the longest, most difficult road to become fully skilled and respected. There are two reasons for this.

First, sushi chefs prepare seafood for raw consumption. They must be sure that the seafood is absolutely fresh when they buy it; they must know how to handle and store it properly; and they must maintain a completely hygienic kitchen. They must know which fish may contain potentially harmful parasites and how to eliminate those parasites. Sushi chefs must also acquire a detailed knowledge of the biochemical changes in seafood after it is slaughtered. From the muscle contractions at death to full rigor mortis, the texture and flavor of fish change. Sushi chefs must understand this process and know how to control it so they can serve each fish not just within a window of safety but when it tastes most delicious.

During my own training as a sushi chef, I tackled hundreds of samples of sushi seafood. I had many questions: How can I know whether this fish is fresh enough to serve raw? How long will it stay fresh enough? In what stage of rigor mortis is a fish so stiff it seems frozen? How can I know whether to trust the fishmonger? Why was the fish I filleted yesterday firmer and easier to slice than the fish of the same species that I filleted today? When will this fish reach its peak flavor?

Usually my instructor avoided answering. Learn by experience, he said. Fish vary, not only among species but among individuals—in diet and health, in the method of catching and killing, and in the degree of struggle at death. Some fish are wild, some cultivated; some come from warmer waters, some from cooler. Storage time and conditions vary, too. With so many variables, general rules don't help. Only long hours and months of practice could lead me to the answers to my questions.

The second reason sushi chefs need long training is that they do more than make sushi. Whereas other chefs can

weep, laugh, or explode behind the kitchen door, sushi chefs entertain an audience. They must take orders directly from their customers, explain the menu, make recommendations, keep tabs, and check whether diners like what they are served. Sushi chefs must also engage politely and attentively in conversations that have nothing to do with the meal.

The first time I worked as a sushi chef, I struggled to keep a smile on my face. Rice grains stuck to my hands. Because I was tense, my knife wouldn't cooperate, and I knew I couldn't serve badly filleted fish. Diners called out a cascade of orders, and while I tried to converse in a

knowledgeable-sounding way (what do I know about the latest baseball game statistics?), I worried about getting the right sushi to the right diners, keeping the ingredients chilled, and pleasing the customers with my performance and my sushi. I finished the shift mentally and physically exhausted.

Later that night, the faces of my favorite Tokyo and New York sushi chefs appeared in my mind. How did they get where they are? I learned that most of the older chefs in Japan apprenticed for fifteen years or longer; they started by sweeping the restaurant floor. Younger chefs have been trained at chain sushi restaurants or in schools such as the one I attended. In the United States, some sushi chefs have worked their way up in sushi restaurants; some have trained in other cuisines before learning to make sushi; and others have simply decided to "do it" despite the long odds against success. However a sushi chef learns, that patience and devotion are key both to mastering the craft and to staying calm and charming while practicing it.

After my training, I did not become a sushi chef; instead, I incorporated this new area of expertise into my work as a cooking instructor, food consultant, and food writer. My mission is to share this culinary art with all sushi devotees, diners, and home cooks as well as professional chefs.

A Sushi Chef's Odyssey

Zhong Zhen Seki was nineteen years old when his father sent him from his native province of Fujian, China, to study the Japanese language in Japan. As a student in Tokyo, he found part-time work at a small restaurant that served *sashimi* (sliced raw fish) and thin rolls as well as other popular Japanese dishes. Since his homeland was far from the sea, he was amazed at the Japanese custom of eating uncooked fish.

Three and a half years later, with no particular career in mind, Mr. Seki moved to New York City. Although he had mastered the Japanese language, he spoke no English, and so he took a job in a Japanese restaurant. After several months there, he decided that if he wanted to be successful in the Japanese food business, he should be trained as a sushi chef.

He began as an *oimawashi,* a person to be driven by senior chefs. At a little restaurant called Kenzo Zushi, he ran errands, swept the floors, polished the sushi bar, washed and cut vegetables, and did anything else his seniors asked. He was soon promoted to *wakai-shuu,* junior chef. For five years, he cleaned, scaled, and filleted small fish, and he learned to cook rice in the correct way for sushi.

Then Mr. Seki took a job at Akasaka Restaurant, just across the Hudson River from New York City in Fort Lee, New Jersey. Fort Lee is a bedroom community with a large population of Japanese expatriate businesspeople, a demanding clientele. Mr. Seki recalls Akasaka's sushi chef, Chef Sasaki, as an influential teacher. "He knew exactly how to bring out the maximum natural flavor and texture of each fish and shellfish, with minimal disguise. Even now I follow Mr. Sasaki's approach every day."

One day, Mr. Seki received a telephone call from Sushi of Gari, a restaurant in Manhattan. Since its opening in 1997, Sushi of Gari had become one of the most popular sushi restaurants in New York. Mr. Seki joined the staff and worked his way up to *chuken,* a midrank among sushi chefs.

Now he was entrusted with handling and preparing larger fish. He was eventually promoted to *waki-ita* (number three chef) and then *hana-ita* (number two chef). Finally he could stand behind the sushi bar and make *nigiri-zushi* to order for customers.

Mr. Seki dreamed of being his own boss. His chance arrived in 2001, when he heard that a sushi restaurant on the Upper East Side of Manhattan was going to close and the owner was looking for a buyer. He moved quickly to take it over. His restaurant, Sushi Seki, opened in 2002.

Today Sushi Seki is usually packed with customers and is favorably reviewed. Three chefs work under Mr. Seki, whose own training hasn't ended yet. "Every day is another day of learning and polishing my skill," he says. "The more I learn, the more I feel that I know so little. This is excellent motivation, since it keeps me working hard."

Female Sushi Chefs

Until recently, women were forbidden to work as sushi chefs. It was said that their hair oil and makeup had no place in a sushi kitchen, where no odor is permitted and total cleanliness is the rule. It was also said that women have a higher body temperature, especially during menstruation, and that warm hands are unsuitable for handling chilled fish.

Nonsense, I say. Women certainly can become sushi chefs. Their hands are generally cooler than men's, according to scientists, and women are as free as men are to go without hair oil and makeup. But whether you are male or female, becoming a chef at a top-class sushi restaurant requires years of training, practice, and discipline as well as enormous physical and mental strength and commitment. In the past, sushi apprenticeships were unbearably harsh for most people, male and female, but today's sushi schools and chain sushi restaurants train young devotees of both sexes more democratically and more efficiently. For men and women fit for the job, being a sushi chef is a very rewarding occupation.

A *nigiri-sushi* dinner platter

Chapter 3
Sushi Restaurant Etiquette 1 to 9

Sitting at a sushi bar and watching a chef make a *nigiri-zushi* or *maki* (roll) is like watching a soap bubble getting larger and larger and suddenly bursting in the air. In a few miraculous seconds, the chef crafts the sushi and passes it to you, and then you eat it.

The tips that follow will help you connect with the chef behind the counter and fully appreciate his or her performance. Whether you eat at the bar or at a table, it will make your sushi dining experience much more pleasurable. But these tips are not meant to be a set of immutable rules. Use your common sense to modify them according to the situation. Above all, enjoy.

Etiquette Point 1:
Sushi Bar or
Table Seating?

Whereas, in Japan, we fight to sit at the sushi bar, in American sushi restaurants, the bar is often deserted. This is too bad. When you sit at a sushi bar, you can study the day's fish and shellfish in the refrigerated case, consult with the chef about your dinner, and watch him or her prepare it. You can please the chef by making a special order. For instance, my husband loves to order a roll with *anago* (conger eel), cucumber, and sweet *tare* sauce, but without rice. No sushi chef in Japan or in

America has ever refused this order; in fact, chefs smile broadly when they receive it. And each chef constructs the roll in a slightly different way. Watching a creative chef interpret an unusual order is part of the fun of sitting at the bar.

Sitting at the bar may seem scary at first, but as soon as you begin to interact with the chef, you will start to enjoy yourself. You and your chef will become collaborators in your meal.

If you are in a group of four or more, I recommend that you sit at a table. It is difficult to interact with the chef when you are talking with several friends.

Etiquette Point 2:
How to Begin

When you are ushered to the sushi bar, make eye contact with the nearest chef. *"Irasshai,"* he or she will say; Welcome! If you are a regular, you will be taken to the chef who has served you in the past. With a big smile, he or she will shout, *"Maido!"* Welcome back!

How should you respond? With the simple phrase *Yoroshiku*—How do you do, and please treat me kindly. You will likely get a big grin in return. Any ice will have melted away.

If you are being seated at a table, make a detour to exchange greetings with the chefs.

Etiquette Point 3:
Chef's Choice, *O-makase*

If you are sitting at the sushi bar and do not know how to order, treat your chef like a private chauffeur who can drive you to any destination. Tell him or her, if you know, what you especially like or dislike, ask about the day's choices, and indicate your price range (write it on a napkin if you must). The chef will then prepare sushi to suit you, one kind after another, describing each as he or she presents it. If the restaurant is a good one, with an experienced chef, you absolutely cannot go wrong ordering *o-makase,* chef's choice. I order this way myself, even at restaurants I frequent, so the chef can build my dinner around what's best and special on that day.

In the United States, *o-makase* meals start at about $50, but they may range from $80 to $140 at high-end restaurants. When you make a reservation, you might casually ask about the price range.

The typical *o-makase* meal begins with a few *sashimi* (sliced raw fish) dishes. These are followed by seven to twelve *nigiri-zushi* pieces and then a traditional thin roll. But even after your *o-makase* dinner begins, its progress depends on your participation. If you particularly liked something, speak up. If you want more of the same, ask for it. If you were unimpressed with some dish, tell your chef. If you want to start with

Classes of Sushi Seafood and Omelet

GROUP	CHARACTERISTICS	SPECIES
Akami (red flesh)	Red-fleshed fish, with a metallic flavor and tender flesh. Tuna cuts are classed as *akami* (red meat), *chu-toro* (the fatty back), or *o-toro* (the fattier belly). Skipjack tuna is usually seared with its skin on. Eat these species with dipping sauce.	**Maguro** (tuna) **Katsuo** (skipjack tuna)
Shiromi (white flesh)	Firm, pale-fleshed fish, low in fat and mild and sweet in flavor. Yellowtail, the fattiest fish in this group, is best with dipping sauce, but other varieties may be served with sea salt instead.	**Buri, hamachi** (yellowtail) **Hirame** (flounder) **Kampachi** (great amberjack) **Ma-dai** (red sea bream) **Shima-aji** (striped jack) **Suzuki** (sea bass)
Hikari-mono (shiny thing)	Silver-blue, oily-fleshed fish with a strong, rich flavor. These varieties are often cured with salt and vinegar to prevent spoilage and balance their oiliness. Sardine and mackerel are served with grated ginger rather than *wasabi*.	**Kohada** (Japanese gizzard shad) **Iwashi** (sardine) **Saba** (mackerel) **Sayori** (halfbeak)
Nimono (simmered seafood)	Certain fish and shellfish have always been favored cooked. Simmering them in *shoyu* (soy sauce), *mirin* (sweet rice wine), and *sake* (rice wine) brings out their flavor and tenderizes their flesh.	**Anago** (conger eel) **Unagi** (eel) **Hamaguri** (hard-shell clam) **Tako** (octopus)
Tamago-yaki (omelet)	There are two kinds of omelet. One is rolled; the other looks like sponge cake and contains puréed shrimp and fish. Neither requires dipping sauce.	
Ebi (shrimp) **Ika** (squid and cuttlefish)	Boiled shrimp are available at sushi bars, but do try shrimp raw. Good, fresh raw shrimp is tender and a little jellylike but with a noticeable bite, and heavenly sweet. Many people think raw squid is rubbery, but varieties such as *aori-iki* and *sumi-ika* are tender and sweet. Both shrimp and squid are delicious either with dipping sauce or with a squeeze of lemon and a little salt.	**Kuruma-ebi** (*kuruma* prawn) **Ama-ebi** (northern shrimp) **Botan-ebi** (humpback shrimp) **Shiro-ebi** (white prawn) **Aori-iki** (big-fin reef squid) **Sumi-ika** (golden cuttlefish)
Kai-rui (clams, scallops, and abalone)	There are many varieties of edible clams. Depending on the variety, we may eat the muscle meat, the meaty siphon, or the long strip of flesh surrounding the muscle. Whichever part we eat, raw clams generally have a tender texture and a rich, sweet flavor. They are delicious with either dipping sauce or sea salt and lemon.	**Miru-gai** (gaper clam) **Hokki-gai** (surf clam) **Hotate-gai** (scallop) **Aoyagi** (hen clam) **Awabi** (abalone) **Akagai** (bloody clam)
Sono-ta (others)	Seafoods that don't belong to any of the above categories are lumped together as *sono-ta*. Each has its own distinctive flavor and texture.	**Ikura** (salmon roe) **An'kimo** (monkfish liver) **Uni** (sea urchin)

nigiri-zushi rather than *sashimi,* or if you prefer more rolls and less *nigiri-zushi,* say so. You may think you are being a pain in the neck, but in fact, you are letting the sushi chef do what he or she loves to do—please the customer. After you have visited the restaurant several times, the chef will know your preferences and your dinners will be even more relaxed.

Etiquette Point 4:
Ordering a Dish at a Time

When you choose your own dishes, there are no rules about which should come first or which should follow.

Here is the way I order my dinner. Since I love *sashimi,* I always start with a mixed platter of it, called *o-tsukuri* (to arrange several things as one component). Although there may be fixed *sashimi* platters on the menu, I prefer to study the refrigerated case, ask the chef for the day's recommendation, and make my own choices. You could instead ask the chef to assemble a custom platter of his or her choice.

After I have enjoyed the *sashimi,* I move on to *nigiri-zushi.* I order the day's specials and my personal favorites. I choose seafoods of different classes (see the accompanying table, "Classes of Sushi Seafood and Omelet") so I can enjoy a broad variety of textures and flavors. I might start, for example, with a piece of raw shrimp, with its slightly jellylike texture and melting sweetness, and follow the shrimp with meaty, metallic-flavored tuna. Then I might savor the refreshing flavor and firm texture of vinegar-cured mackerel and move on to a white-fleshed, clean- and lean-flavored fish such as flounder. After that, I might sample tender cooked conger eel with its rich basting sauce and then more delicate sea urchin. I

finish my dinner with a refreshing hand roll with cucumber or a mixture of *daikon* sprouts and pickled *daikon.* What a good sushi dinner!

Etiquette Point 5:
One Piece of Sushi or Two?

When you order *nigiri-zushi* in Japan, the chef normally makes you two pieces. Some people feel this is so the restaurant can make more money, but others say that the first piece is to taste, the second to satisfy the hunger.

Even in Japan today, you can usually order one piece of sushi at a time if you prefer. *Ik-kan* means "one piece"; *ni-kan* means "two pieces." Ordering *ik-kan* lets you enjoy as many different kinds of *nigiri-zushi* as possible. If a restaurant allows only *ni-kan* orders, share each plate of sushi with a friend.

Etiquette Point 6:
Sushi and *Sashimi* Condiments

During your meal, you will be presented with a variety of condiments.

Tsuke-joyu, a sweet, smoky blend of *shoyu* (soy sauce) and *mirin* (sweet rice wine), is served as a dipping sauce with *sashimi* and sushi.

Wasabi, pungent, aromatic Japanese horseradish, is served with *sashimi* and sometimes with sushi. In Japan, and often in the United States, chefs preparing *nigiri-zushi* add a dab of *wasabi* between the rice and the seafood; customers specify whether they want a little more or less than usual or none at all. When *nigiri-zushi* is prepared without *wasabi,* many customers stir a little into their dipping sauce.

For *sashimi,* as with sushi, you can stir *wasabi* into the dipping sauce, but I keep

these condiments separate so I can better appreciate the individual flavors, especially if the *wasabi* has been freshly grated. Here is how I eat *sashimi:* With my chopsticks, I pick up a tiny amount of *wasabi* and place it on one end of a slice of *sashimi.* I then use my chopsticks to fold the slice in half with the *wasabi* on the inside, and I lightly dip the very tip of the fish in the sauce before carrying the morsel to my mouth.

A *sashimi* platter also comes with julienned *daikon,* long white radish, and *shiso* or another seasonal herb. These are not just visual garnishes; they also clean your palate. Munch them a bit at a time after each bite of fish and shellfish. Some types of *sashimi* also come with grated fresh ginger, sea salt, or lemon.

Nigiri-zushi is always served with *gari,* sweet pickled ginger, which serves to refresh the mouth. When you sit at the sushi bar, your chef will renew your pile of *gari* from time to time without being asked. Better restaurants generally pickle their own ginger, from tender young roots, rather than buying a factory-produced product. (You can easily pickle your own by following the recipe on page 66.) Good *gari* is mild in flavor, tender, and pale, not red.

Etiquette Point 7:
Sushi, a Finger Food

Since sushi was first sold from street stalls, it has always been a finger food. Using chopsticks is fine, but watching someone struggle to pick up sushi with chopsticks and dropping or crumbling it on the way to the mouth is painful—and, to the chef, insulting. Besides, when you feel the warm sushi rice and chilled fish in your hand, you add to your sensual enjoyment of the meal. So please use your (clean) fingers. You can wipe them occasionally on your napkin or *o-shibori,* a moist washcloth provided by some restaurants.

To dip your *nigiri-zushi* in sauce, hold the sushi with your thumb and middle finger on either side and your index finger over the slice of fish. Turn the sushi upside down so that the tip of one end of the fish touches the dipping sauce. Don't dip the rice; it would immediately get soggy and fall apart. And please don't remove the fish from the rice, dip it in the sauce, and put it back on the rice. Your sushi chef would weep, since all of the chef's long years of perfecting the art of putting the sushi rice and fish together in his or her hand would seem for naught. Besides, dipping just the tip of the fish gives you all the sauce you need to balance the flavors.

In a special type of *nigiri-zushi* called *gunkan,* sea urchin, salmon roe, or chopped spiced tuna is placed on top of a *nori*-wrapped block of sushi rice. If you tilted this kind of sushi, the loose topping would tumble off. For sea urchin *gunkan,* take a slice of sweet pickled ginger from the pile before you, lightly dip it in the sauce, and use the damp ginger to sprinkle or paint a little sauce on the sea urchin. Salmon roe and spiced tuna need no sauce.

Etiquette Point 8: *Oishii,* Delicious!

After finishing a piece of *nigiri-zushi* or *maki* that you have really enjoyed, give a friendly cheer to your sushi chef: *"Oishii!"* Delicious!

Not all sushi is worthy of this praise. The seafood must, of course, be excellent, but the sushi rice is just as important. It must not be too tender, too sticky, or too firm, and it must be seasoned properly. It should be slightly warm; warm rice is tender and moist, with a pleasant bite, and best complements the chilled fish or shellfish.

Since sushi can be delicious only if eaten fresh, you should stop chatting when a dish is placed in front of you. Immediately pick up the sushi and eat it. Your mother always told you to drink your soup before it got cold; it is the same with sushi. When you eat it at the perfect temperature, it may truly be *oishii.*

Etiquette Point 9: Closing the Curtain

Toward the end of my *nigiri-zushi* ordering, I finish any alcoholic beverage I'm drinking. Before switching to green tea, *o-cha,* I order a soothing, satisfying *miso* soup, *o-wan.* Ask your chef about the day's soup; ingredients may vary from clams to fish to tofu and *wakame* sea vegetable.

In Japan, dessert is seldom on the menu, although some chefs now please diners (usually women) by offering a small cup of ginger or *yuzu* (citron) sherbet or a fruit-flavored gelatin. American sushi restaurants usually offer a variety of desserts.

Ask the chef for the *o-kanjo,* the bill, and sip another cup of green tea. Before leaving, even if you have been sitting at a table, pay the chef a final compliment: *"Gochiso-sama!"* This was a feast! A wonderful ending for both parties.

Using *Hashi,* Chopsticks

Although sushi is a finger food, you will want to know how to use chopsticks when you eat *sashimi* and other Japanese dishes. The rules are simple:

1. When not in use, chopsticks are traditionally placed parallel to the edge of the table or counter right in front of the diner. A little stand may be provided on which to rest the chopsticks, at your left if you are right-handed and at your right if you are left-handed. Because chopsticks in the traditional position often fall on the floor, many restaurants now place them on the right side perpendicular to the table or counter edge, like a Western knife and spoon.

2. If you are sharing a communal platter, turn your chopsticks around so you can pick up foods and transfer them to your plate with the ends that haven't touched your mouth. Don't forget to turn your chopsticks around again before eating.

3. Because disposable wooden chopsticks can be rough, some people rub them together to remove any splinters. Doing this at a good restaurant, though, is considered poor manners.

4. Drink your soup directly from the bowl and use your chopsticks to pick up solid ingredients. Disregard the soup spoon if you are given one.

5. Do not lick your chopsticks in an obvious way or point with them or play with them. My mother would be very upset!

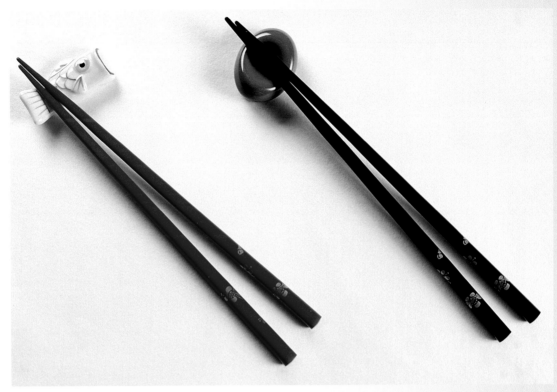

Chopsticks for eating. Note that the man's chopsticks (*on the right*) are slightly larger than the woman's.

Conversation in a Japanese Sushi Bar

THE CHEF:

Irasshai!   Welcome!

Maido!   Welcome back!

THE CUSTOMER:

Yoroshiku   How do you do (Hello),
     and please treat me kindly

. . . onegashimasu   Please give me . . .

sake   rice wine

biiru   beer

o-cha   green tea

o-mizu   water

o-makase   chef's choice

ik-kan   one piece of sushi

ni-kan   two pieces of sushi

o-shibori   (hot or cold) towel

o-kanjo   the bill

Itadakimasu.   Thank you (and all who made it)
     for the food.

Oishii!   Delicious!

Gochiso-sama!   This was a feast!

Part Two
Kitchen Essentials
for Sushi Making

Chapter 4
The Sushi Pantry

To make sushi in your own kitchen, you need just a few basic ingredients: rice, rice vinegar, *nori* for rolls, and *wasabi* and pickled ginger as condiments. This chapter introduces you to each of these special foods. For the best selection of each, visit a large Japanese or general Asian food store.

Su
Vinegars

Properly flavored rice is the foundation of good sushi, and rice vinegar, *komezu,* is the most important sushi flavoring. At 4.2 to 4.5 percent acetic acid, *komezu* is a little milder than commercial cider and wine vinegars, but it is acidic enough to suppress bacterial growth in both the rice and the raw seafood used in sushi. With certain fish, rice vinegar also serves to soften strong smells and flavors and firm the flesh.

The production of *komezu* begins much like that of *sake:* Rice is mixed with mineral water and *koji* mold (*Aspergillus oryzae*). The *koji* converts the starch and protein in the rice into sugar and amino acids, producing a sweet liquid. Yeast metabolizes the sugar in this liquid to alcohol and carbon dioxide. The result is a kind of *sake,* though no one drinks it. At this point, a bacterial culture is added to convert the alcohol to acetic acid.

In the sushi kitchen, vinegar is used not only for flavoring rice but also for rinsing and curing certain fish and shellfish and for moistening the chef's hands. Since *komezu* is relatively expensive, low-cost grain vinegar, *kokumotsu-zu,* is used for these purposes instead.

Shopping Tips. Most supermarkets carry at least one brand of rice vinegar, but large Japanese markets often carry several. Look for one labeled *jun-komezu,* pure rice vinegar. It will have a golden color and a richer flavor and aroma than ordinary *komezu,* which is made from a combination of rice and other grains. Grain vinegar has only one type. Look for *kokumotsu-zu.*

Be sure you don't mistakenly buy *sushizu,* a ready-made sushi dressing consisting of vinegar, sugar, and salt. Making your own blend allows you to use exactly as much sugar and salt as you like.

Storage Tips. For the best flavor and fragrance, store an opened bottle of vinegar in the refrigerator or in a cool, dark, dry place and use it up within three months.

Kasuzu
Red Sushi Vinegar

Although rice vinegar was marketed in Japanese cities in the sixteenth century, commercial production remained small until the nineteenth century, when the sudden popularity of *nigiri-zushi* created a surge in demand. In response, breweries began to make rice vinegar from *sake* lees, the solids left over from fermenting rice to make *sake*. Since the new vinegar, *kasuzu*, was both more flavorful and less expensive than *komezu*, sushi chefs immediately adopted it as the vinegar of choice for sushi.

To make *kasuzu, sake* lees, smelling strongly of alcohol, are packed in a wooden barrel, which is sealed tightly with a paper lid and stored for two to three years. During this period, the sugars and amino acids in the *sake* lees react to form a brown, rich-flavored mass. This is mixed with spring water, and the mixture is left for a week. It is then stirred and strained, and half of the strained alcoholic liquid is boiled down and mixed with the rest of the liquid. The blend is left to ferment. Through natural bacterial action, the alcohol is transformed to acetic acid.

Compared with *komezu, kasuzu* is both more colorful and more flavorful. It is also called *akazu,* red vinegar, because of its reddish tint, which faintly colors the rice prepared with it. *Kasuzu* also has a lot of *umami*—savory flavor—and a distinctive sweetness. This is why, in the era when sushi rice was prepared solely with *kasuzu,* no sugar was added.

After World War II, nearly colorless *komezu* became the favored vinegar for sushi. Most diners simply preferred their sushi rice pearl-white, as they still do. I suspect that Japanese reject tinted sushi for the same reason they disdain natural brown rice: White represents purity and prosperity. Tinted rice is associated with lack of refinement and poverty.

Kasuzu hasn't disappeared, however. About 15 percent of Japanese sushi restaurants still use it instead of *komezu,* and an additional 10 percent use a mixture of *kasuzu* and *komezu.* This blend is distributed to restaurants in America, so without knowing it, you may have tasted *sake* lees vinegar in your sushi rice.

Kome
Rice

Japanese sushi chefs take as much care in choosing and preparing rice as they do fish and shellfish. You, too, will want to choose your rice with care.

But shopping for rice in a Japanese market can be bewildering. How do all those bags differ? Whether in Japanese characters or Roman letters, the labels may mean nothing to you. Here is what you need to know.

Rice varieties differ in their proportion of two types of starch, amylose and amylopectin. All Japanese rice is of the short-grained "Japonica" type, which has a higher proportion of amylopectin than does long-grained "Indica" rice and so is more moist, tender, and sticky.

Japanese cooks use two basic varieties of Japonica rice, *uruchi-mai* and *mochi-gome*. The starch in *mochi-gome*, also known as sticky rice, sweet rice, or glutinous rice, is nearly entirely amylopectin. When cooked, *mochi-gome* is very sticky; this is the rice that is pounded into soft, gooey rice cakes, *mochi*. *Mochi-gome* is too sticky for use in sushi.

Rice for sushi is *uruchi-mai,* the same type of rice that Japanese eat every day. All *uruchi-mai* varieties are descended from two parent seeds selected in the Meiji era (1868 to 1911) and so are closely related. But the differences among these varieties are sometimes quite noticeable. Today the Japanese rice family tree has two branches, *koshihikari* and *sasanishiki*. The principal difference, again, lies in the proportion of the two kinds of starch. *Sasanishiki* has less amylopectin and so is less sticky and more firm when cooked than *koshihikari*. Many chefs prefer *sasanishiki* for *nigiri-zushi,* but others like to use a blend of the two types. For *oshi-zushi* (pressed sushi), tender, moist *koshihikari* is indispensable. Most Japanese prefer *koshihikari* as a daily table rice, too, and so its production is much higher than that of *sasanishiki*.

If you're shopping in an ordinary supermarket, you can still buy perfectly suitable rice for sushi, from California. Until recently, California produced only long-grain and medium-grain rice. The medium-grain varieties, such as Nishiki and Kokuho, are Indica-Japonica crosses, developed in the 1960s by a Japanese company. Medium-grain California rice has long been used by Japanese Americans for sushi rolls, and it is still a good choice for this purpose (although Italian or Spanish medium-grain rice is not). Better still are the short-grain Japanese varieties, mostly *koshihikari* types, now grown in California by Japanese companies. In flavor, fragrance, and appearance, the short-grain varieties are all superior to the medium-grain varieties, especially for *nigiri-zushi*.

Rice sold soon after harvest, from October through February, is labeled *shin-mai,* new harvest. Exceptionally moist, tender, and fragrant, *shin-mai* is delicious as table rice, like fresh corn on the day it is picked. But in fall and early winter, *shin-mai* is too moist and tender for sushi. If no other rice is available during these months, spread the *shin-mai* in a broad, flat-bottomed colander and leave it in an airy, dry place for two or three days before using it for sushi. *Shin-mai* rice sold after the New Year should be dry enough to use immediately.

Rice Varieties for Sushi

Koshihikari has many children and grand-children, whose names—*hitomebore, akita-komachi, hae-nuki, hi-no-hikari,* and *kirara,* for example—often appear on the labels of Japanese rice bags. *Koshihikari* varieties grown in California are *tama-nishiki, kaga-yaki, tamaki-mai, hitomebore,* and *kirara*.

Drier, firmer *sasanishiki* rice has fewer offspring. On Japanese rice bags, *sasani-shiki* is generally identified only by the generic name. California-grown *sasanishiki,* if you can find it, may be identified by a varietal name, such as *nozomi*.

I have found all of these varieties—*koshihikari* and *sasanishiki,* Japanese- and California-grown—quite suitable for sushi.

Shopping Tips. For *nigiri-zushi,* choose short-grain rice from either Japan or California; for sushi rolls, medium-grain California rice will do. If the rice is from Japan, make sure it isn't labeled *mochi-gome* (sticky rice) or *shin-mai* (new har-vest). Be sure the packaging is airtight, and check the "use by" date or the date of packaging to be sure that the rice hasn't been sitting in the store for many months unsold. If you can see the rice grains through the packaging, make sure they are unbroken, smooth, clean, and shiny white.

Storage Tips. Keep rice in an airtight container in a cool, dry, dark place. For the best flavor and fragrance, use the rice within a month or two.

Bugs in Your Rice?

If you buy organically grown rice, *yu-u-ki-mai,* you may one day find tiny black bugs moving around in it, especially if the weather has been hot and humid. Don't panic; remember that only rice grown with heavy applications of pesticide is totally bug-free. To get rid of the bugs, spread the rice on paper outdoors in bright sunlight; they will walk away and disappear. Let the rice cool and then pack it in a clean container with a few dried red chile peppers. Store it in the refrigerator or a cool, dry place. Any eggs remaining will be washed away when you prepare the rice for cooking.

Mirin
Sweet Cooking Wine

The delicious flavor of *tsuke-joyu,* the dipping sauce for sushi or *sashimi,* comes from blending *shoyu,* soy sauce, with *mirin,* sweet rice wine. The sugars in *mirin,* glucose and maltose, mellow the sharp saltiness of *shoyu,* and the amino and other organic acids created in the maturation of this wine add savor and balance to the sauce. *Mirin* is also a partner for *shoyu* in other Japanese sauces, such as *tsume,* a velvety, golden brown sauce that is brushed over a slice of cooked conger eel or eel *nigiri-zushi. Mirin,* like *sake,* is usually brought to a simmer before it is incorporated in a sauce, to cook off the alcohol and add a subtle caramel flavor.

Once enjoyed as a beverage, *mirin* is traditionally made by leaving rice cultured with *koji* mold (*Aspergillus oryzae*) and steamed *mochi-gome* (glutinous rice) in a 40 percent solution of distilled alcohol for two to three months. During this period, the rice starch converts to sugar, while the alcohol prevents any wild yeast from converting the sugar to additional alcohol. The result is a sweet, sherrylike liquor with an alcohol content of 14 percent.

Unfortunately, very little authentic *mirin* is made in Japan today. What is labeled as *mirin* in markets is usually a cheap, synthetic, mass-produced brew with a low alcohol content and poor flavor. It is unpalatable as a drink.

Shopping Tips. In Japanese and general Asian markets, *mirin* is stocked near the vinegar and *shoyu.* Read the bottle labels to find a brand that is made mostly from rice and that has a relatively high alcohol content. Avoid any *mirin* whose main ingredient is corn syrup or another form of sugar.

Storage Tips. Store an opened bottle of *mirin* in the refrigerator or a cool, dark, dry place and try to use it up within three months or so. *Mirin* stored for a long time will darken and lose both flavor and nutritional value.

Nori
Laver

The inside-out roll was born thirty years ago because some American sushi diners complained that *nori* was fishy and unpleasant to bite. Instead of omitting the *nori,* clever chefs buried its flavor and texture in the rice. Today the situation has changed: American diners are enjoying *nori-maki,* traditional thin rolls, and *temaki,* hand rolls, made with crisp, fragrant, and delicious *nori*— on the outside, where it belongs.

Nori has been an indispensable food in Japan since ancient times. It was first listed in the tax code in AD 701. In the twelfth century, Zen Buddhism spread the consumption of *nori* along with vegetarianism to all the aristocrats and monks. In 1717, the Japanese began cultivating *nori* in Edo Bay. *Nori* finally reached the commoners' tables in the latter part of the eighteenth century, when it became popular in *nori-maki.*

Grades of *nori* differ in color, flavor, fragrance, crispness, and thickness. The

Where *Nori* Comes From

An alga, *nori* grows naturally in bays where fresh water from rivers meets the salt water of the sea. *Nori* spores begin life resting on the shells of oysters. The spores eventually slip onto the inside surface of each shell, where they keep cool during the heat of summer. When autumn approaches, the spores drift into the water and settle on rocks. There the *nori* grows, dropping new spores into the water. At the beginning of November, the first batch of *nori* is harvested, in 6-inch-long strands. Second and third batches are harvested later in the same month.

Today *nori* cultivation starts on empty oyster shells, from which the spores move to rope nets floating in the water. At harvest time, the *nori* is pulled off the nets, rinsed, minced, and made like paper into thin, dark green sheets. The sheets are mechanically dried until crisp, stacked and bundled, and then sorted into thirty different grades.

differences depend partially on where the *nori* grows. The three *nori*-producing regions of Japan are Ariake Bay, in the south; Seto-uchi Bay, in central Japan; and Tokyo Bay. The high tidal flow of Ariake Bay exposes *nori* to plenty of air and strong sunlight during the long hours of the ebb. This makes Ariake Bay *nori* especially sweet, crisp, and thin and therefore well suited for *temaki,* hand rolls. *Nori* from Seto-uchi Bay is glossy black and relatively thick; its thickness makes it suitable for *onigiri,* rice balls, and *futo-maki,* thick rolls. *Nori* from Tokyo Bay is medium-thick and has the best flavor and fragrance of all. Since the invention of *nori-maki* in old Edo, Tokyo Bay *nori* has been used for thin rolls, although Ariake Bay *nori* is even better for this purpose. Although Tokyo Bay is at the center of one of the most densely populated urban regions in the world, pollution control measures have preserved the high quality of Tokyo Bay *nori.*

Like other sea vegetables, *nori* is highly nutritious. One sheet provides 20 percent of the minimum daily adult requirement of vitamin A and as much vitamin B$_1$ as is found in 3 ounces of cow's milk. *Nori* is also a good source of balanced protein, calcium, and iron. Although its fat content is very small, *nori* is rich in eicosapentaenoic acid (EPA), the fatty acid in fish oil that lowers LDL ("bad") cholesterol and raises HDL ("good") cholesterol. Our Japanese ancestors were wise to start each day with a bowl of rice and *nori.*

Shopping Tips. A package of *nori* usually contains ten sheets, each about 7½ by 8¼ inches. Don't buy an economy-size package, of fifty or a hundred sheets, unless you are going to throw a big sushi party. Once a package is opened and *nori* is exposed to the air, flavor, texture, and aroma quickly deteriorate.

The price for a package of ten *nori* sheets can range from two to ten dollars, and at a Japanese market, you may be bewildered by the number of brands. Look first for the name of the bay of origin—Seto-uchi, Ariake, or Tokyo. If you know you'll be making *nori-maki* (thin rolls) or *temaki* (hand rolls), thin, crisp Ariake Bay *nori* or medium-thin Tokyo Bay *nori* is best; if you plan to make *futo-maki* (thick rolls) or *onigiri* (rice balls), thick Seto-uchi *nori* is preferable. For inside-out rolls, medium-thick Tokyo Bay *nori* is good.

Unfortunately, few brands of *nori* are identified by their bay of origin. Another way of narrowing your choice is to look at the photographs of prepared sushi on the package. Choose the package that has a picture of the kind of sushi you plan to make.

To learn more about *nori,* buy two or three brands that look suitable, one with a higher price. Open the packages at home and compare the sheets. Good *nori* is glossy, dark green (or reddish brown, if it is from Ariake Bay), smooth, even in thickness, free of holes, and fragrant as a sea breeze. Try a small bite. The *nori* should be mellow-sweet, savory, and crisp, and it shouldn't stick to your mouth.

Storage Tips. Higher-priced *nori* comes in a resealable, airtight package. If your *nori* package isn't resealable, store the leftover sheets, along with the small bag of desiccant with which *nori* is

Toasting *Nori*

Nori sheets are toasted before they are packaged, and until the package is opened, the sheets stay crisp. By toasting the *nori* just before you use it, though, you can revive its fragrance and make it even crisper. Don't bother doing this for *futo-maki,* thick rolls, which are usually prepared several hours in advance of serving, or for inside-out rolls. With these rolls, the *nori* won't stay crisp. But do try toasting *nori* for *nori-maki* (traditional thin rolls) and *temaki* (hand rolls).

I used to toast *nori* by passing it over the flame of a gas stove. This improved the flavor, but moisture from the gas combustion softened the *nori* a little. A better way is to use a toaster or toaster oven. I now toast a half-sheet of *nori* at a time in my toaster, at a low heat setting (2 on a scale of 1 to 6), for exactly 10 seconds, or I use a whole sheet and turn it around after 10 seconds. Experiment to find out what works best with your own equipment.

If toasting *nori* doesn't work for you,

be sure to use a new, unopened package of *nori* every time you make *nori-maki* or *temaki.*

always packaged, in a tin if you have one large enough, with a tight lid, or in a freezer-weight bag with a zipper closure. Keep leftover *nori* in a cool place and use it as soon as possible, preferably within a month.

If your *nori* somehow becomes damp or misshapen, you don't have to throw it away. Instead, tear it into small pieces and add them to your omelet, *miso* soup, or steaming hot rice.

Shio
Salt

The word *shio* can refer to granulated salt, but it also means "salt water," "ocean current," or "tide." Although Japan has always had plentiful *shio* in liquid form, the country's humid, rainy climate has never been suited for large-scale production of dry salt. Our ancestors made do with salt ash, which they produced by spreading seaweed on the beach to dry between storms, rinsing the dry seaweed in an isolated saltwater pool, and then boiling the brine over a wood fire to evaporate the water and crystallize the salt, which ended up mixed with ash from the burned seaweed. What a long, laborious task to produce salt on an island surrounded by the salty ocean!

A salty flavor is described in Japanese as *shio-karai*, which literally means "salty-bitter." This term reflects the continuing Japanese preference for salt with a high content of minerals other than sodium chloride. For an authentic Japanese flavor, a natural, mineral-rich salt is essential. I personally prefer salt with approximately a 4 percent content of minerals such as potassium, magnesium, and calcium.

Today Japanese salt is available in four types, all in the form of fine crystals:

1. *Seisei-en,* made by chemically isolating sodium chloride from sea water
2. *Arajio or shizen-en,* imported natural salt that is first rinsed to remove biological impurities and then fortified with minerals
3. *Shizen kaien,* "natural sea salt," produced by boiling concentrated salt water over low heat
4. *Ten'nen kaien,* natural sea salt produced by evaporating sea water in a hothouse

Shopping Tips. Moderately priced *arajio* is available from a few Web sources as well as from Japanese food stores. I use it lavishly for cleaning, salting, pickling, and flavoring seafood and vegetables. When I want a more flavorful salt—for soups, salads, simmered dishes, and some kinds of *nigiri-zushi*—I use *shizen kaien,* which can be ordered over the Internet. So far, the more expensive *ten'nen kaien* is unavailable in the United States. You might instead use gray French or flaky English sea salt or any natural salt that you prefer.

Storage Tips. Generally sold packed in a plastic bag, Japanese salt should be stored in a tight-lidded container. If the salt becomes moist, toast ten or so grains of rice in a skillet and put them into the salt container to prevent clumping.

Japanese Flavor Terms

amami	sweetness
san'mi	tartness
nigami	bitterness
karami	spiciness
shibumi	astringency
umami	savoriness
shio-karai	saltiness (salty-bitter)

Shoyu
Soy Sauce

If you feel thirsty after a sushi meal, perhaps you have overindulged in *tsuke-joyu,* the sushi and *sashimi* dipping sauce whose main component is *shoyu,* soy sauce. *Shoyu* is 60 percent salt.

Shoyu is not simply a salt substitute, however. Through its long fermentation and maturation, it develops numerous aromas (which have been compared to vanilla, coffee, pineapple, rose, hyacinth, and more) and a complex flavor, at once sweet, sour, bitter, spicy, astringent, and savory. The savoriness, or *umami,* of *shoyu* derives from natural amino acids, especially glutamic acid.

In sushi kitchens of the past, *shoyu* was more than a condiment. Its high levels of acids and sodium made it ideal for curing fish for raw consumption. Everyone's favorite sushi fish, *maguro* (tuna), was once always cured in *shoyu* before it was placed on a *nigiri-zushi* rice ball. *Zuke,* the technique of curing in *shoyu,* remains popular in Japan and has spread beyond the country (for *zuke* recipe, see page 185).

Three types of *shoyu* are used in Japanese kitchens. Both *koikuchi,* ordinary *shoyu,* and *usukuchi,* light-colored *shoyu,* are made from soybeans and toasted wheat. For *usukuchi,* the wheat is toasted less and extra salt is added to slow the fermentation, so the result is a less flavorful, slightly saltier *shoyu.* The third type of *shoyu* is *tamari,* which is made from only soybeans and salt and fermented longer than the other two types. *Tamari* is just as salty as *koikuchi* but darker, thicker, and richer in aroma. For sushi making, you only need *koikuchi,* common dark *shoyu.*

Shopping Tips. Buy *koikuchi shoyu,* ordinary dark soy sauce, without extraneous ingredients such as caramel coloring. Look on the label for the word *marudaizu,* whole soybeans; *shoyu* not labeled as *marudaizu* may be made from defatted soybeans, left over from the production of soybean oil. If you want to buy organic *shoyu,* look for the word *yuuki.* In my experience, *shoyu* from Japan is slightly more expensive but also better than American *shoyu,* even when the two are made by the same company. A glass bottle wins over plastic, because glass preserves *shoyu* with minimal quality changes over time. Buy a smaller rather than an economy-size container, because an opened bottle of *shoyu* deteriorates in flavor and nutritional value over time.

Storage Tips. Store an opened bottle of *shoyu* in the refrigerator or in a cool, dry, dark place. Although *shoyu* will keep a very long time without spoiling, you should try to use up the bottle within two or three months, while its flavor is best.

How Good Is Your *Shoyu*?

Check the quality of your *koikuchi shoyu* with these tests:

- Pour some into a small white saucer. The *shoyu* should be dark reddish brown, translucent, and glossy. Bring the saucer to your nose. The fragrance should be round and complex, not sharp or chemical.
- Spill a drop of *shoyu* into a tall glass of cold water. The drop should hold its round shape for a time before gradually spreading and thinning.
- Now pour some *shoyu* into a clear glass jar with a lid and gently shake the closed jar. Tiny bubbles should appear on the surface and remain for a while.

If your *koikuchi* passes these tests, you can be sure it is a very good *shoyu.*

Wasabi
Wasabia

Oh, *wasabi*! With its striking pungency and attractive green color, it has spellbound sushi lovers all over America. Most, though, know *wasabi* only as a prepared relish, not as a plant. This perennial member of the mustard family grows wild nowhere but in the mountains of Japan. The Japanese have been using *wasabi* as a food and medicine for more than one thousand years, cultivating it since the late sixteenth century and eating its grated green root with sushi since the early nineteenth century.

A fastidious plant, *wasabi* is very difficult to grow. It needs a clean running stream with the proper mineral balance, temperature, and fast flow, and just the right mix of shade and sunlight. For this reason, the plant is very expensive to cultivate. Only recently have a few high-tech farms in America begun successfully producing *wasabi*.

In the best sushi restaurants, the chef grates the green *wasabi* rhizome in front of the diners immediately before serving it. Grating the rhizome causes an enzyme, myrosinase, to react with a chemical called sinigrin, a glucoside; the reaction produces a surprising pungency and a delicious aroma. When this happens, you can be sure your dinner will be worth the high price. You will not forget your experience of real *wasabi*.

Cheaper sushi restaurants rely on *wasabi* powder, which is mixed with water, or *wasabi* paste from a tube. These are not really *wasabi* at all; they are mixtures of ordinary white horseradish, mustard powder, and artificial flavor and color. Fake *wasabi* has plenty of pungency but none of the natural aroma, sweet flavor, and delicate color of the real thing. Some tubes are labeled *hon-wasabi,* real *wasabi,* but if they contain any real *wasabi* at all, according to Yoshihiko Shiratori (see the accompanying box, "A Japanese *Wasabi* Farm"), it is the flavorless white rootlets and not the valuable green rhizome. If you must use fake *wasabi,* take a tip from Mr. Tominaga of Hana Japanese Restaurant: add some grated *daikon,* to provide texture and blunt the pungency.

The Japanese food store where I shop in New York City began carrying fresh *wasabi* only last year. *Wasabi* is expensive—about fifteen dollars for a 4-inch-long root. If you can get it, though, I strongly suggest that you try it.

Wasabi deteriorates in flavor and pungency four to five minutes after it is grated, so always grate it immediately before you need it. The best grater for *wasabi* is made from a piece of sharkskin glued to a small wooden board (see "*Oroshiki,* Grater," page 52). If you don't have one of these, use your finest ceramic or metal grater. If the spikes are sharply pointed, as on a box-style grater,

Japanese versus American *Wasabi*

When I was visiting the Hana Japanese Restaurant in Sonoma, California, Ken Tominaga, the restaurant's sushi chef, offered me a special tasting opportunity: Japanese and American *wasabi,* freshly grated from the rhizome and served side by side. They were amazingly different. The Japanese *wasabi* was a lighter green, like pale lime sherbet. The two were equally pungent, but the Japanese root had more fragrance and a mellowing sweetness. The American *wasabi* simply hit my sinuses hard.

Wasabi for Health

Fresh *wasabi* is known to help prevent cancer and tooth decay, work against diarrhea, help fight osteoporosis, thin the blood, and kill microbes. Since *wasabi* prevents the growth of bacteria that cause food poisoning, serving it with raw fish makes perfect sense.

1. Grate the peeled *wasabi* in a slow, circular motion.

2. A pile of grated *wasabi*.

If you take an hour-long ride on the bullet train from Tokyo to Shizuoka Station, then drive twenty miles north along the meandering Abe-kawa River, you will reach Utougi, a village of seventy-nine households situated 2,200 feet above sea level and surrounded by high mountains. All the land in Utougi is cultivated, in tiny plots. In the level areas, tea grows; on the terraces, *wasabi*. This secluded place is where *wasabi* cultivation was born.

Yoshihiko Shiratori is one of fifty *wasabi* farmers in the village. His is the seventeenth generation in Wasabi no Monzen, a business founded by his ancestors four hundred years ago. His farm sits on a steep slope near one of the mountaintops.

When I visited him, every terrace was covered with *wasabi* plants, bursting with deep green leaves and ready to harvest. Clean water flowed naturally from the top of the mountain, sparkling and gurgling as it rushed through the terraced fields. To support the plants and provide efficient drainage, the terraces are built in layers, large stones covered by medium stones covered by small stones, which are in turn covered by pebbles, sand, and soil. The finicky plants take about eighteen months to grow to harvest size. Then, with a great deal of exertion, they are pulled up. Stepping onto a terrace, Mr. Shiratori shouted, *"Yoisho!"* as he pulled out a large *wasabi* plant with thick green leaves, a large plump rhizome, and long, hairy rootlets. Mr. Shiratori handed me the plant, and I hastily pulled off the stalks and leaves. Voilà! Now only a large green rhizome, bearing a smaller attached rhizome and two or three infant plants, the *wasabi* looked just like the one on boxes of *wasabi* powder and tubes of *wasabi* paste.

cover the surface with a piece of sturdy plastic wrap. Rinse and dry the rhizome, and peel off any remnants of the stalk with a knife. Grate the exposed top part of the root with a slow, circular motion, as illustrated; this breaks up the cells more finely and thus produces more pungency and aroma. For even more pungency, sprinkle the grater with sugar, salt, or lemon juice, any of which will extract more flavor from the *wasabi* cells.

You don't have to reserve *wasabi* for sushi or *sashimi.* Try it grated over cold *soba* noodles or, as Mr. Shiratori recommends, over steaming hot rice with julienned *nori* and a little *shoyu* (soy sauce). Mr. Shiratori also likes to sprinkle *wasabi* on steak, on cold tofu cubes, and into *shochu,* a high-proof liquor much like vodka.

Shopping Tips. Fresh *wasabi* is available from some Japanese markets and can be ordered directly from American *wasabi* farms, which you can easily find on the Internet.

If you find fresh *wasabi* in a store, select a rhizome that is plump, heavy for its size, and an attractive green color without dark spots. Look for tiny knobs; they show where stalks grew and dropped off as the plant matured. Closely spaced, small knobs indicate healthy growth, which creates abundant pungency, aroma, and flavor.

Wasabi powders and pastes are available in many ordinary supermarkets and health food stores as well as Japanese and general Asian markets.

Storage Tips. If you cannot use up your rhizome before it begins to dry out and lose flavor, grate the remainder and immediately wrap it in plastic. Put the wrapped *wasabi* into a sealable freezer bag and store the bag in the freezer.

Chapter 5
Tea and *Sake,* Beverages for Sushi

O-cha
Japanese Tea

Until about 1935, when *sake* became the standard drink at sushi restaurants, tea was the only partner for sushi. Still served free of charge in sushi restaurants, Japanese tea is an excellent accompaniment to a sushi meal. Tea refreshes the palate, provides the antioxidant vitamins C and E, raises "good" (HDL) cholesterol, and even has antibacterial properties. Also, sipping hot tea with cold sushi maintains a good thermal balance in the body.

If you get on the bullet train from Tokyo to Osaka, after about an hour you find yourself passing through tea country, where straight hedges of well-trimmed tea plants flash by at more than 160 miles per hour. Tea grown in Japan is the Chinese variety (*Camellia sinensis sinensis*), a low shrub with small leaves and better cold tolerance than the Assam variety (*Camellia sinensis assamica*) of northern India. Each tea shrub grows for five years before its leaves are harvested. The best leaves come from seven-year-old plants.

Since all Japanese tea is processed without fermentation, it is all "green," though some types are not really green in color. At a green-tea factory, freshly harvested leaves are briefly steamed to deactivate the enzymes that would otherwise ferment the leaves. This steaming preserves the green color of the tea, its refreshing "green" aroma, and more tannin than in either partially fermented Chinese *oolong* or fully fermented black tea from India. Tannin provides the pleasant, balanced astringency and bitterness characteristic of Japanese tea.

After they are steamed, Japanese tea leaves are rolled, dried, and twisted. They are then sold to a tea wholesaler, who sorts them by width, length, and quality and dries them a little more. The wholesaler packs the best leaves for sale and processes the inferior leaves to make brown-rice tea (*genmai-cha*) or roasted tea (*hoji-cha*).

The kind of tea served at sushi restaurants is *kona-cha,* from broken leaves that have been left in the processing machines at the end of production. Although *kona-cha* is inexpensive, it has good flavor, and it can be brewed in a quick way that suits a sushi restaurant's busy operation. *Kona-cha* is served at sushi restaurants in big, thick cups rather like American coffee mugs but without handles. Because these cups hold a large quantity of tea and keep it warm for quite a while, they save time and effort for the waitstaff.

To accompany homemade sushi, you don't need *kona-cha;* any Japanese tea is suitable. Each has a unique delicious flavor and its own ideal brewing method.

Most types of Japanese tea are available in tea bags, but I prefer loose

Cut the Caffeine

The caffeine content of most Japanese tea is about 2 percent by weight, or about twice as much as that of coffee beans. The brewing process, however, extracts more caffeine from coffee than from tea, and therefore, a cup of coffee has more than twice as much caffeine as a cup of Japanese tea. For the lowest level of caffeine, choose *genmai-cha* (a blend of tea and puffed brown rice) or *hoji-cha* (roasted tea).

tea so I can check the appearance before I buy. If the tea isn't prepackaged but stored in large bins or jars, I check the aroma as well.

To brew loose tea, put the leaves into a large disposable brewing bag (available in Japanese markets and kitchenware stores) or directly into the pot, rather than into a tea ball, so the leaves can expand fully and speak their loudest. Unless a fine strainer is built into the pot, use a separate tea strainer as you pour the tea into cups.

Shopping Tips. In general, the higher the price, the better the quality. If the tea is packaged rather than loose, the package should be airtight. Don't be tempted by a large package, because once it is opened, the aroma and quality of the tea will deteriorate quickly. Check for production or packaging dates, and choose the freshest tea you can find. To appeal to Americans, some green teas are now sold with added flavorings. I recommend buying pure, good-quality green tea.

Storage Tips. In Japan, we always store tea in a tin with a tight-fitting lid, but you could substitute a plastic container. Store tea in a dry, dark, cool place. For the best flavor and aroma, use up an opened package of tea within a month or so.

If you have stored your tea too long, you can revive its aroma and flavor somewhat by toasting the leaves for about half a minute in a skillet or toaster oven.

Japanese Teas and How to Brew Them

Sen-cha. This is the most widely consumed tea in Japan, with about an 80 percent market share. *Sen-cha* is made from younger, tender leaves and graded according to harvesttime:

- *Ichi-ban-cha:* first harvest, in spring
- *Ni-ban-cha:* second harvest, from early summer through midsummer
- *San-ban-cha:* third harvest, from midsummer through late summer
- *Yon-ban-cha:* fourth harvest, in early autumn

Brewed *sen-cha* has an attractive light green color, a balanced astringency and bitterness with a round finish, and a refreshing "green" aftertaste. The best *sen-cha* is *ichi-ban-cha,* from the first harvest, in late April and May, but this tea is expensive. If you choose to serve *sen-cha* for your sushi dinner, you might serve a lower grade during the meal and reserve the best grade for the end. The caffeine content of *sen-cha* is 2.3 percent by weight; the tannin content, 13 percent.

How to brew sen-cha*:* Fill a teapot with boiling water. After a minute or so, pour the water into porcelain teacups, filling each about two-thirds full. Discard the water remaining in the pot. By this time, the water in the cups should be at about 175° F; at this temperature, the steam spreads toward the side of each cup before rising. Put 2 teaspoons of tea leaves per person into the warm pot and pour the slightly cooled water from the cups back into the pot. Cover the pot and let the tea steep for one minute. Then strain the tea into the cups. To brew a second round of tea with the used leaves, use somewhat hotter water and steep the tea for just twenty seconds.

Ban-cha. Made from the larger, tougher leaves of later harvests, *ban-cha* is an inexpensive tea that may contain some twigs. Compared with *sen-cha, ban-cha* has a little less caffeine and tannin (2 percent and 11 percent, respectively), and when brewed, it has a yellow-green color and a refreshing finish. In Japan, *ban-cha* is an everyday, informal tea.

How to brew ban-cha*:* Put 2 teaspoons of tea per person into a teapot. Pour boiling water into ceramic tea or coffee cups, filling each about two-thirds full. Wait one minute and then pour the cooled water into the pot. Cover the pot and steep the leaves for thirty seconds. Then strain the tea into the cups. For a second round, bring water to a boil and let it cool for three minutes before adding it to the teapot. Steep the leaves for just thirty seconds before serving.

Genmai-cha. *Genmai* is brown rice. *Genmai-cha* is made by blending *ban-cha* or mid- or low-grade *sen-cha* leaves with puffed brown rice, which adds a sweet, nutty, toasted flavor. This tea goes best with American-style sushi rolls or other strongly flavored foods. It contains less caffeine (1.8 percent by weight) than any other Japanese tea, and its tannin content (5 percent) is less than half that of *ban-cha.*

Brew *genmai-cha* just as you would *ban-cha.*

Gyokuro. Like champagne in the West, this most expensive of Japanese teas is reserved for important occasions. *Gyokuro* is produced by covering tea bushes with black cloth when they begin to bear their first spring leaves, thus severely limiting the sunshine that reaches the leaves. This reduces their production of catechin, the source of astringency in tea, and both increases the caffeine level and creates a balanced, round flavor. The brewed tea has an attractive deep green color, a full body, and a refreshing "green" finish. The caffeine is 3.5 percent by weight; the tannin, only 10 percent.

How to brew gyokuro: This tea is steeped in a small pot and served in special small, espresso-size cups. Pour boiling water into a small teapot and let the water cool, uncovered, to about 140° F. I know the temperature is right when I can just bear to hold my fingertip in the water for five seconds. Pour the cooled water into the cups and discard the water remaining in the pot. Put 2 teaspoons of tea leaves per person into the pot. Immediately pour the water in the cups back into the pot. Cover the pot and steep the leaves for two minutes before serving. By the time you begin sipping your tea, it should be just lukewarm. To brew a second round, pour water a little hotter than 140° into the pot and steep the leaves for thirty seconds.

Hoji-cha. To make this tea, *ban-cha* or mid- or low-grade *sen-cha* leaves are roasted until they turn light brown and take on a pleasant, caramelized and smoky flavor and fragrance. An inexpensive, everyday tea, *hoji-cha* is not suited for a *nigiri-zushi*

dinner made with delicate raw seafood, but it can be enjoyed with modern rolls made with mayonnaise or other oily sauces. The brewed tea is golden brown and delicious drunk cold as well as hot. The caffeine content is only 1.9 percent by weight; the tannin, 9.5 percent.

Brew *hoji-cha* in the same way as *ban-cha.*

Kona-cha. Standard at sushi restaurants, this tea has a good flavor but lacks a full-bodied aroma. It is similar to *sen-cha* and *ban-cha* in caffeine and tannin content.

How to brew kona-cha: Hiroyuki Yamanashi, a tea wholesaler, recommends a simple method for brewing *kona-cha* to accompany sushi. Use 2 teaspoons of tea leaves for each half-cup serving. Pour boiling water over the leaves and steep the tea for two minutes. This method extracts from the leaves a maximum amount of catechin, an antibacterial chemical.

Matcha. The tea served at a traditional Japanese tea ceremony, *matcha* is produced like *gyokuro* but ground into a powder in a large stone mortar. *Matcha* comes in two styles, one for thin tea, *o-usu,* and the other, made from even higher-quality leaves, for thick tea, *o-koi-cha.* Used

only for very special occasions, *o-koi-cha* is made by blending *matcha* with hot water to make a thick paste. *O-usu* is made in the same way but with more hot water and much beating with a bamboo whisk. The result is a foamy drink that looks rather like green espresso. Because the tea leaves are actually consumed, *matcha* tastes quite bitter. For this reason, it is often accompanied by a seasonal Japanese sweet. The tannin content of *matcha* is 10 percent by weight; the caffeine content, 3.2 percent by weight.

How to make o-usu (thin matcha): You will need a bamboo whisk (*chasen*) and a *matcha* tea bowl (*matcha jawan*) or another ceramic bowl of a size you might use for breakfast cereal. You can find both a *chasen* and a *matcha jawan* in a Japanese grocery store. Sift the *matcha* through a fine sieve. Pour hot water into the bowl to warm it and then discard the water and wipe the inside of the bowl dry. Put 1/2 teaspoon sifted *matcha* into the bowl. Bring some water to a boil, let it cool to about 195°, and then pour 1/4 cup of the hot water into the bowl. With the bamboo whisk, beat vigorously until a fine, thick foam completely covers the surface of the tea. Pour the tea into a cup. Make additional servings in the same way.

Old Tea Performs Miracles

Hiroyuki Yamanashi, president of a wholesale tea company, offered me several great tips for using tea that has lost its aroma and flavor:

- Tea makes a good household deodorizer. Toast the leaves in a skillet over medium-low heat until they are fragrant. Put them into an open container or a disposable

brewing bag, and put it wherever it's needed, such as in the refrigerator or a pair of shoes.
- Tea removes fishy smells and oily flavors. Before broiling or grilling a smelly fish, rinse it, either sliced or whole, in freshly brewed and cooled tea. Or poach the fish in weak tea.
- Tea is a good sterilizing agent. If you are worried about the safety of eating raw fish, you can rinse the fish in freshly brewed and cooled tea before using it for sushi or *sashimi.* But don't overdo this;

the strong tannins in the tea could destroy the delicate flavor of the fish.
- A traditional way of preparing octopus is to cook it in strong-brewed *ban-cha* with a little salt and vinegar. This keeps the octopus's skin from peeling off.
- A tip of my own: After brewing tea in a disposable bag, squeeze out the liquid and keep the bag by the kitchen sink. Use the tea bag to clean oily spots from a pan or remove stains from cookware.

Sake
Rice Wine

In the past twenty-five years in Japan, *sake* has become a gourmet beverage, available in many varieties for pairing with different foods and for drinking hot, warm, cool, or chilled. Now that they have begun to appear in U.S. markets, these varieties are causing a wave of interest in *sake* across the country.

Sake *Production Styles.* *Sake* is made from rice; spring water; a kind of mold called *koji* (*Aspergillus oryzae*), which breaks down the rice to produce a sweet liquid; and yeast, which converts the sugar in the liquid to alcohol. The resulting brew, with an alcohol content of about 20 percent, is usually diluted with spring water before bottling to between 13 and 18 percent alcohol, not much different from grape wine.

There are two basic styles of *sake*: *junmai-shu,* pure rice wine, and *honjozo-shu,* naturally brewed rice wine. *Honjozo-shu* is different in that a little distilled alcohol is added at the end of production to soften the flavor, stabilize the quality, and preserve the fresh aroma of the newly made *sake. Honjozo-shu* has a rounder, smoother flavor and more fragrance than *junmai-shu,* which is more acidic, fuller-bodied, and earthy. Less *honjozo-shu* than *junmai-shu* is imported to the United States.

Sake *Grades.* The following grading system by which *sake* is labeled applies to both basic styles, *junmai-shu* and *honjozo-shu:*

Premium	*dai-ginjo-shu*
Superior	*ginjo-shu*
Third-ranked special	*tokubetsu-shu*
Ordinary	labeled only by its production style, *junmai-shu* or *honjozo-shu*
Low-grade, "table *sake*"	*futsu-shu*

Sake Culture in Japan

Sake was once drunk, mostly by men, just to get drunk. Being drunk in public was pardoned by Japanese society, because only when drunk could a man express his true thoughts and feelings. Most important, he could speak directly and critically with his boss. After everyone sobered up, the men regarded all that had happened during their drunkenness as if it had never occurred.

Sake once put women into a kind of slavery. While the men were getting drunk, women were repeatedly warming the *sake* in its little flask, serving it in tiny cups, and when necessary, taking care of the drunks.

Since those days not so long ago, the Japanese have both refined and democratized *sake* drinking. The introduction of French wines brought with it the concept of enjoying an alcoholic beverage for its aroma, color, and flavor and for the way it complements various foods. Because dining with wine seemed elegant, it had mass appeal for the Japanese. As wine drinking spread, *sake* breweries began to fear for their survival. And so they began to produce better kinds of *sake,* kinds that go well with food. Superior (*ginjo*) and premium (*dai-ginjo*) grades became popular. Improvements in brewery technology and transportation made possible the marketing of seasonal and other specialty types of *sake* to *sake* lovers far away, even overseas.

Special Kinds of *Sake*

Nigori-zake, *Cloudy* Sake. This is made by filtering newly brewed *sake* through coarse cloth, so that tiny particles of rice, *koji,* and yeast remain in the *sake,* giving it a slightly sweet-sour, almost yogurtlike flavor. The cloudiness varies from that of milk with 1 percent butterfat to a much denser white. If the bottle is undisturbed, however, most of the residue settles.

Because unpasteurized *nigori-zake* is very vulnerable to spoilage, it is sold in America only after heat treatment. *Nigori-zake* should be refrigerated at or below 41° F, even if the bottle is pasteurized and unopened. Before serving this *sake,* let it stand at room temperature for five minutes and then shake the bottle to mix the sediments thoroughly in the liquid.

Genshu, *Undiluted* Sake. This *sake* is diluted only slightly before bottling, to an alcohol content of about 19 percent. The strong body of *genshu* is balanced by the sweet, savory flavor of the rice from which it is made. *Genshu* is excellent to drink on the rocks; as the ice melts, you can taste the *sake* at different strengths.

Kimoto. This traditional *sake* may be a bit challenging for beginners. Whereas most modern *sake* brewers add lactic acid to the *shubo,* or yeast mash, to shorten to ten days the period during which *sake* yeast and bacteria multiply, *kimoto* brewers nurture the yeast for a full thirty days. The result is a more robust microbial mix, which extracts more aroma and sweetness from the rice in the fermentation tank. With its strong body and distinctive flavor, *kimoto* is the *sake* for the real *sake* drinker.

Koshu, *Aged* Sake. Although *sake* has always been consumed primarily within a year of its production, some Japanese brewers were aging *sake* as early as the thirteenth century. They stopped completely in the late nineteenth century, when the Japanese government began funding its wars with a tax on all *sake* that was produced, regardless of whether it was sold. With this severe tax and rice shortages besides, it made no sense for brewers to withhold *sake* for aging. But when in 1954 the government began taxing *sake* sales rather than production, some breweries resumed the old art of producing *koshu,* aged *sake.*

Generally, aged *sake* has a rich body, concentrated flavors, and an attractive amber hue. *Koshu* makes an excellent dessert drink. The quality of this *sake* varies widely, however, as there is no uniform standard for its production. You may have to try a few brands before you find one that is to your liking.

Kijoshu, *Nobly Brewed* Sake. Invented in 1975 by a chemist at the Research Institute for Breweries, this is another exception to the rule that *sake* is bottled and consumed soon after production. With its amber color, thick texture, and sweet, rich flavor, *kijoshu* reminds me of sweet sherry. To produce *kijoshu,* a portion of the spring water used in the final fermentation is replaced with *sake,* and then the mixture is aged for several years. Like *koshu, kijoshu* is a very good dessert drink.

The higher the grade, the more labor, time, and money have been spent on production. For instance, making premium-grade *sake* requires small batches, a long, low-temperature fermentation, a special yeast, and high-quality rice that is polished more than for lower grades. The choice of yeast determines the strength of the *sake*'s fragrance and the subtlety and refinement of its flavor. The amount of polishing matters because the outer layer of rice is mostly protein, whereas the interior is mostly starch. Since the protein gives *sake* a rough, unpleasant flavor, the more the rice is polished, the better the *sake. Dai-ginjo-shu* (premium *sake*) is made with rice polished to 50 percent of its original volume; *ginjo-shu* (superior *sake*) is made with rice polished to 60 percent of its original volume. Ordinary *sake* and *futsu-shu* (low-grade *sake*) are made with rice polished to 70 percent of its original volume. For both *junmai-shu* and *honjozo-shu,* premium and superior grades have more fragrance, lower acidity, and a lighter, more refined flavor. *Tokubetsu-shu* (third-ranked special *sake*) has unique characteristics, which differ from one brewery and one batch to another. I use *futsu-shu,* table *sake,* mainly for cooking.

Beyond production styles and grades, other elements that affect the taste of *sake* are pasteurization and length of storage. *Sake* has traditionally been made and consumed in accordance with the yearly cycle: the fermentation process begins with the rice harvest in October and continues until spring, and the *sake* is drunk within a year. From the fifteenth century until quite recently, fresh *sake* was always filtered and pasteurized, allowed to mature through the summer, and then pasteurized again before bottling and distribution. Thanks to technological advances, however, some *sake* is now bottled in spring or

summer, with or without pasteurization. As a result, *sake* drinkers can enjoy different brews to suit each season.

Until recently, only a few devotees got to taste *sake* before it was pasteurized. By dropping by the brewery at the right time in winter, they could drink *shiboritate,* new brew, whose flavor is like an untamed horse—young, rough, vibrant, and refreshing. Now superfine filtering, cold storage, and refrigerated transportation have made it possible to taste *shiboritate* far from the brewery, even in America. To stabilize the quality, the alcohol content of *shiboritate* is kept on the high side, about 18 percent.

Connoisseurs' favorite *shiboritate* is *arabashiri,* rough run. For each batch of *sake,* only a few bottles bear this label, because *arabashiri* comes from the first cloudy drips through the filtering bag, before the *sake* flows clear. *Arabashiri* tastes even wilder than other *shiboritate.* On my first sip, a slight carbonation tickled my mouth, a fresh, fruity bouquet entertained my nose, and a lively flavor danced down my throat. A bottle of *arabashiri* pairs well with the pleasant bitterness of young spring mountain vegetables and plant buds, which are harvested just at the time that *sake* filtering begins.

Today newly brewed *sake* is sometimes stored without pasteurization. After several months of storage, some of this *sake* is pasteurized just before bottling, and some is bottled with no pasteurization at all. Unpasteurized *sake,* or *nama-zake,* has a half-matured character, with a vibrancy provided by the living microorganisms and active enzymes in the bottle. As with *shiboritate,* a relatively high alcohol content ensures stable quality. *Nama-zake* is mostly distributed in the summer, when its flavors go well with dishes such as cold noodles, chilled tofu, vegetable *tempura,* and salt-grilled fish. Since it

requires refrigeration, *nama-zake* is drunk chilled.

Sake that is pasteurized only just before bottling is *nama-chozo-zake,* another summertime favorite. Although the heat treatment eliminates some of the fresh aroma and flavor, this *sake* is still very refreshing to drink chilled in hot weather.

Sake that is pasteurized in spring is stored longer, until cool autumn breezes replace the blazing heat of summer. In the fall, the stored *sake* is fully mature, with the smoothest, most balanced flavor characteristics. It is ready for bottling now, with or without a second pasteurization. Without heat treatment, it is *nama-zume,* a kind of *sake* cherished for its full, smooth flavor and nicknamed *hiya-oroshi,* autumn bottling. *Nama-zume* is a perfect match for the rich-flavored foods of the fall harvest.

Sake pasteurized in both spring and fall has no special name, since most *sake* falls into this category. Bottles of twice-pasteurized *sake* are identified only by production style and grade. The mature flavor of this *sake* is enjoyed throughout the winter.

***Tasting* Sake.** As with grape wine, connoisseurs have developed tasting methods for *sake;* some have written books on the subject. Here is my distillation of the experts' advice:

1. Even if the *sake* is of a type usually drunk warm or chilled, for tasting have the bottle at about 68° F. At this temperature, the *sake*'s vapor will be most noticeable and its sweetness and other flavors most neutral.
2. Pour some *sake* into a glass and observe the color. Unless you're tasting *nigori-zake* (cloudy *sake*), the liquid should be clear and glossy.
3. Holding the glass in both hands, slowly rotate it and then bring it to your

nose. Sniff and enjoy the complex fragrance without sipping right away. From a higher-grade *ginjo* or *dai-ginjo* brew will burst forth many distinctive fragrances, which may be reminiscent of flowers, fruits, nuts, caramel, mushrooms, fallen leaves, and of course, rice.

4. Sip about a teaspoon and roll the liquid over your tongue. From the warmed *sake,* more fragrances will fly up and hit your olfactory nerves. Breathe in and enjoy this second round of fragrances.

5. Swallow the *sake,* take another sip, and consider the acidity, sweetness, alcohol content, and amino acid content.

All *sake* is very low in acid compared with grape wine, but *junmai-shu* (pure rice *sake*) is generally more acidic than *honjozo-shu* (naturally brewed *sake*), and *honjozo-shu* is generally a little more acidic than *ginjo-shu* and *dai-ginjo-shu.*

A number on the bottle, preceded by a + or −, indicates sweetness on a chemically accurate scale; a value of 0 is neutral, +7 is very dry, and −7 is very sweet. Your own perception, however, may not match this scale. Even +1 seems very sweet to some people. Your perception of sweetness will vary according to the serving temperature, the acidity,

and the alcohol content of the *sake.*

The alcohol content is always identified on the label. In general, the higher the alcohol content, the rounder and richer the flavor of the *sake.*

You can taste the organic acids in *sake*—glutamic, lactic, malic, succinic, and others—as the savoriness that we Japanese call *umami. Kombu* (kelp), mushrooms, tomato, and parmesan cheese are examples of foods high in *umami.* Since the outer part of a rice grain has the most protein, ordinary-grade *junmai-shu* and *honjozo-shu,* made from less polished rice, have more *umami* than premium brews.

Pairing *Sake* with Sushi

Composed of the freshest, most delicate ingredients from the sea and the field, sushi is light and lean, but each tiny mouthful is full of distinct, natural flavors. *Sake,* likewise, has a light body and a clean, lean taste. Because *sake* and sushi are both made primarily of rice, *sake* is a low-key supporting character for the sushi meal. And because of its low acidity, *sake* never competes with the unembellished flavors of raw seafood.

Some American restaurants have begun to recommend *sake* as a partner for raw oysters, caviar, or aged ham. Grape wine might speak too loudly with these foods or make their strong characteristics—fishiness, saltiness, greasiness, a metallic flavor—stand out too much. *Sake* better complements such foods.

There are no prescriptions for matching *sake* with sushi, but here are my suggestions:

- *Junmai-shu* (pure rice *sake*): Choose fatty fish or fish parts, such as *toro* (fatty tuna), *buri* or *hamachi* (yellowtail), *kampachi* (great amberjack), *sake* (salmon), *katsuo* (skipjack tuna or bonito), *ikura* (salmon roe), broiled or basted *anago* (conger eel), and *anko no kimo* (monkfish liver). Most of the modern rolls—California, *tempura,* eel and avocado, and spicy tuna—also go very well with this style of *sake. Junmai-shu* tastes best at about 59° to 68° F, and this lukewarm temperature complements a cold sushi dinner.

- *Ginjo-shu* and *dai-ginjo-shu* (superior and premium *sake*): Choose sushi seafoods that are lean, fragrant, clean-tasting, and naturally sweet, such as *uni* (sea urchin), *awabi* (abalone), *hirame* (flounder), *suzuki* (sea bass), *kai-rui* (clams), and *ebi* (shrimp).

- *Nama-zake* (unpasteurized *sake*) and *nama-chozo* (*sake* pasteurized only at bottling): Choose any of the fish recommended for pairing with *junmai-shu* or try lean but strong-flavored seafoods such as oyster, *uni* (sea urchin), vinegar-cured fish, and *shoyu-* or *kombu-*cured fish.

6. Before you've drunk enough to dull your tastes, consider the *kire,* finish. When you swallow a sip of *sake,* your mouth and throat are left with some sensation—a taste that lingers or suddenly fades, a stickiness, a smoothness or roughness. A good finish—*kire ga ii*—is a clean aftertaste, without a sensation of sweetness or roughness. A bad finish—*kire ga warui*—is unpleasantly rough, sticky-sweet, or burning.

Serving Sake. *Chibiri chibiri to sake o nomu* goes the old saying: "Drink *sake* tiny sip after tiny sip." *Sake* is traditionally poured from a small ceramic flask, *tok-kuri,* which is first put into a hot bath until the *sake* reaches the desired temperature. The *sake* is served in a tiny cup, *o-choko,* which holds only 2 to 3 tablespoons. Each diner takes with chopsticks a morsel or two from five to ten small dishes before him or her, then takes a sip of *sake,* then takes another morsel or two. By tiny bites and tiny sips, the meal progresses. The hostess or server refills the tiny cups until the flask is empty and then returns to the kitchen to refill and rewarm the flask. This ensures that everyone can enjoy their *sake* at just the right temperature through the entire dinner.

Today *sake* may be served at a wide range of temperatures, from chilled (41° F) to hot (131° F). The ideal temperature for a particular *sake* depends on production style, grade, and personal preference. In place of a *tok-kuri* and *o-choko,* glasses of various sizes and shapes may be appropriate. Here are some general guidelines for serving *sake:*

• *Ginjo* (superior) and *dai-ginjo* (premium) *sake:* These brews are slightly bitter when warmed. To best enjoy their delightful aroma and flavor, serve them at 50° to 59° F, in small, stemmed glasses such as those used for port or Chardonnay.

• *Junmai-shu* (pure rice *sake*): This *sake* is refreshing at 50° F, but its acidity, sweetness, bitterness, and astringency are in best balance at a slightly warmer temperature, 59° to 68°. To bring out the sweetness, heat *junmai-shu* to as high as 114°. *Junmai-shu* is generally drunk from *sake* cups, *o-choko,* but when I serve it at 50°, I use small glasses instead.

Sake Temperature Terms

Just as Americans have a special vocabulary related to the serving of alcoholic beverages—"neat," "on the rocks," "straight up," and so on—the Japanese use specific terminology in the endlessly discussed subject of cooling and warming *sake.*

Try one of these terms with your Japanese bartender, sushi chef, or waiter:

Yuki-hie	snow cold, 41° F
Hana-hie	flower cold, 50°
Suzu-hie	cold, 59°
Hinata-kan	sunshine warm, 86°
Hitohada-kan	body temperature, 98°
Nuru-kan	lukewarm, 104°
Jo-kan	warm, 113°
Atsu-kan	hot, 122°
Tobikiri-kan	superhot, 131°

- *Nama-zake, nama-chozo-shu,* and *genshu* (unpasteurized, once-pasteurized, and undiluted *sake*): These vibrant brews, high in alcohol content, are delicious quite cold, at about 40°. You can even serve them on the rocks. Use small, straight-sided glasses.
- *Kimoto:* The robust, mature flavor of this *sake* is best expressed at a warm temperature, 113° to 131° F. Use *o-choko* cups.

Shopping Tips. Make sure the *sake* you buy has been kept sufficiently cool or chilled. Twice-pasteurized, nonpremium *sake* should be stored at 59° F or below. Premium and unpasteurized brews require refrigeration and so are always marked *yo-reizo,* refrigerate. Unfortu- nately, this is written in Japanese charac- ters. If you are selecting a fairly expen- sive *sake* and no one in the store can identify the *yo-reizo* mark for you, you might better shop elsewhere.

With the increasing varieties of *sake* imported from Japan, more and more bottles are labeled in English. As with grape wine, the description on the label may be no more than a glorified sales pitch. But keep in mind the basics of production methods and grades and you won't go wrong. As your knowledge and experience increase, you can explore the subtle variations among brands, brew- eries, and regions. For sources, see pages 261–264.

Storage Tips. Store twice-pasteurized, nonpremium *sake* in a dark, cold place. Refrigerate premium brews. Under these conditions, unopened bottles will main- tain good quality for two years if they are nonpremium, one year if they are premium. If you don't finish a bottle, pour the remaining *sake* into a smaller bottle (to eliminate excess air), refriger- ate the bottle, and drink the remaining *sake* as soon as possible. If you don't drink it up quickly, use it in cooking. I keep opened bottles of *futsu-shu,* the lowest grade of *sake,* in the refrigerator for as long as a month or so for use in cooking.

Unpasteurized *sake* should be kept under refrigeration (at or below 41°) and drunk as soon as possible after pur- chase. Finish the bottle on the day it is opened.

Sake for Skin Care

If a forgotten bottle of *sake* has sat on the shelf too long, you might try it in a hot bath. Pour in the entire bottle. The organic acids in the *sake* will make your skin moist and smooth, and the *sake* will help warm your body.

Chapter 6
A Sushi Chef's Tools

You can make sushi with ordinary Western kitchen implements, but Japanese tools designed for the task will enable you to work more efficiently and produce superior results. I recommend you buy at least a *makisu* (bamboo rolling mat) and a *tawashi* (hard brush). These and the other tools described in this chapter can be obtained from large Japanese food stores, Asian supermarkets, some kitchen supply stores, and several Internet vendors (for help in locating suppliers, see "Sources for Japanese Food Products" and "Sources for Japanese Kitchen Equipment," pages 261 and 265). You will also need a *sushi-oke* (wooden tub) or large, unfinished wooden salad bowl and a good, sharp knife. If you plan to slice fish for *sashimi* or *nigiri-zushi,* you should get one of the long-bladed Japanese knives made for this purpose.

Fukin
Kitchen Cloth

This thin, tightly woven, snow-white cotton cloth is very absorbent and lint-free. It is used for wiping, for wrapping foods, and for straining broth and other liquids. A cook cuts a *fukin* to a suitable length from a *sarashi,* a roll of cloth typically 13½ inches wide and about 30 feet long. In the United States, rolls of *sarashi* cloth are now marketed only for restaurant use, but they are so useful that I wouldn't be surprised if they soon appeared in home-kitchen supply stores. In the meantime, a good substitute for a *fukin* is a piece of tightly woven, lightweight muslin or a very high-quality paper towel.

Hocho
Japanese Knife

Japanese chefs believe that a good knife has a soul, *tamashii,* that was implanted by the craftsmen who made, sharpened, and fitted the blade. Only chefs who have polished their knife skills over many years can discover this soul. For this reason, Japanese chefs treat their knives with the utmost care and respect.

A Japanese chef needs good knives and the skill to use them, first of all, because Japanese foods must be cut into pieces manageable with chopsticks. And since each dish must satisfy all five of the senses—taste, smell, touch, hearing, and sight—foods must be cut so they are visually appealing. The quality of the knife and the chef's skill in using it also affect texture, aroma, taste, and even the sound of the food as it is being eaten.

Traditionally, Japanese knives are made of carbon steel or a mixture of carbon steel and soft iron. A carbon steel knife is called a *hon-yaki;* a knife made of carbon steel and iron is called a *tanzo.* A *hon-yaki* blade can hold a sharper cutting edge, but since the blade is very vulnerable to rust, it must always be kept dry, and if it is dropped or used on something hard, such as bone, it may chip or break. A *tanzo*

In my left hand, the *deba* knife; in my right hand, the *yanagiba* knife

blade, which is more flexible and therefore more durable than a *hon-yaki,* also holds its edge longer and costs much less. So a *tanzo* knife is my choice.

Among *tanzo* knives, according to Junro Aoki of Knife System Company, the best are made of *ao-ni-ko,* or blue number 2 carbon steel. This alloy contains tungsten and chrome, which give knives more resistance to shock and lessen their tendency to rust. *Ao-ni-ko* blades also maintain a sharp cutting edge longer than other *tanzo* blades.

Rust is a problem with both *hon-yaki* and *tanzo* knives. Japanese chefs have long spurned stainless steel blades, though, because they can't be honed to a really sharp edge. But today Mr. Aoki's company is producing a new type of stainless steel knife, made of an alloy called Inox. An Inox blade won't rust, and it can be honed to a very sharp edge. The blade requires only occasional sharpening, but when it does, much

strength and energy are needed to restore the hard blade to excellent condition.

With few exceptions, Japanese knives are ground on one face only, on the right for right-handed users or on the left for left-handed users.

Sushi chefs use three styles of knives:

1. *Yanagiba-bocho,* willow-blade knife: Shaped like a willow leaf and also called a *sashimi* knife, this long, narrow, thin-bladed knife is a must for slicing fish thin for *sashimi* or *nigiri-zushi.* A good *yanagiba* knife is heavy enough that, when it is well sharpened, the cook can use it without pressing down. *Yanagiba* knives come in lengths between 9 and 13 inches. Choose a longer one if you have plenty of counter space, since it will work for fillets both big and small. A *sashimi* knife is also good for slicing other things, such as roasts.

2. *Deba-bocho,* fish-butchering knife:

With its thick, triangular blade, this knife is designed for filleting fish; it is also excellent for butchering and cutting up chicken and other fowl. A *deba* blade ranges from 5 to 10 inches, and its weight increases according to its size. A large Western chef's knife is generally a good substitute.

3. *Usuba-bocho,* thin-bladed knife: With a rectangular blade and a straight cutting edge that is parallel to the handle, this knife looks like a thin, slender cleaver. The top edge may be cut off squarely or curved downward to meet the cutting edge. Although indispensable in the professional kitchen for peeling, slicing, and chopping vegetables, this knife is not a necessity in the home kitchen. A good, well-sharpened Western chef's knife will be equally effective.

Many Japanese home cooks today employ only one type of knife, the *santoku-bocho,* or three-values knife.

(continued on page 49)

How to Sharpen Your Japanese Knife

Professional chefs in Japan sharpen their knives every night after closing, but many home cooks do their sharpening only when their knives are really dull. Keeping your knife well sharpened is worth the little time required. With a sharp knife, you can cut foods with the least effort; you avoid crushing fibers and muscle meat and losing juices; and the cut foods will have attractive, clean surfaces.

The following instructions are for right-handed people with right-handed knives. If you are left-handed, reverse the instructions. If you are sharpening knives ground on both sides, follow the instructions as given and then reverse them to sharpen the other side of the blade.

Soak your sharpening stone in water for about fifteen minutes. Wet an old kitchen towel, and squeeze out the excess water. Spread the towel on the counter. Place the stone, short edge facing you, on the towel (the towel will keep the stone in place).

Sprinkle the stone with water. With your thumb extended slightly over the blade, hold the knife in your right hand diagonally to the stone. Place the third of the blade closest to the handle over the stone and raise the top of the blade slightly so the cutting edge lies against the stone's surface. With the middle three fingers of your left hand on the edge of the blade, press the cutting edge against the stone. As you firmly press with your fingers, push the blade away from you across the stone, keeping the angle of the blade constant to maintain the original cutting edge. Take care not to cut your fingers! Release the pressure and draw the blade back to the starting point. Repeat this twenty times.

Now sharpen the middle third of the blade in the same way, and finally the far end, following the illustration.

Lift the knife and very gently touch the edge of the unsharpened side of the blade. You should feel a slight roughness, a bit of metal pushed up by the sharpening. If you don't feel this burr, sharpen the blade some more. Then lay the unground side of the blade flat against the stone and, pressing lightly, run the blade across the stone once or twice. The edge should be smooth now.

Clean the knife with mildly soapy cold water to remove any metallic residue. With a towel, wipe the knife completely dry.

1. Place the third of the blade closest to the handle over the wet stone and, with three fingers pressing down on the edge of the blade, push it away from you.

2. After sharpening the center of the blade, when you get to the tip, push it across and off to the right to sharpen the point.

Repeat the process with the long knife.

The Enduring Art of Japanese Knife Making

Some of the best cooking knives in Japan come from Sakai, a city about eleven miles south of Osaka. Sakai is home to one of the largest of the ancient Japanese royal tombs, the Nintoku-ryo, which were built in the fifth century as resting places for the emperors and their families. The construction of Sakai's tomb complex required skilled craftsmen, who made and used many kinds of iron tools. Their descendants applied the blacksmith's art to implements such as hoes and plows, first made from iron and later from steel. Soon after the Portuguese introduced tobacco into Japan in the sixteenth century, Sakai craftsmen began producing and selling the country's highest-quality tobacco knives. Today Sakai's knife craftsmen remain the best in Japan. Many of the older workers are designated by the government as Dento Kogeishi, Living Important Traditional Arts Craftsmen.

Junro Aoki grew up in this city of knives and has worked here all his life. At the age of thirty-seven, he began to worry about the future of Sakai's knife industry: the aging workers were retiring without training successors, because young people didn't want to do such hard, dirty, low-paid work. So Mr. Aoki left his father's wholesale company to found his own business, the Knife System Company, which makes fine knives to order for professional chefs.

At the Knife System Company workshop, I watched seventy-six-year-old Keijiro Doi make a *tanzo* blade. Standing in a small clay pit before a clay oven, Mr. Doi heated an iron bar over a coal and pine-charcoal fire. Then he took the red-hot softened bar from the oven and pounded it on an anvil with a small iron hammer. He placed a block of carbon steel on top of the iron bar, heated both together in the clay oven, and then put them into the hammering machine that stood beside him in the pit. While the machine pounded at tremendous volume, Mr. Doi continually moved the metal piece, back and forth and left and right. He heated the beaten bar again until it was as soft as hot candy, cut off the end so that he had a piece the right size for a knife blade, and then put the bar back under the mechanical hammer until the metal began

Blade maker

to take on the rough shape of a knife blade.

Abruptly, the noise of the machine ceased, and small, slender, white-haired Mr. Doi jumped out of the pit to greet me with a charming smile. The process I'd just observed, he explained, was a crucial part of knife making. The temperature inside the clay oven, the length of time the bar was heated before hammering, the way it was hammered, and how long it was hammered would determine the quality of the finished knife. After so many years of performing these tasks, said Mr. Doi, he does them well without even thinking.

When he was young, the work was more difficult. Mr. Doi began his career at the age of nineteen, performing in his father's forge the role now played by the mechanical hammer. When Mr. Doi turned forty, his father simply walked out of the forge and did not return. Suddenly, Mr. Doi was in charge of the entire production process, including parts that his father had never taught him. Mr. Doi has struggled ever since to produce knives of the best quality possible. Without pencil, paper, or computer, he can design in his head a new

Knife sharpening at factory

knife of the size, weight, and shape to meet each customer's needs.

On the hottest days of summer, when the thermometer outdoors hits 95° F, the temperature in the forge reaches 122°. It is too hot to eat, so Mr. Doi skips his lunch and drinks cold tea instead. "I get back to my full weight of ninety-two pounds by the beginning of the year," he told me.

Mr. Doi sat down on a low stool beside the oven. He hammered the blade to flatten and smooth it. Next to him, his son, Itsuo, further smoothed his father's blades with an electric grinding wheel. They worked harmoniously but without conversation, and I imagined Mr. Doi and his own father in the same scene. Soon all the rough blades were smoothed, and Mr. Doi was adding more pine charcoal and coal to the oven. When the flame turned reddish orange, he beckoned me closer to watch the process of *yaki-ire,* treating the knife with heat. His son dipped each smoothed blade into a muddy liquid, dried the blade momentarily on top of a clay pot, and handed the blade to his father. Checking the color of the flames, Mr. Doi lifted a clay-covered blade with long pliers and buried it deep into the sparking fire. He pushed the knife to and fro, pulling it out now and then to examine it intensely. Then, with a look of great confidence, he yanked the blazing, reddish orange blade from the oven. He made a quick final inspection and plunged the blade into a pool of cold water. The water spattered as steam filled the air. Immediately, Mr. Doi drew the blade from the water and threw it on the dirt floor. He repeated this process until all the knives were treated. The hot fire strengthens the carbon steel, Mr. Doi explained, so the blades will hold an excellent cutting edge.

But the blades were still hard and brittle and therefore vulnerable to shock. To correct this problem, they would need one more treatment, *yaki-modoshi.* Again, they would be heated, but at a lower temperature, and then they would be left to cool gradually in the air. *Yaki-modoshi* relaxes the carbon steel and makes the blade more resistant to shock.

At about two o'clock each day, Mr. Doi and his son finish their work and hand the blades to a neighboring craftsman, Yukinori Oda, the knife sharpener. In Mr. Oda's workshop are four large grindstones, of different degrees of roughness and each almost 4 feet in diameter. Sharpening a blade on a stone spinning at four hundred revolutions per minute in a continuous water bath, Mr. Oda stood so close to the wheel that he seemed to be perched on top of it. The touch of the knife on the wheel created a shower of sparks and hurled slurry at the wall, where a long metal stalactite grew.

Looking relaxed and happy, Mr. Oda stepped away from the wheel and presented the roughly sharpened knife for my inspection. After forty years as a *togishi,* a knife sharpener, he could distinguish knives made by each of the several *tanzo* craftsmen with whom he works. The better the quality of the forging, the easier his task, he explained. A poorly made blade "is hell to work with."

About the same age as Mr. Doi, Mr. Oda usually works from four in the afternoon until ten at night. When he doesn't feel like working, he stays out of the shop for several days or even weeks, but then he must put in ten-hour days until he catches up. Ever since he got married, he says, his wife has been jealous of his knives. She says he puts more time and care into them than into his marriage.

The final craftsman in the knife-making process is Mr. Aoki. He collects the ground blades from Mr. Oda and fits them with handles of ebony, Japanese yew, or magnolia wood. He examines each completed knife from every angle, as a father might examine his newborn baby. By watching his eyes, I sensed his great appreciation for the skills of each of the craftsmen. Beautiful knives come from beautiful people.

A Bride Needs a Groom

After buying your knife, a "bride," you must find her a "groom," a sharpening stone. Japanese sharpening stones are available in three degrees of roughness: rough, *aratoishi;* medium-rough, *naka-toishi;* and fine, *shiage-toishi.* A rough *aratoishi* stone is primarily for repairing a knife with cracks, dents, or chips on the cutting edge. A fine *shiage-toishi* stone is for the final sharpening of high-quality knives. What you need is the medium-rough *naka-toishi* stone. If you buy a *tanzo* knife, you will use your *naka-toishi* stone every day that you use your knife.

When you sharpen your knife, pay attention to the *ura-suki,* the depression on the unground side of the knife, from the top of the blade to the cutting edge. The *ura-suki* creates a little air pocket between the blade and the food you are slicing, which prevents the slices from sticking to the blade. Be careful to maintain the depression when you sharpen the blade.

(continued from page 45)

This multipurpose knife, with its pointed blade and one-sided cutting edge, is good for filleting small fish, slicing sushi rolls, and for cutting fish, meat, and vegetables into pieces for grilling or sautéing. This knife is not suitable for filleting medium or large fish or for slicing fish for *sashimi* or *nigiri-zushi.* Because a *santoku* knife is stamped rather than forged, it is relatively inexpensive. I recommend buying one if you don't already have a good general-purpose knife.

Which type of Japanese knife you should buy depends on what types of knives you already own and whether you plan to butcher and fillet fish yourself, slice fish that is already filleted, or slice only vegetables and sushi rolls. Once you know which type of knife you want, make your choice according to quality, style, and price.

Makisu
Bamboo Rolling Mat

Available at nearly all Japanese and general Asian food markets and at many kitchen supply stores, bamboo mats are indispensable for forming sushi rolls. These mats are also useful for squeezing water out of cooked spinach and shaping cooked or uncooked foods. Sushi mats come in various styles; some are made of thin, round bamboo sticks and other, better ones, of larger, flat sticks. Sizes vary, too. The mat I use is 9 1/2 inches square.

After you've used your mat for making sushi rolls, it may have rice residue stuck to it. Soak the mat in lukewarm water long enough to soften the rice. Rinse the mat while scrubbing it with a hard *tawashi* or vegetable brush and let the mat dry completely before putting it away.

Oshi-zushi no kata
Sushi Box Mold

This rectangular wooden or plastic mold is used for *oshi-zushi,* pressed or boxed sushi, one of the easiest kinds of sushi to prepare. The standard wooden mold is 4 by 7 by 1 3/4 inches; my plastic mold is a little smaller, 3 1/2 by 7 by 2 inches. The lid of an *oshi-zushi* mold is always slightly smaller than the frame so you can slide the lid inside to press the sushi. The bottom board is separate, too, so that after pressing the sushi, you can lift the frame off the base. I prefer the plastic mold, because its heavier lid makes it easy to do a proper pressing job. With either of these molds, though, a novice can produce perfect sushi every time.

As a substitute for a sushi mold, you can use two small, shallow plastic or metal containers from your kitchen, one to hold the sushi and the other to press it. If you improvise this way, however, you'll have to pry the sushi out of the container in which you have pressed it—and it does not always come out clean—so it's better to buy a real *oshi-zushi no kata.* These days, sushi presses can be found even at kitchen supply stores that don't specialize in Japanese cookware.

To keep rice from sticking to a wooden *oshi-zushi* mold, soak the frame and lid in cold water for thirty minutes. Rice tends to stick less to a plastic mold, especially if you wipe the mold just before using it with a clean, moist cloth. Either kind of mold can be cleaned by soaking it in lukewarm water and then scrubbing it with a hard *tawashi* (see page 53) or vegetable brush. You can use mild soap or detergent if you like. Dry the mold completely before putting it away.

Clockwise starting at two o'clock:
sharkskin grater, wooden paddles, wooden pestle,
and bamboo rolling mat all resting in the mortar, with a fan behind

Otoshi-buta
Drop Lid

Otoshi-buta is a wooden disk-shaped lid for a cooking pot. It should be about 1 inch smaller in diameter than the pot. The lid is placed directly on the food, which is simmering in just a little broth below. During cooking, the broth boils up to the lid, hits it, and then falls back on the simmering food. This continuing process ensures even flavor, uniform color, and moist texture.

A good substitute for an *otoshi-buta* is a parchment paper disk, which you should cut 1 inch smaller in diameter than the pot you use.

Shamoji
Rice Paddle

Small *shamoji,* about 9½ inches long, are used for spooning rice from a pot or rice cooker. Sushi *shamoji* are much larger, about 12 inches long for home use and nearly 17 inches long for restaurant use. These bamboo or wooden paddles, shaped like flattened spoons, are used for turning steaming, tender rice and moving it from one side of a tub to the other while mixing in the sushi dressing. If a small *shamoji* came with your rice cooker, you can use it for making a small quantity of sushi rice—say, 2 cups. For a larger quantity of rice, the best substitute for a sushi *shamoji* is a broad, shallow-bowled wooden spoon.

After you use a *shamoji,* soak it in water until the rice residue has softened and then scrub it with a hard *tawashi* (see page 53) or vegetable brush. Use only very mild detergent, if any, and rinse it away completely. Do not put the *shamoji* in the dishwasher.

Suihanki
Rice Cooker

You can cook rice in a lidded pot on the stove, but an electric rice cooker is a wonderful convenience. An inexpensive one with a separate lid is not a good investment, because as the rice cooks, steam can push the lid up and escape, resulting in improper cooking. Much better is a model with an attached lid, and best of all is one of the new machines with marks that show the proper amount of water to add for sushi rice as well as for ordinary steamed rice. These machines also have an electronic sensor to ensure that the rice cooks to the proper texture for sushi.

Once sushi rice is prepared, it must be kept warm, about 98° F. Sushi chefs used to keep their prepared rice in a thick wooden container wrapped in a thick blanket and placed in a thick straw basket. Today they use a special insulated container that keeps as much as 4 gallons of rice warm for up to six hours. For home sushi making, though, you don't need an insulated container. Just put your warm rice into a plastic food-storage container, cover the rice with a folded paper towel, put on the lid, and float the container in a bowl of warm water. Change the water when it gets cold.

Sushi-oke
Wooden Tub

Big, shallow wooden tubs called *hangiri* are used in making various Japanese foods, such as *sake* and *miso. Hangiri* are made like barrels, consisting of vertical staves held together by metal rings. *Sushi-oke* is the particular kind of *hangiri* used for mixing sushi rice.

A *sushi-oke* is designed to keep rice at the right levels of moisture and warmth. The tub is usually made of *sawara* cypress, a soft, porous wood that absorbs excess moisture from the rice and also keeps it from drying out. The tub's large, unfinished surface helps moisture to evaporate quickly, so the rice ends up light and loose rather than sticky and gelatinized. And the thick walls and base of the *sushi-oke* keep the rice warm.

Sushi restaurants use very large *sushi-oke,* but the most convenient size for a home cook is 14½ inches across and 3¾ inches deep. With this size, you can comfortably handle about 10 cups of cooked rice (prepared from 4 rice-cooker cups of dry rice).

A newly purchased *sushi-oke* smells wonderfully of cypress, but this aroma is a little too strong for sushi rice. To remove the smell, set the tub in a sink, add a cup of distilled vinegar, and fill the tub to the brim with boiling water. When the water has cooled, rinse and dry the tub.

After mixing sushi rice in your tub, clean it as described under "*Shamoji,* Rice Paddle" (see left column). Dry the bowl thoroughly with a cotton cloth.

There is one problem you may encounter with your *sushi-oke.* Because in most of the United States, the climate is drier than in Japan, the wood may shrink so that the copper rings loosen.

Unless your tub is one of the new ones made for export, with small nails to hold the rings in place, the rings may even drop off. To restore your *sushi-oke,* soak the tub in cool water for as long as eight hours. The wood will expand, and the rings will be tight again.

The best substitute for a *sushi-oke* is a big wooden salad bowl, as close as possible to 20 inches in diameter and preferably unfinished.

Oroshiki
Grater

The best grater to use for fresh *wasabi* is a piece of sharkskin glued to a small wooden board. The abrasive skin will grate much more finely than a standard metal grater. You can easily find a sharkskin *oroshiki* on the Web.

After using your sharkskin grater, clean it with a mild detergent, rinse it well, and let it air-dry away from direct sunlight. Never put a sharkskin grater in the dishwasher. Store your grater in a cool, dark place.

A good substitute for a sharkskin *oroshiki* is a ceramic *oroshiki* with small, closely spaced spikes. Widely available in Japanese and general Asian markets, these graters are good for *daikon,* ginger, and garlic as well as *wasabi.*

If you have only a steel grater, use the surface with the finest, most closely spaced spikes and cover the spikes with sturdy plastic wrap before you grate *wasabi* or ginger.

Tamago-yaki nabe
Omelet Pan

A Japanese omelet is made by stacking layers of cooked beaten egg, rolling them together into a loglike form, and then pressing the log to give it a rectangular shape. To make a Japanese omelet, you need a square skillet, a *tamago-yaki nabe.* Square skillets made for home use are 6 to 7 inches across and usually nonstick. Those for professional kitchens are bigger, 8½ inches or more across, and are made of copper plated on the inside with tin. A professional *tamago-yaki nabe* comes with a heavy wooden lid that fits inside the pan and is used to square the sides of the rolled omelet.

You can make a Japanese omelet with a nonstick 6-inch round omelet or sauté pan, although your log will end up thicker in the middle than at the ends.

Instructions for making and shaping a Japanese omelet can be found on page 68.

Suribachi and *Surikogi*
Japanese Mortar and Wooden Pestle

Japanese mortar and pestle are not required for making sushi, but they are frequently called for in part 5, "Great Sushi Accompaniments." The *suribachi* is a ceramic bowl, 6 to 14 inches in diameter, with a rough, combed pattern on its unglazed interior surface. The size of the wooden pestle, *surikogi,* varies; the longest is 24 inches. For home use, the best choice is a 12-inch mortar and a 12-inch pestle.

With a *suribachi* and *surikogi,* you can do things you can't do with an electric food processor. For example, you can grind chopped raw shrimp to a fine, smooth paste without adding liquid. If you do add egg and other liquid, the paste will become looser and smoother without becoming foamy, as it would in a processor. In a *suribachi,* you can also grind sesame seed to a very smooth, very oily paste. If you don't mind a bit of physical labor, you'll find that a *suribachi* and *surikogi* can perform many other tasks exceptionally well, in any cuisine.

Clean your *suribachi* and *surikogi* with a hard *tawashi* or vegetable brush and mild soap. The brush will remove any residue trapped in the comb pattern.

Tawashi
Scrub Brush

In a sushi kitchen, a firm-bristled scrub brush is a real necessity. A *tawashi* works efficiently and thoroughly for removing sticky rice from the inside surface of a wooden sushi tub, from a sushi paddle, from a bamboo rolling mat, and from anything in the kitchen to which the rice has stuck.

Japanese households, and later factories, made *tawashi* from rice straw or hemp until 1907, when the Nishio Company of Tokyo introduced a *tawashi* made from the fibers of the coconut palm. No other brush could, or can, compare. Called a Kamenoko ("child of the turtle") *tawashi* for its resemblance to a small turtle, the coconut fiber brush has more strength, durability, and water resistance than any other kitchen brush I know of. It certainly beats any plastic brush.

Kamenoko *tawashi* are easy to find in Japanese and Asian stores and on the Web. I suggest buying three—one for sushi equipment, one for vegetables such as potatoes and carrots, and one for pots and pans. To tell them apart, store them separately or tie ribbons of different colors to them.

Tane-keisu
Sushi Refrigerator Case

When you sit at a sushi bar, before you is a long refrigerated case full of fish and shellfish. As a home sushi cook, you do not need this expensive piece of equipment, but if you use raw fish and shellfish, you must find another way to keep it continuously chilled at 40° to 41° F until nearly the moment it reaches the mouth. For a home *nigiri-zushi* party, here is how you can create your own countertop refrigerator case: Have a large quantity of ice cubes or chips at hand, or plan to buy a bagful just before the party begins. Neatly arrange the filleted sushi fish, without overlapping, in a sealable plastic container, put on the lid, and store the container in the refrigerator until you need it. Before the party begins, make sure the room temperature is on the cool side. When it's time to make sushi, put the ice cubes into a stainless steel pan or plastic bin, put the container of sushi fish in the ice, and place the whole apparatus on your sushi counter.

Preparing sushi is a little like assembling a car. Before you can begin the final assembly, you need all the parts. In chapter 7, you will find the techniques and recipes for the key components of sushi preparation: the sushi rice (the very foundation of any sushi making), pickled ginger, rolled omelet, simmered vegetables, sushi dipping sauce, and other elements that you will be using over and over again in the chapters that follow.

In chapter 8, I give you the techniques and recipes for producing popular rolls, both traditional and modern creations, such as inside-out styles. After you are comfortable making these, you will want to explore new sushi-making territory in chapter 9. There I will introduce you to new techniques and many delicious, easy-to-prepare recipes. After you have worked with part 3, you will find that sushi rice and all the sushi components are playful tools, and you can begin to create your own original sushi.

Chapter 7
Basic Sushi Preparation Techniques and Recipes

Key Components

Sushi Rice
Sumeshi or *Shari*

Sushi rice is called *sumeshi* (vinegar-flavored rice) or *shari*. *Shari* literally means "Buddha's remains," and it was so named because the very white appearance of the rice reminds people of Buddha's mortal remains, to which the Japanese show great respect.

You can use your freshly made sushi rice right away, but it is better to let it rest for one hour or so (to allow the flavor and texture to settle), covered with a moist paper towel in a Tupperware-like container with a lid. Float the container in a bowl of warm water, changing the water as it gets cold.

The best-tasting sushi rice should be around 98° F when it is used. Never store it in the refrigerator, or the texture of the rice will be too firm and unfit for sushi making.

Master Recipe
for
Sushi Rice

DRY RAW RICE	WATER	COOKED RICE YIELD
2¼ cups	2¼ cups	6 cups (2.3 pounds)*
3 cups	3 cups	8 cups (3 pounds)*

*Approximate; *lightly* packed.

The proper rinsing of the rice is important for its final flavor and appearance. Pour the rice into a fine-mesh strainer, large enough so you can freely toss and turn the grains. Have at hand a larger bowl into which the strainer can easily fit and fill it with cold tap water. Pour the rice into the strainer, then lower the strainer into the large bowl so that the water covers the rice. With both hands, gently rub, turn, and toss the rice. Do not press the grains too hard against the strainer or against one another, or the fragile grains may break, especially if you are using a lower grade of rice. The water will instantly turn milky white, so remove the strainer from the large bowl, discard the water, and refill the bowl with fresh cold water. Return the rice-filled strainer to the bowl and repeat. On the second rinsing, the water will look only slightly milky. Repeat once or twice more. When you have finished, the water will be almost clear, but do not expect 100 percent clarity. Drain the rice and let it sit in the strainer for 10 minutes.

Transfer the rice to a heavy-bottomed pot that is deeper than it is wide and has a heavy, tightly fitting lid

How Much Sushi Rice to Prepare?

The recipes here for making sushi rice yield 6 and 8 cups of cooked rice, made from 2¼ cups and 3 cups of raw rice respectively. They are the standard amounts that I call for throughout the book to prepare many varieties of sushi. You may find that with some recipes you are left with a cup or so of leftover sushi rice. But don't worry. It is always better to have some extra rice to work with, and you'll want to taste a little as you go along. Having some leftover rice in your refrigerator or freezer is like a hidden treasure. You can make a quick lunch by microwaving it and serving it as is, perhaps with a bowl of soup, or use it to prepare quick, delicious rice dishes (page 5, 64, 65, and 73).

For One Thick Roll

If you want to make just one thick roll for your lunch, cook only 1 cup of rice. Adjust the proportion of rice vinegar, sugar, and salt for the sushi vinegar dressing.

Troubleshooting: Rice Cooking

1. If your cooked rice has formed a crust on the bottom of the pan, do not try to scrape that up and incorporate it with the rest. Next time, check that your heat is not too high for the first 10 minutes of cooking. You can tell whether the water is boiling away too rapidly; if so, adjust the heat and sprinkle a little more water over the surface (although adding too much water makes your rice too tender). Also, be sure that the heat is *very* low for the last 10 minutes of cooking.

2. If your cooked rice still has some uncooked firm grains here and there, even after you have sprinkled it with water and cooked it an extra minute or so, probably your lid was not tight enough and steam was escaping during the cooking. Next time, cover your pot tightly with aluminum foil before placing the lid on. Also, watch the heat: it probably was too high, so that moisture evaporated too quickly and some of the grains weren't cooked.

(during cooking, rice swells to as much as two and a half times its original volume, so your pot should be at least three times deeper than the level of the rice and water), add the water, and let it sit for 20 minutes.

Set the rice over medium heat and cook, uncovered, until the water is nearly absorbed by the rice—about 10 minutes. Quickly reduce the heat to very low, cover the pot with the lid, and cook until the rice is plump and cooked through—another 10 minutes. The exact cooking time depends on the heaviness of the pot, the level of the heat, and the quantity and condition of your rice. After a total of 20 minutes' cooking, take a quick look: the rice should be completely transparent. If you see any dry, very white-looking grains, sprinkle a little warm water over the dry spots and cook another couple of minutes or so over very low heat. During the cooking, never stir the rice.

After confirming that all the rice grains are transparent, immediately put the lid back on before the built-up steam can escape. Turn off the heat and let the rice stand for 5 minutes.

Cooking Rice Using a Rice Cooker

If you own a rice cooker, follow these guidelines. Use the cup that came with your rice cooker, which is about four-fifths the volume of a U.S. cup.

Omit the usual presoaking; it makes the rice too tender when you are using a rice cooker. Don't follow the usual water line in the bowl of your rice cooker. Instead, use the guidelines below.

Today some rice cookers have a special built-in sushi rice cooking function. If using, add water to the level designated for cooking sushi rice. Cook the rice according to the manufacturer's instructions, usually for 50 minutes.

DRY RAW RICE	WATER	COOKED RICE YIELD
3 cups*	3 cups	6 cups (2.3 pounds)**
4 cups*	4 cups	8 cups (3 pounds)**
*Rice-cooker cups.	**Approximate; *lightly* packed.	

COOKED SHORT- OR MEDIUM-GRAIN RICE	*KOMEZU* (RICE VINEGAR)	SEA SALT	SUGAR
6 cups (2.3 pounds)*	5 tablespoons	1½ teaspoons	2 tablespoons
8 cups (3 pounds)*	6 tablespoons	2 teaspoons	3 tablespoons

*Approximate; *lightly* packed.

While the rice is cooking, put the rice vinegar, salt, and sugar in a bowl and stir with a whisk until the sugar and salt are almost dissolved.

If you are using a Japanese *sushi-oke* (wooden sushi tub) and *shamoji* (flat wooden paddle), soak them in a bath of cold water for half an hour while the rice is cooking (dry wood will absorb a good portion of the sushi vinegar dressing, and the rice will stick to the wood).

Drain the water and wipe the tub and paddle with a dry kitchen towel. If you are using a large unfinished wooden salad bowl, moisten it just before using (soaking for a long time might cause it to crack). Other bowls made of metal, glass, or porcelain can be substituted, but they tend to make the sushi rice watery, mushy, and lumpy.

Transfer the steaming hot cooked rice all at once to the sushi tub or salad bowl.

Following the illustrations, 1. quickly and gently break up the rice, crisscrossing it with the side of your paddle. 2. Pour the prepared vinegar dressing evenly over it and, with the paddle, break up the lumpy clumps and turn the rice over, working one area at a time. Repeat once or twice until you can tell by looking that the vinegar dressing is roughly distributed throughout the rice. 3. Push the rice toward one side of the tub.

1. Break up the rice, crisscrossing it with the side of your paddle.

2. Pour the prepared vinegar evenly over the rice.

3. Turn the rice over and push it to one side of the tub.

Sushi Rice Proportions for the Pro

MAKES 38 CUPS / 15 POUNDS

14 ½ cups rice (20 rice cooker cups)

1 ½ cups rice vinegar

2 ½ tablespoons sea salt

1 cup plus 5 tablespoons sugar

Now hold the paddle horizontally and 4. insert the paddle into the rice in one area, then rapidly move it back and forth with many small strokes. By cutting into the rice this way, you are breaking up the clumps and pushing a portion of rice toward the opposite side of the tub. Now work on the remaining areas of the rice one at a time in the same way, until you have moved all of the rice to the other side of the tub.

Rotate the tub or bowl 180 degrees and repeat the process. You can see at the end of the second "cutting" that each grain looks evenly plump, when all the vinegar dressing has been evenly absorbed. The whole procedure should take about 2 minutes. With a hand fan or with a magazine or folded news-paper, 5. fan the rice for about 30 seconds. This quick fanning gelatinizes the surface of the rice to give it a glossy

appearance and also cools it, helping the vinegar dressing to settle inside each grain.

Sushi rice, if it is prepared in a large quantity, tends to remain rather hot, even after being fanned. If so, let it cool to a temperature of 104° F, covered with a moist kitchen cloth to prevent it from drying out.

4. Holding your paddle horizontally, insert it into the rice and rapidly move it back and forth, pushing that portion of the rice to the other side of the tub.

5. Fan the rice briefly.

Troubleshooting: Tossing Rice

If there are clumps in the rice that are hard to break down when you are tossing it, break them up by hand. Next time, make sure that the vinegar dressing is distributed evenly throughout the rice and that you work speedily tossing and turning it. Slowly worked and overworked rice becomes clumpy and pasty.

Simmered Dried Vegetables for Sushi
Sushi yasai no nikata

In traditional sushi preparation, dried *shiitake* mushrooms, dried *kanpyo* gourd, and freeze-dried tofu, *koya-dofu,* are indispensable. These dried vegetables are valued over fresh varieties for their concentrated flavor and aroma, and the unique texture that comes from drying. You will find many uses for this preparation throughout the book.

Simmered *Shiitake* Mushrooms
Shiitake no nikata

When you purchase dried *shiitake* mushrooms, choose ones with thick, meaty, and plump caps that are not spread open. On the surface of these plump caps, you will see a cracked pattern resembling the shell of a turtle. Bring a piece close to your nose; it should smell sweet and aromatic. This is the *donko* mushroom (the Mercedes of *shiitake* mushrooms), and the price is twice that of lesser varieties—those with thin, flat, opened caps and thin stems—but the flavor and aroma are at least four times better. I highly recommend this extravagance.

The prepared mushrooms will keep their taste and quality for three to four days in the refrigerator. Simmered mushrooms are used over and over again in this book, so I suggest that you prepare a batch and freeze them, or cook half the portion. The mushrooms are used whole, sliced, or chopped.

⅛ pound dried *shiitake* mushrooms (about 14), preferably *donko* variety

¼ cup sugar

3 tablespoons *shoyu* (soy sauce)

1½ tablespoons *mirin* (sweet cooking wine)

Rinse the *shiitake* mushrooms under cold running tap water and soak them in a large bowl of cold water overnight.

The next day, remove the mushrooms from the water, reserving the soaking liquid. Put the mushrooms in a medium pot with enough of the reserved soaking liquid to barely cover them. Set the pot over medium heat and bring to a boil; turn the heat to medium-low and cook, covered with a drop lid (page 51) or a parchment paper disk, for 30 minutes. Skim off any foam that rises during cooking. Add the sugar and cook, covered, for 10 minutes. Add half the soy sauce and continue to cook, covered, for 10 minutes, or until about 85 percent of the liquid is absorbed. Add the remaining soy sauce (*shoyu*) and the sweet cooking wine (*mirin*); turn the heat to medium-high and cook the mushrooms, stirring with a wooden spoon, until the liquid is almost absorbed and the mushrooms are coated with a layer of glossy, syrupy sauce. Drain the mushrooms in a strainer and turn them over several times to cool them quickly, discarding the cooking liquid. Store the cooled mushrooms in the refrigerator or freezer. Before using, cut off the stems. The cook can enjoy them as a snack.

Simmered
Kanpyo Gourd
Kanpyo no nikata

They may look like the shoelaces of a sneaker, as some of my students have remarked, but the long dried thin strips of *kanpyo* come from a large round gourd called *fukube.* The vegetable grows to an average weight of 12 pounds. After the harvest during the hot and humid summer in Japan, a machine peels the skin of the gourd and cuts its flesh into 1½-inch-wide strips. The strips are then bathed in strong sunlight for two days, which produces a concentrated unique flavor with a sweet acidic smell and bite. Good-quality *kanpyo* is the color of fresh cow's milk with a slight yellowish tinge. Avoid brown strips, which have been stored too long, or ones that are too white, indicating that they may have been processed with bleach.

Prepared *kanpyo* maintains its taste and quality for three to four days in the refrigerator. Simmered *kanpyo* gourd is used over and over again in this book, so I suggest that you prepare a large batch and freeze it.

Before cooking the gourd, cut the strips into 8-inch lengths—the length of the short side of a whole sheet of *nori,* so the gourd strips fit precisely across it when you are making a sushi roll. In general, one package contains 1 ounce of dried *kanpyo.* When that quantity is cut into 8-inch lengths, you usually have 17 to 23 strips.

MAKES ABOUT 36 SIMMERED STRIPS

2 ounces *kanpyo* (dried *kanpyo* gourd) (2 packages), cut into 8-inch-long strips; you will have about 36 strips
2 teaspoons salt
¼ cup plus 1 tablespoon sugar
¼ cup plus 1 tablespoon *shoyu* (soy sauce)
2 tablespoons *mirin* (sweet cooking wine)

Place the *kanpyo* strips in a large bowl and add cold tap water to submerge and moisten them. Pour off all the water and sprinkle about 2 teaspoons of salt over the strips, then rub them in order to soften the fibers and also to clean the strips. Rinse under cold running tap water to remove the salt. Drain the strips and soak them in a bowl of cold water overnight.

The next day, drain the *kanpyo* strips and transfer them to a medium pot. Add enough water to cover them by 2 inches. Cook, covered with a drop lid (page 51) or a parchment paper disk, for 15 minutes, or until the strips are firmly done. To check, extract one strip and gently press it with your thumbnail. A sharp nail mark should be left on the surface (overcooking at this stage turns the strips unpleasantly soft so they tear easily).

Drain the *kanpyo* strips, discarding the cooking liquid. Pour the sugar and soy sauce into the cleaned cooking pot and bring to a boil over medium heat, stirring with a wooden spatula. When the sugar is dissolved, add the *kanpyo* strips and cook them over medium-high heat, turning the strips frequently with a pair of cooking chopsticks (spiky metal tongs can puncture the gourd strips and damage them). When the cooking liquid is almost all absorbed, add the sweet cooking wine (*mirin*) and cook until it is almost all absorbed and the strips are coated with a layer of glossy, syrupy sauce. Drain the *kanpyo* strips in a strainer, discarding the cooking liquid. Turn the strips over several times to cool them off quickly. Store the *kanpyo* in the refrigerator or freezer.

A Delicious
Quick Rice Dish for Two

Toss 1 cup of leftover sushi rice (or plain, hot cooked rice) with 1 tablespoon each finely chopped simmered *shiitake* mushrooms, sweet pickled ginger (page 66), toasted white sesame seeds, and minced walnuts. Enjoy as is or wrapped in a *nori* sheet.

Simmered Freeze-Dried Tofu
Koya-dofu no nikata

Koya-dofu, freeze-dried tofu, comes in flat, creamy white squares, each weighing virtually nothing. When it is soaked in warm water, the tofu quickly absorbs a large amount of liquid and takes on a slightly spongy character. It has a distinctive, intense soybean fragrance but almost no flavor. It absorbs flavor from the condiments with which it is cooked. When you are preparing a vegetarian sushi, this sweet simmered tofu offers everything—meaty texture, nutrients, and it has now developed a rich flavor.

You can easily find koya-dofu in the dried-food section at a Japanese or Asian food store. In addition to the standard-sized cakes of 2 by 2 3/4 inches, there are packages with smaller 1-inch-square cakes.

MAKES 6 SIMMERED CAKES

6 dried *koya-dofu* cakes (freeze-dried tofu), 2- by 2 3/4-inch rectangles
3 cups *dashi* (fish stock) (page 74)
1/4 cup *sake* (rice wine)
1/4 cup *mirin* (sweet cooking wine)
1 tablespoon sugar
1 tablespoon *usukuchi shoyu* (light-colored soy sauce) or ordinary *shoyu*
1 teaspoon *shoyu* (soy sauce)

Soak the tofu cakes in a bowl of lukewarm water for 10 minutes. Drain the tofu and run water over it, pressing each cake between your palms and rinsing until the water from the cakes becomes clear. Squeeze the cakes to remove excess water.

Pour the fish stock (*dashi*) into a medium pot, add the tofu cakes, and cook over medium heat, covered with a drop lid (page 51) or a parchment paper disk, for 10 minutes. Add the *sake, mirin,* and sugar and cook over medium-low heat, covered, for 10 minutes. Add the soy sauces, turn the heat to low, and cook the tofu cakes, covered, for 30 minutes.

Remove from the heat and let the tofu cakes cool in the cooking liquid. Refrigerate them in their cooking liquid in a sealable container for up to three days. To freeze, drain the tofu cakes, discarding the cooking liquid, and store in a sealable container.

Another Delicious Quick Rice Dish for Two

Toss 1 cup of leftover sushi rice (or plain, hot cooked rice) with 1 tablespoon each chopped gourd, simmered *shiitake* mushrooms (page 63), sweet pickled ginger, and *shiso* or coriander leaves.

Sweet Pickled Ginger
Gari

14 ounces young ginger (after peeling and slicing, about 3 cups) or ordinary mature ginger
1/2 cup *komezu* (rice vinegar)
2 1/4 teaspoons salt
1/4 cup plus 1 tablespoon sugar

S*hoga,* ginger, is an indispensable component of sushi dining because of its antiseptic properties. Ginger's spiciness also suppresses the strong flavor and oiliness of fish and mellows the particularly strong aroma of certain kinds of fish. Ginger is used fresh, grated or julienned, or pickled in sweet vinegar marinade. Biting into slices of pickled ginger after eating fatty *toro nigiri-zushi* or mayonnaise-filled rolls, for example, certainly refreshes your palate.

In a sushi restaurant, the pickled ginger is called *gari.* Making *gari* at home is simple and quick, and the result is so much better than buying already prepared *gari* in a jar. Commercial products often contain preservatives and artificial food coloring and have inferior flavor. If you own a good mandoline that can cut ginger into translucent, paper-thin slices, the preparation is even easier. If you have reasonable knife skills and have a well-maintained knife, the slicing is easily accomplished by hand. The best choice of ginger for this recipe is *shin-shoga,* a young ginger. Unlike the ordinary, more mature brown variety, young ginger has a very thin skin, which is a creamy white color. The root has knobs with a slight pink tinge, and the flesh is juicy, tender, and not stringy. In Japan, young ginger appears in the market from early May through August. Visit your neighborhood Asian food store to look for the young ginger, which was grown in and shipped from Hawaii, Jamaica, and Puerto Rico. You can also use ordinary mature ginger by cooking it slightly longer.

Remove the little knobs from the ginger, then peel the main part and the knobs with a knife or vegetable peeler. Cut the ginger lengthwise into *paper-thin* slices, 2 inches long.

Mix the rice vinegar, 1/4 cup of water, 2 teaspoons of the salt, and sugar in a small saucepan and bring to a boil, stirring to dissolve the salt and sugar. Turn off the heat and pour this pickling liquid into a 2-cup-size jar.

Bring about 1 1/2 quarts of water to a boil in a pot. Add the ginger slices all at once and cook them for 20 seconds. If you are using mature ginger, cook for 40 seconds or until the slices are translucent. Drain the slices in a large colander; sprinkle the remaining 1/4 teaspoon of salt over them, tossing them thoroughly. Shake the colander and remove as much water as possible from the ginger slices. While they are still hot, transfer the slices to the jar and submerge them in the liquid. The ginger will immediately acquire a faint pink color, although sometimes this does not happen and it may remain golden yellow. Do not be disappointed; the flavor will not be affected.

Pickled ginger tastes better after resting overnight or for two days. Refrigerate it for an additional two to three weeks (for longer storage, freeze it), but I am certain it will not last that long. You and others who visit your refrigerator will find it hard to keep from opening the jar and taking a slice or two as a refreshing snack anytime.

Sushi Egg Preparation
Sushi no tamago

Eggs are indispensable in the sushi kitchen, and there are three basic preparations: *dashi-maki tamago,* rolled thick omelet; *tamago-yaki,* egg cake with puréed fish or shrimp; and *usuyaki tamago,* thin omelet.

How the Chicken Came to Japan

Chickens were brought to Japan from the Asian continent between the fourth and the sixth century AD. They were soon domesticated and kept as a sacred bird serving the gods. The rooster's unique ability to announce the time of day by crowing about the same time each morning was considered remarkable and very convenient. For this reason, slaughtering chickens and consuming their eggs was banned while other wild birds were freely eaten. In the Nihon Reiki, a collection of tales compiled at the beginning of the ninth century, it states that "a person who has consumed chickens and their eggs is destined to be sent to hell after death."

This attitude clearly changed when the Portuguese arrived in the sixteenth century and introduced new dishes that used eggs, such as pound cake, *kasutera,* and *tempura.* By 1770, both of these dishes had become favorites of the citizens of Edo, and people began to explore many new ways to enjoy eggs. In 1785, a landmark cookbook entitled *Manbo-ryori-himitsubako* was published, in which the egg chapter, *"Tamago hyakuchin"* (One Hundred Ways to Prepare Egg Dishes), contains 103 egg recipes.

Rolled Thick Omelet
Dashi-maki tamago

Rolled thick omelet, *dashi-maki tamago,* contains a substantial amount of *dashi,* fish stock, as its name suggests. The stock adds good flavor to the eggs and also dilutes the egg protein, so the resulting omelet is tender and juicy, as you probably know from tasting one at sushi restaurants in your neighborhood. Unlike the Western omelet, a Japanese rolled omelet is made up of four to five layers, which, when rolled together, become indistinguishable.

To prepare the rolled omelet efficiently, you should use a Japanese rectangular omelet pan, 6½ by 5½ inches by 1½ inches deep. For more information on the omelet pan, see page 52. With some manipulation, a 6-inch-diameter Western skillet will also do the job.

The rolled omelet tastes best on the day of preparation. Refrigeration firms the egg protein in the omelet and destroys the fragrance and taste.

MAKES 1 ROLLED OMELET, 2 BY 6 INCHES AND 1 INCH THICK

Vegetable oil for greasing the omelet pan
4 large eggs, broken into a large bowl
3 tablespoons *dashi* (fish stock) (page 74)
1½ tablespoons *mirin* (sweet cooking wine)
¼ teaspoon salt
1 tablespoon sugar
1 teaspoon *shoyu* (soy sauce)

If you are using a Japanese omelet pan, temper it by following the instructions in the accompanying box. In my experience, nonstick Japanese omelet pans that have been used several times still need tempering each time they are used.

1. Pour in the egg mixture and swirl to coat the bottom of the pan.

2. Using your chopsticks, roll the thin layer of omelet toward you.

3. Push the roll to the far end of the pan.

6. Lift the first roll so that some of the new layer of egg flows under it.

7. Roll the first omelet toward the front of the pan over the second layer of egg to make a two-layered roll.

8. Repeat the process with the final layer of the egg.

Break the eggs into a large bowl and, with a whisk, gently stir (do not beat) until the egg white is broken up. Add the *dashi, mirin,* salt, sugar, and soy sauce and mix together gently (you do not want to create much foam).

Set the tempered pan with 1 tablespoon of the reserved oil over medium-high heat and, when hot, wipe out the excess oil with a paper towel (leaving too much oil makes the omelet taste greasy). Following the illustrations, 1. pour in ¼ cup of the egg mixture. It should make a sizzling sound. Quickly swirl the eggs to coat the bottom of the pan and then cook them over medium-high heat until the bottom is cooked and barely golden and the surface is still moist. During this stage, bubbles from trapped steam may push the thin layer of egg up from the bottom, making it inflate like a balloon here and there. With chopsticks or with the sharp edge of a flat stainless steel spatula, poke a small hole through the bubbles to deflate them and let the uncooked egg liquid run through the holes and under the omelet.

2. Roll the thin omelet toward you with chopsticks or a spatula. 3. Push the rolled omelet to the far end of the pan.

4. Grease the entire bottom of the pan again using an oil-soaked paper towel. 5. Add another ¼ cup of the egg mixture. Spread it over the bottom of the pan. 6. With chopsticks or a spatula, lift the rolled omelet you have just made so that some of the new egg flows underneath. Cook until the bottom is firm and the surface is moist, poking the steam vents if necessary. 7. With chopsticks or a spatula, loosen the second thin omelet from the pan along with the first omelet, then lift them up over the second sheet of omelet and turn them both together to make a two-layered omelet. Return it to the back of the pan. Repeat this process with another ¼ cup of the egg and 8. finally with the remaining egg. 9. With the help of a spatula, press and form the hot tender omelet into a neat rectangular shape in the pan. Remove the omelet from the pan and let it stand to cool to room temperature. The omelet tastes best after 3 to 5 hours at room temperature.

4. Coat the pan with oil.

5. Ladle in another ¼ cup of the egg mixture.

9. When all four layers have been rolled together, press the omelet into a rectangular shape.

Egg Cake with Minced Fish or Shrimp
Surimi-iri tamago-yaki

Sushi chef Hiroaki Sasaki, who provided the history of *dashi-maki tamago* (rolled thick omelet), gave me his recipe. This traditional restaurant favorite was a natural development in the sushi kitchen, where there was always leftover fish and shrimp. Puréed, these seafood scraps were mixed with eggs and then made into an egg cake, *tamago-yaki,* that has an oven-baked cake appearance and a smooth, light texture. You feel as if you are eating a moist and slightly dense pound cake. On your next visit to your favorite sushi restaurant, ask your sushi chef if he or she makes this true *tamago-yaki* (egg cake). It is yet another signature of a real sushi restaurant.

Usually the egg cake is cooked in a skillet like a Spanish tortilla, over low heat. That is the way Mr. Sasaki does it, but I have adapted his technique so that the egg cake can be baked in the oven.

I use an 8½-inch-square, 1½-inch-deep professional Japanese omelet pan made of tinned copper, but you may use a good-quality metal baking pan of similar size.

MAKES ONE 8-INCH-SQUARE AND ³/4-INCH-DEEP EGG CAKE

Cooking oil for greasing the omelet pan
¼ pound shelled, deveined shrimp
¼ pound filleted, skinned, and boned fresh flounder or fluke
¼ cup plus 1 tablespoon *sake* (rice wine), and ½ cup *mirin* (sweet cooking wine), brought to a simmer
½ cup sugar
1 teaspoon sea salt
½ teaspoon *shoyu* (soy sauce)
2 tablespoons (or 1½ ounces) grated *nagaimo* yam (page 115) or 2 tablespoons potato starch mixed with 1 tablespoon water
11 medium eggs

Preheat the oven to 325° F. If you are using the traditional Japanese omelet pan, temper it by following the instructions on page 71. If you are using a Western cake pan, preheat it, unoiled, in the heated oven for a few minutes.

Process the shrimp and flounder in a food processor until finely puréed. Transfer the purée to a large Japanese *suribachi* mortar or a large bowl. Pour the warmed *sake* and *mirin,* sugar, salt, and soy sauce into a small bowl and stir well with a whisk. Add the *sake* mixture little by little to the shrimp and fish and grind with a *surikogi* pestle or stir with a whisk until smooth. Add the *nagaimo* yam or potato starch mixed with water and blend. Break the eggs one at a time into the mortar or bowl and incorporate with the pestle or the whisk. When using the whisk, be careful not to whip, because that produces too much foam. Set a fine-mesh sieve on top of a bowl and strain the egg and puréed fish, pressing the seafood through the sieve with a rubber spatula. You will get about 3 cups of strained purée.

How Rolled Thick Omelet Came into Being

When I talked with Hiroaki Sasaki, an owner chef at the venerable sushi restaurant Sasaki in Tokyo, he told me, "*Dashi-maki tamago* [rolled thick omelet] was adopted into sushi restaurants from the *sobaya,* a buckwheat noodle restaurant. *Soba* restaurants traditionally made their own noodles from scratch several times a day on the premises. So the customers sometimes had to wait a while until the *soba* dough was kneaded, rolled out, cut into strips, cooked, and finally served. But they were willing to wait because no *soba* tasted better than when the noodles have been just made and immediately cooked. In order to keep these hungry waiting customers happy, the *sobaya* developed a tradition of serving collections of simple appetizers and a flask of *sake,* rice wine. And the *dashi-maki tamago* has long been one of the most popular such appetizers. It was a natural move for the chef, since the *soba* kitchen was always stocked with copious quantities of daily-made high-quality *dashi* [fish stock] and eggs, both of which are prime ingredients."

The following steps should be done quickly so the warmed pan cools as little as possible. Make sure that the surface of the pan is well coated with a thin layer of the oil. If not, grease the entire inside surface of the pan with a paper towel. Put the Japanese omelet pan back on the stove top over low heat (if you can heat your cake pan on the stove top, do the same) and pour in the egg-seafood purée. Leave the pan for 5 minutes over the low heat, then transfer it to the heated oven. The egg cake will take 70 minutes to bake. After 40 minutes of cooking, the batter begins to acquire a light golden color on the surface. After 60 minutes, the batter increases in volume and becomes browner. By 70 minutes, the surface of the egg cake looks like a typical flour dessert cake—plump and golden. Remove the pan from the oven, loosen the sides first with a small knife, and carefully remove the egg cake with a spatula onto a wooden chopping board to cool.

Tempering the Japanese Omelet Pan

If using a conventional omelet pan, pour ¼ cup of vegetable oil into it and warm over medium-low heat. When the oil is hot, turn the heat to low and continue warming it for 20 minutes. If the outer edge of the pan is not covered with oil, using tongs pick up a piece of paper towel, dip it into the heated oil, and smear a little of the oil onto the outer edge (be very careful not to ignite the paper towel). This tempering of the pan is done so that the omelet won't stick to the pan during cooking. After tempering, pour off all the oil from the pan into a heat-resistant cup and reserve.

Large Omelet Proportions for the Pro

In the professional sushi kitchen, a larger square tin-coated copper omelet pan, 8½ inches square and 1½ inches deep, is used. The ingredients to make one large omelet are:

10 large eggs
5½ tablespoons *dashi* (fish stock) (page 74)
3½ tablespoons *mirin* (sweet cooking wine)
½ teaspoon salt
3 tablespoons sugar
2 teaspoons *shoyu* (soy sauce)

Thin Omelet
Usuyaki tamago

There are two types of thin omelet, *usuyaki tamago.* One is made with potato starch and the other without. The thin omelet without potato starch is usually cut into fine julienne strips and used to garnish *chirashi-zushi,* decorated sushi, like Cherry Blossom Celebration Decorated Sushi (page 140) and Fisherman's Sushi (page 146). Adding potato starch to the egg strengthens the prepared thin omelet, so this type is used to wrap sushi rice, both plain and flavored, to create unique forms of sushi, such as Elegant Yellow Pouch Sushi (page 149).

The thin omelets freeze well, so I suggest making a large number and keeping them for later use. Or reduce the amounts and make fewer omelets.

THIN OMELETS WITH POTATO STARCH

MAKES TWELVE 8-INCH-DIAMETER THIN OMELETS

12 large eggs
1½ tablespoons sugar
1 teaspoon salt
1 tablespoon potato starch or corn-starch mixed with 1½ tablespoons *dashi* (fish stock) (page 74) or water
Vegetable oil for greasing the skillet

Crack the eggs into a bowl and beat thoroughly with chopsticks or a fork. Add the sugar, salt, and potato starch with *dashi* or water, stirring, then transfer to a measuring cup.

Heat a 10-inch skillet over medium heat and add 3 tablespoons of vegetable oil, swirling it to coat the bottom of the pan. When the oil is hot, pour off the excess into a small heat-resistant cup and reserve. Pour ¹⁄₁₂ of the egg liquid, about ¼ cup, into the pan, swirling it to cover the bottom. Turn the heat to very low and cook until the bottom is firm but not browned and the top is almost dry. Turn the omelet over with a spatula and cook the other side for 3 seconds. Transfer the omelet to a cutting board. Heat the skillet again over medium heat and coat the entire bottom surface with part of the reserved oil. Wipe off any excess oil from the skillet with a paper towel and repeat the cooking process, making an additional eleven thin omelets and stacking them one on top of the other. Let the omelets cool before using.

THIN OMELETS WITHOUT POTATO STARCH

MAKES FOUR 8-INCH-DIAMETER THIN OMELETS

4 large eggs
1 tablespoon *dashi* (fish stock) (page 74) or water
1 tablespoon sugar
¼ teaspoon salt
Vegetable oil for greasing the skillet

Crack the eggs into a bowl and beat thoroughly with chopsticks or a fork. Add the *dashi,* sugar, and salt and mix well. Transfer the eggs to a measuring cup and figure out how much one-quarter of it will be.

Heat a 10-inch skillet, add 2 table-spoons of vegetable oil, and when the oil is hot, swirl it to coat the entire inside surface. Pour off the excess into a heat-resistant cup and reserve. Add one-quarter of the egg, about ¼ cup, and swirl it to cover the bottom. Turn the heat to very low and cook the omelet until the bottom is firm but not browned. Turn it over with a spatula and cook the other side for 3 seconds. Transfer the omelet to a cutting board. Make three additional omelets in the same way. Let them cool for 20 minutes. Now cut each omelet into four quarters.

Stack up the four quarters, roll each pile of omelet into a tight cylinder, and cut it into needle-thin julienne strips.

Sweet-Simmered Thin Tofu
Abura-age no nikata

Sweet-simmered, golden brown, thin tofu is the major component of *inari-zushi,* the brown tofu "bag" packed with sushi rice (pages 148 and 160). You can buy prepared thin tofu packed in a plastic bag at Japanese or Asian food stores. But these prepre-pared products are often made with too much soy sauce and sugar, and they also have off flavors, probably because of chemical additives and preservatives. Preparation of sweet-simmered tofu bags is a simple task, and the results are both delicious and healthful. Cook a large batch and freeze some for later use.

MAKES 40 BAGS

20 *abura-age* sheets (fried thin tofu) (1 sheet is about 3 by 6 inches; one package contains 3 to 5 sheets)

⅔ cup sugar

¼ cup *mirin* (sweet cooking wine)

½ cup plus 3 tablespoons *shoyu* (soy sauce)

Bring plenty of water to a boil in a medium pot and add the tofu sheets. Push them down into the water with a wooden spatula without poking into them and cook for 30 seconds (this removes any excess oil). Remove the tofu sheets from the pot, put them in a colander and cool them under cold tap water, then press gently between your hands to remove excess water. Transfer them to a chopping board and cut each tofu sheet in half crosswise in the center, into two 3- by 3-inch pieces.

Carefully open up the cut side of each piece and separate to form a pocket or bag.

Combine 6 cups water, the sugar, and *mirin* in a medium pot and bring to a boil over medium heat, stirring to dissolve the sugar. Add the tofu bags and simmer for 10 minutes, covered with a drop lid (page 51) or a parchment paper disk. Add the soy sauce and cook until the liquid is 80 percent absorbed. During the cooking, to get even color and flavor, carefully turn the tofu bags several times with a wooden spatula (do not use steel tongs with sharp teeth, or you might puncture the tofu bags). Drain the tofu bags in a colander, discarding the cooking liquid, and let them cool. They are now ready to use in *inari-zushi* preparations (pages 148 and 160). Refrigerate the bags and use within three days or freeze.

A Quick Lunch or Snack for Two

Defrost 5 simmered tofu bags. Finely chop 1 of the tofu bags. Toss 1 cup of leftover sushi rice (or plain, hot cooked rice) with 1 tablespoon each chopped tofu bag, chopped walnuts, chopped coriander leaves, toasted white sesame seeds, and chopped sweet pickled ginger. Pack the rice into the remaining 4 tofu bags.

Sweet Fish Flakes
Sakana no oboro

Sakana no oboro is made from lean, white-fleshed fish cooked in water, drained, crumbled, and dry-toasted in a pan with sugar, *mirin* (sweet cooking wine), and a little salt. The result is a dry, sweet, flaked fish with a faint pink color because of the addition of some red food coloring. This is another of those recipes born out of necessity—what to do with accumulated leftover whitefish in the sushi kitchen, most of which consists of end pieces or odd parts of the fish that could not be served to the sushi diners. This delightful sweet delicacy solves the problem.

Since, in our home kitchens, we seldom accumulate enough fish scraps to prepare these sweet fish flakes, here is the home version using a can of tuna, adapted from a recipe of my sister, Keiko Arakawa.

One 6-ounce can tuna in water, chunk-type, or 6 ounces accumulated cooked fish
1 tablespoon *shoyu* (soy sauce)
1 tablespoon *mirin* (sweet cooking wine)
1 tablespoon *sake* (rice wine)
1 tablespoon sugar
Red food coloring (optional)

Place the tuna meat in a cotton cloth bag made of *fukin* (page 44) or muslin. Close the top of the bag tightly, secure with a rubber band, and put it under cold running tap water. Press the tuna in the bag several times until the water runs clear (this cleans the fish and removes excess fat and fishy flavor). Turn off the tap water and firmly press the fish in the cloth bag to remove excess water. Put the tuna in a bowl and add the soy sauce, *mirin, sake,* and sugar, stirring and mixing thoroughly with chopsticks. Transfer the tuna to a heated skillet (no oil is added) and cook over low heat, moving the fish around in the skillet, until all the moisture is cooked away and the fish becomes light and flaky, about 8 minutes. At the very end, add a small drop of red food coloring if you like and stir thoroughly. Transfer the sweet fish flakes to a bowl and let them cool. Store them in a sealable container in the refrigerator and use within two weeks or freeze.

Fish Stock Preparation
Dashi

Dashi is a lean, aromatic, nutritious, and flavorful stock that is made from water, *kombu* (kelp), and *katsuobushi* (bonito fish flakes). It is simple, quick, and easy to make. Freshly made *dashi* is like freshly brewed coffee. As time passes, the quality deteriorates dramatically. So prepare it as you need it. If you have some *dashi* left over, refrigerate it in a sealed container for two to three days. It is also very handy to have frozen dashi available packed in a small container or in an ice cube tray, since many recipes in this book call for a small quantity of it (2 tablespoons or ¼ cup).

1½ ounces *kombu* (kelp) (about one 10- by 4½-inch rectangle
2 ounces *katsuobushi* (dried bonito flakes) (about 2¼ cups, firmly packed)

Soak the kelp in a large bowl overnight (about 10 hours) with 3 quarts of water. Remove the kelp, reserving it for making a second round of *dashi.* This soaking

A Cloud of Sweet Fish Flakes

Oboro in Japanese means "vague" or "dim" in a visual sense as well as in thought—a dim memory. The following somewhat poetic depiction of the moon aptly illustrates how the word is used: a moon that is covered with a thin layer of cloud or haze is called *oboro-zuki,* a cloudy, dim moon.

My interpretation of the connection between *vague* or *dim* and "sweet dry fish flakes" is this: When we decorate prepared sushi rice with these sweet fish flakes, we use a very thin coating of flakes so that the snow-white rice is barely covered. That reminds us of a vague, indistinct sight, *oboro;* the rice is no longer clearly visible, but we can perceive it is there.

liquid is the *kombu dashi* (kelp stock) and is used when a recipe calls for kelp stock.

Pour the kelp stock into a cooking pot and set it over medium-high heat. When it comes to a boil, add the fish flakes all at once. Count 10 seconds, then quickly turn off the heat. Remove any foam that rises. Let the stock rest with the fish flakes for 2 minutes, then strain it through a *fukin,* tightly woven cotton cloth (page 44), or a strainer lined with a strong paper towel. Discard the bonito flakes or reserve them along with the reserved kelp for making a second round of *dashi.*

If you forgot to soak the kelp overnight, put the kelp and measured cold water in a pot, set it over medium-low heat, and cook for 10 minutes. Remove the kelp and turn the heat to medium. When the kelp stock comes to a boil, add the bonito fish flakes and follow the preceding instructions.

To prepare a second round of *dashi,* combine 3 quarts of cold water and the reserved kelp and bonito fish flakes in a pot, set it over medium-low heat, and cook for 10 minutes. Strain the *dashi* through a *fukin* or a strainer lined with a strong paper towel, discarding the bonito flakes and kelp. Use the second round of stock to prepare a *miso* soup whenever you like. Refrigerate or freeze the unused second round of *dashi* in sealable containers in small batches.

Grated *Daikon* Radish
Daikon oroshi

Snow-white finely grated *daikon* radish, *daikon oroshi,* is important as a mouth refresher and also as an aid to digestion. Grated *daikon* is seldom used directly in sushi cuisine but is served with many different dishes that accompany the sushi meal—fried, grilled, steamed, raw, and cured protein or vegetables. During autumn and winter, *daikon* is grated together with a small Japanese dried red chile pepper, *aka-togarashi.* This tints the grated radish a pretty red color, reminding us of autumn leaves, *momiji,* so it is called *momiji oroshi.* The red chile pepper also adds a pleasant spiciness to the sweet *daikon* radish.

Choose a *daikon* that is heavy for its size, so it will be juicy. If the *daikon* is already cut for sale, buy the thicker top. Grate only the top half of the radish, which is sweeter than the lower half. For a very fine grating, use a Japanese porcelain grater (page 52). If using the standard box-type steel grater, cover the whole grating face with good-quality plastic wrap and grate using the smallest spikes. Not only will you get finer grating, but collecting the grated *daikon* is easier. Grated radish is full of juice, so let it rest in a sieve over the bowl for 10 seconds or so to remove excess liquid. But do not let it become too dehydrated. The collected juice is full of vitamin C, so drink it diluted with some water—another cook's treat.

For the red-tinged *momiji oroshi,* soak two dried red chile peppers in cold water for 20 minutes. Using a cooking chopstick, make two deep holes on the cut surface of the *daikon* radish that will be grated. Insert one red chile pepper into each hole and grate the *daikon* and chile together. Follow the same instructions for removing excess juice.

Sweet Fish Flakes Proportions for the Pro

This large quantity used at sushi restaurants makes about 10 cups of sweet fish flakes.

3 pounds skinned and boned fillet from white-fleshed fish
1¼ cups sugar
2 cups *mirin* (sweet cooking wine)
1 teaspoon salt
1 teaspoon *shoyu* (soy sauce)
Red food coloring

Traditional Dips and Sauces

Here are two staple sauces that you should prepare and have on hand for use—*tsuke-joyu,* sushi dipping sauce, and *ponzu, yuzu*-flavored *ponzu* sauce—as well as several other traditional dips and sauces with distinct flavor and texture that are used in sushi and in accompanying dishes throughout this book. Prepare these homemade dips and sauces ahead of time and have them ready in jars and bottles in your refrigerator.

Sushi Dipping *Shoyu*
Tsuke-joyu

At a sushi bar, you will always find small pots every 3 feet or so along the counter. You will want to pour some liquid from one of these pots into a small individual saucer for dipping your *sashimi* or sushi. The sauce looks like pure *shoyu,* soy sauce, but it is a blend of *shoyu, mirin* (sweet cooking wine), and bonito fish flakes. The quality of *tsuke-joyu* (sushi dipping sauce) can vary widely from one restaurant to another. Indeed, it is true that the flavor of *tsuke-joyu* at a sushi restaurant can tell you a lot about the overall quality of the place.

Tsuke-joyu is quite handy. You can use it as a base for a dressing, a dipping sauce for noodles, or to season a broth.

1 cup *mirin* (sweet cooking wine)
2 cups *shoyu* (soy sauce)
4 ounces *katsuobushi* (dried bonito fish flakes) (about 4 cups)

Pour the *mirin* into a medium pot, set it over medium heat, and bring it to a simmer. Add the *shoyu* and bring it to a gentle boil, then add the fish flakes and quickly turn off the heat. Let stand until the fish flakes all sink to the bottom of the pot. Strain the liquid through a strainer lined with a *fukin,* finely woven cotton cloth (page 44), or a doubled paper towel and discard the fish flakes. Transfer the liquid to a sterilized bottle and store, capped, in the refrigerator. The sauce will keep for half a year. The longer it is stored, the milder and better the flavor becomes.

Tsuke-joyu, a More Contemporary Embellishment

The widespread use of *tsuke-joyu* (sushi dipping sauce) developed in Japan around the beginning of the Showa era (1926–1989). From back in the nineteenth century when *nigiri-zushi* first appeared until the introduction of refrigeration, the sushi did not need additional dipping sauce, since the fish and shellfish used in its preparation were cured or cooked with salt, vinegar, kelp, *shoyu* (soy sauce), *mirin* (sweet cooking wine), or *sake* (rice wine).

Yuzu-Flavored Ponzu Sauce
Ponzu

Ponzu is made with the juice of a kind of citron, yuzu—a tangerine-sized citrus fruit with a thick, bumpy rind. Bright green in summer, yuzu turns golden yellow in autumn when it is ripe. Like lemon, yuzu is valued for its rind and juice, which are bursting with fragrance and a slightly tart and bitter flavor. The yuzu is not generous, producing only a little less than a tablespoon or so of juice per fruit. To get ½ cup of yuzu juice, as is suggested in this recipe, is expensive and difficult, especially outside Japan. So purchase three yuzu fruits and, for the rest, substitute good-quality komezu, rice vinegar. Adding even a small quantity of yuzu juice to the vinegar creates the distinctive flavor of ponzu. If yuzu fruit is not available, use the juice of other citrus fruits such as lemon, lime, or grapefruit. Japanese and Asian food stores carry freshly squeezed plain yuzu or the juice from other Japanese citrus fruits, such as kabosu or dai-dai, packed in small bottles. This is a good substitute when the fresh fruit is not in season or is unavailable. But watch out for the salted variety, since you will then need to adjust the recipe in order to avoid making your sauce too salty.

This aromatic sauce brightens many Japanese dishes. In part 5, "Great Sushi Accompaniments," you will find dishes that are flavored or served with ponzu sauce. So try to have homemade ponzu available in your refrigerator. It keeps about two months but after that loses its flavor.

MAKES 2 CUPS

¼ cup mirin (sweet cooking wine)

1 cup shoyu (soy sauce)

½ cup yuzu juice, bottled plain yuzu, kabosu, or dai-dai juice; or good-quality komezu (rice vinegar)

½ cup freshly squeezed lemon or grapefruit juice

2 inches kombu (kelp)

1 cup katsuobushi (bonito fish flakes)

Fill a large bowl with cold water and ice cubes. Pour the mirin into a small saucepan and bring it to a simmer over medium heat. Add the shoyu and cook over low heat for 5 minutes. Remove the saucepan from the heat and set it in a large bowl of ice water. When it has cooled, add the yuzu juice or rice vinegar, lemon juice, kelp, and fish flakes. Pour the sauce into a clean jar and refrigerate, covered with a tight lid, for one week. Strain the ponzu sauce through a fukin, tightly woven cotton cloth (page 44), or a strainer lined with a strong paper towel, discarding the kelp and fish flakes. Refrigerate in a clean bottle, capped.

The Story of Ponzu

Ponzu provides an interesting insight into Japanese history. The word ponzu came from the Dutch word ponsen, punch. The Dutch, with a small base in Nagasaki, along with the Chinese, were the only people allowed to enter Japan and trade with the Japanese when our country was closed to foreigners during most of the Edo era (1600–1868). Ponzu was originally simply freshly squeezed juice from the dai-dai citrus fruit, which resembles yuzu citron. Shoyu, soy sauce, was later added to it to become the ponzu that we know today.

Quick Rich Brown *Shoyu* Sauce
Tsume

Many of you are familiar with the rich, brown, slightly sweet *shoyu*-based sauce that is used to baste broiled eel. The sauce is called *tsume* and is made from very basic ingredients. Commercially prepared *tsume* may contain some chemical ingredients, including monosodium glutamate, so it is better to prepare your own sauce from scratch using the quick and easy recipe below. This version has no eel flavor because it does not use the leftover eel cooking stock of the traditional recipe. If you want to try genuine *tsume* as it is prepared in a lengthy process in good sushi restaurants, refer to the eel sauce recipe on this page.

MAKES ¼ CUP

½ cup *mirin* (sweet cooking wine)
¼ cup *sake* (rice wine)
¼ cup *shoyu* (soy sauce)
2 tablespoons sugar
4 garlic cloves, peeled
2 *akatogarashi* (Japanese dried red chile peppers)

Pour the *mirin* and *sake* into a small saucepan, set it over medium heat, and bring to a simmer. Add the *shoyu,* sugar, garlic, and red chile pepper and cook, stirring to dissolve the sugar. Turn the heat to low and cook for 8 minutes. Remove the saucepan from the heat and cool. Store the sauce in a clean jar with a lid. The next day, remove the garlic (but leave the red chile pepper). The sauce keeps several months in the refrigerator.

Eel Sauce, *Anago no tsume,* for the Pro

Eel sauce is a by-product of a sushi restaurant's daily preparation of conger eel. Every day, chefs fillet conger eels, *anago,* and cook them in a broth made from the eel bones and head seasoned with *sake* (rice wine), *shoyu* (soy sauce), and *mirin* (sweet cooking wine). When the conger eel is cooked until tender, the cooking broth is saved and recycled to cook the next day's batch of conger eel, and then again the third day's batch. By this time, the cooking broth is full of good flavor, so it is cooked down until reduced by half and then stored in the refrigerator. When the chef has a total of about five quarts, he or she cooks down that quantity again in a large pot until it is reduced to one-fifth of its volume. By the end of cooking, the broth becomes a thick, glossy, dark brown color—a delicious sauce. This eel sauce can be stored for a year in the refrigerator. Here is my best version of the recipe for chefs who prepare conger eel on a regular basis.

MAKES ABOUT 3½ CUPS

4 pounds *anago* (conger eel), filleted and blanched, reserving the heads and bones (page 197)
3½ cups *sake* (rice wine)
¾ cup sugar
1½ cups *shoyu* (soy sauce)
¾ cup *mirin* (sweet cooking wine)

Put the reserved bones and heads on a grill over a gas or charcoal fire or under the broiler and cook until lightly browned. Pour 8 cups of water into a large cooking pot and add the conger eel bones and heads. Set over high heat and bring to a boil. Reduce the heat to medium and cook for 20 minutes. Strain the cooking broth through a fine sieve, then discard the bones and heads.

Transfer the conger eel broth to the cleaned cooking pot, add the *sake* and sugar, and bring to a simmer. Add the blanched conger eel fillets and cook for 15 minutes. Pour the *shoyu* and *mirin* into the pot and cook for 20 minutes. Turn off the heat and let the fillets cool in the cooking broth. Remove them from the cooking broth and drain in a strainer, reserving the broth. Store the eel fillets in a sealable container and use as a sushi topping or as *sashimi.* Use the reserved broth the next day to cook an additional batch, and on the third day as well. Each time, you will prepare a new batch of eel bone and head broth to add to the reserved broth.

On the third day, after removing the cooked and cooled eel fillets, set the broth over medium-high heat and reduce it to half the volume. Preserve the reduced broth in a sealable container in the refrigerator until you have collected about 5 quarts in total.

Pour the 5 quarts into a large pot, set it over low heat, and cook it down to one-fifth of the volume. This will take 5 hours or so, and you may need to add additional sweet cooking wine and soy sauce to the pot during the reduction to adjust the flavor of the final sauce. Toward the end of the cooking, watch closely so that you do not burn the precious sauce. Refrigerate.

The best way to judge the taste of your prepared eel sauce is to visit your favorite sushi restaurant, order some conger eel sushi, and taste the chef's sauce. Try it several times, and when you get back to your kitchen, let your taste buds guide you, remembering the flavor of the sauce you want to emulate.

Rich Brown Chicken *Shoyu* Sauce
Tori no tsume

Cooking charbroiled chicken wings in quick rich brown *tsume* sauce (page 79) makes a delicious sauce for basting chicken. The chicken wings render much flavor, and since the wings also absorb the flavor of the *shoyu*, soy sauce, and *mirin,* sweet cooking wine, as they cook, they are a great treat for everyone. This sauce goes very well with sushi rolls containing chicken, such as Chicken *Teriyaki* Roll (page 117), or save some for your own *teriyaki* chicken preparation.

MAKES ½ CUP

8 chicken wings
1 small, thin whole leek, cut in half crosswise
3 garlic cloves, peeled
½ cup *sake* (rice wine)
1⅓ cups *mirin* (sweet cooking wine)
3 tablespoons sugar
1⅓ cups *shoyu* (soy sauce)

Arrange the chicken wings on a broiler pan and broil, turning over once, until both sides are golden brown. Cook the leek and garlic on a broiler pan and broil until all sides are lightly golden. Pour the *sake* and *mirin* into a cooking pot, set it over medium heat, and bring to a simmer. Add the sugar, soy sauce, chicken wings, garlic, and leek and cook over low heat for 15 minutes, occasionally checking the pot to make sure the liquid is not burning. Strain the sauce through a fine sieve, reserving the chicken wings for your snack. Cool the sauce and refrigerate in a sealed jar or freeze.

Rich Brown Beef *Shoyu* Sauce
Gyuniku no tsume

Since I have included sushi rolls and *nigiri-zushi* using beef, I have created this recipe for a matching basting sauce.

MAKES ⅓ CUP

1 tablespoon vegetable oil for greasing the pot
½ pound ground beef
½ cup *sake* (rice wine)
½ cup *mirin* (sweet cooking wine)
2 tablespoons sugar
¼ cup *shoyu* (soy sauce)

Set a medium cooking pot over medium-high heat and pour in the oil. When the oil is hot, swirl it around and add the ground beef, stirring with a wooden spatula to break it up. When the beef is no longer rosy, add the *sake* and *mirin.* When hot, add 1 cup of water and the sugar and cook for 10 minutes over medium-low heat, constantly skimming off any foam that rises. Add the *shoyu* and cook for 20 minutes. Strain the liquid through a sieve, reserving the liquid (about 1 cup) and the ground beef separately. Return the beef liquid to the cooking pot and reduce it to ⅓ cup over medium-low heat, about 20 minutes. Store the beef sauce in a lidded container in the refrigerator. See the next page for a quick and delicious rice bowl recipe that uses the reserved ground beef.

Yuzu-Flavored *Miso* Sauce
Yuzo miso

In part 5, "Great Sushi Accompaniments," you will find several dishes that use this delicious sauce, *yuzu miso,* prepared either with sweet white *miso* (*Saikyo shiromiso*), or with the salty *akamiso,* brown *miso.* Either way, the *yuzu* citrus fruit flavor clearly stands out. This traditional sauce is a fine addition to modern sushi rolls.

When *yuzu* is not available, use grapefruit, lemon, or lime instead.

BROWN *MISO*-BASED *YUZU MISO* SAUCE

MAKES 1/2 CUP

2 large *yuzu* (*yuzu* citron) or 1 large lemon

3 1/2 ounces *akamiso* (brown *miso*) (about 1/2 cup)

3 tablespoons sugar

2 tablespoons *sake* (rice wine)

1/4 cup *mirin* (sweet cooking wine)

1 egg yolk from large egg

Using a fine grater, grate the rinds of 2 *yuzu* or 1 lemon into a cup. Squeeze the *yuzu* or lemon to obtain about 2 tablespoons of juice.

   Put the brown *miso*, sugar, *sake*, *mirin*, and egg yolk in a saucepan and mix with a whisk until smooth. Set the saucepan over low heat and cook, stirring constantly with a wooden spoon, until the sauce is no longer watery, about 8 to 10 minutes. Add the grated *yuzu* or lemon rind and juice and cook until the liquid is absorbed, about 5 to 7 minutes, stirring constantly. Remove the saucepan from the heat and let it cool. Store the sauce in a clean lidded jar in the refrigerator.

SWEET WHITE *MISO*-BASED *YUZU MISO* SAUCE

MAKES 1/2 CUP

2 large *yuzu* (*yuzu* citron) or 1 large lemon

3 1/2 ounces *Saikyo shiromiso* (sweet white *miso*)

1/4 cup *sake* (rice wine)

2 tablespoons honey

2 tablespoons *dashi* (fish stock) (page 74)

1/4 teaspoon salt

Using a fine grater, grate the rinds of 2 *yuzu* or 1 lemon into a cup. Squeeze the *yuzu* or lemon to obtain about 2 tablespoons of juice. Put the sweet white *miso*, *sake*, honey, *dashi*, and salt in a saucepan and whisk until smooth. Set the saucepan over medium-low heat and cook, stirring with a spatula, until the sauce is no longer watery, about 8 minutes. Add the *yuzu* or lemon rind and juice and cook over low heat for 3 to 4 minutes or until the liquid is absorbed, stirring constantly. Remove the saucepan from the heat and let it cool. Store the sauce in a clean lidded jar in the refrigerator.

Superquick Ground Beef Rice for Four

Using just-cooked ground beef from preparing Rich Brown Beef *Shoyu* Sauce makes a tasty rice lunch, but if you have an additional 1/4 pound of hamburger meat left in your refrigerator, it is even better. Cook 2 cups of brown rice in a cooking pot with measured water (twice the amount of water per volume of dry rice and soaked for 1 hour) over medium heat on the stove top following the instructions for cooking rice on page 58. Please note that it will take 15 to 20 minutes for brown rice to absorb the water. While the rice is cooking, heat a skillet and warm up the leftover cooked ground beef, crumbling it and stirring it with a spatula. Add the uncooked ground beef and 1 tablespoon of freshly grated ginger with its juice and continue to cook over medium-low heat (no additional oil is required) until the beef is no longer rosy.

   When the water in the rice cooking pot is almost absorbed, turn the heat to *very* low, spread the cooked ground beef over the rice (do not stir at this time), quickly return the lid, and cook another 12 minutes. Two minutes before the end of cooking, add 1 cup of blanched, freshly shelled, or frozen green peas. After the rice is cooked, let it stand, covered, for 10 minutes. Now stir the rice, mixing it with all of the ingredients in the pot. Serve in four individual rice bowls garnished with fresh julienned ginger. You can also add some chopped green herbs to the rice for additional color and flavor; parsley, coriander, chives, or *shiso* are all excellent.

Sauces for Modern Rolls

Yuck! That was my original reaction to mayonnaise-based spicy chile sauces used for popular inside-out rolls in America. With the passage of time, these innovations have become classics in the American sushi repertoire, and I have become more tolerant. Well made and properly used, such sauces add a new flavor dimension. So here are some modern sauces that can be used with the sushi rolls or other side dishes in this book.

Wasabi-Mayonnaise Sauce

Adding *wasabi* paste to your homemade mayonnaise makes a good *wasabi*-mayonnaise sauce, but real grated *wasabi* rhizome is even better. In order to make the color of this sauce a more intense green and to add a little pleasant bitterness, I stir in some Japanese green tea powder, *matcha* (page 37).

MAKES ¼ CUP

2 tablespoons *wasabi* powder or *wasabi* paste from a tube
1 teaspoon *matcha* (Japanese green tea powder) (optional)
¼ cup mayonnaise, preferably homemade

When using the powdered form of *wasabi,* mix the powder in a small cup with 1½ tablespoons of water and stir well with a spoon until you have a smooth paste. In another small cup, mix the Japanese green tea powder with 1 teaspoon of hot water, stirring with a spoon until smooth. Now mix the two together with the mayonnaise. Store the sauce in a clean lidded jar in the refrigerator.

Spicy *Sriracha* Mayonnaise Sauce

Every restaurant has its own version of spicy mayonnaise sauce. *Sriracha,* the Vietnamese red chile sauce, seems to be the most popular chile sauce used for this American signature sushi sauce. You can also use plain *toban jiang,* Chinese chile bean sauce, or Italian red chile flakes.

MAKES ¼ CUP

¼ cup mayonnaise
2 tablespoons to ¼ cup *Sriracha* (Vietnamese chile sauce) or 2 tablespoons *toban jiang* (Chinese chile bean sauce)

Put the mayonnaise and *Sriracha* in a cup and stir with a spoon to mix. Store the sauce in a clean lidded jar in the refrigerator.

Spicy Sesame *Shoyu* Sauce

This is a mixture of toasted sesame oil, *Sriracha* sauce, and *shoyu* (soy sauce). Use ordinary golden brown toasted sesame oil, which has a pronounced nutty flavor—not the refined "boutique" clear light sesame oil.

MAKES ¼ CUP

2 tablespoons sesame oil
2 tablespoons *Sriracha* (Vietnamese chile sauce)
2 teaspoons *shoyu* (soy sauce)

Pour the sesame oil into a small skillet and heat it over medium heat until it is fragrant, but don't let it smoke. Transfer the sesame oil to a jar, add the *Sriracha* sauce and soy sauce, and mix well. Cool the sauce and store it tightly closed in the refrigerator.

Hiroko's Hot Chile and *Miso* Sauce

The mixture of Chinese chile bean sauce, Japanese brown *miso*, sugar, and rice vinegar produces a spicy and very flavorful sauce. Use as a sauce or condiment for a roll, raw vegetable sticks, steamed hot rice, or *miso* soup.

MAKES ½ CUP

2 to 3 tablespoons *toban jiang* (Chinese chile bean sauce)
¼ cup *akamiso* (brown *miso*)
¼ cup sugar
¼ cup *sake* (rice wine)
2 garlic cloves, finely grated
1 tablespoon *komezu* (rice vinegar)
1 tablespoon sesame oil

Put the Chinese chile bean sauce, brown *miso,* sugar, *sake,* and garlic in a small saucepan and mix with a whisk until smooth. Set the saucepan over medium-low heat and cook, stirring with a wooden spoon, until the sauce is no longer watery, about 10 minutes. Add the rice vinegar and cook for 3 to 5 minutes. Add the sesame oil and cook for 1 minute. Cool the sauce and store it in a lidded jar in the refrigerator.

Vegetable Garnishes
Kazari-kiri

There are several easy-to-master basic vegetable-cutting techniques. These attractively cut vegetables can greatly improve your sushi dinner, providing additional color, texture, and a charming appearance.

Daikon Radish

Here are the two most popular *daikon* radish cutting techniques. The first is *katsura-muki,* the technique of cutting *daikon* into a transparent paper-thin sheet. The proper knife to use is a *usuba-bocho* (thin-bladed knife) or *yanagiba-bocho* (*yanagiba* knife), both of which have a cutting edge on only one side (see page 45). If you are using a Western knife, choose one that is well sharpened and has a thin blade. The paper-thin *daikon* sheets are then stacked up and cut into fine julienne strips. Julienned *daikon* is an indispensable component of *sashimi* presentations. You will frequently find a mound of it on the plate propping up the *sashimi* slices to make an appealing display of the sliced fish.

Transparent *daikon* slices also play another role today. An innovative chef will use them to wrap the outside of an ordinary sushi roll made with a sheet of *nori* so that the black color of the *nori* is hidden under a white sheet of crisp *daikon.* Especially when there are oily materials inside the roll, *daikon* offers a refreshing component.

The second *daikon* flower is made using the thinly cut *daikon* sheet, so you should master the *katsura-muki* technique first.

Cutting *Daikon* Radish into a Paper-Thin Sheet
Katsura-muki

Cut the *daikon* into 4-inch-long pieces. When you look at the cut surface, you will notice a white circle area about $1/8$ inch all around the circumference. Peel this off along with the skin, using a well-sharpened knife.

Following the illustrations, 1. hold the knife in your right hand with the blade toward you and cut using a slight sawing motion around the length of the *daikon,* rotating as you go. Continue to move the knife around the *daikon* in this way to produce a long, transparent paper-thin sheet. And do watch your left thumb.

2. Drop the slices into a bowl of cold water.

For a *sashimi* presentation, stack up several sheets and 3. cut them crosswise or lengthwise into fine julienne strips. When you cut across the grain, the julienned *daikon* is flexible and tender to bite. When it is cut with the grain, the *daikon* stays crisp and can make a sturdy, taller presentation. In either case, the *sashimi* fish or shellfish is rested on the julienned *daikon.* The *daikon* absorbs excess water from the seafood, so it remains fresh. You will find that after biting into several slices of raw fish, munching some *daikon* is refreshing.

You can produce a paper-thin cucumber sheet using the same technique.

Daikon Flower

1. Cut a thin slice by going all the way around the *daikon* with your knife, using a slight sawing motion.

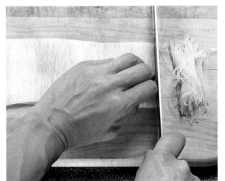

2. Soak the slices in a bowl of cold water.

3. Cut the *daikon* along the grain into julienne strips.

Prepare a 2½- by 8-inch rectangular *katsura-muki daikon* sheet. Following the illustrations, 1. with a very sharp pointed knife, make diagonal cuts about 1½ inches long, spaced about ¼ inch apart along the length of the sheet. Do not cut through to the edges of the sheet; you want an uncut border, about ½ inch wide on top. 2. Fold the sheet in half lengthwise and then 3. roll it around the tip of your index finger and work it into a flower shape. 4. Secure the end of the roll with a toothpick. Use the flowers, which look like the paper decorations on a French crown roast, to garnish your sushi dinner or any Japanese dish.

1. Make 1½-inch-long diagonal cuts, ¼ inch apart.

2. Fold the *daikon* sheet in half lengthwise.

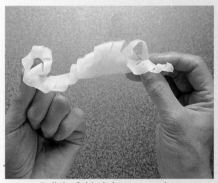

3. Roll the folded sheet around your index finger.

4. The finished flower.

Cucumber

Here are three standard, easy cucumber cutting techniques. Each makes a lovely addition to a sushi platter. You can use the same techniques for carrots and *daikon* radish.

Cucumber Flower Cup

Cut off the very end of a thin cucumber. Stand the cucumber vertically on its cut end and hold it in place on the chopping board. Following the illustrations, 1. insert a paring knife into the cut end of the cucumber to form a petal, taking care not to cut all the way through the bottom of the cucumber. Rotate the cucumber and make three more such petals around the circumference of the cucumber. Hold the bottom end of the cucumber and 2. twist it several times until the "flower" breaks off. You now have a small cucumber cup with four petals. Again, cut off the bottom of the cucumber to flatten it and repeat the process to make additional cups. 3. Fill the cup with *wasabi,* salmon roe, or other sauce and place it on the plate with the sushi or *sashimi.*

1. Insert a paring knife into the cut end of the cucumber to form a petal.

2. After forming petals all around, twist the bottom end of the cucumber until it breaks open.

3. Fill the cup with salmon roe.

Cucumber Fan

Cut a cucumber into 2-inch-long pieces. Cut each piece in half lengthwise, following the illustrations, and 1. cut them in half again lengthwise, producing four broad sticks. Place the cucumber pieces on the chopping board skin side down and cut off the seedy inside part with a knife. Now turn them so the green skin sides are up and make fine lengthwise cuts, not going through the skin end, leaving $1/2$ inch of it intact. Press the cucumber flat and 2. open up the finely sliced parts into a fan shape. Use to garnish your sushi or any dinner plate.

1. Cut a cucumber piece into four 2-inch sticks. After making fine cuts on each piece, leave the end intact.

2. Open up the finely sliced parts of the cucumber into a fan shape.

Cucumber Triangle Points

Cut off a 2-inch piece of a thin cucumber. Following the illustrations, 1. using a knife with a blade about 1 inch wide, stab through the cucumber to the right of center and cut to the left, leaving $1/2$ inch at either end intact. Leave the knife in place. 2. With a second knife, make a diagonal cut in the side of the cucumber, cutting down until the blade hits the first knife. Turn the cucumber piece over, leaving the first knife in place, and 3. make a second similar cut with the second knife. 4. The cucumber piece will now come apart, each section having two attractive "mountain" triangles facing in opposite directions. Use to garnish your sushi or any Japanese dishes.

Cucumber Cups

1. Make the first stab into the cucumber with your knife, leaving the ends intact.

2. With a second knife, make a diagonal cut in the side of the cucumber.

3. After turning the cucumber over, make a second similar cut with the second knife.

4. Pull the cucumber apart.

To create cucumber cups, follow these illustrations. 1. Peel off enough skin at one end of the cucumber to leave a 1-inch cone of unpeeled cucumber.

2. Insert the blade of your knife so that it lies flat against the exposed flesh of the cucumber, cutting into the skin 1/8 inch, then rotate the wide end of the blade one and a quarter times around the cone to shave off a thin cuplike shape with a slim border of green peel. Drop the cup into a bowl of ice water and repeat the process to make as many cucumber cups as you want.

1. Peel off enough skin at one end of the cucumber to leave a 1-inch cone of unpeeled cucumber.

2. Cut into the skin 1/8 inch, then rotate the wide end of the blade one and a quarter times around the cone to shave off a thin cuplike shape.

Lemon Saucer

Cut a lemon in half lengthwise and then in half again lengthwise, to make four wedges. Trim some of the pulp in an even line so that when you turn the wedge over, skin side up, it will lie flat. On the skin side, cut out a deep wedge from the center of the lemon along its length. Use the trench as a container for ikura, salmon roe, or any other ingredient that is attractive and will benefit from contact with the lemon juice in the trench (crab meat? caviar?).

Bamboo Leaf Cutting
Sasa-giri

You may be familiar with the green plastic faux bamboo leaf with its notched upper edge that is frequently tucked into take-out sushi packages. They should, of course, be real bamboo leaves, as they were in the past, when the refrigeration that we take for granted today did not exist, and they were used for years in Japan because of their sterilizing properties. Prepared food can be kept edible longer surrounded by bamboo leaves.

Here I will show you one of the simpler bamboo cutting techniques. Just follow the illustrations carefully. It is worth the time and trouble to practice the design. Cut bamboo leaves can change a simple sushi dish into something quite extraordinary. There are, of course, entire books in Japanese devoted to *sasa-giri,* but that is really the advanced course.

Ask for fresh bamboo leaves packed in an airtight plastic bag at your local Japanese or Asian food store. Usually fifty or one hundred sheets come in one package, so buy a package and share them with a friend. After the package is opened, the sheets keep in the refrigerator for about two weeks. Even if you don't make decorative cuts, the bamboo leaf provides a stunning tray for displaying your sushi.

The Art of Bamboo Leaf Cutting and Sushi Apprenticeship

At sushi restaurants in Japan, fresh bamboo leaves were always packed with sushi for home delivery. When I talked with Hideo Kuribara, the owner and sushi chef at Ushi Wakamaru in New York City, he told me that, for customers, the bamboo leaf was a sign of freshness, conveying the message that sushi is perishable and should be eaten before the bamboo leaf dries out. As is often the case in Japan, the simple act of including bamboo leaves with home-delivery sushi developed into an intricate art form.

Mr. Kuribara went on to tell me about his early days as an apprentice at Kintaro Zushi in Tokyo. Every day he and his colleagues were put to work practicing the art of bamboo leaf cutting, *sasa-giri.* In fact, they were not allowed to move up to do a real sushi kitchen apprenticeship until they mastered this skill. The restaurant, Kintaro Zushi, did a big business in delivering sushi, so hundreds of bamboo leaves were cut daily. If you visit Ushi Wakamaru in New York, you will notice a framed display of Mr. Kuribara's *sasa-giri* collection. The cutouts include a crane, turtle, shrimp, bird, gourd, and green shrub, many of which are symbols related to good fortune. If you ask him when he is not too busy, he will enthusiastically show you how to make a basic *sasa-giri.*

Fold the bamboo leaf in half lengthwise, then follow the series of cuts as illustrated here.

Finally, open up the bamboo leaf.

The finished leaf.

An assortment of bamboo shoot cuttings.

Chapter 8
Popular Sushi Rolls

Throughout this chapter, I use classic recipes as the master recipes for making each type of roll. In the recipes that follow, you will use the same techniques that are spelled out in detail and illustrated in the master recipe.

Traditional Thick and Thin Rolls
Futo-maki (Maki-zushi) and
Nori-maki (Hoso-maki)

Traditional" means that the roll has a sheet of *nori* on the outside. Thick rolls are about 2 to 3 inches in diameter and made by using one whole sheet of *nori*. My mother's traditional filling ingredients included rolled omelet (page 68), blanched *mitsuba* (trefoil greens), simmered *shiitake* mushrooms (page 63), simmered *kanpyo* gourd (page 64), and cooked shrimp. Thick rolls were often made at home for lunch outdoors—picnics, autumn school athletic meets, school field trips, and family day trips to the countryside. By lunchtime, the thick rolls that were made early in the morning had a matured flavor, and the *nori* covering prevented the rice from becoming dry, so it was pleasantly chewy. With every bite, we could enjoy the varied flavors and textures of the fillings.

The thin roll is made into a rectangular log, 1 inch in diameter. Thin rolls are an essential part of a traditional sushi meal. A typical set menu at a sushi restaurant in Japan usually consists of eight to ten pieces of *nigiri-zushi* and one thin roll cut into six pieces. Even when we do not order a set menu and enjoy one piece of *nigiri-zushi* after another, we often finish our dinner with one or two thin rolls. One thin roll equals about three to four pieces of *nigiri-zushi* in rice volume, so a roll satisfies our remaining appetite at the end of the meal. At the same time, thin rolls are refreshing because they use light fillings such as raw cucumber, salt-pickled plum and *shiso* leaves, or crisp pickled *daikon* radish. They complement and add final punctuation to a dinner of sushi and *sashimi* that has been seafood-oriented.

A platter full of sushi rolls and more.
First row, left to right: cucumber flowers, sweet pickled ginger, Thin Roll with Cucumber (page 102),
Thin Roll with Red Bell Pepper (page 105), and a cucumber triangle point;
second row: Caterpillar Roll (page 113);
third row: Pressed Sushi with Eel (page 130) and Smoked Salmon Pressed Sushi (page 126);
last row: California Roll (page 108) and *wasabi*

Master Recipe
My Mother's Classic
Thick Roll
Futo-maki

This thick roll is stuffed with sweet simmered *shiitake* mushrooms, *kanpyo* gourd, sweet fish flakes, and thick rolled omelet, all of which require advance preparation before you push up your sleeves to begin making rolls. The good news is that these ingredients can be prepared in advance and kept refrigerated or frozen. I make my thick roll a little thinner than the traditional one, so it is lighter and easier to eat.

If you would like a shortcut for the sweet fish flakes, there is an already prepared product sold at Japanese or Asian food stores. It is not called *oboro*, though, but *denbu* and is made with much sugar and pink food coloring. It is acceptable, but I still recommend that you make your own, using the recipe for *Sanaka no oboro* (sweet fish flakes) on page 74.

MAKES 4 THICK ROLLS
(2-INCH-DIAMETER ROLLS)

1 *dashi-maki tamago* (rolled thick omelet), 6 inches by 2 inches by 1 inch (page 68)

16 medium-thick asparagus spears

16 medium shrimp in their shells (31 to 35 count per pound)

Sea salt, sugar, and *komezu* (rice vinegar)

1 cup *sanaka no oboro* (sweet fish flakes) (page 74)

6 simmered *shiitake* mushrooms (3 ounces) (page 63)

16 strips 8-inch-long simmered *kanpyo* gourd (page 64)

6 cups (lightly packed)* prepared sushi rice (1½ cups, 9.5 ounces, per roll) (page 58)

4 whole sheets *nori* (laver); choose the thick variety

*Rough cup measurement based on lightly packed rice. In time, after lots of sushi making, you will be able to judge visually the correct quantity of rice.

Cut the omelet in half lengthwise. Cut each half of the omelet in half again lengthwise, then cut each quarter piece in half again lengthwise. You will have eight even-sized logs.

Bring plenty of water to a boil in a large pot and add a little salt. Add the asparagus and cook for 1 minute. Drain and cool the spears under cold tap water. Drain them again and cut off the hard bottom ends.

Make shallow cuts on the belly side of the shrimp, as described on page 111, and bend the shrimp backward. Cook in salted boiling water for 2 to 3 minutes, or until cooked through. Drain the shrimp and cool them briefly under cold tap water. Drain them again and remove the shells. Toss the shrimp in a bowl with ¼ teaspoon salt, ¼ teaspoon sugar, and 2 teaspoons rice vinegar. Remove the shrimp from the bowl.

My Mother's Classic Thick Roll

STEP 1
Setting Up

Following the illustrations, 1. line up all the filling ingredients—rolled omelet, asparagus, shrimp, sweet fish flakes, *shiitake* mushrooms, and *kanpyo* gourd—on a tray. Have at hand the sushi rice, *nori,* and a small bowl containing 1 cup of cold water with 2 tablespoons of rice vinegar or grain vinegar for moistening your hands, and a moistened clean cotton cloth, *fukin* (page 44), or synthetic or paper material (to wipe away excess water or any rice residue stuck to your hands). Have a well-sharpened knife at hand. Place a bamboo rolling mat on a working counter in front of you, with a short side facing you. If using a mat composed of bamboo strips that are flat on one side (and green-colored), be sure the flat side is faceup.

STEP 2
Spreading the Sushi Rice and Filling Ingredients and Rolling

Place a whole sheet of *nori,* shiny side down, on the bamboo rolling mat. Moisten your hands lightly with the vinegar water and pick up the sushi rice—about 1½ cups. Form the rice into a roughly egg-shaped ball and 2. place it on the *nori,* 1 inch below the upper left edge. 3. Spread the measured sushi rice evenly to the right (do this by supporting the rice ball with your right hand and pushing the rice with your left hand toward the right side of the *nori*) until you have made a band of rice along the *nori,* leaving 1 inch of the *nori* uncovered. 4. Now, using all your fingers, spread the rice toward you, until you have covered the whole sheet of *nori* (except for the 1-inch strip at the top).

(If you are using *wasabi* paste or other sauce in the roll, smear the measured portion across the center of the sushi rice from left to right.)

5. Spread one-quarter of the fillings across the center of the sushi rice from left to right in the following order: sweet fish flakes, *shiitake* mushrooms, omelet, asparagus, shrimp, and *kanpyo* gourd. When finished, you will have covered the lower half of the *nori* with fillings.

To roll, pull up the bamboo rolling mat near you and fold it over the fillings. 6. Pull back the edge of the bamboo rolling mat (so that you do not roll it into the sushi) and 7. continue to roll tightly until the whole roll is complete. The 1 inch of exposed *nori* at the top will seal the roll. 8. Now place the bamboo mat over the roll, holding the mat securely, to firm up the roll and square off the edges slightly. Remove the sushi from the bamboo rolling mat.

1. Line up all the fillings and the tools you will need.

2. Place the rice ball on the *nori* 1 inch below the upper left edge.

3. Spread the rice to the right.

5. Spread one-quarter of the fillings across the center of the rice.

6. Pulling back the bamboo mat, continue to form the roll.

7. Now you have almost completed the roll.

To cut the roll into eight pieces, first cut across the center with a sawing motion, not pushing down too hard, **9.** then cut each half-roll into quarters, wiping the blade of the knife with the moist cloth to remove the rice residue when neces-sary. Serve the rolls without a dipping sauce (as most of the fillings are fully flavored). You can prepare this roll half a day in advance.

When you store the rolls, wrap them (before or after slicing) in plastic wrap and put them in a sealable container. Keep the rolls in a cool, dry, dark place for short-term storage. Or for longer storage, refrigerate in the warmest part of the refrigerator, the vegetable bin. Remember that long refrigeration makes the plump, juicy rice dry and no longer pleasant. If you are using raw fish fillings, prepare the rolls just before serving, or if you can't, always keep the rolls at about 40° to 45° F. Remove the refrigerated sushi from the refrigerator at least 20 minutes before serving.

Important Tips

ROLLING

• When spreading sushi rice over the *nori,* do not press the rice tightly onto the *nori.* The sushi rice should have an appearance of new snow just fallen to the ground.

• If your hands are covered with rice, wipe them with the moist cloth. Or dip your hands into the vinegar water and remove the rice grains, but do not forget to blot your hands with the moist cloth. If your hands are too wet, the sushi rice becomes soggy, and then wet *nori* becomes soft and misshapen. A little experience will guide you.

• Do not squeeze or push down on the roll while shaping it.

• Although you may be tempted, do not lick your fingers to remove stuck rice.

4. Using your fingers, spread the rice toward you to cover the whole sheet.

8. Place the bamboo mat over the roll to firm it up and square the edges.

9. Cut across the center of the roll.

Hiroko's Thick Roll
Hiroko no futo-maki

Here I use my favorite filling ingredients, all of which take little effort to prepare. I cook the shrimp in their own shells, so they absorb the color pigments of the shells, making them an attractive bright reddish pink. But you can substitute already prepared shrimp from your fishmonger or supermarket.

MAKES 4 THICK ROLLS

4 large eggs

16 medium shrimp in their shells (31 to 35 count per pound)

Sea salt, sugar, and *komezu* (rice vinegar)

1 medium carrot (3½ ounces), cut into fine julienne, 4 inches long (about 1 cup)

12 asparagus spears, with tough bottoms removed

6 simmered *shiitake* mushrooms (3 ounces) (page 63), cut in thin slices, or 8 brown mushrooms

1 tablespoon vegetable oil

THE SAUCE: *Sriracha* mayonnaise sauce (page 82) (optional)

Sixteen ½-inch-square and 4-inch-long cucumber sticks from 1½ Japanese cucumbers or other cucumbers (for cutting instructions, see page 99)

6 cups (lightly packed) prepared sushi rice (1½ cups, 9.5 ounces, per roll) (page 58)

4 whole sheets *nori* (laver); choose the thick variety

Put the eggs in a pot with water to cover, set over medium heat, and bring to a boil. Reduce the heat to simmer and cook the eggs for 12 minutes. Plunge the eggs into a bowl of ice-cold water and cool immediately. Shell the eggs and cut each into quarters lengthwise.

In order to minimize curling up of the shrimp during cooking, make several very shallow diagonal cuts across the belly side of each shrimp, pull on the ends, and bend it backward (page 111).

Bring water to a boil in a medium cooking pot and add a little salt. Add the shrimp and cook for 2 to 3 minutes, or until cooked through. Drain and cool briefly under cold tap water. Drain the shrimp again, remove the shells, and toss them in a bowl with ¼ teaspoon salt, ¼ teaspoon sugar, and 2 teaspoons rice vinegar.

Mix ¼ teaspoon salt, ¼ teaspoon sugar, and 2 teaspoons rice vinegar in another bowl, add the julienned carrots, and toss (what you are making is quick-pickled carrots). Let the carrots sit for 10 minutes, then drain and squeeze them gently to remove excess liquid.

Cook the asparagus in salted boiling water for 1 minute, then drain and cool under cold tap water. If you are using brown button mushrooms instead of *shiitake,* cut them into thin slices and cook them in a heated skillet with a little oil and salt for 1 minute.

Line up the filling ingredients— *Sriracha* mayonnaise sauce (optional), shrimp, carrot, asparagus, cucumber, *shiitake* mushrooms, and hard-boiled eggs—on a tray. Now follow the instructions in the Master Recipe (page 94).

ADDITIONAL INSTRUCTIONS

1. If you are using the *Sriracha* mayonnaise sauce, smear 2 to 3 teaspoons across the center of each roll.

2. Spread one-quarter of the fillings in the following order: asparagus, hard-boiled eggs, mushroom slices, shrimp, cucumber sticks, and carrot.

3. You can prepare this roll half a day in advance.

4. Serve the rolls with the additional *Sriracha* mayonnaise sauce, or if you have not used *Sriracha* sauce in the rolls, *tsuke-joyu* (page 77) makes a nice dipping sauce.

Eel and Avocado Thick Roll

Thick rolls are ideal for your lunch. In this roll, pleasantly bitter arugula leaves, mild spicy *daikon* sprouts, richly flavored eel, good-quality crabmeat, and avocado create a sensational color, flavor, and texture experience. Put this in your lunch bag and enjoy an amazing midday treat.

MAKES 4 THICK ROLLS

1 package *unagi no kabayaki* (prepared eel) (1/2 pound) (for heating instructions, see below) or cured fish such as gravlax or smoked salmon (choose a less salty variety)

THE SAUCE: 3 tablespoons *tsume* (quick rich brown *shoyu* sauce) (page 79), or *Sriracha* mayonnaise sauce (page 82)

2/3 package *kaiware* (*daikon* sprouts) (2 ounces) or other seed sprouts
Sixteen 1/2-inch-square, 4-inch-long cucumber sticks (below)
1 1/2 cups good-quality canned crabmeat or cooked crabmeat (7 ounces)
16 avocado sticks from 1 ripe but firm avocado (for cutting instructions, see below)
2 cups arugula or baby salad green leaves (about 2 ounces)
6 cups (lightly packed) prepared sushi rice (1 1/2 cups, 9.5 ounces, per roll) (page 58)
4 whole sheets *nori* (laver); choose the thick variety

Remove the reheated eel from its package and cut it into three pieces crosswise, each about 4 inches long.

Cut the head end and the middle pieces into 6 long strips lengthwise and cut the narrower tail section into 4 long strips, to make 16 strips.

Line up all the filling ingredients—*tsume,* eel, *daikon* sprouts, cucumber, crabmeat, avocado, and arugula—on a tray. Now follow the instructions in the Master Recipe (page 94).

ADDITIONAL INSTRUCTIONS

1. When you are using *tsume* in the roll, smear 1 1/2 to 2 teaspoons across the center of each roll.
2. Spread one-quarter of the fillings in the following order: eel, *daikon* sprouts, arugula, crabmeat, cucumber, and avocado.
3. You can prepare this roll half a day in advance.
4. Serve with or without an additional sauce.

Important Tips

CUTTING CUCUMBER FOR ROLLS

One standard Japanese cucumber is about 8 inches long, 1 to 1 1/4 inches in diameter, and weighs around 3 1/2 ounces. In order to cut the unpeeled cucumber into sticks for the rolls, first cut off 1/4 inch from both ends and cut in half crosswise. Cut each piece in half lengthwise and cut each of those pieces into 3 even long sticks, giving you 12 sticks from one Japanese cucumber. When you use other cucumbers, adapt the instructions to the different size. Japanese cucumbers are less seedy than Western varieties, so we do not remove the seeds, but if you use an American cucumber, remove the seeds. Don't peel the cucumbers. And try not to buy waxed ones.

HEATING PREPARED *UNAGI*, EEL

Prepared *unagi,* eel, packed in a plastic bag is sold either frozen or already defrosted. It should be reheated before using. Either microwave it in its own plastic package (make sure there are no foil packs inside the plastic wrapper) or heat it wrapped in aluminum foil for 10 minutes in an oven preheated to 325° F.

CUTTING AVOCADO FOR SUSHI

Cut the avocado into halves lengthwise and remove the pit. Do not remove the skin at this stage. Cut each half into 8 even, long segments and then peel off the skin from each segment.

Crisp Pork Thick Roll
Tonkatsu-maki

Tonkatsu, pork coated with *panko* bread crumbs and fried, originated in Japan at the beginning of the twentieth century. At that time, Japan opened its door to foreign trade and ideas, and new Western preparations suddenly flooded into the country. The idea behind the creation of *tonkatsu* probably came from Austrian Wiener schnitzel. A complete *tonkatsu* dinner consists of fried pork served with mounds of crisp shredded Western cabbage and a sweet, spiced sauce. *Tonkatsu* quickly became one of the signature dishes of Japan and later gave birth to the *tonkatsu* sandwich.

So here is my crispy, juicy *tonkatsu* roll, inspired by this ever popular dish. Since cabbage is too firm in the roll, I use radicchio. It adds a pleasant bitter flavor and an attractive color. If you are not a pork eater, try making this with jumbo shrimp, beef tenderloin, or whitefish fillet.

It is best to bread and fry the pork just before making the roll. If that is not convenient, cook the pork in advance and microwave or reheat it in the oven before making the rolls. Or bread the pork half a day ahead and refrigerate, then dredge the prepared pork once more in the bread crumbs just before frying.

MAKES 4 THICK ROLLS

MAKES 1/3 CUP
TONKATSU SAUCE:
1/2 cup Worcestershire sauce
1/4 cup sugar
1/4 cup *shoyu* (soy sauce)
1/4 cup tomato ketchup
2 teaspoons smooth French mustard
1 teaspoon *umeboshi* paste (salt-pickled plum) or *komezu* (rice vinegar) to taste

1/2 cup cake flour
2 large eggs, lightly beaten with 2 tablespoons water
2 cups Japanese *panko* bread crumbs or homemade bread crumbs
Salt and pepper
1/2 pound pork tenderloin, cut into eight 4-inch-long strips
Vegetable oil for frying
Mustard (optional)
1 small radicchio (6 ounces) or other similar slightly bitter salad greens, cut into fine julienne strips
1 sprig parsley or coriander leaves picked from the stems
6 cups (lightly packed) prepared sushi rice (1 1/2 cups, 9.5 ounces, per roll) (page 58)
4 whole sheets *nori* (laver); choose the thick variety

Combine all the sauce ingredients in a small saucepan and cook over low heat, stirring with a wooden spatula, until the volume is reduced by 20 percent. Remove from the heat and let cool to room temperature. Refrigerate the sauce in a sealed jar.

Put the flour in one bowl, the egg and water mixture in another, and the *panko* bread crumbs in a third. Salt and pepper the pork strips and dust them with the flour, then shake off the excess. With a fork (using a fork keeps your fingers dry), pick up one strip of pork and pass it through the egg mixture, shake off the excess, dredge in flour again, and once more pass it through the egg (a double layer of egg and flour makes the crust very crispy). Cover the pork with the bread crumbs. Finish breading all the pork strips.

Heat 2 inches of vegetable oil in a deep pot to 330° F. Cook the pork in small batches in the heated oil over low heat until it begins to acquire a light golden color, about 3 to 4 minutes. Remove the pork from the oil and cook the remaining batches. After all the pork has been deep-fried, increase the temperature of the oil by about 10° and refry the pork for 10 to 20 seconds or until the outside acquires a golden brown color and is crisp to the touch. Drain the pork strips and rest them on a steel strainer.

Line up all the filling ingredients—*tonkatsu* sauce, mustard (optional), fried pork, julienned radicchio, and parsley—on a tray. Now follow the instructions in the Master Recipe (page 94).

ADDITIONAL INSTRUCTIONS

1. Smear 1/2 to 1 tablespoon *tonkatsu* sauce across the center of each roll. Dot the *tonkatsu* sauce with mustard for more spiciness.
2. Spread one-quarter of the fillings on each roll in the following order: radicchio, fried pork, and parsley.
3. You can prepare this roll several hours in advance, but it tastes best just after the pork is fried and rolled into the sushi.
4. Serve with additional *tonkatsu* sauce.

Healthy Brown and Red Rice Roll

Brown rice is not a good choice for sushi rice. It is impossible to make *nigiri-zushi* with it because it is too firm and its nutty flavor and brown color are not what is expected in a delicate sushi. Brown rice can be cooked until tender, but then it becomes too mushy. Some health-conscious food stores and supermarkets today, however, are carrying rolls made with brown rice, in which the *nori* sheet wraps around the looser brown rice and holds it inside.

I make a brown sushi rice by combining it with Asian red rice—a glutinous or waxy variety, which is available at Asian food stores or large supermarkets. Red rice, when it is cooked, becomes moist and very sticky, providing a suitable texture when combined with the brown rice. Another bonus is that the cooked rice acquires a lovely deep purple color. When cooking brown rice and red rice together in my rice cooker, I use the ordinary white rice cooking setting (the brown rice setting makes the rice too soft), and for stove top cooking, I add

5 cups of water to the 2¼ cups of dry rice, which was rinsed and soaked in water for 1 hour, then follow the instructions on page 58. Please note that it will take about 15 to 20 minutes for the rice mixture to absorb water.

The classic combination of sweet simmered *shiitake* mushrooms, rolled omelet, and boiled spinach makes this roll the ultimate healthy lunch.

MAKES 4 ROLLS

1 rolled thick omelet (6 inches by 2 inches by 1 inch) (page 68)
1 pound spinach, preferably with stems and roots
Salt
¼ cup toasted black sesame seeds mixed with ¼ teaspoon salt
6 simmered *shiitake* mushrooms (3 ounces) (page 63), cut into thin slices
16 strips simmered *kanpyo* gourd (page 64)
6 cups (lightly packed) prepared sushi rice made from 1¼ cups brown rice and 1 cup sticky red rice (1½ cups, 9.5 ounces, per roll) (see above)
4 whole sheets *nori* (laver); choose the thick variety

Cut one whole omelet into 8 equal-sized long logs (page 94).

Bring plenty of water to a boil in a large pot and add a little salt. Add the spinach, plunging the root and stem part in first and gradually submerging the leaves in the water. Cook for 1 minute. Drain and cool the spinach under cold tap water. Drain it again, squeeze out excess water, and cut off the root.

Line up all the filling ingredients—black sesame seeds, omelet, spinach, *shiitake* mushrooms, and *kanpyo* gourd—on a tray, then follow the instructions in the Master Recipe (page 94).

ADDITIONAL INSTRUCTIONS

1. Spread one-quarter of the fillings on each roll in the following order: black sesame seeds, omelet, *shiitake* mushrooms, spinach, and *kanpyo* gourd.
2. You can prepare this roll half a day in advance.
3. Serve without a dipping sauce.

Why is the Cucumber Roll Called *Kappa*?

The *kappa* is not a cucumber but an imaginary humanlike tortoise-shaped animal, similar to the elves of Western folklore, who lives near the water. He has a little bald depression, like a saucer, on top of his head, and fine hair hangs from it. The depression catches the water, and if there is no water, he dies. The *kappa,* whose feet and hands are webbed like a duck, stands and walks like a human being. But this description gives no clue as to why the thin roll filled with cucumber is named after this creature. Maybe it is because of the *kappa*'s color. He is deep green like cucumber skin.

Master Recipe
Thin Roll
with Cucumber
Kappa-maki

This roll is pictured on page 93.

MAKES 12 THIN ROLLS
(EACH 1 INCH IN DIAMETER)

Twenty-four ½-inch-square and 4-inch-
long cucumber sticks (for cutting
instructions, see page 99)

THE CONDIMENT: 3 to 4 tablespoons
wasabi paste

6 cups (lightly packed)* prepared sushi
rice (½ cup, 2.8 ounces, per roll)
(page 58)

12 half-sheets *nori* (laver); choose the
crisp variety

3 tablespoons toasted white sesame
seeds

THE SAUCE: *tsuke-joyu* (sushi dipping
sauce) (page 77)

*Rough cup measurement based on lightly
packed rice. In time, after lots of sushi
making, you will be able to judge visually
the correct quantity of rice.

STEP 1
Setting Up

Following the illustrations, 1. line up the
filling ingredients—cucumber sticks and
wasabi paste—on a plate. Have at hand
the sushi rice, half-sheets of *nori*
stacked up in a tin or in a closed sealable plastic bag, a small bowl containing 1 cup of cold water with 2
tablespoons of rice vinegar or grain
vinegar for moistening your fingers, and
a moistened clean cotton cloth, *fukin*
(page 44), or synthetic or paper material (to wipe away excess water or any
rice residue stuck to your hands). Have
a well-sharpened knife at hand. Place
a bamboo rolling mat on a working
counter in front of you, with a short side
facing you.

STEP 2
Spreading the Sushi Rice and
Filling Ingredients and Rolling

Arrange one half-sheet of *nori,* shiny
side down, on the bamboo rolling mat,
with a long side facing you. Moisten
your hands with a small amount of the
vinegar water and pick up the sushi rice
(about ½ cup). Form it into a roughly
egg-shaped ball without squeezing it,
and 2. place the ball on the *nori* on the
left side, ½ inch below the far edge of
the *nori.* Spread the sushi rice evenly to
the right (do this by supporting the rice
ball with your right hand and pushing
the rice with your left hand toward the
right side of the *nori*) to make a band
across the *nori,* leaving ½ inch of the far
end uncovered. 3. Now spread the rice

1. Line up all the ingredients and the tools
you will need.

2. Place the rice ball on the far left side of the
nori, leaving ½ inch uncovered at the top.

5. After sprinkling on the sesame seeds,
arrange 2 cucumber slices in the center.

6. Pick up the bamboo mat and start rolling

from the band toward you, covering all the *nori* except for a ½-inch strip closer to you. With your fingers, make a slight depression in the center across the sushi rice. 4. Smear about ⅛ to ¼ teaspoon *wasabi* (or other sauce, if you are using it) across this depression. Sprinkle sesame seeds over the rice.

5. Arrange 2 cucumber sticks along the center of the sushi rice. 6. Pick up the bamboo mat and fold it over the ingredients so that the edge of the rice-covered *nori* just meets the top edge of the rice farther from you, leaving the ¼ inch of the *nori* at the top exposed. Pull back the edge of the bamboo mat (so that you do not roll it into the sushi) and 7. continue to roll tightly until the whole roll is completed. The ½ inch of exposed *nori* at the top will seal the roll (too much rice won't leave room for this

flap, and the roll won't be sealed at the end). 8. Now place the bamboo mat over the roll and hold the roll (put your index fingers along the top of the mat to keep the roll flat while you shape the roll on its sides with your thumbs and other fingers) to firm it up and square off the edges slightly. Unroll the bamboo rolling mat and remove the sushi.

STEP 3
Cutting, Serving, and Storing

To cut the roll into six pieces, first cut across the center in a sawing motion, not pushing down too hard, then cut each half-roll into three pieces, wiping the blade of the knife with the moist cloth to remove the rice residue when

necessary. Serve the rolls with cut surface up with the sushi dipping sauce or other appropriate sauce or without a sauce, as you like.

You can prepare the cucumber roll several hours in advance: wrap it uncut in plastic wrap and put it in a sealable container. Place rolls in a cool, dry, dark place for short-term storage. For longer storage, refrigerate in the warmest part of the refrigerator, the vegetable bin. Remember that long refrigeration makes the plump, juicy rice dry and no longer pleasant.

If you are using raw fish fillings, prepare the rolls just before serving. If you do it one hour in advance, always keep the rolls at about 40° to 45° F. Remove the refrigerated sushi from the refrigerator at least 20 minutes before serving.

3. Spread the rice out to cover all the *nori* except for ½ inch at the top and bottom.

4. With your finger, smear the *wasabi* down the length of the depression.

7. Continue rolling until the *nori* meets the top border of the rice, leaving ½ inch of *nori* uncovered.

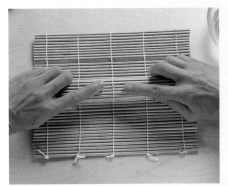
8. Place the mat over the roll to firm it up and square the edges.

Thin Roll with *Kanpyo* Gourd
Kanpyo-maki

The thin roll filled with *kanpyo* gourd, *kanpyo-maki,* was the first traditional roll made in Edo (now Tokyo) in the mid-nineteenth century. *Kanpyo-maki* is unique in two ways. All other thin rolls are rolled and then generally shaped into a square log, but the *kanpyo-maki* is made into a round form. All other thin rolls are cut into six bite-sized pieces, but a *kanpyo-maki* is cut into four pieces. Since each piece is longer than pieces of other rolls, *kanpyo-maki* is presented lying down on its side rather than standing up like its colleagues. A good *kanpyo-maki* prepared by a skilled sushi chef is as delicious and worthwhile as a piece of well-crafted *nigiri-zushi.* Find out more about *kanpyo* and how to prepare it on page 64.

MAKES 12 THIN ROLLS

Forty-eight 8-inch-long strips simmered *kanpyo* gourd (page 64)

6 cups (lightly packed) prepared sushi rice (1/2 cup, 2.8 ounces, per roll) (page 58)

12 half-sheets *nori* (laver); choose the crisp variety

Have the simmered *kanpyo* strips ready, then follow the instructions in the Master Recipe (page 102).

ADDITIONAL INSTRUCTIONS

1. Remember, a *kanpyo-maki* roll is cut into quarters.

2. Serve without a dipping sauce.

3. You can prepare this roll several hours in advance.

Thin Roll with Pickled *Daikon* Radish
Oshinko-maki

My husband's favorite way to finish his sushi dinner is with *oshinko-maki,* pickled *daikon* radish roll. He calls it his dessert. Sushi chefs from one restaurant to another prepare slightly different versions, but the best is a combination of crunchy pickled yellow *daikon* radish mixed with crisp *daikon* sprouts, nutty white sesame seeds, and some smoky julienned bonito fish flakes. When you purchase the pickled *daikon* radish, *takuwan,* at a Japanese or Oriental food store, avoid those that are a very bright yellow (a sign of excessive use of artificial food coloring). Also, study the ingredients list on the package and choose products with the shortest list of ingredients, preferably those that have no artificial coloring or monosodium glutamate additives. The average size of a pickled radish is 7 ounces in one package. Thinly julienned bonito fish flakes are called *ito-katsuo,* which literally means "thread bonito," and have a more delicate taste and fewer fishy characteristics than the larger flakes that are used to prepare Japanese *dashi.* Both types are sold in the dry foods department of Japanese, Asian, or large American supermarkets, usually side by side.

MAKES 12 THIN ROLLS

6 ounces *takuwan* (pickled *daikon* radish) or use julienned carrot instead

1 package *kaiware* (*daikon* radish sprouts) (3 ounces), with the very bottom root removed, or other seed sprouts

2 small packets *ito-katsuo* (julienned bonito fish flakes), each containing about 1/3 cup (1/8 ounce), or larger fish flakes

2 tablespoons toasted white sesame seeds

6 cups (lightly packed) prepared sushi rice (1/2 cup, 2.8 ounces, per roll) (page 58)

12 half-sheets *nori* (laver); choose the crisp variety

Cut the pickled *daikon* into julienne strips, 4 inches long. Mix the pickled *daikon, daikon* sprouts, bonito fish flakes, and toasted sesame seeds together in a bowl, then follow the instructions in the Master Recipe (page 102).

ADDITIONAL INSTRUCTIONS

1. You can prepare this roll several hours in advance.

2. Serve without a dipping sauce.

Thin Roll with Tuna
Tekka-maki

A thin roll with a strip of tuna in the center is called *tekka-maki*. *Tekka*(-*ba*) means gambling place, so this is food for gamblers who only have time to grab a bite-sized *tekka-maki*. If this story sounds familiar, remember the card-playing Lord Sandwich, for whom, it is said, the sandwich was invented because he couldn't stop playing.

MAKES 12 THIN ROLLS

Twenty-four 1/2-inch-square and 4-inch-long tuna logs cut from a 1 1/3-pound sushi *maguro* (tuna) block or blocks (for information on shopping for sushi fish, see page 168; for sushi tuna, see page 185)

4 tablespoons *wasabi* paste

6 cups (lightly packed) prepared sushi rice (1/2 cup, 2.8 ounces, per roll) (page 58)

12 half-sheets *nori* (laver); choose the crisp variety

THE SAUCE: *tsuke-joyu* (sushi dipping sauce) (page 77)

Have the tuna logs and *wasabi* at hand, then follow the instructions in the Master Recipe (page 102).

ADDITIONAL INSTRUCTIONS

1. Since raw fish is used, prepare the rolls just before serving.
2. Serve with the dipping sauce.

Thin Roll with Red Bell Pepper
Shojin tekka-maki

Invariably my students and guests will say, "Is this tuna?" when they see the red-colored filling. Smoky roasted red bell pepper makes a wonderful vegetarian version of *tekka-maki* (tuna rolls). If you want to make it spicy, use the spicy sesame *shoyu* sauce (page 83). These rolls are pictured on page 93.

MAKES 12 THIN ROLLS

2 medium red bell peppers (5 to 6 ounces each)

4 tablespoons *wasabi* paste

6 cups (lightly packed) prepared sushi rice (1/2 cup, 2.8 ounces, per roll) (page 58)

12 half-sheets *nori* (laver); choose the crisp variety

THE SAUCE: *tsuke-joyu* (sushi dipping sauce) (page 77)

Roast the bell peppers over an open gas flame or other heat source until the skins are charred. Immediately put the peppers into a plastic bag and seal for 10 minutes so they can steam. Remove the peppers and peel off the skins without using water. If you need to clean off the charred skin, use a paper towel. Cut off the stems, remove the seeds, and cut each bell pepper into 10 strips, for a total of 20 strips.

Have the *wasabi* and red bell pepper at hand, then follow the instructions in the Master Recipe (page 102).

ADDITIONAL INSTRUCTIONS

1. You can prepare this roll several hours in advance.
2. Serve with the dipping sauce.
3. For a spicy roll, before filling, toss the red bell pepper strips in a bowl with a generous amount of spicy sesame *shoyu* sauce (page 83).

Thin Rolls with Pickled Plum and *Shiso* Leaves
Ume-shiso-maki

Even though travelers and workers carried cooked rice packed with a salt-cured plum long before refrigeration existed, this particular delightful roll was born after World War II.

12 large *umeboshi* (salt-pickled plums), to yield approximately 1 teaspoon of plum paste per *umeboshi*

2 tablespoons *mirin* (sweet cooking wine)

24 *shiso* leaves (perilla), julienned, or 1/2 cup coriander leaves, julienned

1/2 Japanese cucumber (about 2 ounces) or other small cucumber, cut into 4-inch-long julienne strips, with any seedy parts removed

6 cups (lightly packed) prepared sushi rice (1/2 cup, 2.8 ounces, per roll) (page 58)

12 half-sheets *nori* (laver); choose the crisp variety

Mix the mashed *umeboshi* in a small cup with the *mirin* and julienned *shiso* leaves. Have the *umeboshi* sauce and cucumber sticks at hand, then follow the instructions in the Master Recipe (page 102).

ADDITIONAL INSTRUCTIONS

1. You can prepare this roll several hours in advance.

2. Serve without a dipping sauce.

About *Ume*

Ume-shiso-maki, pickled plum roll, offers a refreshingly tart flavor to cleanse your palate and aid digestion, so it is a good choice for finishing your sushi dinner.

Ume are Japanese green plums that mature to plump fruit during the early summer rainy season in Japan. The matured fruits are firm to the touch and more than anything resemble a hard green unripe apricot. When raw, the *ume* is inedible because of its strong astringency and the presence of a small amount of a toxic substance. So we have had to come up with several delicious ways to enjoy this seasonal delicacy. One is curing the fruit in salt to make *umeboshi,* a practice that goes back to the Muromachi era (1393–1573). Since that time, cured plums have played an important role as a nutritious and medicinal food. The plum is rich in several organic acids and is full of vitamins (A, B_1, B_2, and C) and minerals, including calcium, phosphorus, and potassium, all of which help to promote proper metabolism. Salt-pickled plums can also suppress bacteria that cause spoilage and fight dysentery, tubercle, and typhoid bacilli.

Inside-out Rolls
Uramaki

Since their debut, many inside-out rolls have been created, and some have already become classics that are nearly universally available—California roll, spicy tuna roll, *tempura* roll, salmon skin roll, and caterpillar roll. The list continues to grow. Here I give you a collection of my favorite inside-out rolls. The key to success in creating your own is selecting a well-matched, appealing combination of ingredients. A good rule is to choose ingredients of different colors, textures, flavors, and aromas, so that they harmonize and complement one another. Selecting the freshest and best-quality ingredients is no doubt the most important single element in the preparation.

I have tried many inside-out rolls at different sushi restaurants across the country and have decided that *thin* inside-out rolls are the winners. One slice of a roll is about 1¼ inches in diameter and 1¼ inches thick. This one-bite size is easy and pleasant to pick up and eat. When the roll is medium-thick (1¾ inches in diameter), it takes two bites to eat, so you struggle after the first— holding on to a sticky piece of sushi while the fillings fall out (there is no sushi rice inside to bind the fillings together, and *nori* does not do the job).

In this section, therefore, all the recipes except one are *thin* inside-out rolls. If you wish to make them medium-thick, use the larger volume of sushi rice indicated in the accompanying box and double the quantity of filling ingredients used to make the thin rolls. Instead of seven thin rolls, you will have five medium-thick rolls. The rolling instructions are exactly the same.

The exposed sushi rice of the inside-out roll is sticky, so the surface is always decorated with toasted white sesame seeds or *tobik-ko* (flying fish roe). You can also use black sesame seeds, *aonori* (freshwater algae flakes), *ito-katsuo* (julienned bonito fish flakes), or finely chopped peanuts or other nuts.

To make inside-out rolls, you must wrap your bamboo rolling mat tightly in plastic wrap.

Nori Size for the Medium-Thick Roll

You will need three-quarters of a sheet of *nori* to make a medium-thick inside-out roll. With scissors, cut off one-quarter of the *nori* sheet crosswise. You will need five trimmed sheets and 6 cups prepared sushi rice for five rolls.

Master Recipe Classic California Roll

This is the Adam *and* the Eve of today's inside-out rolls. It is filled with the now conservative-sounding mixture of crabmeat, cucumber, and avocado. The crabmeat can be mock or real, but the real, more expensive crabmeat, of course, makes the rolls taste much better. This roll is pictured on page 93.

MAKES 7 ROLLS (EACH THIN ROLL 1 1/4 INCHES IN DIAMETER; EACH MEDIUM-THICK ROLL 1 3/4 INCHES IN DIAMETER)

1 1/2 cups crabmeat (7 ounces) or 7 sticks faux crabmeat

Fourteen 1/2-inch-square, 4-inch-long cucumber sticks (for cutting instructions, see page 99)

1/2 pitted large avocado (3 1/2 ounces), cut into 14 long sticks and then peeled

THE GARNISH: 1/2 cup toasted white sesame seeds or *tobik-ko* roe

THE SAUCE: 3 tablespoons *Sriracha* mayonnaise sauce (page 82) or 1 tablespoon *wasabi*

7 half-sheets *nori* (laver); choose the thicker variety

6 cups (lightly packed)* prepared sushi rice (7/8 cup, 4.2 ounces, per roll) (page 58)

*Rough cup measurement based on lightly packed rice. In time, after lots of sushi making, you will be able to judge visually the correct quantity of rice.

Following the illustrations, **1.** line up all the filling ingredients—crabmeat, cucumber, avocado, white sesame seeds, and *Sriracha* mayonnaise sauce—on a tray along with the sushi rice and half-sheets of *nori,* stacked up in a tin or in a closed sealable plastic bag. Have at hand a small bowl containing 1 cup of cold water with 2 tablespoons of rice vinegar or grain vinegar for moistening your hands and moistened clean cotton cloth, *fukin* (page 44), or synthetic or paper material (to wipe away excess water or any rice residue stuck to your hands). Open up your bamboo rolling mat and wrap it tightly in plastic wrap. Have a well-sharpened cutting knife at hand.

Place one half-sheet of *nori,* shiny side down, on the rolling mat with a long side facing you. Moisten your hands slightly with the vinegar water and pick up the sushi rice (about 7/8 cup), forming it into a roughly egg-shaped ball without squeezing. **2.** Place the rice ball on the *nori,* 1/2 inch from the upper far left edge of the *nori.* Supporting the rice with your right hand, spread the rice evenly to the right, leaving 1/2 inch of the far end of the *nori* uncovered. Now, using all your fingers, spread the rice toward you, until you have covered the whole area (except for the 1/2 inch at the top). **3.** Sprinkle the surface of the rice evenly with 1 tablespoon of white

1. Line up all the filling ingredients and the tools you will need.

2. Place the rice ball on the far left side of the *nori,* leaving 1/2 inch uncovered at the top.

5. Pile up the filling ingredients on the sauce-smeared area.

6. Pick up the bamboo mat and fold it over the fillings.

sesame seeds to form an outer coating for the roll.

4. Flip the rice-covered *nori* sheet over onto the rolling mat, lining up the bottom edge of the mat and the *nori* sheet evenly. The *nori* is now on top of the rice.

Smear about 2 teaspoons of the *Sriracha* mayonnaise sauce across the *nori* from left to right, one-quarter of the way up the side nearer to you.

5. Arrange the crabmeat over the sauce-smeared area. Place two sticks of cucumber over the crabmeat and then two sticks of avocado on top of the cucumber sticks. 6. To roll, lift up the bamboo mat near you and fold it over the fillings. As you roll and the bamboo mat reaches to the surface of the *nori,* pull back the edge of the bamboo mat (so that you do not roll it into the sushi) and continue to roll tightly until the whole roll is completed, leaving the seam down the roll. Now place the bamboo mat over the roll, hold it securely to firm it up, and square off the edges slightly. 7. Unroll the rolling mat.

STEP 3
Cutting, Serving, and Storing

It may be easier for you to cut the inside-out roll covered in plastic wrap. To cut the roll into six to eight equal pieces, first cut across the center with a sawing motion, not pushing down too hard, then cut each half-roll into thirds or quarters, wiping the blade of the knife with the moist cloth to remove the rice residue when necessary. Serve the rolls with additional *Sriracha* mayonnaise sauce or without a sauce.

You can prepare this roll several hours in advance. For short-term storage, wrap each uncut roll in plastic wrap, put it in a sealable container, and store it in a cool, dry, dark place. Or for longer-term storage, refrigerate it in the warmest part of the refrigerator, the vegetable bin. Remember that long refrigeration (even 1 hour) makes the plump, juicy rice dry and no longer pleasant. If you are using raw fish fillings, prepare the rolls just before serving. Or if you cannot, always keep the rolls at about 40° to 45° F.

3. Sprinkle sesame seeds over the surface of the rice.

4. Flip the rice-covered *nori* sheet over onto the mat.

7. Unroll the mat.

New World Roll

As I have noted, numerous rolls have been invented in America using ingredients that were unheard of in the Japanese sushi kitchen. Usually such innovations occurred out of necessity. When chefs could not find authentic ingredients, they had to rely on what was available locally, such as avocado, salmon, packaged *unagi no kabayaki* (prepared eel), and cream cheese. In this New World Roll, I combine sushi salmon, eel, and roe.

MAKES 7 THIN ROLLS

1/2 pound *unagi no kabayaki* (prepared eel) (1 package)

1/2 pound sushi salmon (for instructions on shopping for sushi fish, see page 168; for sushi salmon, see page 176) or not too salty smoked salmon

1/2 cup *tobik-ko* (flying fish roe) or faux caviar

THE GARNISH: 1/2 cup toasted white sesame seeds

1/4 cup *wasabi* paste

6 cups (lightly packed) prepared sushi rice (7/8 cup, 4.2 ounces, per roll) (page 58)

7 half-sheets *nori* (laver); choose the thicker variety

THE SAUCE: 2 tablespoons *tsume*, quick rich brown *shoyu* sauce (page 79)

Follow the instructions on page 99 for reheating the prepared *unagi*, eel. Cut the eel into three pieces crosswise. Cut the top piece into 6 long sticks, the middle piece into 5 sticks, and the bottom narrow tail piece into 3 sticks, for a total of 14 eel sticks, each about 4 inches long. Cut the salmon into 14 sticks, preferably in 4-inch lengths.

Line up all the filling ingredients—eel, salmon, *tobik-ko,* white sesame seeds, and *wasabi*—on a tray, then follow the Master Recipe (page 108).

ADDITIONAL INSTRUCTIONS

1. If you are using sushi salmon, prepare it just before serving.
2. Use the *tsume* sauce to garnish the platter.

Shrimp *Tempura* Roll

Shrimp *tempura* roll was quite shocking to me when I first heard about it. I have since tried the rolls at several restaurants and found that there are good ones and bad ones. The good ones are crisp and not greasy.

For a successful *tempura* preparation—crisp results—I suggest you use Japanese *tempura* flour, which contains a little starch and some powdered egg. The ratio of *tempura* flour and water is usually 1 cup of flour and 3/4 cup of ice-cold water. If *tempura* flour is not available, make your own batter following the recipe in the accompanying box. No matter which flour you use, start with one small batch and prepare another batch as you go. Batter that was made, stirred, and left too long becomes heavy when it is fried (gluten builds up). Also, dust each shrimp lightly in additional flour before dredging it in the prepared batter so that the runny batter adheres. Always use fresh oil and maintain a constant temperature of 335° F during cooking. Cook the shrimp in small batches, occupying less than half the surface area of the oil at a time. During frying, remove with a fine-mesh skimmer any bits of batter flakes floating on the surface of the oil.

Make the roll with freshly fried shrimp and enjoy it as soon as possible.

Homemade *Tempura* Batter

1 egg
1 cup cake flour
3 tablespoons potato starch or cornstarch

Beat the egg in a 2-cup measuring cup and add about 1/2 cup ice water, enough to make 3/4 cup of liquid. Transfer the egg liquid to a medium bowl and add the cake flour and starch, whisking roughly.

14 large shrimp (21 to 30 count per pound), peeled, tails intact

Vegetable oil for frying

1¾ cups *tempura* flour or homemade *tempura* batter (see the accompanying box)

3 sprigs of coriander, with leaves picked off and stems discarded

1 green jalapeño chile, charbroiled, skinned, seeded, and chopped

6 cups (lightly packed) prepared sushi rice (⅞ cup, 4.2 ounces, per roll) (page 58)

THE GARNISH: ½ cup toasted white sesame seeds

7 half-sheets *nori* (laver); choose the thicker variety

THE SAUCE: *tsuke-joyu,* sushi dipping sauce (page 77), mixed with freshly squeezed lemon juice

Prepare the shrimp following the directions in the accompanying box.

Heat 3 inches of vegetable oil in a heavy-bottomed skillet to 335° F. If you are using the *tempura* flour, mix ½ cup of the flour and ¼ cup plus 2 tablespoons of ice-cold water in a bowl, stirring with a whisk until smooth. Have at hand ¼ cup of the remaining *tempura* flour in another medium bowl for dusting the shrimp (when you are using homemade batter, use ¼ cup of cake flour for dusting). Pick up one shrimp by its tail, dredge it first in the bowl of flour, then, still holding it by the tail, dip it in the batter (the tail remains unbattered). Lightly shake off the excess batter, then lower the shrimp into the heated oil. This should all take less than 10 seconds. Quickly do the same with a few more shrimp. Cook, turning the shrimp once or twice, until they are golden and, when you test one with chopsticks, you feel crispiness, about

2 minutes. Drain the shrimp on a rack. Continue frying all the shrimp in batches. As you go along, the batter may become thicker, because of the flour that you used to dust the shrimp. If this happens, add a little ice-cold water. When the batter is all gone, make a second batch using the remaining *tempura* flour.

Line up all the filling ingredients—shrimp *tempura,* coriander leaves, jalapeño, and white sesame seeds—on a tray, then follow the Master Recipe (page 108).

ADDITIONAL INSTRUCTIONS

1. Use two *tempura* shrimp per roll. Arrange them so that a tail sticks out from each end of the roll.

2. Serve sushi with dipping sauce to which lemon juice has been added.

Preparing Shrimp (So It Doesn't Curl Up)

Place a peeled shrimp, with the tail attached, on a chopping board belly side up. Following the illustrations, **1.** with a

cutting knife, make three to four shallow diagonal cuts on the belly, without cutting through the shrimp. **2.** Pick up the shrimp

and pull both ends, bending backward. This prevents the shrimp from curling up during cooking.

1. Make three or four diagonal cuts across the belly of the shrimp.

2. Pull both ends and bend the shrimp backward.

King Crab Dynamite Roll

This uniquely named sushi was born out of a sushi chef's professional struggles. Enjoy the tiny explosions and the dynamite flavor.

MAKES 7 ROLLS

MAKES 1¼ CUP
DYNAMITE SAUCE:
1 cup mayonnaise
¼ cup *tobik-ko* (flying fish roe)
1 tablespoon plus 1 teaspoon sesame oil
1 teaspoon *shoyu* (soy sauce)

1½ cups high-quality crabmeat (Dungeness, blue, or Alaskan king) (7 ounces) or canned crabmeat

THE GARNISH: ½ cup toasted white sesame seeds

6 cups (lightly packed) prepared sushi rice (⅞ cup, 4.2 ounces, per roll) (page 58)
7 half-sheets *nori* (laver); choose the thicker variety

Mix the mayonnaise, *tobik-ko,* sesame oil, and soy sauce in a bowl. Have the crabmeat, dynamite sauce, and white sesame seeds on a tray, then follow the Master Recipe (page 108).

ADDITIONAL INSTRUCTIONS

1. Preheat the broiler or toaster oven. Cut each roll into six equal pieces. Arrange the pieces cut side down on an oven dish and smear the top of each piece with the dynamite sauce. Cook the sushi briefly until the surface acquires a golden brown hue.

2. You can prepare the rolls several hours in advance. After removing them from the refrigerator, cut them into pieces and follow the instructions above.

How the Dynamite Roll was Born

When I talked to Hiroshi Shima, at the Katana Restaurant in Los Angeles, he told me, "Every day at our restaurant when we first started, we prepared plenty of excellent raw seafood, arranged and stored it in our sushi counter case, and waited for the customers. Our motto was to do our best to bring the finest quality, authentic, damn good sushi and *sashimi* to our diners. But back seven years ago, people were less adventurous, and we had months of watching the fish go unsold. At first, we cooked it up in our kitchen for staff meals. It was great for us but was a huge waste for the business. Finally, I bent my pride and forced myself to make sushi such as California rolls and salmon skin rolls, which customers requested. Then my own creativity began to tickle me." Mr. Shima devised a new California roll with an Alaskan king crab filling, by decorating the finished cut roll pieces with a traditional Japanese egg and oil sauce (very similar to mayonnaise) and crunchy *tobik-ko* (flying fish roe) and browning it in a toaster oven. The sauce gave a golden brown hue and caramelized flavor. It was during this browning period that he and his chefs heard a little popping noise in the oven. "*Tobik-ko* was exploding!" Thus, the dynamite roll was born.

Caterpillar Roll

A roll filled with meaty, smoky *unagi* (eel) topped with thinly sliced avocado has an enticing and succulent appearance. The selection of a perfectly ripe, yet firm avocado, a well-sharpened knife, and good knife skill are essential to creating this sushi. If the avocado is too soft, the slices are simply mashed during the shaping of the sushi. In contrast, too firm or too thick avocado slices will not adhere to the surface of the sushi, giving a sloppy appearance. When all works well, it really does look like a caterpillar (see page 93).

MAKES 7 ROLLS

10 ounces *unagi no kabayaki* (prepared eel) (1½ packages) (for heating instructions, see page 99)

3½ avocados, ripe but still firm, cut in half, pit removed, and peeled

14 chives, 7 inches long

14 salmon roe or carrot cut into ⅛-inch cubes for "eyes"

6 cups (lightly packed) prepared sushi rice (⅞ cup, 4.2 ounces, per roll) (page 58)

7 half-sheets *nori* (laver); choose the thicker variety

After heating the eel, remove it from its foil. Cut one whole eel into three pieces crosswise. Cut the top piece into 6 sticks, the middle piece into 5 sticks, and the narrow tail part into 3 sticks. Cut the top third of the second eel into 7 sticks, making 21 sticks in all.

Cut each avocado in half, remove the stone, and peel. Cut 2 of the half avocados lengthwise into 7 sticks (you will have 14 in total). Cut the remaining 5 half avocados crosswise into paper-thin slices, which will be used to cover the top of the roll (the nice green "skin" of

the caterpillar). To make the "skin," following the illustrations, 1. spread about 14 slices on a piece of plastic wrap, overlapping them in a line, the length of which will be the same as the sushi roll. Place 2 chives on the sheet of avocado, protruding at one end of the avocado band (these are the "antennae" of your curious caterpillar). Make 7 such "skins." Since the avocado slices are not all the same size, be creative in designing the look of your caterpillar.

Line up all the filling ingredients—eel, avocado, and chives—on a tray and the avocado slices on the pieces of plastic wrap, then follow the Master Recipe (page 108).

ADDITIONAL INSTRUCTIONS

1. First prepare seven inside-out rolls *without* garnish on the sushi rice surface.
2. Following the illustration, 2. place each roll, rice side down, on top of an avocado "skin." 3. Carefully flip the roll with the avocado over onto the plastic wrap, so that the slices of avocado are now on top of the roll. Place the bamboo rolling mat over the plastic wrap protecting the avocado and gently press and shape the roll, so that the avocado slices drape over and adhere to the roll. 4. Remove the mat and place the salmon roe "eyes" on the head of the caterpillar.
3. Cut the caterpillar roll with a piece of plastic wrap draped over it (so that you do not mush the thin avocado slices on top).
4. To serve, line up the slices as though the roll were uncut. No dipping sauce is necessary.
5. You can make the roll without the avocado toppings several hours in advance. Once the avocado is in place, it begins to discolor, so do the final decoration just before serving.

1. Arrange on the plastic wrap about 14 avocado slices, overlapping, in a line the length of your *nori* sheet.

2. Place an inside-out roll, rice side down, on top of the row of avocado slices.

3. Flip the roll over onto the plastic wrap so the avocados are now on top.

4. After removing the mat, decorate the head of the caterpillar with salmon roe "eyes."

Spicy Tuna and *Nagaimo* Yam Roll

Spicy tuna roll has been popular in America for the past twenty-five years. Today some creative chefs are adding *nagaimo* yam to this classic.

MAKES 7 ROLLS

½-pound sushi *maguro* (tuna) block, cut into strips ¼ inch by 4 inches long (for information on shopping for sushi fish, see page 168; for sushi tuna, see page 185)

1 tablespoon spicy sesame *shoyu* sauce (page 83)

½ pound peeled *nagaimo* yam, cut into sticks ¼ inch by 4 inches long, or jicama, shredded

¼ cup thinly sliced scallion rings

THE GARNISH: ½ cup toasted white sesame seeds

6 cups (lightly packed) prepared sushi rice (⅞ cup, 4.2 ounces, per roll) (page 58)

7 half-sheets *nori* (laver); choose the thicker variety

Toss the tuna in a bowl with the spicy sesame *shoyu* sauce. Line up all the filling ingredients—tuna, *nagaimo* yam, scallions, and white sesame seeds—on a tray, then follow the Master Recipe (page 108).

ADDITIONAL INSTRUCTIONS

1. Serve without a dipping sauce.
2. Since raw fish is used, prepare the sushi just before serving.

Vegetarian FSP Roll

The Vegetarian FSP Roll recipe is from Cape Cod restaurant owner and sushi chef Andrew Semler, who was actually trained in vegan cuisine. *FSP* stands for "*f*ried *s*weet *p*otato." Finely julienned, golden crispy sweet potato is rolled with traditional sweet simmered *shiitake* mushrooms and blanched and grilled asparagus. If you want to enjoy even more crispiness from the sweet potato, make the roll medium-thick (see page 107), using twice the amount of crisp sweet potato in each roll.

MAKES 7 ROLLS

½ medium sweet potato (¼ pound), peeled and cut into matchstick-thin strips, 1½ inches long

Sea salt and sugar

Vegetable oil for frying

14 thin asparagus (2 ounces), blanched, with the tough bottoms removed

6 simmered *shiitake* mushrooms (3 ounces) (page 63), sliced thin

THE GARNISH: ½ cup toasted white sesame seeds

2 tablespoons *wasabi* paste (optional)

6 cups (lightly packed) prepared sushi rice (⅞ cup, 4.2 ounces, per roll) (page 58)

7 half-sheets *nori* (laver); choose the thicker variety

THE SAUCE: *tsuke-joyu* (sushi dipping sauce) (page 77)

Soak the julienned potatoes in a bowl of cold water for 30 minutes to remove excess starch (this makes the fried potatoes crisper). Drain the potatoes, spread them out on a paper towel, and dry them well. Before frying, sprinkle pinches of salt and sugar over the potatoes and toss by hand.

Heat 3 inches of vegetable oil in a deep, heavy-bottomed skillet to 320° F. Add one-third to half the sweet potatoes (according to the size of your skillet) and cook over low heat until they are crisp and begin to acquire a light golden color, about 10 minutes. During cooking, maintain the temperature of the oil at about 260° F (slow frying removes moisture gradually and completely without browning). Remove the fried strips from the oil all at once using a large fine-mesh skimmer and transfer them to a paper towel laid on top of newspaper. While they are hot, separate the sticks with chopsticks or with your fingers. Sprinkle an additional pinch of salt over the strips and toss. Fry the remaining batch or two.

Heat the grill or other heat source and cook the asparagus until the outside begins to blister, 30 seconds or so.

Line up all the filling ingredients—fried sweet potato, asparagus, *shiitake* mushrooms, white sesame seeds, and *wasabi* paste (optional)—on a tray, then follow the Master Recipe (page 108).

ADDITIONAL INSTRUCTIONS

1. You can fry the sweet potatoes half a day in advance, but prepare the rolls just before serving to ensure the most crispy sweet potatoes.
2. If you wish, smear a small quantity of *wasabi* on the *nori* before adding the potatoes.
3. Serve with the sushi dipping sauce.

Salmon Skin Roll

To prepare this roll, you need the skin of a smoked salmon. Because they live in cold water, salmon build up a particularly delicious thick layer of fat under the skin, making their skin best for this preparation. Purchase smoked salmon with the skin or ask for the skin at your local fishmonger or food store. In many food shops where smoked salmon is cut to order from a large fillet, this delicious skin may simply be thrown away. I cook the skin in a skillet (no oil is added). The layer of fat attached to the skin gradually melts during cooking and makes it crisp.

The pickled mountain burdock—a long, thin, orange-colored root vegetable about 8 inches in length, often packed in a plastic bag containing eight to ten pieces with pickling solution—can be found at Japanese or Asian food stores. If it is not available, use carrot instead.

½ pound skin of smoked salmon

1 package *yamagobo no tsukemono* (pickled mountain burdock) or 5 ounces julienned carrot, 3 inches long

1 small Kirby cucumber (2 ounces), julienned, 3 inches long

⅔ package *kaiware* (*daikon* radish sprouts) (2 ounces), roots removed

1 scallion, finely sliced

THE GARNISH: ½ cup toasted white sesame seeds

6 cups (lightly packed) prepared sushi rice (⅞ cup, 4.2 ounces, per roll) (page 58)

7 half-sheets *nori* (laver); choose the thicker variety

Put the salmon skin in a skillet, skin side down, and cook over medium-low heat until it is golden and crispy, turning it over once. Remove from the skillet and cut it into ¼-inch-wide strips, 8 inches long. Cut the pickled mountain burdock in half crosswise and then cut each piece in half lengthwise.

Line up all the filling ingredients—salmon skin, cucumber, pickled mountain burdock, *daikon* sprouts, scallion, and white sesame seeds—on a tray, then follow the Master Recipe (page 108).

ADDITIONAL INSTRUCTIONS

1. You can prepare the rolls several hours in advance.

2. Serve without a dipping sauce.

Nagaimo

Nagaimo is the tuberous root of a climbing vine. When it is peeled, the snow-white flesh inside appears, and when you touch it, you will feel a slight sliminess, a bit like the juice that comes from okra. *Nagaimo* has no distinctive flavor, but its refreshing color and very crisp texture have long made it an excellent partner for soft tuna in sushi and *sashimi* preparations in Japan. If *nagaimo* is not available, use fresh jicama instead.

Beef and Crisp Sweet Potato Roll

Beef is not a traditional filling ingredient for rolls, but this recipe proves that your favorite beef can be part of a delicious sushi roll. Here the juicy beef, which is seared and marinated in a Japanese broth overnight, is rolled up with crisp sweet potato and Western horseradish. Serve it with *gyuniku no tsume,* rich brown beef *shoyu* sauce (page 80). This roll is best when made medium-thick, so you get more beef and crispy potatoes. You could also use leftover sliced steak (without marination).

MAKES 5 ROLLS (*MEDIUM-THICK*)

MARINADE:

1 cup *kombu dashi* (kelp stock) (page 74)

1 tablespoon *shoyu* (soy sauce)

2 tablespoons *mirin* (sweet cooking wine)

¼ cup *komezu* (rice vinegar)

2 pieces *akatogarashi* (dried red chile pepper) or 1 tablespoon red chile pepper flakes

1 tablespoon vegetable oil

⅔ pound boneless rib eye steak

1 medium sweet potato (5 ounces), peeled, cut into matchstick-thin strips, and deep-fried crisp (see below)

2 stalks coriander, with leaves picked off and stems discarded

THE GARNISH: ¼ cup plus 1 tablespoon toasted white sesame seeds

THE SAUCE: *gyuniku no tsume* (rich brown beef *shoyu* sauce) (page 80)

6 cups (lightly packed) prepared sushi rice (1 cup, 6.3 ounces, per roll) (page 58)

Five ¾-sheets *nori* (laver); choose the thicker variety

Pour the kelp stock into a pot along with the soy sauce, *mirin,* and rice vinegar and bring to a boil. Turn off the heat and add the dried red chile peppers. Let the broth stand to cool.

Heat a skillet and pour in enough vegetable oil to coat the bottom. Add the beef and cook, over medium-low heat, until it is lightly browned on both sides. Continue to cook for 8 minutes, until it is medium done (too rare could be too chewy in a sushi roll). Transfer the beef to the cooled marinade and refrigerate, covered with plastic wrap, overnight.

The next day, remove the beef from the marinade, wipe it with a paper towel to remove excess liquid, and cut it into thin sticks, about ¼ inch thick and 3 inches long.

Line up all the filling ingredients—beef, sweet potato, coriander leaves, white sesame seeds, and rich brown beef *shoyu* sauce—on a tray, then follow the Master Recipe (page 108).

ADDITIONAL INSTRUCTIONS

1. This sushi is better if it is put together just before serving to ensure the crispness of the sweet potato. But you can prepare the sweet potato and the beef in advance.

2. Serve with the *gyuniku no tsume* sauce.

Tips for Crisp Fried Potato

Andrew Semler passes on these tips for producing *very* crisp fried potatoes: "Toss the shredded sweet potatoes with a little salt and sugar and then fry in the oil. When the sweet potatoes start to acquire a light golden color, quickly remove them from the oil. Drain and spread over a paper towel that is backed by newspaper and separate the potato sticks from each other." He makes crisp fried beets in the same way for use in another delightful vegetarian roll.

Chicken *Teriyaki* Roll

Perfectly prepared popular *teriyaki* chicken (there are so many bad versions!) rolled in properly made sushi rice is quite a winner. To give this roll a special flavor, I use beer to marinate the chicken and then cook the bird with it. The result is a *teriyaki* chicken that is perfect for a well-fashioned roll.

MAKES 7 ROLLS

MARINADE:

1 cup beer, Pilsner or lager

2 tablespoons honey

3 tablespoons and 2 teaspoons *shoyu* (soy sauce)

1 tablespoon freshly grated ginger, juice and pulp

¾ pound chicken thighs, without bone and skin

2 thumb-sized pieces of ginger (about 1 ounce), peeled and finely julienned

2 tablespoons vegetable oil

7 *shishitogarashi* (Japanese *shishitogarashi* green peppers) or ½ medium frying pepper*

2 teaspoons *shoyu* (soy sauce)

THE GARNISH: ½ cup toasted white sesame seeds

6 cups (lightly packed) prepared sushi rice (⅞ cup, 4.2 ounces, per roll) (page 58)

7 half-sheets *nori* (laver); choose the thicker variety

*If using the frying pepper, remove the seeds and cut into ¼-inch-wide strips.

Mix in a bowl the beer, honey, 3 tablespoons soy sauce, and ginger juice and pulp, add the chicken, and marinate for 30 minutes.

Meanwhile, bring a small saucepan of water to a boil and cook the ginger strips for 10 seconds. Drain them in a colander and spread them out to cool.

Remove the chicken from the marinade and wipe dry with a paper towel, reserving the marinade. Heat the oven to 350° F. Heat a cast-iron skillet or heavy-bottomed skillet, pour in 1 tablespoon vegetable oil, add the chicken, and cook over medium-low heat until it is golden on both sides. Put the skillet with the chicken in the oven and cook another 8 minutes. Remove the chicken, transfer it to a platter, and cover it with aluminum foil. Wipe out any excess oil in the skillet with a paper towel and add the reserved marinade. Cook the marinade over medium-high heat until it begins to bubble and lightly thicken. Return the chicken to the skillet and cook it with the sauce over medium-low heat until it is well coated with the sauce. Transfer the chicken to a platter and let it sit for 10 minutes, covered, reserving the sauce in the skillet. Cut the chicken into sticks ¼ inch thick and 3 inches long.

Brush the whole *shishitogarashi* peppers with a little vegetable oil and cook them in the skillet until the skin blisters. Pour on 2 teaspoons soy sauce, quickly toss with the peppers, then remove the skillet from the heat. Cut the peppers into halves lengthwise.

Line up all the filling ingredients—chicken, reduced chicken sauce, blanched julienned ginger, peppers, and white sesame seeds—on a tray, then follow the Master Recipe (page 108).

ADDITIONAL INSTRUCTIONS

1. You can prepare the chicken a day in advance. Reheat before using it. This sushi is best when the roll is made just before serving.

2. Garnish the serving plate with the remaining thickened sauce.

Spicy Cod Egg and *Daikon* Roll

Japanese salt-cured cod roe, *tarako,* is similar to Greek *tarama,* cured cod roe, which is used to prepare a signature dish, *tarama* salad. In addition to the traditional salt-cured cod roe, in Japan we have a spiced-up version made with red chile pepper, *karashi mentaiko.* It is available in all Japanese food stores here. This roe is a wonderful addition to sushi preparation. A crisp, juicy *daikon* provides a refreshing taste and texture complement to the spicy cod roe.

MAKES 7 ROLLS

2 large pairs of *karashi mentaiko** (spicy salt-cured cod eggs) or the nonspicy variety

1½ tablespoons mayonnaise

½ teaspoon freshly squeezed lemon juice

7 *shiso* leaves (perilla), cut into julienne strips, or ⅓ cup coriander leaves

5 ounces *daikon* (*daikon* radish) (1 medium potato size), cut into fourteen 4-inch-long sticks

THE GARNISH: 7 tablespoons toasted white sesame seeds

6 cups (lightly packed) prepared sushi rice (⅞ cup, 4.2 ounces, per roll) (page 58)

7 half-sheets *nori* (laver); choose the thicker variety

*One pair weighs about 1 ounce, about 1 tablespoon roe; the size varies.

Remove the thin filmlike skin from the cured cod roe sacs and put the roe in a bowl. Add the mayonnaise and lemon juice and mix well.

Line up all the filling ingredients—cod roe with mayonnaise, *shiso* leaves, *daikon* sticks, and white sesame seeds—on a tray, then follow the Master Recipe (page 108).

ADDITIONAL INSTRUCTIONS

1. You can prepare this roll several hours in advance.
2. Serve without a dipping sauce.

Korean Barbecued Beef Roll

The influence of Korean food can easily be spotted when you walk around the cities of Japan. There are many Korean barbecue restaurants, *yakiniku-ya,* where such popular dishes as *bulgogi* (skillet-cooked marinated beef and vegetables) and *kalbi* (barbecued beef) are cooked up for hungry diners. These imports are no longer authentically Korean but have been "Japanized" and transformed into different, but quite delicious dishes. Koreans living in both Japan and Korea have also taken up our sushi roll culture and prepare their own unique rolls with their favorite Korean ingredients such as beef and *kimuchi,* fermented pickles. When they are well made, these rolls offer a great taste and texture experience. Here is my Korean-style roll.

In this recipe, beef is marinated overnight in a garlic-and-chile-flavored sauce, then browned in a skillet and rolled with sliced onion.

MAKES 7 ROLLS

½ pound rib eye steak

MARINADE:

2 tablespoons toasted black sesame seeds, roughly ground through a sesame seed grinder or in a mortar

2 tablespoons *shoyu* (soy sauce)

2 tablespoons *mirin* (sweet cooking wine)

2 tablespoons *sake* (rice wine)

2 tablespoons honey

1 tablespoon Hiroko's hot chile and *miso* sauce (page 83) or 2 teaspoons *toban jiang* (Chinese chile bean sauce)

3 large garlic cloves, pressed through
   a garlic press
1 tablespoon sesame oil

½ small purple onion (about 3 ounces)
Vegetable oil for cooking the beef
2 cups small salad leaves (about 1½
   ounces)

THE GARNISH: ½ cup toasted white
   sesame seeds

6 cups (lightly packed) prepared sushi
   rice (⅞ cup, 4.2 ounces, per roll)
   (page 58)
7 half-sheets *nori* (laver); choose the
   thicker variety

Cut the beef into thin slices, ⅛ inch
thick. Mix together in a bowl the black
sesame seeds, soy sauce, *mirin, sake,*
honey, Hiroko's hot chile and *miso*
sauce, garlic, and sesame oil. Toss in
the beef and marinate overnight.

   Cut the onion crosswise into paper-
thin slices, then soak in a large bowl of
cold water for 30 minutes. Drain the
onion slices and gently squeeze to
remove excess water.

   Drain the beef, discarding the marinade, and pat dry with a paper towel.
Heat a skillet, pour in a little vegetable
oil, and cook the beef slices over
medium-high heat until golden on both
sides. Cut each beef slice into ⅔-inch
strips.

   Line up all the filling ingredients—
cooked beef, onion slices, salad leaves,
and white sesame seeds—on a tray, then
follow the Master Recipe (page 108).

ADDITIONAL INSTRUCTIONS

1. You can prepare this roll several hours
in advance.
2. Serve without a dipping sauce.

Collection of Hand Rolls
Temaki

T*emaki* rolls, which the chef forms
in his or her hands, using no tools,
and immediately presents to the
diner, who consumes it on the spot,
come in two different styles: one is cone-
shaped, and the other, a simple cylindri-
cal roll. The *nori* for *temaki* should be
thin, crisp, and full of fragrance. Spend
a little more for a high-quality product.

   A *temaki* should be consumed immediately to appreciate the crisp *nori,*
which flakes into your mouth and then
melts on biting, at the same time as you
are enjoying the rice and the fillings. So
plan a *temaki* dinner party where the
ingredients are spread out, everyone
rolls their own, and eats together at the
table.

Master Recipe
Vegetarian
Cone-Shaped
Hand Roll

In this recipe, I roll asparagus, avocado, *kaiware* (*daikon* sprouts), pickled carrot, and spicy *Sriracha* mayonnaise sauce together into a cone-shaped roll. Use any favorite vegetable combination you wish.

MAKES 16 HAND ROLLS
(TOP DIAMETER 1 1/2 INCHES;
LENGTH 5 INCHES)

16 thin asparagus spears
1 small carrot (5 ounces), peeled
    and cut into julienne strips
Sea salt, sugar, and *komezu* (rice
    vinegar)
16 avocado sticks (for cutting instruc-
    tions, see page 99)
1 package *kaiware* (*daikon* sprouts)
    (3 1/2 ounces), roots removed
Spicy *Sriracha* mayonnaise sauce
    (page 82)
4 cups (lightly packed) prepared sushi
    rice (1/4 cup, 1.4 ounces, per roll)
    (page 58)
16 half-sheets *nori* (laver); choose
    the thin and crisp variety

Bring a large skillet of lightly salted water to a boil, drop in the asparagus, and cook for 1 minute. Drain and cool the asparagus under cold tap water. Drain the asparagus and wipe it dry with a paper towel. Cut each spear into 2 1/2-inch lengths. Toss the carrot in a bowl with a pinch of salt and sugar and 1 teaspoon rice vinegar. Let stand for 10 minutes, then drain the carrot and squeeze gently to remove excess liquid.

Temaki Party!

All the preparations can be done beforehand in the kitchen—the sushi rice, rice balls, filling ingredients, condiments, and sauces. Arrange the prepared items on platters or in bowls and carry them to the table. Have a moistened washcloth for each person and the necessary implements, such as small spatulas or spoons.

Call your guests and family to the table and lead the party by demonstrating how to make the rolls and cones. They will catch on quickly. Then you can relax and enjoy the dinner with everyone else. To complete a *temaki* dinner party, you may wish to serve several side dishes, all prepared in advance, and a bowl of *miso* soup. You will find easy-to-make, suitable side dishes and soups in part 5.

STEP 1
Setting Up

Following the illustrations, 1. line up all the filling ingredients—asparagus, pickled carrot, avocado, *daikon* sprouts, and *Sriracha* mayonnaise sauce—on a tray. Have at hand the sushi rice and a small bowl containing 1 cup of cold water with 2 tablespoons of rice vinegar or grain vinegar for moistening your hands, and moistened clean cotton cloth, *fukin* (page 44), or synthetic material (to wipe away excess water or any rice residue stuck to your hands). Make the sushi rice balls as follows. Slightly moisten your hands, pick up the sushi rice (¼ cup), and mold it in your hand, without squeezing, into an egg-shaped ball, 2½ inches long and 1¼

inches in diameter. Continue shaping all the sushi rice into balls, place them in a single layer on a tray without overlapping, and cover with plastic wrap to prevent drying out. Have half-sheets of *nori,* stacked up, on several dry platters. For a sushi party, carry everything to the table.

STEP 2
Spreading the Sushi Rice and Filling Ingredients and Rolling

Pick up one half-sheet of *nori* and put it shiny side down on the palm of your dry left hand, one long edge facing you. Pick up a rice ball and arrange it on the left side of the *nori* (the sushi rice ball looks as if it were falling toward the left

edge of the *nori* sheet). 2. Make a depression along the center of the rice from top to bottom, smear the *Sriracha* mayonnaise sauce in the trench, then 3. pile on the asparagus, pickled carrot, avocado, and *daikon* sprouts one by one. (If some ingredients are long, it is nice to have them protrude beyond the top of the *nori,* but not the bottom.) 4. With your right hand, pick up the bottom left corner of the *nori* and fold it over the rice and fillings. 5. Finish by rolling the remaining *nori* over the fillings to make a cone. 6. Enjoy it immediately.

1. Line up all the fillings and the tools you will need.

2. Place a rice ball at an angle on the left side of the *nori* and make a trench in it.

3. Pile the filling ingredients into the trench.

4. Fold the left corner of the *nori* over the fillings.

5. Continue rolling the *nori* over the fillings to make a cone shape.

6. The finished hand roll.

Cone-Shaped *Tatsuta* Shrimp Hand Roll

In this recipe, I make a cone-shaped hand roll using my favorite *tatsuta* shrimp. The shrimp are lightly marinated in a mixture of *shoyu* (soy sauce), *mirin* (sweet cooking wine), *sake* (rice wine), and ginger juice, dredged in potato starch, and then deep-fried. The potato starch adds a slightly chewy texture to the crisp fried shrimp. You can substitute cornstarch, which will produce a lighter texture.

MAKES 16 HAND ROLLS

MARINADE:

2½ tablespoons *shoyu* (soy sauce)

2 tablespoons *mirin* (sweet cooking wine)

2 tablespoons *sake* (rice wine)

1 tablespoon ginger juice from freshly grated ginger (see the accompanying box)

20 large shrimp (21 to 30 count per pound), peeled but with tails attached; deveined

½ cup potato starch or cornstarch

Vegetable oil for frying

2 springs coriander, with leaves picked off and stems discarded, or 10 *shiso* (perilla) leaves, cut into julienne strips

4 cups (lightly packed) prepared sushi rice (¼ cup, 1.4 ounces, per roll) (page 58)

16 half-sheets *nori* (laver); use a good-quality thin and crisp variety

Mix together in a bowl the soy sauce, *mirin, sake,* and ginger juice. Add the shrimp with tails attached and marinate for 20 minutes.

Remove the shrimp from the marinade, discarding the marinade, and wipe them with a paper towel. Place a shrimp on a chopping board belly side up and prepare following the instructions in the box on page 111.

Heat 2 inches of vegetable oil in a heavy-bottomed skillet or a wok to 320° F and cook the shrimp in batches, over medium heat, for 2 to 3 minutes or until golden. Remove the shrimp from the oil and drain on a steel rack. Increase the temperature of the oil to 350° F and refry the shrimp a few seconds in small batches to make them crispy. Drain on a steel rack.

Have at hand the fried shrimp and coriander, then follow the Cone-Shaped Hand Roll Master Recipe (page 120). Serve without a dipping sauce.

Master Recipe Fermented Soybean Cylinder-Shaped Hand Roll
Natto-temaki

Natto, a fermented product, is made from only soybeans and a fermentation starter, *natto-kin.* It is extremely nutritious, being very rich in calcium and potassium and easily digestible protein. The fermentation also improves the quality of B vitamins in soybeans and produces vitamin B_{12}.

The idea of rolling the *natto* into a *temaki* hand roll originated after World War II, and this roll is now one of the most popular classics in Japan. At Japanese or Asian stores, you can find refrigerated *natto* (shelf life is about three days after purchase) packed in small, square Styrofoam trays. It is commonly sold in a stack of two or three trays bound by a plastic wrapper. Each individual tray contains about 1¾ ounces, or ¼ cup, of fermented soybeans. *Natto* is said to be an acquired taste largely because of its texture. Sampling it in a *temaki* is a good way to discover this nutritious food.

Making Ginger Juice with a Box-Type Grater

Wrap a layer of sturdy plastic wrap around the spikes of your grater. Grate the peeled ginger over the smallest, most closely placed spikes to produce finely grated ginger and juice. Transfer the ginger to a fine-mesh strainer, squeeze to catch all the juice, and discard the pulp.

MAKES 16 HAND ROLLS (DIAMETER 1¼ INCHES; LENGTH 4 INCHES)

4 small packages *natto* (fermented soybeans), or 7 ounces (1 cup)

2 teaspoons *shoyu* (soy sauce)

⅔ cup thinly sliced green part of scallions cut into rings

4 cups (lightly packed) prepared sushi rice (¼ cup, 1.4 ounces, per roll) (page 58)

16 half-sheets *nori* (laver); choose the thin and crisp variety

Put the *natto* into a bowl along with the soy sauce and scallions and stir lightly with chopsticks to break up lumpy parts.

STEP 1
Setting Up

Follow the setting-up instructions for rolling cone-shaped hand rolls (page 121).

STEP 2
Spreading the Sushi Rice and Filling Ingredients and Rolling

Pick up one half-sheet of *nori* and put it shiny side down on the palm of your dry left hand, one long edge facing you. Following the illustrations, 1. pick up a rice ball and place it on the left side of the *nori*, ½ inch from the left edge of the *nori*. Make a depression along the center of the rice from top to bottom and 2. spoon the fermented soybeans and scallions into the depression. With your right hand, pick up the left end of the *nori* and roll it over the rice. Stop rolling halfway and hold the sushi tightly. 3. With scissors, cut a 1-inch strip from the right side of the *nori* sheet. Continue to roll another 90 degrees. With your right hand, place the 1-inch strip of *nori* on the right bottom corner of the sheet you are rolling so that three-quarters of the *nori* strip hangs down. Complete the roll, then 4. pick up the *nori* strip, covering the bottom and press it against the roll to seal the open end. This prevents the fillings from squirting out when you bite into the roll.

1. Place a rice ball on the left side of the *nori* and make a depression along the center of the rice.

2. Spoon the fermented soybeans and scallions into the depression.

3. After rolling halfway, cut a 1-inch strip of *nori* from the right edge of the *nori* sheet.

4. Pick the *nori* strip up and press it against the roll.

Popular Sushi Rolls • 1 2 3

Tuna and Scallion Hand Roll
Negi-toro temaki

When preparing this sushi at home, the choice of tuna is nearly always the *akami,* the nonfatty red meat, because of its availability and reasonable price. So in this recipe, I devise my own "faux *toro*" (fatty tuna) by tossing the chopped tuna with spicy sesame *shoyu* sauce to simulate the fattiness of real *toro.*

MAKES 16 CONE OR CYLINDER HAND ROLLS

10 ounces *maguro akami* (red meat tuna) (for information on shopping for sushi fish, see page 168; for sushi tuna, see page 185), chopped

2 to 3 tablespoons spicy sesame *shoyu* sauce (page 83)

²⁄₃ cup chopped green part of scallions

4 cups (lightly packed) prepared sushi rice (¼ cup, 1.4 ounces, per roll) (page 58)

16 half-sheets *nori* (laver); choose the thin and crisp variety

Toss the chopped tuna in a bowl along with the spicy sesame *shoyu* sauce and scallions. Then follow the Cone-Shaped Hand Roll Master Recipe (page 120) or the Cylinder-Shaped Hand Roll Master Recipe (page 122). Serve without a dipping sauce.

A Chef's Accident

The tuna and scallion hand roll, *negi-toro temaki,* which is popular both in and outside Japan, was born by accident. One day, a sushi chef at the Kintaro Zushi restaurant in Tokyo, as was his daily routine, was scraping and collecting in a bowl the small fatty bits of tuna clinging to parts of the fish, such as the head and tail, that could not be used for slicing. After finishing this laborious job, the chef went to chop some scallions to use as part of the staff lunch. While carrying the chopped scallions to another station in the kitchen, he acci-dentally dropped them over the bowl of scraped tuna meat. Though upset, the chef, who had his staff food budget to consider, had to use the scallion-tainted tuna for the meal—so he produced a dish composed of sushi rice topped with scallion-tuna and a little *shoyu* (soy sauce). Everyone in the kitchen loved it, and soon afterward, under the owner's guidance, the tuna and scallion hand roll appeared on the menu for the public. It became an instant hit, and all the other sushi restaurants quickly adopted the dish.

Chapter 9
Sushi Beyond the Rolls

*M*aki (rolls) are fun to prepare and eat, and now they are very well known around the world. There are, however, other wonderful varieties of sushi that a home chef can easily prepare and enjoy for an ordinary meal or a special occasion. Some are, in fact, even less trouble to prepare than rolls. These sushi fall into three categories: pressed sushi, called *oshi-zushi;* tossed sushi, known as *chirashi-zushi;* and craft sushi, *sonota no sushi.* Here is a chance to discover the greater sushi family.

Pressed Sushi
Oshi-zushi

*P*ressed sushi, *oshi-zushi,* is made in a wooden or plastic mold. Sushi rice and topping ingredients are pressed to form a clean-cut rectangular shape, which is then removed from the mold and cut into bite-size pieces. Try these delicious morsels for your next party as a canapé or an appetizer.

To make *oshi-zushi* efficiently, I suggest that you purchase a special plastic sushi mold. The mold, which is sturdy and easy to use and clean, consists of a rectangular frame, a flat base on which the frame is placed, and a pressing lid that fits just inside the frame. Sizes vary. I use a 2-inch-high mold whose inner dimensions are about 2 × 5 inches, which is what determines the size of the sushi. For a possible substitute, see page 49.

Raw seafood is not a choice for *oshi-zushi,* since the pressing would crush such delicate materials. Popular toppings are cooked or cured seafood, vegetables, and omelet, many of which can be prepared half a day in advance.

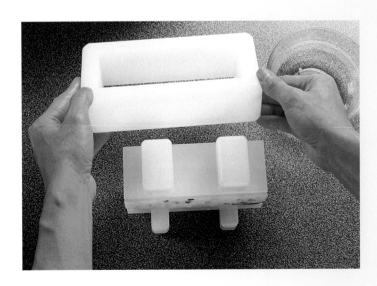

Master Recipe
Smoked Salmon
Pressed Sushi
Kunsei sake no oshi-zushi

MAKES 4 PRESSED SUSHI, EACH 2 × 5 × 2 INCHES, WHICH ARE CUT INTO 20 BITE-SIZE OR 40 MINISIZE PIECES IN TOTAL

9 ounces smoked and roasted salmon fillet or smoked salmon fillet

¼ pound shelled fava beans (about ½ pound in the shells)

1 ear corn

½ Japanese cucumber (2 ounces) or 1 small Kirby cucumber, cut into ⅛-inch cubes

Sea salt

4 cups (lightly packed)* prepared sushi rice (1½ cups, for each pressed sushi) (page 58)

Wasabi paste

THE GARNISH: ¼ cup *ikura* (salmon roe) (optional)

THE SAUCE: *tsuke-joyu* (sushi dipping sauce) (page 77)

*Rough cup measurement based on lightly packed rice. In time, after lots of sushi making, you will be able to judge visually the correct quantity of rice.

S moked salmon is wonderful in pressed sushi. My favorite is smoked salmon with skin from Maine that comes packaged in a 4-ounce piece. It is meaty, moist, and only moderately salty (with the leftover skin, you can make salmon skin roll, page 115). If you cannot find it, then the second choice would be unsliced, less salty smoked salmon that you can cut into thicker slices. If you can only get pre-sliced smoked salmon, which is available nearly everywhere, use a double layer of fish. Here the smoked salmon is pressed with summer vegetables—fava beans and corn. Create your own delicious seasonal combination. See photograph on page 93.

Cut the salmon into 20 slices, about 2- × 1¼-inch rectangles. Bring a pot of lightly salted water to a boil, add the fava beans, and cook for 3 minutes. Drain and remove the thin skin from the beans.

Grill the corn on the cob over an open gas flame or other heat source for 1 to 2 minutes, rotating it a quarter turn at a time until the surface is lightly browned. Remove the kernels from the cob with a knife.

Toss the cucumber in a bowl with a pinch of salt and let it stand for 5 minutes. Drain the cucumber on a paper towel and squeeze to remove excess liquid. Toss the sushi rice with the corn and cucumber.

STEP 1
Setting Up

Following the illustrations, 1. line up all the ingredients—salmon, fava beans, *wasabi,* salmon roe (optional), and sushi rice. Have at hand a small bowl with

1. Line up all the ingredients and tools.

2. Arrange 5 salmon slices, *wasabi,* and fava beans in the bottom of the mold.

3. Place the rice in the mold and spread it out by pushing from the center toward the four corners of the mold.

1 cup of cold water and 2 tablespoons of rice vinegar or grain vinegar for moistening your hands. If your sushi mold is wooden, first soak it in cold water (sushi rice sticks to dry wood) for half an hour. Plastic molds should be wiped with a moistened cloth just before filling. If you are using plastic containers, line one of the inside containers with plastic wrap, leaving a 2-inch additional length hanging over the sides. Have a well-sharpened knife at hand.

2. Arrange 5 salmon slices slightly overlapping in the bottom of your mold or plastic container. (If the ingredients have a front side and back side—for example, cooked butterflied shrimp: pink-colored outside is the front and white inside is the back—always place the front side down for a prettier appearance when unmolded.) When you are using the presliced thin smoked salmon, double the layer. Rub the center of each salmon slice with a dab of *wasabi* (less than 1/8 teaspoon) with your finger and spread one-quarter of the fava beans over the salmon slices. Moisten your hands with the vinegar water, pick up the sushi rice (about 1 cup), and form it into a rough egg shape. 3. Put the rice in the mold and spread it out, by pushing from the center with your fingers toward the four corners of the mold. 4. Place the lid or another plastic container on top of the rice and press firmly once. Rotate the mold 180 degrees and press firmly again. Repeat rotating 180 degrees and pressing until you have pressed four times. If you are using a sushi mold, 5. leave the lid in place and unmold the sushi by lifting the frame from the base. 6. Turn the sushi rice over with the base so that the toppings are now on top and remove the lid. If you are using the plastic containers, remove the top container and lift out the sushi in the plastic wrap carefully, then flip it over so that the toppings are facing up. Wrap the sushi in plastic wrap. Make three more pressed sushi.

With a very sharp knife, using a sawing motion, cut the pressed sushi (still wrapped in the plastic wrap) into 5 even bite-size pieces. Each piece can be cut further into two squares to give a total of 10 approximately 1- × 1-inch squares. These minisushi make lovely appetizers or hors d'oeuvres. Decorate the top of each with 3 to 5 pieces of salmon roe, if desired. Serve the sushi with *tsuke-joyu* (sushi dipping sauce).

You can prepare this pressed sushi, without the salmon roe garnish, half a day in advance. When you store it, wrap uncut sushi in plastic wrap and put it in a sealable container. For short-term storage, keep the sushi in a cool, dry, dark place. For longer storage, refrigerate in the warmest part of the refrigerator, the vegetable bin.

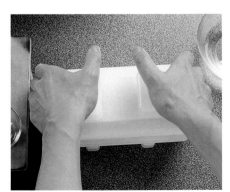

4. Place the lid on and press firmly.

5. Unmold by lifting the frame from the base.

6. Turn the sushi rice over so that the toppings are on top and remove the lid.

Pressed Sushi with Vinegar-Cured Mackerel (*saba-zushi*)

Pressed Sushi with Vinegar-Cured Mackerel
Saba-zushi

*S*aba-zushi, mackerel sushi, the pressed sushi that is very popular in Japan, has been made in the old imperial capital of Kyoto for several hundred years. It is prepared with excellent-quality *saba,* mackerel, which is caught seasonally in nearby Wakasa Bay on the Sea of Japan, about 45 miles from Kyoto. Today the journey takes less than one hour by road, but in the past, the fish, which was caught early in the morning, packed with salt in barrels, then rushed to the capital by strong male porters on foot, would arrive in Kyoto the next morning. By then, the perfectly cured mackerel was ready for vinegar pickling and after that was packed with cooked rice and pressed for a day or so before being sold.

This historic sushi is easily prepared in your kitchen using *shime-saba,* mackerel cured in salt and vinegar, which comes packed in a plastic bag and is sold in the refrigerated or frozen foods case at Japanese or Asian food stores. Some of these products may have chemical additives, such as monosodium glutamate or preservatives, so check the label. If you wish to make your own cured mackerel, see page 188.

MAKES 4 PRESSED SUSHI
(20 BITE-SIZE OR 40 MINISIZE PIECES)

2 packages cured mackerel (average size 3 1/2 ounces per package) or 1 prepared, cured mackerel fillet (*shime-saba*) (page 188)

1/3 cup *gari* (sweet pickled ginger) (page 66), cut into julienne strips

4 cups (lightly packed) prepared sushi rice (1 cup for each pressed sushi) (page 58)

THE SAUCE: *tsuke-joyu* (sushi dipping sauce) (page 77)

Place the cured mackerel fillet, skin side up, on a chopping board. Peel off the thin, transparent skin carefully from the head part to the tail, trying to leave as much as possible of the silvery covering between the skin and the flesh. Turn the fish over so it is flesh-side up and cut it into four flat pieces by running the knife parallel to the chopping board. As you cut the fillets, each succeeding slice will be larger in dimensions. Cut the largest fillet sheet diagonally into 4 strips; it

will have the silver blue pigment attached. Repeat for the second fillet if you are using the commercially prepared mackerel. These silver-faced strips (one piece for the larger home-made mackerel and two pieces for the smaller commercially prepared fillets) will become part of the attractive surface of the sushi.

Have at hand the mackerel slices and pickled ginger on a tray, then follow the Master Recipe (page 126).

ADDITIONAL INSTRUCTIONS

1. Place one or two slices of the fillets, silvery side down, on the bottom of each mold. Fill the empty space with the remaining thin sheets of mackerel. Plan it so that all four molds will have an equal number of slices. Spread out one-quarter of the sweet pickled ginger strips over the fish. Put the measured sushi rice (about 1 cup) on top and press. **2.** The pressed sushi tastes best the next day. Prepare it a day in advance. **3.** Serve with the dipping sauce.

Dressed-up Mackerel Sushi

Prepared mackerel sushi is usually covered with a paper-thin shaved kelp sheet, *shiro-ita kombu* (white sheet kelp), that has been pickled in sweet vinegar marinade. The kelp prevents the surface of the fish from drying and also adds a sweet-tart flavor to the matured sushi. These kelp sheets are not yet available at retail stores in America, but they may appear soon.

Pressed Sushi with Eel
Unagi no kabayaki oshi-zushi

Velvety, glossy, rich-tasting eel basted with sweet sauce is nearly everyone's favorite. In this pressed sushi, sweet pickled ginger hidden underneath the eel and *sansho* pepper powder sprinkled on top offer a refreshing taste. See photograph on page 93.

MAKES 4 PRESSED SUSHI
(20 BITE-SIZE OR 40 MINISIZE PIECES)

2 packages *unagi no kabayaki* (prepared eel) (each 6 ounces)
½ Japanese cucumber (2 ounces) or 1 small Kirby cucumber, cut into ⅛-inch cubes
Sea salt
⅓ cup *gari* (sweet pickled ginger) (page 66), cut into julienne strips
Tsume (quick rich brown *shoyu* sauce) (page 79)

THE GARNISH: *sansho* pepper powder (see the box below)

4 cups (lightly packed) prepared sushi rice (1 cup for each pressed sushi) (page 58)

THE SAUCE: *anago no tsume* (eel sauce) (page 79), or *tsume* (quick rich brown *shoyu* sauce) (page 79)

Reheat the eel as instructed on page 99. When it has cooled, remove the skin, discarding it, and cut the eel into four rectangles—the same size as the lid or the bottom surface area of your mold. Toss the cucumber cubes in a small bowl with a pinch of salt and let stand for 5 minutes. Strain the cucumber, rinse quickly under cold water, and drain well. Wipe the cucumber pieces with a paper towel and squeeze to remove excess water. Toss the prepared sushi rice with the cucumber pieces.

Line up all the ingredients—eel, cucumber, sweet pickled ginger, *tsume* sauce, and *sansho* powder—on a tray, then follow the Master Recipe (page 126).

ADDITIONAL INSTRUCTIONS

1. Spoon the measured tossed sushi rice (1 cup) into the mold and spread it out. Place the lid or another container on top of the sushi rice to level the surface. Arrange the cut-out eel on top of the rice, return the lid or the other container, and press gently.
2. Cut the unmolded sushi into bite-size pieces and, with a pastry brush, paint the *tsume* sauce over the surface, then sprinkle the top with a little *sansho* powder.
3. You can prepare the sushi half a day in advance.

Colorful Pressed Sushi
Iro-dakusan oshi-zushi

Shrimp, octopus, smoked fish, and asparagus—these four colorful ingredients are bound to please both the eyes and the stomach. Boiled octopus is a very popular sushi ingredient and is available already prepared at Japanese food stores. If you cannot find it, substitute a small cooked squid or a few scallops, or prepare your own octopus following the instructions on page 193.

MAKES 4 PRESSED SUSHI
(20 BITE-SIZE OR 40 MINISIZE PIECES)

4 large shrimp (21 to 30 count per pound)
4 thick asparagus spears (2 ounces)
¼ pound smoked trout or other smoked fish, skin removed
¼ pound cooked sushi octopus or cooked scallops or squid
Wasabi paste
4 cups (lightly packed) prepared sushi rice (1 cup for each pressed sushi) (page 58)

THE SAUCE: *tsuke-joyu* (sushi dipping sauce) (page 77)

Sansho Pepper

Sansho are berries from the Japanese prickly ash shrub, which is related to Chinese fagara, the source of Szechuan pepper. *Sansho* has a sharp, slightly bitter, mintlike flavor and fragrance. The green husks are dried, powdered, and used in dishes that have a natural oiliness. Eel (noted for its fatty sweet flavor) and *sansho* make the best of partners.

Peel the shrimp and cook them in salted boiling water over medium heat for 2 minutes. Drain the shrimp and spread them out in a colander to cool. Cut each shrimp in half lengthwise.

Cook the asparagus over an open gas flame or other heat source until the outside is lightly golden, about 1 minute. Cut the asparagus into 2-inch lengths crosswise and then cut each piece in half lengthwise.

Cut the smoked trout and sushi octopus into 2- × 1¼-inch slices.

Line up all the ingredients—shrimp, asparagus, smoked fish, octopus, and *wasabi* paste—on a tray, then follow the Master Recipe (page 126).

ADDITIONAL INSTRUCTIONS

1. In the bottom of each 2 × 5-inch mold, make a pattern of the fillings using one-quarter of the shrimp in one corner, one-quarter of the asparagus in another corner, one-quarter of the octopus in another, and one-quarter of the smoked fish in the final corner. With your right index finger, scoop up some *wasabi* (about ⅛ teaspoon) and smear it over the seafood. Put the measured sushi rice (about 1 cup) on top and press.

2. You can prepare the sushi half a day in advance.

3. Serve with the dipping sauce.

Roast Beef Pressed Sushi
Rosuto biifu oshi-zushi

In this recipe, medium-rare tender filet mignon is basted with delicious rich brown beef *shoyu* sauce, cut into thin slices, and pressed with sushi rice. Sweet simmered *shiitake* mushrooms add a depth of flavor.

MAKES 4 PRESSED SUSHI
(20 BITE-SIZE OR 40 MINISIZE PIECES)

Sea salt and ground black pepper
1 pound filet mignon, sliced into
    4 steaks
2 tablespoons olive oil
2 sweet simmered *shiitake* mushrooms
    (1 ounce) (page 63), chopped
⅓ cup *gari* (sweet pickled ginger)
    (page 66) or ginger, cut in julienne
    strips and blanched for 20 seconds
    in boiling water
¼ cup plus 1 tablespoon rich brown
    beef *shoyu* sauce (page 80)

THE GARNISH: ¼ teaspoon *yuzu-kosho*
    (salt-cured green chile and *yuzu*)
    (page 227) or *wasabi* paste

4 cups (lightly packed) prepared sushi
    rice (1 cup for each pressed sushi)
    (page 58)

Preheat the oven to 350° F. Salt and pepper the steak. Heat 1 tablespoon of olive oil in a cast-iron skillet or heavy-bottomed skillet, add the beef, and cook over medium-low heat until both sides are golden brown. Transfer the skillet to the oven and roast the meat for 6 minutes, to medium-rare. Remove the beef from the oven, transfer it to a plate, and let it sit for 10 minutes, covered with aluminum foil. Cut the beef into 20 slices, about 2- × 1¼-inch rectangles.

Line up all the ingredients—beef, *shiitake* mushrooms, pickled ginger, rich brown beef *shoyu* sauce, and the *yuzu kosho*—on a tray, then follow the Master Recipe (page 126).

ADDITIONAL INSTRUCTIONS

1. Fill the bottom of each mold with 5 slices of beef. With a pastry brush, paint the slices once or twice with the rich brown beef *shoyu* sauce. Sprinkle the *shiitake* and ginger over the beef and spread them out evenly. Put one-quarter of the measured sushi rice (1 cup) on top and press.

2. You can prepare this sushi half a day in advance.

3. Cut the unmolded sushi into bite-size pieces and paint the top of each square with the additional rich brown beef *shoyu* sauce and garnish with a tiny dab of the *yuzu kosho*.

4. Serve without a dipping sauce.

Summer Vegetable Pressed Sushi
Natsu yasai no oshi-zushi

When our neighborhood farmers market at Union Square in New York City is at its most colorful, filled with wonderful just-picked summer vegetables and fruits, I make this sushi to celebrate the season. Creamy eggplant, sweet bell peppers, and juicy corn are delicious and beautiful on top of snow-white sushi rice.

One day after loading my shopping bags with summer vegetables, I stopped at the shop of a local cheese maker, Mr. Tonjes, who was selling his hand-made selection of cheeses and yogurt. I purchased the variety he called "aged farmstead cheese," a creamy cow's milk cheese with a notable sharpness, and I decided to add it to my summer vege-table sushi. It made the ordinary version much more flavorful and satisfying. Enjoy this sushi with a crisp sauvignon blanc, outside, under the sun.

**MAKES 4 PRESSED SUSHI
(20 BITE-SIZE OR 40 MINISIZE PIECES)**

1 medium red bell pepper (about 6
    ounces)
1 medium green bell pepper (about 6
    ounces)
1 small ear sweet corn
1 tablespoon *mirin* (sweet cooking wine)
2 teaspoons *shoyu* (soy sauce)
1 Japanese or Italian eggplant or ½
    small American eggplant
Olive oil for cooking the eggplant
¼ pound mildly sharp creamy cow's
    milk cheese, cut into 8 slices

THE GARNISH: brown *miso*-based *yuzu* sauce (page 81)

4 cups (lightly packed) prepared sushi rice (1 cup for each pressed sushi) (page 58)

Cook the red and green sweet bell peppers over an open gas flame or other heat source until the outsides are charred. Place them in a bowl, cover the bowl with plastic wrap, and let them stand for 10 minutes. Grill the corn in the same manner until the outside is lightly golden. Cut the kernels off the cob.

Peel off the charred black skin from the peppers with paper towel; do not rinse the peppers. Remove the ribs, stems, and seeds from the peppers and cut each into eight 2- × 1½-inch rectan-gles. Mix together in a bowl the bell peppers, *mirin,* and soy sauce and let them stand for 5 minutes. Scoop out the peppers from the marinade, then add the grilled corn kernels to the bowl and toss them with the marinade.

Cut off ¼ inch from both ends of the eggplant. Cut the eggplant into four slices lengthwise (you do not need to

peel it). Heat a little olive oil in a skillet and cook the eggplant, over medium-low heat, until both sides are lightly golden. Cut the eggplant into eight 2- × 1½-inch rectangles.

Line up all the ingredients—red and green bell peppers, corn, eggplant, cheese, *yuzu miso* sauce, and *tsuke-joyu*—on a tray, then follow the Master Recipe for Pressed Sushi (page 126).

ADDITIONAL INSTRUCTIONS

1. In the bottom of each 2 × 5-inch mold, make a pattern of the fillings using one-quarter of the red bell pepper in one corner, one-quarter of the green bell pepper in another corner, one-quarter of the corn in another, and one-quarter of the eggplant in the final corner. Spread out one-quarter of the cheese, put the measured sushi rice (about 1 cup) on top, and press.
2. After cutting each sushi into pieces, garnish the top of each piece with a dab of *yuzu miso* sauce.
3. You can prepare the sushi half a day in advance.
4. Serve without a dipping sauce.

Decorated or Tossed Sushi
Chirashi-zushi

You can prepare delicious, attractive sushi by tossing sushi rice with other ingredients and serving them in a bowl. This colorful style of sushi is called *chirashi-zushi,* or just *chirashi,* literally, "scattered sushi." It is regional in character and is some-times related to particular festivities, each local version drawing on seasonal ingredients from the nearby waters, mountains, and fields. So enjoy this new style of sushi with your family and friends. The best part of *chirashi-zushi* is that you can create your own with your favorite locally available ingredients.

When making *chirashi-zushi,* have at hand a small bowl with 2 cups of cold water and 2 tablespoons of rice vinegar for moistening your hands.

Clockwise, from top right: Kansai-Style Decorated Sushi (page 137), Western Vegetarian Summer Tossed Sushi (page 145), and Fisherman's Sushi (page 146)

Tokyo-Style Decorated Sushi
Edo-mae chirashi

This *Edo-mae* (Tokyo-style) *chirashi-zushi* (pictured on page 136) is prepared by packing a bowl with sushi rice, slicing up the same seafood that is used in *nigiri-zushi,* and presenting the bowl with the slices beautifully arranged on top. It is especially popular as a quick, satisfying meal in a bowl and is also a welcome relief for busy chefs, especially during crowded lunch hours, because there is no need to take orders for individual piece-by-piece *nigiri-zushi.*

This style of sushi is eaten differently, since the sushi is not bonded together as in a roll or *nigiri-zushi.* Usually, you pick up one of the toppings—a slice of fish, for example—with your chopsticks, lightly dip a small edge in the *tsuke-joyu* (sushi dipping sauce), then drop the fish onto the rice and pick it up again together with some rice. A small mound of *wasabi* is always served in each sushi bowl, so if you like, put a generous dab of it on the fish before dipping.

At a sushi restaurant that carries twenty to thirty varieties of sushi topping ingredients, preparing the attractive *chirashi-zushi* is very easy. When you do this at home, your choices are naturally more limited. So make it with easily available ingredients such as tuna, prepared eel, smoked fish, omelet, avocado, crabmeat, and/or cooked shellfish. This sushi is pictured on page 106.

1 package *unagi no kabayaki* (prepared eel) (6 ounces) (for heating instructions, see page 99)

1 rolled thick omelet (6 inches × 2 inches × 1 inch) (page 68), cut into 8 pieces

1 lemon, made into 4 lemon saucers (page 90)

1/4 cup *ikura* (salmon roe)

1/2 pound sushi *maguro* (tuna) (for information on shopping for sushi fish, see page 168; for sushi tuna, see page 185)

1/2 pound sushi salmon (for information on shopping for sushi fish, see page 168; for sushi salmon, see page 176) or smoked salmon, the least salty type

1/3 cup *gari* (sweet pickled ginger) (page 66), finely minced

1 sheet *nori* (laver), cut with scissors into quarters lengthwise and then into julienne strips crosswise

4 large simmered *shiitake* mushrooms (page 63), cut into halves

4 *shiso* (perilla) leaves or 8 baby salad leaves

1/2 avocado, pitted, peeled, and cut into 4 sticks lengthwise

1 Japanese cucumber or 2 Kirby cucumbers, cut into fans (page 88)

1 tablespoon plus 1 teaspoon *wasabi* paste

6 cups (lightly packed) prepared sushi rice for small bowls or 8 cups (lightly packed) prepared sushi rice for large bowls (page 58)

THE SAUCE: *tsuke-joyu* (sushi dipping sauce) (page 77)

Reheat the prepared eel following the instructions on page 99. Cut the fillet into 3 pieces crosswise. Cut the upper and middle sections into 3 strips and the narrow tail piece into 2 strips, for a total of 8 strips. Cut the rolled omelet into 8 even pieces crosswise. Pack each lemon saucer with 1 tablespoon salmon roe.

Just before making the sushi, cut the tuna and salmon into twelve 1 1/4- × 2 3/4-inch rectangular slices, using the *hira-zukuri sashimi* cutting technique (page 218).

Following the illustrations, 1. line up all the ingredients on a tray—ginger, *nori, shiitake* mushrooms, *shiso,* eel, omelet, sliced tuna and salmon, avocado, lemon saucers with salmon roe, cucumber fans, and *wasabi* paste. Have at hand the sushi rice and four shallow soup bowls, about 1 1/2- or 2 1/2-cup size.

Spoon the measured sushi rice— 2 cups for the large bowl or 1 1/2 cups for the small bowl—into each bowl, making gently sloping mounds with a flat top in the center. Arrange the ingredients on top as follows:

1. Line up the ingredients on a tray.

2. Place one-quarter of the eel slices and of the avocado sticks in the bowl.

1. Scatter one-quarter of the minced sweet pickled ginger over the rice and then the julienned *nori.*

2. Place two pieces of omelet at the far end of the sushi rice. Arrange a *shiso* leaf over the omelet pieces but do not completely hide them.

3. Lay two halves of *shiitake* mushroom partially leaning against the *shiso* leaf.

4. Following the illustrations, **2.** Place one-quarter of the eel slices and an avocado stick at the left front of the bowl and the tuna slices at the front center, followed by the salmon. Use a cucumber fan to separate the tuna and salmon. Place a lemon saucer with salmon roe at the left front of the bowl where the sushi rice is still exposed. Put 1 teaspoon of the *wasabi* paste on the right front so that you cover the remaining exposed sushi rice. Take care not to flatten your sushi ingredients; the bowl should have a voluminous appearance.

ADDITIONAL INSTRUCTIONS

1. Since raw fish is used, the bowls should be put together just before serving. You can, however, do all the preparations far in advance, keeping the ingredients—especially the raw fish— properly chilled in the refrigerator.

2. At the time of serving, the rice should be warm and the fish should be chilled. Serve with the dipping sauce.

Rice Proportions for Tossed Sushi

4 LARGE BOWLS (2 ½ CUPS/16 OUNCES)** AS MAIN DISH

Prepared Sushi Rice	*Sushi Rice for each bowl*
8 cups* (3 pounds)	2 cups* (12.6 ounces)

4 SMALL BOWLS (1 ½ CUPS/12 OUNCES)** AS SIDE DISH

Prepared Sushi Rice	*Sushi Rice for 1 sushi*
6 cups* (2.3 pounds)	1 ½ cups* (9.5 ounces)

*Rough cup measurement based on lightly packed rice. In time, after lots of sushi making, you will be able to judge visually the correct quantity of rice.

**The large bowl sushi contains more rice. The quantity of the toppings used for both presentations—large or small—is the same.

Tokyo-Style Decorated Sushi (*edo-mae chirashi***)**

Kansai-Style Decorated Sushi
Bara-zushi

Kansai is the southwestern part of Japan, in the center of the Japanese archipelago, and it includes the second largest commercial city, Osaka, and the old imperial capital, Kyoto. Kansai-style decorated sushi is called *bara-zushi,* and it bears little resemblance to the preceding *Edo-mae chirashi.* The Kansai style employs all cooked ingredients, including simmered *shiitake* mushrooms, *kanpyo* gourd, freeze-dried tofu, sweet pickled ginger, omelet, prepared *anago* (conger eel), and cooked shrimp. These ingredients are usually cut into small cubes or pieces and are tossed with the sushi rice, while a portion of the remaining ingredients is scattered attractively on top. *Bara-zushi* frequently reminds me of looking at a gorgeous *kimono* (traditional Japanese garment) fabric with intricate patterns and colors. The dish is not only a stunning presentation but also provides a very satisfying complete meal. Serve in individual plain shallow soup bowls or in a large bowl from which individual portions are served. It will make a great addition to your next buffet party or picnic. See photograph on page 133.

MAKES 4 SMALL OR 4 LARGE SUSHI BOWL SERVINGS

½ pound *unagi no kabayaki* (prepared eel) (for heating instructions, see page 99)

8 large shrimp (21 to 30 count per pound), boiled, shelled, and deveined

1 Japanese cucumber or 2 small Kirby cucumbers, cut into ½-inch cubes

2 simmered 2- × 2¾-inch dried *koya-dofu* (freeze-dried tofu) (page 65)

1 rolled thick omelet (6 inches × 2 inches × 1 inch) (page 68)

12 strips simmered *kanpyo* gourd (page 64), minced

6 simmered *shiitake* mushrooms (3 ounces) (page 63), minced

8 *shiso* (perilla) leaves, minced, or ¼ cup minced coriander leaves

¼ cup minced *gari* (sweet pickled ginger) (page 66)

¼ cup *ikura* (salmon roe)

6 cups (lightly packed) prepared sushi rice for small bowls or 8 cups (lightly packed) prepared sushi rice for large bowls (page 58)

Reheat the prepared eel following the instructions on page 99 and cool it for 10 minutes. Remove the skin and cut the eel into 1-inch squares, using a very well sharpened knife so that the eel meat has clearly, cleanly defined edges. Cut the shrimp, cucumber, and freeze-dried tofu into 1-inch pieces and the omelet into about 4 dozen pieces.

Following the illustrations, 1. line up all the ingredients—eel, shrimp, cucumber, simmered freeze-dried tofu, omelet, minced *kanpyo* gourd, *shiitake* mushrooms, *shiso,* sweet pickled ginger, and salmon roe—on a tray. Have at hand the sushi rice and four shallow soup bowls, about 1½- or 2½-cup size.

2. In a glass bowl, toss all the sushi rice with the minced *kanpyo, shiitake, shiso,* sweet pickled ginger, and half of the cucumber, eel, tofu, omelet, and shrimp. Spoon the measured sushi rice—2 cups for a large bowl or 1½ cups for a small bowl—into each bowl, making gently sloping mounds with a flat top in the center. Arrange on top equal portions of the eel, tofu cubes, omelet, cucumber, shrimp, and salmon roe.

ADDITIONAL INSTRUCTIONS

1. This sushi can be prepared several hours in advance. Place it in a sealable container and store in a cool, dry, dark place. When the room is hot, refrigerate it in the vegetable bin, but for no longer than 30 minutes.

2. Serve at room temperature without a dipping sauce.

1. Line up all the ingredients.

2. Toss together the sushi rice, *kanpyo* gourd, *shiitake* mushrooms, *shiso,* and pickled ginger.

Cured Salmon, Gravlax, Decorated Sushi
Sake no marine chirashi

Homemade gravlax (salt-and-sugar-cured salmon) makes an ideal *chirashi-zushi* topping. It is important to purchase *absolutely* fresh salmon that is also *free of parasites.* Go to a trusted fishmonger and ask for the right variety among the many types of salmon that may be for sale. If your fishmonger does not understand precisely what you are asking for, try another shop. For more about sushi salmon, see page 176.

Start marinating the salmon a day in advance. Prepared gravlax keeps in the refrigerator for a couple of days.

MAKES 4 SMALL OR 4 LARGE
SUSHI BOWL SERVINGS

FOR THE GRAVLAX:

1 pound *absolutely* fresh Norwegian or Scottish Atlantic farmed salmon fillet for gravlax preparation, skin attached
1 tablespoon sea salt
2 tablespoons sugar

¼ cup plus 2 tablespoons white wine vinegar
2 tablespoons olive oil
¼ cup white wine or *sake* (rice wine)
2 ounces radicchio, cut into julienne strips, or other salad greens (about 1 cup)
2 ounces chive sprouts or other seed sprouts (about 1½ cups)
8 cherry tomatoes, cut into thin slices
Ponzu sauce (page 78)
6 cups (lightly packed) prepared sushi rice for small bowls or 8 cups (lightly packed) prepared sushi rice for large bowls (page 58)
⅓ cup *gari* (sweet pickled ginger) (page 66), chopped fine

Cut the salmon in half crosswise. Spread a sheet of plastic wrap on your working counter. Mix the salt and sugar together and sprinkle one-quarter of it on the plastic wrap. Arrange the salmon, skin side down, over the salt and sugar mixture. Sprinkle two one-quarter portions of the salt and sugar mixture over the salmon flesh and place the remaining piece of the salmon fillet, skin side up, on top. Sprinkle the remaining salt and sugar mixture on the skin of the upper fillet. Wrap the salmon tightly in plastic wrap. Place it in a shallow stainless steel pan, skin side down, and set another stainless steel pan on top as a weight. Secure the two pans together with strong rubber bands in three or four places, which will give added pressure. Refrigerate about 14 hours.

Remove the salmon from the plastic wrap and rinse it quickly in a large bowl of salty water, then drain and wipe dry with a paper towel. Mix 2 tablespoons of the white wine vinegar with ¼ cup water in a small bowl. Rinse the salmon with the vinegar water, then wipe it dry with a paper towel. With a pastry brush, paint a thin coat of olive oil on the bottom of a large platter. Remove the skins from the salmon and cut the fillets at an angle (see the illustration on page 202), starting at the narrow end, into 32 thin slices—16 from each fillet. As you cut the slices, place them on the oiled platter without overlapping. After you have arranged all of them, paint the slices with additional olive oil. Mix the remaining white wine vinegar and white wine in a small cup and pour it over the salmon slices. Let stand for 15 minutes in the refrigerator, then remove from the platter and drain.

Mix the radicchio, chive sprouts, and sliced tomato in a bowl with a little olive oil and then with a generous amount of *ponzu* sauce. Have at hand the sushi rice and four shallow soup bowls, about 1½- or 2½-cup size.

Toss the sushi rice with the sweet pickled ginger in a sushi tub or wooden bowl.

Spoon the measured sushi rice—2 cups for a large bowl or 1½ cups for a small bowl—into each bowl, making gently sloping mounds with a flat top in the center. Arrange the slices of salmon, like the spokes of a wheel, on top. Garnish the very center of the sushi rice with the radicchio mixture.

ADDITIONAL INSTRUCTIONS

1. You can prepare the sushi rice, the salmon, and other ingredients in advance. Do the final assembly just before serving.
2. At the time of serving, the rice should be warm and the fish should be chilled. Serve without a dipping sauce.

Salmon Roe and Sea Urchin Decorated Sushi
Zeitaku chirashi

Zeitaku means "extravagant." Here sushi rice is completely covered with expensive *ikura,* salmon roe, and *uni,* sea urchin.

When you purchase the pickled salmon roe at a specialty shop or fish market, try to get those that look like orange pearls. Each roe should be shiny and plump with lots of juice; none should be broken or crushed.

As with all raw fish or cured items for sushi preparation, make sure that you purchase absolutely fresh, high-quality sea urchin (see the accompanying box) and cured salmon roe.

MAKES 4 SMALL OR 4 LARGE SUSHI BOWL SERVINGS

2 wooden trays *uni* (sea urchin) or 16 sea urchins

1 cup Japanese *ikura* (salmon roe) or ordinary cured salmon roe

1 whole sheet *nori* (laver), cut with scissors into needle-thin julienne strips 2 inches long

1/2 cup *gari* (sweet pickled ginger) (page 66)

THE CONDIMENT: 4 cucumber flower holders (page 87) with *wasabi* paste

6 cups (lightly packed) prepared sushi rice for small bowls or 8 cups (lightly packed) prepared sushi rice for large bowls (page 58)

THE SAUCE: *tsuke-joyu* (sushi dipping sauce) (page 77)

Line up all the ingredients on a tray—sea urchin, salmon roe, julienned *nori,* sweet pickled ginger, and cucumber flower holders with *wasabi.* You will need four Western-style shallow soup bowls, about 1 1/2- or 2 1/2-cup size.

Spoon the measured sushi rice—2 cups for a large bowl or 1 1/2 cups for a small bowl—into each bowl, making gently sloping mounds with a flat top in the center. Arrange the sea urchin and the salmon roe on top, each occupying half of the surface. Garnish the sushi with the julienned *nori,* cucumber flower holder with *wasabi,* and sweet pickled ginger on the side.

ADDITIONAL INSTRUCTIONS

1. Prepare the sushi just before serving.
2. At the time of serving, the rice should be warm and the fish should be chilled. Serve with the dipping sauce *only* for the sea urchin. Dip a slice of sweet pickled ginger in the sauce, shake it over the sea urchin, and sprinkle just a few drops or so on each bite of sea urchin.

Uni, Sea Urchin, on a Wooden Tray

At Japanese food stores or large fish markets, you can find shelled sea urchin, packed in a small wooden tray (3 1/2 × 6 1/2 inches) containing about 1/4 pound of sea urchin. If not available, try to get sea urchins in the shell. Slice off the top of the shell and remove the orange meat with a small spoon.

Cherry Blossom Celebration Decorated Sushi
Hanami chirashi

This cherry blossom celebration sushi is my creation to celebrate our New York spring and cherry blossoms. I toss the sushi rice with locally available springtime ingredients from the farmers market—shelled peas, fava beans, and fiddlehead ferns—and I decorate the sushi with a gimmick: some little *daikon* radishes, lightly dyed and cut to resemble cherry blossom petals.

MAKES 4 SMALL OR 4 LARGE
SUSHI BOWL SERVINGS

3 tablespoons *komezu* (rice vinegar)
1 tablespoon sugar
¼ teaspoon salt
1-inch-thick *daikon* radish, top part, cut out into thin "cherry blossom petals"
Dash of red food coloring (optional)
¼ pound freshly shelled green peas (1 cup), fresh or frozen
¼ pound freshly shelled fava beans or other beans
¼ pound fiddlehead ferns

Four 8-inch-diameter thin omelets without potato starch (page 72)
6 cups (lightly packed) prepared sushi rice for small bowls or 8 cups (lightly packed) prepared sushi rice for large bowls (page 58)
¼ cup minced *gari* (sweet pickled ginger) (page 66)
6 simmered *shiitake* mushrooms (3 ounces) (page 63), minced
8 strips simmered *kanpyo* gourd (page 64), minced
2 whole sheets *nori* (laver), cut with scissors into needle-thin julienne strips, 2 inches long

Put the rice vinegar, sugar, and salt in a small saucepan and bring to a boil. Turn off the heat and pour the liquid into a bowl. Add the sliced *daikon* petals and pickle them for 30 minutes. If you have red food coloring, add a dash to the pickling liquid to give the *daikon* petals a faintly pink hue.

Bring a medium pot of lightly salted water to a boil and cook the green peas for 1 minute. Remove them with a slotted spoon, drop in the fava beans, and cook for 3 minutes, and finally the fiddlehead ferns for 30 seconds to 1 minute. When the vegetables are done, transfer them to a colander and cool

under running cold water. If using fava beans, remove their skins. Cut the fiddlehead ferns in half. Cut the omelets into short (about 2 inches long) julienne strips.

Have at hand the sushi rice and four shallow soup bowls, each about 1½- or 2½-cup size.

Toss the sushi rice in a sushi tub or wooden bowl with the minced sweet pickled ginger, *shiitake* mushrooms, and *kanpyo.* Add the green peas and fava beans and toss thoroughly, being careful not to break the beans.

Spoon the measured sushi rice—2 cups for a large bowl or 1½ cups for a small bowl—into each bowl, making gently sloping mounds with a flat top in the center. Distribute the topping ingredients over the rice in the following order: fiddlehead ferns, *nori,* omelet, and *daikon* "cherry petals."

ADDITIONAL INSTRUCTIONS

1. You can prepare all the ingredients half a day in advance. Do the final assembly and presentation just before serving.
2. Serve at room temperature without a dipping sauce.

Sakura and the Japanese

Cherry blossoms, *sakura,* represent the joy of welcoming the height of spring in Japan. The gorgeous blossoms are a symbol of the cycle of our lives. The tiny, firmly closed flower buds in the cold winter represent the birth and start of new life. The fully blossomed elegant, gorgeous flowers in the warm spring sun are a metaphor for the beauty, energy, and success in our lives. The gently falling petals represent our inevitable end. To celebrate the blossoms in full bloom, we do *hanami* (literally, the act of flower viewing)—simply walking under a long arched passageway of a cherry tree–lined avenue and enjoying a picnic with family, friends, or office mates beneath the branches of the cherry trees in full bloom. Among the dishes we prepare for the occasion, *chirashi-zushi* is always popular.

Festive Tossed Sushi
Gomoku chirashi

One of the most popular tossed sushi is *gomoku chirashi* (*gomoku* means "random, various kinds of things"). For this dish, we add and toss whatever we have available and choose to eat with our sushi rice. Of course, this being Japan, there are rules governing the limits of "whatever." My mother's version is a very traditional one—sushi rice tossed with cooked *shiitake* mushrooms, *kanpyo* gourd, carrot, lotus root, and omelet. It is all presented on a large communal platter or, as my mother did, in a wooden sushi tub, decorated with additional colorful toppings that include pickled ginger, needle-thin crisp julienned *nori,* and strips of golden yellow thin omelet. All the ingredients are so simple, but they must be properly cooked, flavored, cut, and presented to make the difference between an excellent *gomoku chirashi* and an indifferent one.

½ small carrot, cut into 1½-inch-long julienne strips (about ⅔ cup)

½ teaspoon salt

2 tablespoons sugar

½ cup *komezu* (rice vinegar)

1 large fresh lotus root (about ¼ pound)

2 cups freshly shelled green peas or frozen green peas

6 cups (lightly packed) prepared sushi rice for small bowls or 8 cups (lightly packed) prepared sushi rice for large bowls (page 58)

8 strips simmered *kanpyo* gourd (page 64), minced

6 simmered *shiitake* mushrooms (3 ounces) (page 63), minced

6 cakes simmered *koya-dofu* (freeze-dried tofu) (page 65), cut into ½-inch cubes

⅓ cup walnuts, toasted and roughly chopped

⅓ cup *gari* (sweet pickled ginger) (page 66), cut into julienne strips

2 whole sheets *nori,* cut with scissors into needle-thin 2-inch-long julienne strips

Put the carrot strips in a small saucepan with enough water to cover them by ½ inch and set over medium heat. Add ¼ teaspoon of the salt and 1 teaspoon of the sugar, and cook for 2 minutes. Drain the carrots.

Mix together in a bowl 2 cups of water with 2 tablespoons of the rice vinegar. Peel the lotus root with a vegetable peeler, removing a thin layer of skin, and cut the root into paper-thin slices. If the lotus root's diameter is greater than 2 inches, cut it first in half lengthwise, and then into thin semicircular slices. Soak the slices in the vinegar water, which will prevent them from turning brown. Drain the lotus root, place in a medium pot with enough water to cover it by 1 inch, and cook over medium-low heat for 10 minutes. Add the remaining rice vinegar, sugar, and salt and continue cooking for an additional 1 minute. Transfer the lotus root with its cooking liquid to a bowl and let it cool.

Cook the fresh green peas in a medium pot of boiling water with a little salt for 1 minute. Drain.

Toss the sushi rice in a sushi tub or wooden bowl with the carrot, *kanpyo* gourd, *shiitake* mushrooms, half the lotus root, half the green peas, and half the simmered freeze-dried tofu and walnuts. Spoon the measured sushi rice—2 cups for a large bowl or 1½ cups for a small bowl—into each bowl, making gently sloping mounds with a flat top in the center. Garnish the top with the remaining lotus root, tofu cubes, green peas, sweet pickled ginger, and *nori.*

ADDITIONAL INSTRUCTIONS

1. You can prepare all the ingredients half a day in advance. If you assemble this dish several hours in advance, do not add the *nori,* which will soften, until just before serving.

2. Serve at room temperature without a dipping sauce.

Cooked Seafood *Chirashi-zushi*

Cooked Seafood
Chirashi-zushi
Shin-kaisen chirashi

During sunny, gorgeous, cool autumn days, when I want to feed my family or guests a good seafood sushi with a nice glass of white wine, I prepare a modern *cooked* seafood *chirashi-zushi*.

MAKES 4 SMALL OR 4 LARGE
SUSHI BOWL SERVINGS

VEGETABLE SALSA:

1/2 red bell pepper (about 1/4 pound), cut into 1/4-inch cubes

2/3 avocado, firm but ripe, peeled and cut into 1/4-inch cubes

2 ounces Japanese cucumber or 1 small Kirby cucumber, cut into 1/4-inch cubes

1/4 pound tomato (about 1/2 medium), seeded and cut into 1/4-inch cubes

1 green jalapeño, grilled until the skin is charred, peeled and minced

1/3 cup chopped coriander leaves

Sea salt, olive oil, lemon juice, black peppercorns, and cayenne pepper

1 cup *sake* (rice wine) or white wine, mixed with 1/2 cup water

4 large scallops (each about 2 1/2 ounces), each cut crosswise into 4 disks

4 baby squid (each about 1 ounce) or 1 large squid (about 4 ounces), cleaned

12 large shrimp (21 to 30 count per pound) in their shells

1/2 pound salmon fillet, cut into 12 thin slices

1/2 pound monkfish fillet, cut into 12 thin slices

Rice vinegar

6 cups (lightly packed) prepared sushi rice for small bowls or 8 cups (lightly packed) prepared sushi rice for large bowls (page 58)

To make the salsa, toss the red bell pepper, avocado, cucumber, tomato, jalapeño, and coriander in a bowl. Stir in 1/2 teaspoon salt, 1 tablespoon olive oil, 1 tablespoon freshly squeezed lemon juice, and freshly ground black pepper and cayenne pepper to taste. Let the salsa rest in the refrigerator for one hour to overnight.

Pour the *sake* and water into a small saucepan and bring to a simmer. Add a little salt and the scallop disks, and cook over medium-low heat for 1 to 2 miutes, or until the scallops are briefly cooked through, turning them over several times. Scoop out the scallops with a slotted spoon, reserving the *sake* broth, and transfer to a paper towel–lined platter. Drop in the squid, cook for 2 minutes, remove, and cut it into rings. Cook the shrimp in their shells for 2 minutes in the same pan, then cool, remove the shells, devein, and butterfly. Cook the fish in the same way for 1 to 2 minutes. Place all the cooked seafood on a platter, paint with a layer of olive oil and rice vinegar, cover with plastic wrap, and refrigerate.

When you are ready to serve, have at hand the sushi rice and four Western-style shallow soup bowls, about 1 1/2- or 2 1/2-cup size.

Spoon the measured sushi rice— 2 cups for a large bowl or 1 1/2 cups for a small bowl—into each bowl, making gently sloping mounds with a flat top in the center. Decorate the top of the sushi rice with the vegetable salsa and then arrange the seafood.

ADDITIONAL INSTRUCTIONS

1. You can prepare the seafood and other ingredients in advance and refrigerate them. Do the final presentation just before serving.

2. This sushi can be eaten more easily with a fork, knife, and spoon. Serve at room temperature.

Beef *Tataki* Sushi
Gyuniku no tataki chirashi

MAKES 4 SMALL OR 4 LARGE
SUSHI BOWL SERVINGS

For this dish, beef is cooked until the outside is nicely browned. After marinating in a spicy marinade overnight, it is cut into thin slices and placed on the sushi rice to make a delicious and satisfying *chirashi-zushi*. As with raw seafood *chirashi*, the temperature of the sushi rice should be around 98° F, so that the juicy, plump, and tender sushi rice perfectly complements the cold sliced beef.

MARINADE:

¼ cup plus 1 tablespoon *sake* (rice wine)
½ cup *shoyu* (soy sauce)
¼ cup *komezu* (rice vinegar)
1 tablespoon sugar
1 large thumb-size piece of ginger, peeled and cut into fine julienne strips
1 teaspoon *toban jiang* (Chinese chile bean sauce)
1 tablespoon sesame oil

1 pound boneless rib eye steak
3 tablespoons vegetable oil
¼ pound watercress, hard stem part discarded
2 ounces chive sprouts (⅓ package) or other seed sprouts
Ponzu sauce (page 78)
6 cups (lightly packed) prepared sushi rice for small bowls or 8 cups (lightly packed) prepared sushi rice for large bowls (page 58)
⅓ cup pine nuts, toasted in a skillet until lightly golden
6 simmered *shiitake* mushrooms (3 ounces) (page 63), minced
¼ cup *shiso* (perilla) leaves or coriander leaves, minced

Put the *sake* in a medium pot and bring to a simmer over medium heat. Add the soy sauce, rice vinegar, and sugar and bring to a boil. Remove the pot from the heat and add the ginger, chile bean sauce, and sesame oil.

Heat the oven to 350° F. Salt and pepper the beef. Heat a cast-iron skillet or heavy-bottomed skillet over medium heat until hot. Add the vegetable oil and, when the oil is hot, sear the beef over medium-low heat until both sides are browned. Transfer the skillet to the oven for 6 minutes. Remove the beef from the oven and, while it is hot, put it in the marinade. When cool, transfer the beef and marinade to a sealable container and refrigerate overnight.

Remove the beef from the marinade, drain, and wipe off excess liquid. Cut the beef into 32 thin slices. Toss the watercress and chive sprouts in a bowl with a little *ponzu* sauce.

Have at hand the sushi rice and four Western-style shallow soup bowls, about 1½- or 2½-cup size.

Toss the sushi rice with the pine nuts, *shiitake* mushrooms, and *shiso* in a sushi tub or a wooden bowl. Spoon the measured sushi rice—2 cups for a large bowl or 1½ cups for a small bowl—into each bowl, making gently sloping mounds with a flat top in the center. Arrange one-quarter of the beef slices in each bowl to resemble the spokes of a wheel. Garnish the center with the vegetables.

ADDITIONAL INSTRUCTIONS

1. You can prepare the beef and other ingredients in advance and refrigerate them. Do the final assembly just before serving.
2. Serve at room temperature without a dipping sauce.

Western Vegetarian Summer Tossed Sushi
Seiyo-fu gomoku chirashi

This is a more Western version of my mother's traditional *gomoku chirashi*. The ingredients are all familiar—bell peppers, corn, cucumber, green peas, eggplant, and avocado—and easy to prepare. This dish will also help you understand how to select and assemble various ingredients to produce your own version, using what is locally available in each season. See photograph on page 133.

See photograph on page 133.

MAKES 4 SMALL OR 4 LARGE
SUSHI BOWL SERVINGS

1 small American eggplant

Olive oil

¼ pound fresh or frozen green peas (1 cup)

½ red bell pepper, cut into ¼-inch cubes (about 1 cup)

½ green bell pepper, cut into ¼-inch cubes (about 1 cup)

2 seeded Kirby cucumbers, cut into ¼-inch cubes (about 1 cup)

1 medium ear of corn, briefly grilled, kernels removed from the cob

½ firm avocado, halved, pitted, peeled, and diced into ¼-inch cubes

1 to 2 tablespoons minced, cured, and pitted black olives

¼ pound sharp cheddar cheese, cut into ¼-inch cubes

¼ teaspoon salt

1 tablespoon lemon juice or vinegar

1 teaspoon honey

6 cups (lightly packed) prepared sushi rice for small bowls or 8 cups (lightly packed) prepared sushi rice for large bowls (page 58)

THE GARNISH: ¼ cup julienned basil leaves

Remove the stem and cut the eggplant into ¼-inch slices lengthwise. Heat a little oil in a skillet and cook the eggplant over medium-low heat until both sides are golden and cooked through. Cool and cut each slice into ¼-inch cubes.

Cook the fresh green peas in a medium pot of lightly salted boiling water for 1 minute. Drain in a strainer, spread out, and cool.

Toss the eggplant, red and green peppers, cucumber, corn, avocado, black olives, green peas, and cheese in a large bowl with 2 teaspoons oil, salt, lemon juice, and honey. Let stand for 30 minutes.

Have at hand four Western-style soup bowls, about 1½- or 2½-cup size.

In a sushi tub or wooden bowl, gently but thoroughly toss the sushi rice with the vegetables and cheese. Spoon the measured sushi rice—2 cups for a large bowl or 1½ cups for a small bowl—into each bowl, making gently sloping mounds with a flat top in the center. Garnish the top with the basil strips.

ADDITIONAL INSTRUCTIONS

1. You can prepare the sushi several hours in advance.

2. Serve at room temperature without a dipping sauce.

Fisherman's Sushi
Tekone-zushi

Since sushi skipjack tuna, *katsuo,* is not readily available in America to most home chefs, I suggest that you use sushi tuna. This dish is pictured on page 133.

MAKES 4 SMALL OR 4 LARGE
SUSHI BOWL SERVINGS

1/4 cup *sake* (sweet cooking wine)
1/4 cup *mirin* (rice wine)
1/2 cup *shoyu* (soy sauce)
1 pound sushi *maguro* (tuna) (for information on shopping for sushi fish, see page 168; for sushi tuna, see page 185)
1 ounce ginger (1/4 cup), peeled and cut into fine julienne strips
1 bunch *mitsuba* greens (trefoil) (1 1/2 ounces) or 1/3 cup coriander leaves
6 large fresh *shiitake* mushrooms, preferably the plump *donko* variety (see page 63), stems removed
6 cups (lightly packed) prepared sushi rice for small bowls or 8 cups (lightly packed) prepared sushi rice for large bowls (page 58)

Four 8-inch-diameter thin omelets without potato starch (page 72)
4 *shiso* (perilla) leaves, cut into fine julienne strips, or 1/4 cup coriander*
2 tablespoons white sesame seeds
1 whole sheet *nori* (laver), torn by hand into 1-inch pieces
2 scallions, green part, cut into thin rings

*If substituting for both the *mitsuba* and the *shiso,* use a total of 1/4 cup coriander.

Pour the *sake* and *mirin* into a saucepan and bring to a gentle simmer. Add the soy sauce and bring to a gentle boil. Turn off the heat, transfer the liquid to a bowl, and cool in a larger bowl of ice water.

Cut the tuna into 40 slices, each about 1/4 inch thick. When the soy sauce liquid is cool, add the tuna and marinate for 20 minutes.

Meanwhile, bring water to a boil in a cleaned saucepan and blanch the julienned ginger for 10 seconds. Drain the ginger in a strainer and cool it under cold tap water. Drain again. Remove the root ends of the *mitsuba* greens and cut the stems and greens into 1-inch lengths. Cook the *shiitake* mushrooms over an open gas flame or other heat source until both sides are lightly golden. Cut into thin slices.

Have at hand the sushi rice and four shallow Western-style soup bowls, about 1 1/2- or 2 1/2-cup size. Now you will use your hands to toss the rice, so wash them thoroughly. In a sushi tub or wooden bowl, toss all the sushi rice with the tuna, ginger, *mitsuba, shiitake* mushrooms, omelet, *shiso,* and white sesame seeds. Spoon the measured tossed sushi rice—2 cups for a large bowl or 1 1/2 cups for a small bowl—into each bowl. Spread the rice out and decorate the top with the *nori* and scallion rings.

ADDITIONAL INSTRUCTIONS

1. If you wish to add *wasabi* flavor to the sushi, stir a generous amount (1 to 2 teaspoons) into the marinade when you marinate the tuna.
2. You can prepare all the ingredients half a day in advance. Do the final tossing and assembly just before serving the sushi.
3. At the time of serving, the rice should be warm and the fish should be chilled. Serve without a dipping sauce.

Fishermen's Treat

Tekone-zushi literally means "hand-tossed sushi" and comes from the Shima Peninsula, Mie Prefecture, which is the home of the famous skipjack tuna and Pacific oyster. Of course, there is a story attached to the name and the dish.

One day, some fishermen were very busy landing skipjack tuna, *katsuo,* one after another on their boat. When it was time for a brief lunch break, one of the fishermen picked up a freshly caught *katsuo.* He skillfully gutted, filleted, and boned it, then cut it into small pieces and tossed it with *shoyu* (soy sauce). His mates suggested he share this treasure for lunch, and so he tossed it with the ration of rice that each fisherman brought with him on board. As with the sandwich, necessity truly is the mother of invention. It tasted so good that the dish was adopted by the locals and has since become nationally famous. So think of those fishermen while you are enjoying this sushi.

Craft Sushi
Sonota no sushi

Just as we change our appearance with a different outfit or hairstyle, sushi, too, can completely change its look. The main ingredient, sushi rice, and even some of the other ingredients may be the same, but the assembly produces a different sushi. In this craft sushi section, you can play with some of these different styles and gain an appreciation of the breadth of the world of sushi.

Sushi Rice Packed in a Golden Tofu Bag
Inari-zushi

This more than 150-year-old sushi still remains very popular today in Japan as a casual snack, quick lunch, or picnic fare. *Inari-zushi* is sushi rice stuffed into a sweet-simmered tofu bag. It is delicious because the simmered tofu bag imparts its rich flavor to the sushi rice—a perfect combination of tart rice and sweet fried tofu. My students who have learned to make these home-style sushi adore them.

Once you have made a large batch of sweet-simmered tofu bags, *abura-age* (page 73), and stored them in the freezer, making *inari-zushi* is a quick three-step process: (1) prepare the sushi rice, (2) microwave the tofu bags or rewarm them in the oven wrapped in aluminum foil, and (3) pack the sushi rice in the tofu. That's all.

In Tokyo, plain sushi rice is used for the stuffing. In the Kansai region (Osaka and Kyoto), they are a bit more creative, mixing the rice with cooked vegetables to make the stuffing more interesting and nourishing. Here is my unique version for a casual get-together with friends along with some glasses of cold beer. If you are not nuts about nuts, choose other ingredients.

MAKES 16 SUSHI

8 pieces sweet-simmered *abura-age* (tofu bags) (page 73), cut in half

⅓ cup cashew nuts, toasted and cut into ½-inch pieces

½ cup walnuts, toasted and cut into ½-inch pieces

⅓ cup hulled pistachio nuts, toasted

⅓ cup currants or raisins

6 pieces dried apricot, cut into ¼-inch pieces

2 tablespoons toasted white sesame seeds

⅓ cup minced *shiso* (perilla) leaves or coriander

¼ cup minced *gari* (sweet pickled ginger) (page 66)

6 cups (lightly packed) prepared sushi rice (page 58)

Following the illustrations, 1. line up the seasoning ingredients and tofu bags. 2. Mix all the chopped nuts, currants, apricots, white toasted sesame seeds, *shiso,* and pickled ginger in a sushi tub or wooden bowl with the rice.

Have at hand a small bowl containing

1. Line up the seasoning ingredients for the filling and the tofu bags.

2. Mix the seasonings with the rice.

3. Open up a tofu bag and stuff it with a portion of the rice mixture.

4. Fold in the top edge of the tofu bag.

5. Finish filling the remaining bags.

2 cups of cold water and 2 tablespoons of rice vinegar for moistening your hands. Pick up a small handful of rice (about one-sixteenth, or slightly more than $1/3$ cup) and form it into an egg-shaped clump that will fill about two-thirds of the pouch. **3.** Open one half-sheet of the tofu bag so that it forms a pocket and pack the rice ball into it. **4.** Fold in the top edges to make a small pillow-shaped container. **5.** Fill the remaining fifteen pockets the same way.

ADDITIONAL INSTRUCTIONS

1. You can prepare the sushi half a day in advance and store it in a sealable container in a cool, dry, dark place. **2.** Serve at room temperature without a dipping sauce.

Elegant Yellow Pouch Sushi
Chakin-zushi

This sushi acquired its name because sushi rice is wrapped in a sheet of thin omelet to form a pouch. The omelet resembles the square tea ceremony cloth, the *chakin*—hence, the name. The top third of the omelet is squeezed to make a neck, and then the pouch is tied with a blanched chive. The top is left loosely open, resembling a golden yellow gift pouch that conceals some valuable treasure. Whenever it is served, people are curious to discover what is hidden inside. To eat it, gently remove the chive with your chopsticks or fingers. The omelet naturally spreads open and exposes the "treasure." Cut the omelet into 2-inch squares with your chopsticks, wrap one bite-size amount of sushi rice in the omelet square, pick them up together, and enjoy the wonderful combination. See photograph on page 213.

Here I wrap my mother's *gomoku chirashi* (page 141) along with cooked shrimp in the golden yellow pouch.

MAKES 12 *CHAKIN-ZUSHI* POUCHES

1 recipe of Festive Tossed Sushi, *gomoku chirashi* (page 141)*
Twelve 8-inch-diameter thin omelets with potato starch (page 72)
12 medium shelled shrimp (31 to 35 count per pound), boiled in salted water for 2 minutes
$1/2$ cup *ikura* (salmon roe)
12 chives, blanched in boiling water for 1 second and cooled in cold water

THE CONDIMENT: $1/2$ cup *gari* (sweet pickled ginger) (page 66)

*Use only half the amount of simmered *koya-dofu* (freeze-dried tofu). Cut the tofu into tiny cubes and toss with the sushi rice along with the other vegetables.

Have available a bowl with 2 cups of cold water and 2 tablespoons of rice vinegar for moistening your hands. Divide the sushi rice into twelve portions (each about $1/2$ cup) and form each into a ball. Put one of the thin omelets on your working counter and place a rice ball in the center. Arrange one shrimp and some salmon roe on top of the rice, then with both hands pull up the rim of the omelet all around to form a pouch. Gently hold the neck of the pouch with one hand and, with the other hand, tie one chive string around it. If this is hard to do by yourself, ask someone to help: one person holds the egg omelet while the other ties the knot. Serve the sushi with the sweet pickled ginger on the side.

ADDITIONAL INSTRUCTIONS

1. You can prepare the sushi half a day in advance and store it in a lidded container in a cool, dry, dark place. Or refrigerate it in the vegetable bin. **2.** Serve at room temperature without a dipping sauce.

Toy Ball Flower Sushi
Temari-zushi

This sushi is named after the 200-year-old toy ball, *temari,* simply because of its shape and attractive appearance (see page 213). The sushi is made in a moist cotton cloth in which a topping—a slice of fish, for example—and a small squeezed sushi rice ball are shaped together (the moist cloth prevents the sushi rice from sticking to your hands). Try making this easy sushi for your next sushi party.

MAKES 40 SUSHI WITH 4 DIFFERENT TOPPINGS (10 SERVINGS)

5 1/2 ounces sushi tuna (for information on how to shop for sushi fish, see page 168; for sushi tuna, see page 185)

4 large eggs

10 medium shrimp (31 to 35 count per pound), shells attached

5 sushi-quality scallops or 5 scallops for cooking, 1 inch in diameter

Wasabi paste

10 green peas, cooked for 1 minute in boiling water

Ten 2-inch-square *nori* sheets

1/4 cup *ikura* (salmon roe) or faux caviar

3 *shiso* (perilla) leaves, cut into quarters, or 5 mint leaves

1 cup *gari* (sweet pickled ginger) (page 66); 1/4 cup minced

6 cups prepared sushi rice (page 58)

THE SAUCE: *tsuke-joyu* (sushi dipping sauce) (page 77)

Cut the tuna into ten 2-inch-square slices. Bring water in a pot to a simmer and cook the eggs for 10 minutes. Drop the eggs into a bowl of cold water and, while they are hot, peel them and separate the whites and the yolks. Press each separately through a fine sieve into separate bowls. Bring another pot of lightly salted water to a boil and cook the shrimp for 2 minutes. Drain, shell, and butterfly the shrimp, leaving the tails attached. Cut the sushi-quality scallops in half crosswise. If using scallops that are for cooking, bring 1/4 cup *sake* (rice wine) and 1/4 cup water in a saucepan to a boil, add the scallops, and cook for 2 minutes, turning them over several times. Drain the scallops and cut in half crosswise.

Put the ingredients on four plates: the first for the tuna, *wasabi,* and 1 teaspoon of the sieved egg yolk; the second for the shrimp, *wasabi,* and green peas; the third for the sieved egg white, remaining sieved egg yolk, *nori* squares, and salmon roe; and the fourth for the scallops, *wasabi, shiso,* and sweet pickled ginger. Have at hand the sushi rice, a small bowl with 2 cups of cold water and 2 tablespoons of rice vinegar for moistening your hands, and a clean, finely woven, moistened cotton or synthetic cloth.

Now prepare ten pieces each of four kinds of sushi.

Temari
Toy Ball

The *temari* is traditionally made from paper, cotton string, and finely woven silk threads that are dyed in many colors. It is a girl's toy, and I remember that when I was a small child, I played with it all day long, day after day, simply rolling the ball and chasing it over and over again on the *tatami* mat floor of our house. As the ball rolled, the surface, covered with gorgeous patterns made from glossy silk threads, created a miracle of continually changing patterns and colors. Watching it was like peeking into a kaleidoscope. I now think that this was a great learning experience for me about color, movement, patterns, and textures.

1. *Tuna sushi:* Spread the moistened cotton or synthetic cloth on a clean counter. Place a slice of tuna in the center and a little dab of *wasabi* paste in the center of the fish. Scoop up about 1½ tablespoons sushi rice, shape it into a round ball, and place it on top of the fish. With both hands, pull up the edges of the moistened cloth all around to make a pouch. With one hand, hold the neck, and with the other hand, twist the pouch, gently squeezing and shaping the tuna and sushi rice in the cloth into a round miniball. Do not crush or mash the contents. Before unwrapping the sushi, press the cloth with your finger at the center of the tuna to make a little depression. Unwrap, remove the sushi from the cloth, and place it on a plate, depression side up. With a small spoon, place a dab of sieved egg yolk inside the depression for color. This sushi will make everyone at your table think of a camellia. Make nine more camellia sushi in the same way.

2. *Shrimp sushi:* Place the butterflied shrimp with the tail end attached in the center of the moist cloth. Open the upper half part of the shrimp out to broaden it, as though you were opening a fan. Put a dab of *wasabi* in the center. Scoop up a little less than about 1½ tablespoons sushi rice, shape it into a ball, and place it on top. Form the sushi in the moistened cloth as you did the tuna sushi. Before removing the sushi from the cloth, make the same depression as you did for the tuna in the center of the shrimp. After removing the ball from the cloth, decorate the depression with a green pea. Make nine more sushi in the same way.

3. *Egg sushi:* Prepare 8-inch-long pieces of plastic wrap. Arrange the sieved egg yolk and egg white, half and half, in a disk shape, 1½ inches in diameter, on the moist cloth. Scoop up about 1½ tablespoons sushi rice, shape it into a ball, and place it on top of the egg. Form the sushi in the moistened cloth following the instructions for the tuna sushi, except do not press into the cloth to make a depression. Unwrap the sushi. Spread a piece of plastic wrap, about 8 inches long, on the working counter. Place one *nori* square in the center, then the formed sushi, egg side down, on the center of the *nori.* With both hands, pull up the edges of the plastic wrap to make a pouch. With one hand, hold the neck, and with the other hand, twist the pouch, gently resqueezing the sushi so that the *nori* sticks to the egg and rice ball. Unwrap and turn over the *sushi* so that the top of the *nori* faces up. With a very sharp knife, make an X cut on top of the sushi. It opens like the petals of a flower. Decorate the open area with the salmon roe. This sushi will remind people of a pomegranate. Make nine more sushi in the same way.

4. *Scallop sushi:* Place a scallop slice in the center of the moistened cloth and put a dab of *wasabi* on top. Place a *shiso* leaf, cut into half the diameter of the scallop, and cover with a rice ball formed from about 1½ tablespoons sushi rice. Form the sushi following the directions for the tuna sushi. Make a depression in the center of the scallop with your finger before unwrapping and fill it with a little pickled ginger. Make nine more sushi in the same way.

ADDITIONAL INSTRUCTIONS

1. Prepare the sushi just before serving.
2. At the time of serving, the rice should be warm and the fish should be chilled. Serve with the *tsuke-joyu.*

Bamboo Leaf Pouch Sushi
Sasa-zushi

Here sushi rice is packed in a fresh bamboo leaf, which is known to have sterilizing and antispoilage properties. The leaf also transmits its distinctive sweet aroma to the rice, and its deep refreshing green color induces a good appetite.

Fresh bamboo leaves, about 10 to 12 inches long and 3 to 4 inches wide, are found at Japanese food stores in packages of fifty or more leaves. For more information, see page 90.

MAKES 12 POUCHES

¼ cup plus 2 tablespoons *komezu* (rice vinegar)

12 fresh bamboo leaves, scrubbed and rinsed well

¼ pound smoked salmon, cut into 12 equal-size squares

1 recipe of Festive Tossed Sushi, *Gomoku chirashi* (for small bowls) (page 141)

THE CONDIMENT: ½ cup *gari* (sweet pickled ginger) (page 66)

Wet a paper towel with 2 tablespoons vinegar and wipe the bamboo leaves. Mix ¼ cup vinegar and 2 tablespoons water in a bowl and add the salmon pieces, quickly turning them over several times. Drain through a strainer. Make twelve round rice balls (using about ½ cup each).

In your left hand, pick up a bamboo leaf by the stem, the spine side facing you and the stem side up. Following the illustrations, 1. make an ice cream cone–shaped cup by folding the bottom tip up and across the front of the leaf and continuing to roll. 2. Take a sushi rice ball and place it inside the cone, filling the cup almost to the brim. Arrange a salmon slice on top of the rice. 3. Fold the stem and upper part of the leaf toward you, covering the filling. Insert the stem into the cone, pushing it down until the stem emerges from the hole at the bottom of the cone. Pull the stem a little farther down to tighten the package. 4. Repeat, making eleven more pouches, then pack them all tightly together in a container and let them stand, covered, for half a day in a cool, dry, dark place or refrigerate in the vegetable bin. By letting them rest, the bamboo leaf's flavor and aroma are transmitted to the rice. Serve the sushi with pickled ginger on the side.

ADDITIONAL INSTRUCTIONS

1. To eat, open up the bamboo leaf and pop the sushi ball into your mouth. The bamboo leaf is not edible.
2. Serve the sushi at room temperature without a dipping sauce.

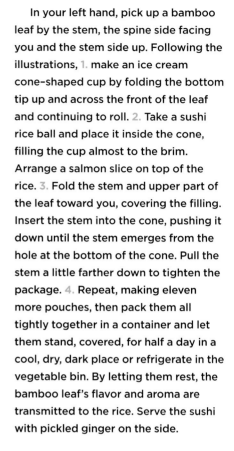

1. Make a triangular cone-shaped cup

2. Place a sushi rice ball inside the cone cup and arrange a salmon slice on top.

3. Fold the stem and cover the rice ball.

4. A platter of 6 pouches.

Steamed Sushi
Mushi-zushi

During cold weather, treating yourself, friends, and family to a steamed sushi is a great pleasure. This one is better prepared with freshly made sushi rice, but you can use day-old, firm sushi rice. Here I top the rice with prepared eel, thin omelet, and green peas and serve it in about 1-cup heatproof bowls—a lovely appetizer to start your dinner party.

14 ounces *unagi no kabayaki* (prepared eel) (for heating instructions, see page 99)

Four 8-inch-diameter thin omelets without potato starch (page 72)

1 cup freshly shelled green peas or frozen peas

10 simmered *shiitake* mushrooms (page 63) (6 ounces), cut into thin slices

2 tablespoons *komezu* (rice vinegar)

THE GARNISH: 1/2 cup *gari* (sweet pickled ginger) (page 66), julienne sliced

6 cups (lightly packed) prepared sushi rice (page 58)

Reheat the eel following the instructions on page 99. Cut the eel down the center into halves lengthwise, then cut each long strip into ten equal pieces crosswise. Cut the thin omelets into julienne strips. Bring a medium pot of salted water to a boil, add the green peas, and cook for 1 minute. Drain in a colander, rinse under cold running water, and transfer them to a bowl.

Line up all the ingredients—eel, thin omelet, green peas, *shiitake* mushrooms, rice vinegar, and sweet pickled ginger—on a tray. Have at hand the sushi rice. Get your steamer going. You need ten 1-cup heatproof bowls.

Toss half the amount of green peas and sweet pickled ginger in a sushi tub or wooden bowl with the rice. Divide the rice evenly among the ten bowls (slightly more than 1/2 cup per bowl). Sprinkle one-tenth of the rice vinegar over each sushi (this additional vinegar compensates for flavor that will be lost when the rice is steamed). Spread equal amounts of the *shiitake* slices on top of each bowl. Do the same with the julienned omelet, the eel, and the remaining green peas. Transfer as many of the bowls to the hot steamer as it will accommodate without crowding and cook over high heat, covered, for 5 minutes. Continue with the rest. Serve the hot sushi in its bowl garnished with the remaining sweet pickled ginger. No dipping sauce is needed.

Tips for Successful Steaming

1. Use plenty of boiling water to generate steam. If you are using a bamboo steamer, choose a deep pot into which the bamboo steamer can fit snugly (a deep pot can hold a lot of water, which ensures vigorous steam for cooking). If you are using a Western-style steamer or the pot does not hold much water, have a kettle of boiling water at hand and add more boiling water as needed to keep the steam going.

2. Before you lower your sushi bowls into the steamer basket or pot, the steamer should be producing plenty of steam (the same principle as preheating an oven).

3. If using a Western-style metal steamer, cover the inside surface of the lid with a cotton cloth, so that the trapped steam can be absorbed (to avoid condensed steam dripping on the sushi).

Oven-Baked Sushi
Yaki-zushi

This oven-baked sushi offers another way to use leftover sushi rice. When you prepare it with freshly made sushi rice, it is, of course, the best. I top the rice with some of my very favorite seafood, yellowtail, and creamy *uni,* sea urchin. I brush the sea urchin with a mixture of *mirin* and *shoyu,* which makes it sizzle and brown during baking. Serve the sushi garnished with a dab of *wasabi* and a sprinkle of additional *shoyu* (soy sauce). If sushi yellowtail is not available, use crabmeat. You need ten about 1-cup heatproof bowls.

Vegetable oil to grease the baking dishes

10 ounces sushi *hamachi* (yellowtail) (for information on shopping for sushi fish see page 168) or crabmeat

2 tablespoons *tobik-ko* (flying fish roe) (optional)

½ cup chopped *mitsuba* (trefoil) greens or coriander leaves

2 tablespoons plus 1 teaspoon *mirin* (sweet cooking wine)

2 tablespoons plus 1 teaspoon *shoyu* (soy sauce)

3 tablespoons *Wasabi* paste

1 whole sheet *nori*

6 cups (lightly packed) prepared sushi rice* (page 58)

3 wooden trays of *uni* (sea urchin) (page 139)

*If you are using leftover, refrigerated sushi rice, first steam it for 10 minutes.

Dip a paper towel in vegetable oil and grease the inside of ten about 1-cup ovenproof baking cups.

Dice the yellowtail and toss it in a bowl with the flying fish roe, *tobik-ko* (optional), *mitsuba,* 1 tablespoon each *mirin* and soy sauce, and ¼ teaspoon *wasabi.* Cut the *nori* with scissors into julienne strips, 1½ inches long. Have at hand the sushi rice and a small bowl with 2 cups of cold water and 2 tablespoons of rice vinegar for moistening your hands. Preheat the oven to 500° F.

Spoon one-tenth (slightly more than ½ cup) of the sushi rice into ten baking cups. Cover the top of each with equal amounts of the diced yellowtail and the sea urchin. Mix the remaining *mirin* and soy sauce in a cup and, with a pastry brush, baste the sea urchin three times. Put the baking cups in the heated oven and cook 5 minutes. Remove from the oven and garnish the sushi with a dab of *wasabi* and the julienned *nori.*

Girls' Day Treat

Hinamatsuri, Girls' Day or Dolls' Day, is a yearly event in Japan that falls on March 3. Parents decorate the house with a set of traditional dolls for a few weeks before the holiday, prepare special meals, and offer a prayer for the happiness and health of their daughters throughout the year. The complete set of dolls, representing the royal court in classical cos-tumes, includes fifteen figures, among them the emperor, empress, ladies in waiting, musicians, warriors, and servants. The tradition is handed down from one generation to another in every family. My mother would put away the dolls in their boxes on the night of the third until the next year, reminding us that if they remained on display after March 3, we would have difficulty finding a husband when we grew up.

In addition to beautiful family dolls, my mother would prepare cute sushi dolls on this special occasion. She would create both emperor and empress sushi dolls, which are really charming and, when the charm wears off, delicious as well.

Kids' Sushi
Kodomo no sushi

This section is devoted to the children in your life. Not only will these dishes provide pleasure and good nutrition, but they will also encourage lifelong healthy eating habits. I hope you will get your children into the kitchen so you will have the fun of preparing these sushi together.

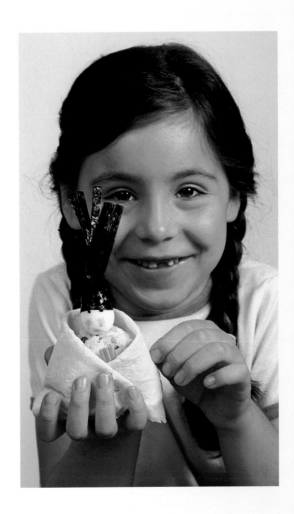

My Mother's Doll Sushi
Hinamatsuri zushi

Treat the girls in your life to this very special doll sushi and get them to help you make them.

MAKES 5 PAIRS OF DOLL SUSHI
(EACH PAIR CONSISTS OF AN
EMPEROR AND AN EMPRESS DOLL)

1 medium carrot, cut into ¼-inch cubes (about ⅓ cup)

1 teaspoon sugar

1 teaspoon *shoyu* (soy sauce)

¼ cup toasted white sesame seeds

½ cup walnuts, toasted and chopped

½ cup raisins

¼ cup minced *shiso* (perilla) leaves or coriander

Ten 8-inch-diameter thin omelets with potato starch (page 72) for cloaks

Five 1-inch-square thin carrot slices for fans

5 small snow peas or string beans for ceremonial batons

10 hard-boiled quail eggs, shelled, for heads

1 tablespoon black sesame seeds for eyes

1 small red beet for drawing lips and cheeks

2 whole sheets *nori* for crowns and hair

6 cups (lightly packed) prepared sushi rice (page 58)

Put the carrot cubes in a small saucepan with water to cover them by ½ inch, bring to a boil over medium heat, and cook for 1 minute. Add the sugar and soy sauce and cook for 1 minute more. Drain the carrot cubes in a colander and cool.

Line up all the ingredients—carrot cubes, white sesame seeds, walnuts, raisins, *shiso* leaves, omelets, carrot slices, snow peas, quail eggs, black sesame seeds, beet, and *nori*—on a tray. Have at hand the sushi rice and a small bowl with 2 cups of cold water and 2 tablespoons of rice vinegar for moistening your hands. You will also need scissors and twenty-five toothpicks.

1. Putting the omelet cloak around the pyramid-shaped sushi rice. *In front:* the whole omelet, a pile of carrot fans, and snow pea batons; *to the left:* two sushi dolls in omelet cloaks; *center left:* the quail eggs (for heads), a bowl of black sesame seeds (for eyes), and sushi rice balls

2. Inserting a toothpick to secure the cloak

3. Putting on the quail egg head

4. Wrapping *nori* strips around the head

5. Putting the crown on the head

Toss the sushi rice in a sushi tub or a salad bowl with the carrot cubes, white sesame seeds, walnuts, raisins, and *shiso* leaves. Divide the sushi rice into ten portions (each slightly more than 1/2 cup) and make pyramid-shaped rice balls. Now call the children to come and assist you. In the illustrations, a young friend, Odessa, and I are making sushi dolls together.

Pick up one omelet and place it on the working counter. Fold the omelet in half with the folded edge away from you. Following the illustrations, 1. place a rice ball on the omelet with the tip of the triangle at the center of the straight edge of the omelet. Fold the right and left sides of the omelet over the rice ball. The rice ball forms the doll's body, and the omelet is a cloak draped over the shoulders. Make nine more bodies with omelet cloaks.

Under the omelet in the front of the doll where the edges of the omelet overlap, insert a carrot slice (showing only an upside-down triangle) for the empress (her fan) and a section of a snow pea for the emperor (his ceremonial baton). 2. Secure the omelet and carrot slice or snow pea with a toothpick. The fan or religious baton should be visible below the cloak.

3. Hold one quail egg pointed end down and insert a toothpick into the other end, but do not let it pierce through the top of the egg. Repeat with the rest of the quail eggs. These are the heads of the sushi dolls. 4. Now we will add hair and crowns to the bald heads using the *nori*. My mother's way of doing this was to make 1/2-inch-wide, 2-inch-long *nori* bands to wrap around the heads for crowns. To glue the ends of the *nori* together, use just a drop of water. But remember that too much water will make the *nori* misshapen. The emperor is bald, poor fellow. For the empress, use one more *nori* strip, hanging it down her back, gluing it with a drop of water to the crown. (5.) Or just create your own hairstyle for the dolls. Finally, they need eyes (black sesame seeds) and lips and rouge, painted with beet juice (stick a toothpick into the beet to get the juice). In order to attach the black sesame seeds to the surface of smooth quail eggs, make a small scratch with a toothpick at the correct locations and insert the seeds, so they are partially buried. The sesame seeds will want to pop out, so you may have to try this several times. 6. Stick a toothpick into the beet a few times. When the tip is nicely covered with red juice, draw the lips of the doll on each quail egg. With additional beet juice, apply some blush for the cheeks. When all the heads are decorated, secure them to the doll bodies with the toothpicks.

ADDITIONAL INSTRUCTIONS

1. As time passes, beet juice spreads out and becomes indistinct. If you have red food coloring, use it in order to avoid this problem.
2. Serve at room temperature without a dipping sauce.

The final treat: biting into it

6. Painting the lips on with beet juice

Log Cabin Sushi

Sushi rolls are round, but by shaping the upper part of the roll into a triangle, you can form a roll with a long peaked roof. This sushi is wonderful to make for children's birthday parties. Their friends will be amazed at what you and your child can do with sushi rice!

MAKES 7 LOG CABIN ROLLS

Fourteen ½-inch-square × 4-inch-long cucumber sticks

6 ounces cheddar cheese, cut into fourteen ½-inch-square × 4-inch-long sticks

¼ cup plus 1 tablespoon toasted black sesame seeds

1 cup *sakana no oboro* (sweet fish flakes) (page 74) or finely minced nuts such as peanuts or walnuts

6 cups (lightly packed) prepared sushi rice (page 58)

4 half-sheets *nori;* crispness is not required

Line up all the ingredients—cucumber, cheddar cheese, sesame seeds, and sweet fish flakes—on a tray. Follow the techniques described in the Master Recipe for Classic California Roll (page 108). After making a roll, place the bamboo rolling mat on top of the roll, pinch the top part of the roll, moving from left to right, and form it into a triangular shape. Make six more rolls in the same way.

Decorate the two angled surfaces of each roll with the fish flakes. Coat the remaining surfaces with a generous amount of black sesame seeds. When the roll is cut into six small pieces, each will look like a miniature log cabin. Serve it at room temperature without a dipping sauce.

Lunch Box Thick Roll
Futo-maki bento

Most children, alas, have a school lunch that consists of something loaded with fat, sugar, and empty calories and leaves them feeling poorly nourished. Why not pack a sushi lunch for them? This sushi is made with brown rice cooked with sticky red rice rolled with delicious Japanese-style chicken. It provides nutrition, energy, and hunger-satisfying appeal.

MAKES 4 THICK ROLLS

MARINADE:

1 tablespoon *shoyu* (soy sauce)

2 teaspoons honey

1 large egg, beaten well

1 tablespoon curry powder

1 pound boneless chicken thighs, cut into 20 long strips, about 4 inches long

½ cup potato starch

Vegetable oil for cooking

5 large salad leaves

1 medium carrot, cut into julienne strips 3 inches long (about 1 cup)

¼ cup *gari* (sweet pickled ginger) (page 66), cut into julienne strips

6 cups (lightly packed) prepared sushi rice made from 1¼ cups dry brown rice and 1 cup dry sticky red rice (page 101)

5 whole *nori* (laver) sheets

Mix in a bowl the soy sauce, honey, egg, and curry powder. Add the chicken, toss thoroughly, and let stand for 15 minutes. Mix in the potato starch, coating the chicken thoroughly.

Heat 1 inch of oil in a skillet to 330° F, add the chicken strips in small batches, and cook over low heat for 2 to 3 minutes, turning them over. Remove the first batch of chicken and drain on a steel strainer. Cook the second and third batches in the same way. Increase the temperature of the oil to 340° F and recook the chicken in small batches until the outside is golden, only about 10 seconds. Drain the chicken on the steel strainer (the chicken is delicious to eat as is).

Line up all the filling ingredients—chicken, salad leaves, carrot, and sweet pickled ginger—on a tray. Follow the techniques described in the Master Recipe for Thick Roll (page 94).

ADDITIONAL INSTRUCTIONS

1. Cut each roll into eight pieces, wrap them in plastic wrap, and put into a sealable plastic bag, then in the school bag. Tell your children to keep the sushi in a cool, dry, dark place and to share with friends.

2. Serve at room temperature without a dipping sauce.

Battleship Sushi
Kodomo gunkan

*G*unkan means "battleship" (page 211). At a sushi bar restaurant, this special style of *nigiri-zushi* is made in order to hold together topping ingredients that are loose and shapeless, such as sea urchin, salmon roe, and chopped tuna. It also makes a wonderful sushi container in which to pack foods that kids love, such as egg or tuna salad. It is important to note that the *nori,* which surrounds the sushi rice ball and supports the topping ingredients, quickly becomes moist and soft, resulting in a less pleasant texture. So make this sushi just before serving.

TOPPING 1:

One 6-ounce can tuna in water
¼ cup finely diced cucumber
¼ cup finely diced carrot
2 tablespoons mayonnaise
Salt

TOPPING 2:

1 cup crabmeat (6 ounces)
1 hard-boiled egg, shelled and finely diced
3 tablespoons minced parsley
2 tablespoons mayonnaise
Salt

5 whole *nori* sheets
6 cups (lightly packed) prepared sushi rice (page 58)

Toss the tuna, cucumber, carrot, and 2 tablespoons mayonnaise together in a small bowl. Add salt to taste.

Mix the crabmeat, hard-boiled egg, and parsley in another small bowl along with 2 tablespoons mayonnaise and salt to taste.

Cut each *nori* into 1¼- × 6½-inch strips. To do this, first cut off a 1½-inch-wide band crosswise from each *nori* (reserve it for later use in other sushi preparations). Cut the remaining 6½- × 7½-inch sheet into six equal strips lengthwise. You will get thirty strips. Store the *nori* in a can or a sealed plastic bag.

Have at hand the sushi rice and a small bowl with 2 cups of cold water and 2 tablespoons of rice vinegar for moistening your hands. Have a moistened cotton cloth to wipe your hands.

Form the sushi rice into thirty mini-football shapes—about 1- × 2-inch ovals and 1 inch high. Place one sushi ball in front of you. Pick up one strip of *nori* and wrap it around the rice. The upper part of the *nori* will protrude above the rice ball, creating an empty space, into which you will stuff either of the two toppings. Wrap all the sushi rice balls with the *nori* strips. With a teaspoon, scoop up a little of the tuna mixture and fill in the empty space. Do the same with the crabmeat and egg mixture. Serve at room temperature.

Treasure Pouch Sushi

Takara sagashi inari-zushi

This is a child's version of *inari-zushi* (page 148), sushi rice stuffed in sweet-simmered tofu bags. Children love to find out what is hidden in the tofu bag.

MAKES 16 SUSHI

6 cups (lightly packed) prepared sushi rice (page 58)

5 simmered *shiitake* mushrooms (page 63), minced

6 dried apricots, cut into ¼-inch-square cubes

⅓ cup sultana raisins

⅓ cup sliced almonds

2 ounces cheddar cheese, cut into tiny cubes (½ cup)

2 tablespoons white sesame seeds

¼ cup minced parsley, coriander, or *shiso* (perilla) leaves

16 half-pieces sweet-simmered *abura-age* (tofu bags) (page 73)

Toss the sushi rice in a sushi tub or wooden bowl with the *shiitake* mushrooms, apricots, raisins, almonds, cheese, white sesame seeds, and parsley. Have at hand a small bowl with 2 cups of cold water and 2 tablespoons of rice vinegar for moistening your fingers.

Divide the tossed sushi rice into 16 portions and shape each one into a ball. Pick up one half-sheet of the tofu bag, open it to make a pocket, and pack one rice ball in it. Fold in the top edge to create a small pillow-shaped container. Fill the remaining fifteen pockets with the remaining rice balls the same way.

ADDITIONAL INSTRUCTIONS

1. You can prepare the sushi half a day in advance. Store it tightly sealed in a container and keep in a cool, dry, dark place.

2. Serve the sushi at room temperature without a dipping sauce.

Pretty Picture Sushi

Watashi no chirashi

The easiest sushi to prepare is *chirashi-zushi,* decorated sushi. Spoon a mound of sushi rice into a cereal bowl, flattening the top, and decorate it with whatever ingredients your child fancies. In this recipe, the toppings are cooked fish and shellfish, in contrast to the adult version with raw fish.

MAKES 4 SUSHI

½ cup freshly shelled green peas or frozen peas

8 large shrimp (21 to 30 count per pound) in their shells

4 large scallops for cooking, cut into 2 disks crosswise

⅓ cup *gari* (sweet pickled ginger) (page 66), minced

8 simmered *shiitake* mushrooms (page 63), sliced thin

½ cup *sakana no oboro* (sweet fish flakes) (page 74)

1 whole sheet *nori* (laver), cut into 2-inch-long julienne strips

6 cups (lightly packed) prepared sushi rice (page 58)

THE SAUCE: *tsuke-joyu* (sushi dipping sauce) (page 77)

Bring a medium pot of lightly salted water to a boil, add the green peas, and cook for 1 minute. With a slotted spoon, transfer them to a small bowl. Drop in the shrimp in their shells and cook, over medium heat, for 2 to 3 minutes. With a slotted spoon, transfer them to a colander and cool. Peel and devein the shrimp, then cut them into 1-inch cubes. Drop in the scallops and cook for 2 minutes. Drain and wipe dry with a paper towel.

Line up all the ingredients—green peas, shrimp, scallops, sweet pickled ginger, *shiitake* mushrooms, sweet fish flakes, and *nori*—on a tray. Have at hand the sushi rice and a small bowl with 2 cups of cold water and 2 tablespoons of rice vinegar for moistening your hands. You also need four shallow 3-cup soup bowls.

Toss the rice in a sushi tub or wooden bowl with the sweet pickled ginger. Spoon equal amounts of the sushi rice into each bowl, making a gently sloping mound with a flat top in the center. Garnish the entire surface of each sushi with one-quarter of the julienned *nori,* then arrange one-quarter of the green peas, shrimp, scallops, fish flakes, and *shiitake* mushrooms in a design resembling the spokes of a wheel or some other interesting pattern of your children's own choosing.

To eat with chopsticks, pick up the ingredients and sushi rice from each area of the design one after the other. Serve the sushi with the dipping sauce to dip shrimp and scallops.

Part Four
Sushi Seafood and How to Prepare It

Chapter 10
Sushi Seafood

You may remember that in the Edo period, when *nigiri-zushi* evolved, only cooked or cured sushi fish and shellfish were used and that it was after the introduction of refrigeration, in the prosperous years following World War II, that raw seafood became widely used. Today modern sushi culture has spread to cities around the globe, and more and more people are eating raw seafood. The expanded market has led to a better distribution system for sushi-quality fish. Working with the world-renowned Tsukiji Wholesale Fish Market in Tokyo and Japanese transportation companies, U.S. distributors are bringing many varieties of fresh, delicious, safe sushi seafood to nearly every part of the United States. Even on a 110° day in Las Vegas, you can enjoy good sushi, though it won't be cheap.

Before you make *nigiri-zushi* yourself, you need to know what kinds of seafood are traditionally used, where to get them, and how to judge whether they are fresh enough for sushi. Even if you only plan to eat restaurant or takeout sushi, knowing the basics of sushi seafood will enrich your dining experience and give you confidence that your sushi is safe as well as delicious.

Memories of the Tsukiji Fish Market

While I was growing up in Tokyo, I loved to visit the city's famous fish market. It was like visiting an aquarium, only better, because I could get very close to the fish and shellfish. Some were alive in tanks; some small, freshly killed fish were in ice water; larger fish were butchered for sushi and neatly placed on a wooden counter; and clams and shrimp were in tubs of water. I particularly loved to watch *aori-ika* swimming in water tanks, each balancing their broad, round bodies by continually rippling the surrounding fine, silky fins. This elegant movement so entranced me that I would stand watching until the wholesalers finally shooed me away.

Seasonal Fish

Because, according to tradition, every Japanese meal should provide a strong sense of the season—spring, summer, fall, winter—Japanese cooks have always favored seasonal fish. In Japan as elsewhere, advances in transportation, refrigeration, and aquaculture have lessened the emphasis on seasonality, but in the professional sushi kitchen, season still matters a great deal. Farmed fish are less expensive than their wild cousins, but their flavor and texture are usually poorer, and their year-round availability numbs our sense of seasonality. For these reasons, many proud sushi chefs in both Japan and America avoid out-of-season, cultured fish.

Fish are in season when they are tastiest and fattest—that is, when they are preparing to spawn—or, if they are migratory, when they are abundant near a certain shore. Migratory fish may be in season in different regions at different times of the year. These fish taste especially good when they are caught in cold waters in which plankton is abundant, in places where cold water surges up from the ocean floor, or where currents collide.

Japan is fortunate to be surrounded by two major currents, Oyashio, a cold current, and Kuroshio, a warm current. Rich in nutrients, cold Oyashio circulates counterclockwise in the northwest Pacific, flowing southward along the east coast of Japan. Warm Kuroshio flows northward, as fast as 11 miles per hour (about the speed you can run), from the south. Near the eastern shores of Japan, the two currents collide, causing much plankton to bloom. The abundant plankton attracts migrating species such as sardines, squid, skipjack tuna, mackerel, and tuna. Fish caught in these waters taste extremely good.

Sushi-Quality Fish

If you worry that the international sushi craze may wipe out all the wild fish in the ocean, consider that seafood destined for the sushi bar is caught, prepared, and consumed in the most ecologically sound ways.

A fish not intended for raw consumption is typically caught in a large net that traps and often kills both desired and undesired species. The fish is dropped onto the deck—bang!—to exhaust itself, suffocate, and die in the sun, where it may lie until the fishermen have stopped fishing and can put all the catch into storage with ice. Eight hours after the fish is caught, it may finally be delivered to a fishmonger and displayed on crushed ice. By this time, it is certainly not suitable for sushi, and perhaps it isn't even suitable for cooking. But the friendly fishmonger

(continued on page 168)

Ike-jime
Proper Slaughter

There are different *ike-jime* methods for different kinds of fish.

Ordinary, inexpensive fish such as sardine, mackerel, and horse mackerel are usually caught in a net. Before they struggle much, they are placed in iced saltwater tanks; this both kills and cools them. After a couple of hours, they are transferred to a box of crushed ice and carried to the fish market.

For expensive sushi fish such as flounder, sea bass, sea bream, great amberjack, yellowtail, and tuna, *ike-jime* consists of cutting quickly behind the head through the spinal column and aorta and inserting a thin steel wire into the spinal column. This instantly kills the fish. The fish is then placed in cold salt water for bleeding and cooling. The time between slaughter and serving is meticulously tracked, so that each type of fish can be served raw at its best.

Tuna from Catch to Port

The Japanese tuna-fishing fleet sails all the world's oceans in pursuit of its huge, highly valuable prey. If tuna are handled swiftly and with immense care, each fish may fetch more than twenty thousand dollars at auction in Tokyo's Tsukiji Fish Market. Tuna for sushi is usually caught by longline, a 60-mile line fitted with more than two thousand baited hooks. When the line is pulled out of the water, one section at a time, every fisherman on board rushes to pull the leaping, 400-pound fish out of the water and lay them gently on the deck. From the trauma they have just experienced, the fish are already accumulating body heat and

lactic acid, which will begin to denature the protein in the flesh. So in just ten minutes per fish, the men quickly kill each tuna in the *ike-jime* style, cut off the tail, remove the gills and intestines, and clean the fish. They stuff the cavity with crushed ice and place the tuna belly side down in a box filled with more ice (storing the fish on its side would damage muscle tissue). Or if the ship is far from port, the fish is placed on a shelf in an ultra-low-temperature freezer. As the fish freezes, it is turned to prevent damaging compression of the flesh. The boat and catch make a speedy trip back to port.

The Development of Flavor in Sushi Fish

The great care taken in catching, killing, storing, and transporting sushi fish is intended to delay and prolong rigor mortis, a contraction of the muscles caused by chemical changes that occur in the body after death. Even after a fish is dead and its flow of blood and oxygen has stopped, its body continues to burn energy, using the glycogen stored in the liver and muscles. This leads to the anaerobic production of lactic acid, which changes the flavor and texture of the flesh. As the production of lactic acid increases, the production of adenosine triphosphate, or ATP, decreases. Essential to the functioning of all animals, ATP is involved in the metabolism of foods, the synthesis of proteins and DNA, and the contraction of muscles. When ATP disappears from the muscles, rigor mortis begins. Until rigor mortis ends, a sushi fish remains fresh enough to eat raw.

How quickly rigor mortis begins after death, and how long it lasts, depends on many things—the species, the size of the

fish, its physical condition, the season, the temperature of the water, the methods of catching and killing, the degree of struggle at death, the handling of the fish afterward, and the storage temperature. In general, rigor mortis begins sooner and lasts a shorter time in small, poorly nourished fish that have died after much struggle and are stored at high temperature. In the worst case, rigor mortis can set in an hour after death and end just a few hours later.

To assure that a fish is safe to eat raw and served at its peak of flavor and texture, sushi chefs carefully track the onset and duration of rigor mortis. Fish arrive at the restaurant before rigor mortis, when their flesh is pliable and resilient. If you press the skin with your thumb, it bounces back without leaving a depression. The body looks plump, the skin damp, the colors strong and natural, and the eyes clear. The gut, which holds enzymes that can cause quick decomposition before the fish is cleaned, is firm, plump, and resilient. Pull up

the gill cover, and you will find blood-red gills through which hemoglobin travels, carrying oxygen to the muscles. The resilience of the flesh makes it hard to cut, and the flavor is mild. As the onset of rigor mortis nears, the flavor intensifies. A chef may choose this moment to serve the fish, so customers can enjoy the still-firm texture along with developing flavor.

When rigor mortis begins and proceeds to its peak, a fish looks frozen stiff. If you try to cut the flesh, you damage it. The muscles begin to relax after the peak of rigor mortis, and toward the end of the process, the flesh becomes quite tender and develops a mature flavor. This is generally the limit of freshness for sushi fish, although tuna and a few other species acquire better texture and flavor after a little further aging. A chef who serves you fish at the end of rigor mortis wants you to enjoy its full, rich flavor.

(continued from page 166)

says, truthfully, that it was caught that morning.

In general, the best fish for sushi is caught by pole and line, gently hauled on board, and quickly transferred, alive, to a tank of sea water. After resting overnight at the port to recover from any stress, the fish is slaughtered by an *ike-jime* method—instantaneously, so that it undergoes the least struggle and stress—to ensure peak quality over the longest period. The fish is then immediately sent to a sushi chef, who treats it with great care and respect. After filleting the fish, he or she slices the fillets for *nigiri-zushi* and *sashimi*. From a 4-pound flounder, the chef can make about one hundred *nigiri-zushi,* which would serve at least ten people if they were to have only flounder for their sushi meal. He or she uses the head and bones (about 30 percent of the fish) and leftover bits of meat to produce soups and dishes such as egg cake with bits of pasted fish, which accompany the sushi meal. The soul of the flounder can take great satisfaction in having fed and nourished so many people.

Where to Buy Sushi Fish

All over the United States today, large and small Japanese food stores carry a variety of sushi fish. Some of these stores are listed in the appendix ("Sources for Japanese Food Products"); you may find others in the phone book or on the Internet. Fish fillets and blocks are packed in Styrofoam trays with plastic lids or wrap and an expiration or sell-by date. The packages of sushi fish are stored in a refrigerator case separate from fish meant for cooking. If you're not sure what fish is for sushi, just ask. If you want a whole fish rather than a piece, your fishmonger should be able to provide it, but be sure to tell him or her that you want the fish for sushi.

Some general Asian supermarkets and non-Asian fishmongers now sell frozen sushi, tuna, yellowtail, and cooked, flavored eel that is also used for sushi. In these stores, though, the label "sushi-grade" doesn't ensure that the fish is safe for raw consumption. If you're in doubt about whether a piece of fish is safe to eat raw, ask for details about its source and handling.

Most fishmongers *don't* sell sushi fish. Don't make the mistake of thinking that the statement "We sell fresh fish" means the fish is necessarily suitable for raw consumption. Even seafood sold by fishermen at the dock may not be sushi-quality, so always ask for details about how a fish has been handled before assuming that it is safe for raw eating.

If you catch or collect your own seafood for sushi, check with local authorities to be sure the water is free of contaminants. Use traditional sushi species and handle them hygienically, according to the guidelines in this book.

Sushi Fish Species

Ma-aji, *Horse Mackerel or Japanese Jack Mackerel. Aji* migrate through the warmer waters of the world's oceans in such large schools—numbering from several hundred to thousands of fish—that fishermen say if you catch one, you will fill your bucket over and over again in a few minutes.

In Japanese waters alone, there are about twenty horse mackerel species. Among them are *ma-aji,* "true horse mackerel," which at sushi restaurants is called simply *aji.* Caught at about 6 to 15 inches long, *ma-aji* has glittering silver-blue skin with a thorny strip of scales running from just behind the gills all the way to the tail. The scale strip, which becomes quite spiky toward the tail, is always removed before the fish is prepared.

The leanest and mildest of oily-fleshed *hikari-mono* fish (see page 18), *ma-aji* taste best in May and June, just before spawning. For sushi, traditionally, 6- to 8-inch *ma-aji* are cured in salt and rice vinegar to mellow their strong flavor and preserve their quality, for these fish are especially perishable. Today, thanks to immediate icing on the boat and modern transportation and refrigeration, we can also enjoy *ma-aji* raw. Cured *ma-aji* are served with *wasabi,* raw *ma-aji* with grated ginger and chopped *asatsuki* chives. *Ma-aji* are also used to make a popular *tataki* (page 219), a *sashimi* dish that is well worth a try.

Most *ma-aji* served in U.S. sushi restaurants are imported from Japan, but you may occasionally find domestic *ma-aji.*

Horse mackerel

Conger eel

Anago, *Conger Eel or Sea Eel.*
Freshwater eel, *unagi,* is grilled and basted with a caramelized sauce to make a pleasantly oily, smoky, and delicious treat that has become popular in sushi restaurants outside of Japan. Traditionally, however, *unagi* isn't used in the sushi kitchen. Eel for sushi is *anago* ("hole fish"), or conger eel, a saltwater eel that thrives in the coastal waters of Japan, Korea, and the East China Sea as well as other places. Once abundant in Tokyo Bay, the birthplace of *nigiri-zushi,* this fish digs a hole in the sand or mud of the seafloor in which to hide, or it takes over a hole in a coral reef. At an aquarium, you may find *anago* living in apartments in a concrete house built by humans. At night, the eels emerge to search voraciously for anything they can eat.

Leaner than *unagi* and more refined in flavor, *anago* become fatter and tastier during summer. They can grow to more than 2 feet long, but in the sushi kitchen, young eels no longer than a foot are preferred. For the U.S. market, *anago* are farmed in Korea, flown to Japan for slaughter, and then flown under refrigeration to the United States (which, to protect the coastal ecosystem, forbids the importation of live conger eels). Frozen *anago* is also imported, from China and Peru.

Besides *anago nigiri-zushi,* try *ana-kyuu maki* (page 226), a popular dish of conger eel and cucumber rolled without rice and drizzled with a delicious sauce.

Buri *and* Hamachi, *Yellowtail.* The Japanese love to give the same fish different names at different ages and sizes, since at each stage, it has a different flavor, texture, and fat content. Yellowtail changes its name six times. But to enjoy yellowtail at a sushi restaurant, you need remember only two names, *buri* and *hamachi. Buri* is full-grown yellowtail, more than 34 inches long. *Hamachi* is the same fish as a young adult, 20 to 24 inches long.

A handsome, masculine-looking fish, yellowtail has the plump shape common to migratory fish. Its back is shiny and dark blue-green, its belly shiny and silver-gray. An earthy yellow brush line runs from below the eye all the way to the tail.

Yellowtail swim in schools off the Japanese shores, moving continuously up and down the coast with the seasons. During the cold months, these fish get fatter, until, at the peak of flavor, their bodies are as much as 20 percent fat. A very fatty piece of yellowtail leaves the same smooth, melting sensation in your mouth as does the fatty part of tuna. Besides enjoying fatty yellowtail in sushi and *sashimi,* we often cook it in the hot pot, in a yellowtail *shabu-shabu.*

The Japanese have been farming yellowtail since 1927, and now production of the cultivated fish is as high as 150,000 tons a year. Except at astronomically expensive sushi restaurants, you are not likely to find wild *hamachi.* If

Filleting Conger Eel, Samurai-Style

There are two ways to fillet long fish like *unagi* (freshwater eel) and *anago* (conger eel): Kanto style and Kansai style. These methods date to the feudal era, when the Kanto region (now Tokyo) had a large population of samurai, warriors who served

the shogun, the most powerful of the warlords. In busy, commercial Kansai, the imperial capital (now the region of Kyoto and Osaka), cooks would begin to fillet the long, swordlike freshwater eel by cutting open its belly. For the people of Kanto,

however, this looked too much like *harakiri,* the ritual suicide practiced by the samurai. So Kanto cooks learned to fillet *unagi* by cutting open the fish's back. These two styles of filleting persist among Japanese cooks to this day.

you do, the white flesh will have a faintly pink tinge and an especially sweet, rich flavor.

Both live and frozen yellowtail are imported to the United States from Japan. Also available in the United States are wild *buri* caught off the Pacific coast of North America and farmed *hamachi* from the Gulf of Mexico.

Hirame, *Olive Flounder, and* Karei, *Marbled Sole.* Flatfish come in many varieties, but the two most popular at sushi restaurants are *hirame* and *mako-garei* (or *karei,* as it is known at sushi restaurants). Next to *tai* (sea bream), *hirame* is the most treasured of white-fleshed sushi fish, because of its delicate, mellow flavor and exceptionally lean meat. *Hirame* tastes best from October through February. The texture can vary from resilient to soft, depending on when the fish is served, either before rigor mortis or toward the end of this natural process.

Hirame live on the seafloor, usually 200 to 400 feet below the surface, in every part of Japan's coastal waters and in all the world's oceans. To fool the fish's predators, the skin of its top side changes in color and pattern to match the surrounding seafloor; the underside of the fish remains snow-white, with dark spots if the fish is a farmed one. Out of the water, the upper side of *hirame* is a dark grayish brown.

Farmed and wild flounder are imported to the continental United States from Japan, Korea, and Hawaii. The output of the *hirame*-farming industry far exceeds the wild catch, but farmed *hirame* has an oiliness that masks its delicate flavor.

Since *hirame*'s season is winter, a sushi chef committed to serving seasonal fish must find a substitute in summer. Nature gives him or her *mako-garei,* the marbled sole from the waters of Japan, China, and North America. In summer, this fish has a flavor and texture similar to that of *hirame* in winter. Another warm-season substitute for *hirame* is a flounder known as fluke, which is caught wild off the eastern coast of the United States.

Ma-iwashi, *Japanese Sardine.* The only sardine species used in the sushi kitchen, this oily, flavorful fish grows to 7 to 8 inches and tastes best from June through autumn. Sardines are extremely perishable, so only those that have been properly slaughtered (*ike-jime*) are used for sushi or *sashimi.*

In the past, *ma-iwashi* was always served lightly cured with salt and vinegar, to prolong the quality, firm the tender meat, and cut its oiliness, and at some restaurants, the fish is still served this way. For raw *ma-iwashi,* grated ginger, not *wasabi,* is the proper accompaniment, to balance the strong flavor and oiliness and to refresh the palate.

Although *ma-iwashi* are caught along both the Pacific and Atlantic coasts of North America, the ones served at sushi restaurants nearly always come from Japan.

Kampachi, *Great Amberjack or Rudderfish.* If you like *buri* and *hamachi, kampachi* is another fish you should try. It looks much like its relative yellowtail and is similarly flavorful but less fatty.

Kampachi swim in the warm currents off Japan, Korea, China, and Hawaii. These fish grow to twice the size of yellowtail, more than 6 feet long. A two- to three-year-old fish, about 20 inches, is the most flavorful.

Wild *kampachi* has always been relatively rare and therefore expensive in Japan, but after World War II, farmed *kampachi* became affordable and popular. Wild *kampachi* tastes best in summer, when its fattier cousin the yellowtail is out of season. Farmed *kampachi* is available year-round, but it tastes a little greasy and less appealing.

After filleting a *kampachi,* a sushi chef cooks the meaty head, the collarbones, and the meaty tail parts in water flavored with *sake, shoyu, mirin, daikon,*

Yellowtail

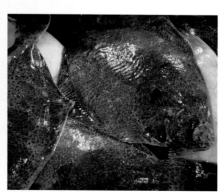

Flounder

Sardine

Flatfish Right and Left

Hirame no engawa "The Flounder's Tasty Edge"

I had my first introduction to flatfish during an elementary school field trip to a local fish market, where fishermen displayed several fish on the water-splashed concrete floor. All the fish eyes faced up; all the bellies faced us children. We giggled and shouted at what we saw: some of the fish had their faces on the left side, the others on the right. Our teacher explained, "The fish with their heads on the left side belong to the *hirame* family, and the fish with their heads on the right belong to the *karei* family. Both are delicious, but they taste different. Find out at home." I later learned that God loves to make exceptions and does so frequently with flatfish; some flounder have eyes on the right, and some sole have eyes on the left. But when I started preparing flatfish myself, this tip from my early school days, buried deep in memory, sprang suddenly to mind.

Voracious species, *hirame* and *karei* lie still in the sand beneath the sea except when they make sudden, quick movements with their fins and tails to chase and catch small prey. The well-exercised fin muscle, *engawa* (edge), develops more fat, flavor, and resilience than the rest of the flesh. If the chef hasn't reserved them for his or her regulars, the four *engawa* strips of a filleted flatfish are quickly snatched by connoisseurs at sushi restaurants.

and ginger. Nothing goes to waste, and the delicious side dish, called *ara-ni,* is a real fish lover's delight.

Wild and cultured *kampachi* is imported to the United States from Japan, Korea, and China.

Katsuo, *Skipjack Tuna.* A member of the mackerel family, *katsuo* migrates along the warm current, Kuroshio, up and down the Japanese coast. With a plump body, *katsuo* has (like tuna, another member of this family) a back fin that retracts for high-speed swimming. This fish usually swims about 20 miles per hour, but when faced with danger, it can speed up to 60 miles per hour. Because *katsuo*'s muscles are rich in oxygen-storing myoglobin, the flesh is deep red and rich in iron, and it has a pleasant metallic flavor. The meat also has a high level of vitamin D.

The Japanese enjoy *katsuo* for several months of the year. Young fish on their northward migration are noted for their lean, mild flavor. Adult fish caught on the southward migration, after swimming in the nutrient-rich, cold waters of the north, have a rich, robust flavor. The price of *katsuo* fluctuates dramatically during these months according to consumers' preferences—for low-fat or high-fat, mild or strong-flavored *katsuo.*

Like other oily fish, *katsuo* is quite perishable, and its deep red meat turns brown quickly. For sushi or *sashimi,* it must be handled swiftly by a well-trained chef, who treats it with the *yakishimo* method—briefly grilling the fillets, with skin attached, close to a flame, and then plunging them into ice-cold water. The skin gets crunchy, smoky, and caramelized, and the combi-nation of still-raw meat and crunchy skin is delicious. For *sashimi—katsuo no tataki*—the sliced fish is served with ginger, garlic, chives, and *ponzu* (sauce made with the juice of *yuzu,* an acidic citrus fruit; see page 78). *Katsuo nigiri-zushi* is always served with ginger, not *wasabi,* and *asatsuki* chives.

In the United States, *katsuo* for sushi comes mainly from Japan and Hawaii and is usually frozen. In the New York area, locally caught *katsuo* is available fresh for a week or two in July.

Great amberjack

Skipjack tuna

Kohada, *Japanese Gizzard Shad.*
This humble-looking member of the herring family, 4 to 5 inches long, is covered with scales like a sardine. Since the birth of *nigiri-zushi, kohada* has been cured with salt and vinegar to sharpen its flavor and firm its texture. Mastering the curing method takes years of practice. How much salt to use, how long to cure the fish in salt, how much vinegar to use, and how long to pickle the fish in vinegar all depend on the size of the fish, its fat content, and the temperature of the kitchen. Properly cured fish is a mark of the sushi chef's skill.

Kohada tastes best from November through February. *Kohada* for sushi is imported to the United States from Japan.

Ma-dai, *Red Sea Bream.* Often called simply *tai,* sea bream, this lean, delicate-flavored species of Pacific waters is one of the most highly praised of white-fleshed sushi fish. With its pink body dotted with shiny blue and what looks like a stroke of fluorescent blue paint over each big eye, a *ma-dai* moves gracefully through the water, displaying greenish and yellowish fluorescent colors on its dorsal fin, reminding me of

Japanese gizzard shad

a woman dressed up and wearing bright blue eye shadow. This fish's amusing appearance, however, is no indication of its personality. With its powerful molars, the *ma-dai* crushes and grinds shrimp, clams, squid, and other small creatures.

For sushi, a 4-pound *ma-dai* is best. Removing the big, thick scales is difficult and messy; I recommend putting the fish into a large, clear plastic bag before scaling it. You can remove the skin, which is too tough to eat raw. If you prefer to keep it, for its lovely pink color, its chewy texture, and the tasty fat beneath, tenderize the skin by the *shimofuri* technique (see page 194). When filleting *ma-dai,* take care not to cut yourself on the sharp dorsal fin.

Sea bream

Today more than 80 percent of the sea bream consumed in Japan is farmed. Cultivated *ma-dai* is more fatty and less flavorful than the wild variety. *Ma-dai* imported to the United States, most of it farmed, comes from Japan and New Zealand.

Maguro, *Tuna.* This fish has been eaten in Japan since ancient times, but until the nineteenth century, it was little appreciated. Then, for some reason, its red meat, cured in *shoyu* (soy sauce), gained favor in Edo as a *nigiri-zushi* topping. Only in the mid-1950s did the Japanese begin to enjoy tuna's fatty muscle meat, *toro,* which is now much in demand by sushi consumers.

Katsuo Is Worth More Than My Wife

During the Edo period (1600 to 1868), the one million citizens of the shogunate capital went crazy every April, when young *katsuo* on their northward migration passed close to Edo. People from every walk of life competed, sometimes spending all that they had, for a taste of the first

katsuo catch. *Haiku* poems of the period depict this passion: *Me ni aoba / yama hototogisu / hatsu-gatsuo* (Lush young green leaves on the trees and the charming voice of little cuckoos in the mountain suggest the long-awaited arrival of this year's first catch of *katsuo*). *Nyobo o /*

shichini iretemo / hatsu-gatsuo (Do not miss the chance to savor the first catch of *katsuo,* even if you need to pawn your wife). Every April, the people of Tokyo still rush to markets and sushi bars for a taste of the first *katsuo* catch.

At American sushi restaurants, four different tuna varieties make their appearance, according to the season and the status of the restaurant: *kuro maguro* (bluefin tuna), *mebachi maguro* (bigeye tuna), *kihada maguro* (yellowfin tuna), and *bin'naga maguro* (albacore). Among these, yellowfin tuna is the most popular, since its flavor is milder and its muscle meat doesn't darken as quickly as does that of bluefin or bigeye. Albacore, sometimes called white tuna, is not a traditional sushi fish but has become popular in *nigiri-zushi* and spicy tuna rolls.

Tuna thrives in both warm and cool waters of the Northern and Southern Hemispheres, including the warm water surrounding the equator. With a plump body streamlined for fast swimming, and built-in pockets for retracting the dorsal and pectoral fins, tuna can maintain a speed of 56 miles per hour for days without rest, just by moving its tail. This fish migrates over enormous distances; for example, a tuna hatched near Taiwan will migrate to Japan, and on the way back, it may decide to make an excursion across the entire Pacific to Baja California. If the tuna isn't caught off the coast of Baja, it will migrate back to Japanese waters. A tuna may conquer all of the world's oceans during its lifetime, which lasts as long as thirty-five years in some species.

One tuna can spawn an astronomical number of eggs—about nine to ten million, in the case of the bluefin. Each egg is as tiny as a cod egg or *tobik-ko,* flying fish roe. The eggs are contained in a very thin-skinned bag that measures up to 16 inches long and weighs up to 5 pounds.

Because it has a slightly higher body temperature than other species of fish, a tuna must not be allowed to struggle much when caught. A long struggle

Tuna

would cause its body temperature to rise enough to denature the protein in its flesh and to increase the secretion of lactic acid, both of which would harm the quality of the flesh. The fish must be killed immediately, gutted, bled, cleaned, and cooled, and if the journey back to port is long, it must be frozen at a very low temperature. If the fishermen take all these measures to protect the fish's quality, it may fetch several tens of thousands of dollars when it reaches the market. The perfectly delicious tuna you may savor by the slice at a sushi restaurant has come a long way and passed through numerous caring hands.

Tuna farming is now practiced in many places, particularly the Mediterranean countries and Australia. This business is controversial, since it may be depleting stocks of mature wild tuna. The farmed fish are not raised from eggs but caught young in the wild, penned, and fattened on a diet of sardines, anchovies, and other fish for three to six months. Unable to swim long distances, the fish develop a lot of fat, or *toro.* The international demand for fatty sushi tuna is fueling this extremely profitable business. Personally, I prefer wild tuna.

Saba, *Mackerel.* A very active migratory fish caught in many of the world's waters, spindle-shaped *saba* grows to

about 20 inches and has a shiny blue back crossed with black stripes. Mackerel tastes best during the cold months, when its body bulks up to 20 percent fat by weight—about the same percentage as in some tuna *toro.* Because of mackerel's high concentration of histidine, one of the amino acids, some people are allergic to this fish, so sample just a little the first time. *Saba* also has gut enzymes that vigorously attack the muscles after death, causing the meat to degrade. Therefore, to use mackerel in sushi, you must find *absolutely* fresh fish that has been properly slaughtered, stored, and handled.

Saba was a popular sushi fish even before the creation of *nigiri-zushi.* The fish was cured with salt and then packed with cooked rice for several months to make *saba-zushi,* pressed mackerel sushi (see page 129).

For *nigiri-zushi, saba* is briefly cured with salt and vinegar to mellow the robust flavor of the fish and to cut its oiliness. As with similar fish, the way *saba* is cured displays the sushi chef's skill and taste; the sweetness and oiliness of the fish must be balanced with just enough salt and acid. Personally, I like *saba* lightly cured, so I can enjoy a

Mackerel

firm, vinegary outer layer along with a "rare," tender red interior.

In the United States, mackerel comes *ike-jime*-killed from Japan, farmed and frozen from Norway and Denmark, and wild and fresh from New England and Canada. If you can buy a really fresh mackerel from a Japanese fishmonger (tell him or her what you want it for), cure it yourself as described on page 188. The process is very simple, and the result is delicious!

Shima-aji, *Striped Jack.* Each year, I can hardly wait for summer to come so I can taste this fish, which is available at sushi restaurants both in Japan and in America. A South Pacific relative of *aji* (horse mackerel), *shima-aji* has a wide, flat body and grows as long as 2 feet. With an attractive yellow stripe (*shima,* brushstroke) running from the gills to the tail, this fish is beautiful to watch swimming in a school. It is a meaty fish with faintly pink flesh and a mellow, sweet flavor, much like that of *hamachi* (yellowtail) or *kampachi* (great amber-jack) but even better tasting, or so most Japanese believe.

Shima-aji first appeared in the sushi kitchen after World War II. Since the catch has always been small, the price has always been high. Farmed fish are available today, but they are too oily and

Striped jack

Tuna Species

Kuro maguro, **Bluefin Tuna.** This fish has a rich metallic flavor and deep red flesh that is slightly firmer than bigeye tuna. *Kuro maguro* is famous for its delicious fatty meat, *toro.* It is caught during the winter months in Japan, from late spring through early summer in the Mediter-ranean, and from July through September in the waters of eastern Canada and New England. The biggest bluefin ever caught—it weighed 1,300 pounds—was taken off the eastern coast of Canada.

Equally valuable is a southern cousin of the bluefin, *minami maguro,* which thrives in the waters of Australia, New Zealand, and South Africa. Weighing about 200 pounds, *minami maguro* is caught from October through November and from February through March. It also packs a good portion of *toro* on its belly and back.

Mebachi maguro, **Bigeye Tuna.** As its English and Japanese names suggest, this fish has quite large eyes, *me.* It swims in equatorial waters, migrating between latitudes 20 degrees north and 20 degrees south. Also red-fleshed, bigeye is generally a second choice to bluefin, which has a firmer texture and a milder flavor. *Mebachi* has an advantage, though, in that its color is slower to oxidize, so in Japan, this fish was once used for takeout *nigiri-zushi,* delivered from the restaurant by bicycle. In Japan, bigeye is caught in spring.

Kihada maguro, **Yellowfin Tuna.** The most frequently used tuna in American sushi restaurants, this fish is sold by fish-mongers and supermarkets as "sushi-grade" tuna. Yellowfin is firm in texture and milder in flavor than bluefin and bigeye, and the pinkish red color is quite stable when the flesh is exposed to air. Because of these characteristics, yellow-fin is favored in Japan mainly for *sashimi.*

Yellowfin primarily are equatorial species, but some of the fish swim to the waters of southeastern Japan and may be caught there in summer. Yellowfin is also caught in the waters of Hawaii, Mexico, Florida, the northeastern United States, and Bermuda.

Bin'naga maguro, **Albacore Tuna.** The favored tuna for canning, albacore is a smaller species; it grows to only about 90 pounds. Its meat, white with a tinge of pink, is very smooth, tender, and pleasantly fatty. Until recently, albacore was considered too white and too tender for Japanese sushi, but now chain sushi restaurants across Japan feature this cheaper tuna, and *bin-toro,* fatty albacore, is a regular item in both American and Japanese sushi restau-rants. Demand for *bin'naga maguro* has been so high lately that this once cheapest tuna is getting expensive.

lacking in flavor, so sushi chefs in Japan prefer pole-and-line-caught wild *shima-aji,* weighing about 5 pounds each. *Shima-aji* in American sushi restaurants tend to be farmed ones from Japan, but wild fish are occasionally flown in from New Zealand, Australia, and Hawaii.

Sayori, *Halfbeak*. I first encountered this fish not in a sushi restaurant but in a fish market in Japan. I saw a small, slender, silvery fish with a long "beak"—the lower jaw stretched three to four times longer than the upper one. The tip of the beak was tinted deep red—an indication, I later learned, of a very fresh fish.

Halfbeak

The snow-white flesh of the *sayori* has a lean, delicate flavor. Since the flesh deteriorates very quickly, the fish must be handled swiftly and efficiently. Traditionally, *sayori* is lightly cured with either salt and vinegar or salt alone. Some sushi chefs roll the delicately flavored skin around a bamboo skewer and grill it, to make a smoky, crunchy, delicious *sayori*-skin lollipop.

Sayori inhabit the western Pacific waters from Sakhalin Island in the north to Taiwan in the south, and their season is early spring. Because the fish is both expensive and laborious to prepare, it reaches the United States only in small numbers.

Fresh or Frozen?

Until recently, most fish was caught locally and sold alive or freshly killed to locals; fish caught far from port was preserved with salt. As ships got larger, and as storage, cooling, and freezing systems advanced, fishermen began sailing farther out to sea and freezing the fish before bringing it home. Fresh fish, if properly handled and quickly brought to the consumer, is far better than any frozen fish. But when fish must be transported a long distance, it may keep its quality better frozen than not.

Most important in proper freezing is the temperature. Until recently, fish intended for raw consumption was frozen at –4° F for a maximum of seven days. This treatment killed parasites and some bacteria that cause spoilage (although other bacteria only become dormant at this temperature), but the treatment also promoted the formation of large ice crystals that damaged muscle tissue. Today most fish is flash-frozen at the much lower

temperature of –31° F. This allows the fish to pass quickly through the critical temperature range at which damaging ice crystals can form, from 30° to 23° F.

Tuna is frozen at an even lower temperature, –50° or even –75° F. At a temperature higher than –50°, the myoglobin in the fish slowly oxidizes, causing the flesh to change from red to brown. The very low freezing temperature can keep tuna as good as fresh for nearly two years.

Even at very low freezing temperatures, not all bacteria are killed. For this reason, fish intended for raw consumption must be hygienically gutted, bled, and cooled at its freshest stage; frozen immediately; and kept frozen at the proper temperature until it reaches the consumer. Then the fish must be thawed under refrigeration and consumed immediately.

Wicked *Sayori*

When the Japanese describe someone as "like a *sayori*," they don't mean that the person is slim, elegant, and handsome. Rather, they mean that he or she is malicious, evil-minded—a *hara-guroi,* or person with black insides. If you ever cut open the belly of a *sayori*, you will understand this expression, for lying against the snow-white belly flesh you will find inky-black entrails.

Suzuki, *Japanese Sea Bass Perch.*
This silver-gray fish more closely resembles the Mediterranean fish Italians call *branzino* than the fish New Yorkers call sea bass. *Suzuki* looks something like a trout, but its back slopes up in the shoulder area and then down to a face smaller than that of a trout. More than 2 feet long at maturity, *suzuki* is caught from early summer through August.

A very fresh slice of *suzuki* has a translucent appearance, firm texture, and subtle sweetness. Because it is extremely lean, the fish is well suited to summer dining. Sushi chefs use *suzuki* not only for *nigiri-zushi* but also for a *sashimi* dish called *arai,* rinsed in cold water. For this dish, very fresh slices of fish, firmed by immersion in ice-cold water, are presented on crushed ice along with a dipping sauce. In hot, humid weather, nothing is more refreshing than a dish of *arai.*

Suzuki is imported to the United States from Japan, Australia, and Spain. Both wild and farmed *suzuki* is available. Some sushi chefs substitute farmed striped bass for Japanese *suzuki.*

Sake, *Salmon.* With a Japanese name pronounced like that of the drink, this tender, oily fish has never been found in the waters near Tokyo, the city where *nigiri-zushi* was born. Salmon took its place in the sushi kitchen only recently, when sushi chefs in the United States started using it. Because of its association with America and modernity, salmon sushi quickly became popular in Japanese sushi restaurants.

Sushi salmon comes to U.S. markets from many waters. Wild king salmon comes from Alaska, and wild chum salmon from various Pacific Northwest waters. Less expensive, farmed Atlantic salmon comes from Maine, British Columbia, Washington, Norway, and Chile. Although salmon is often infested with parasitic worms that can sicken humans, the worms can be killed by freezing. Farmed salmon is generally considered parasite-free, but some experts say that to guarantee safety, all salmon should be frozen (see page 175) before it is eaten raw.

Sushi Clams

In old Edo, various kinds of clams were harvested in abundance from the shores of Edo Bay and cooked or cured for *nigiri-zushi.* Today eight clam varieties are commonly used for sushi, and all are served raw. Some of these varieties, native to the United States as well as Japan, have long been used in America for clam stews, chowders, and cakes.

Clams contain more water and less protein than fish. When properly prepared, all sushi clams have a rich flavor and pleasant bite. Enjoy clam sushi between courses of oily tuna belly, yellowtail, or vinegar-cured mackerel, and you'll appreciate the contrast in flavor and texture.

Clams purchased in the shell should be alive. To be sure they are, tap the shells lightly; they should close tight. Live clams must be opened, cleaned, and stored very carefully to prevent quick spoilage. Most clams sold in American sushi restaurants are locally harvested, but some varieties are imported from Japan.

Akagai, *Bloody Clam.* This species lives all along the Japanese coast, from south to north, and the *akagai* clams from Tokyo Bay are especially noted for their fine quality. Today many *akagai* are also imported to Japan from Korea. The harvest season for this clam is late autumn through early spring.

Akagai has a triangular shell about 4 inches wide and 3 inches high. Deeply grooved and dark brown, the shell makes this clam easy to distinguish from others. The foot of the *akagai* is bright orange, sweet, and pleasantly firm. When you order *akagai* sushi at a high-end sushi restaurant in Japan, the chef shucks a well-cleaned shell in front of you, and red liquid flows out. You may think the chef's hand is bleeding, but what you see is the clam's own hemoglobin-rich liquid, and it is hemoglobin that gives the foot meat its rich color. As you continue to watch, the chef removes the intestines, rinses the meat, cuts the clam in half butterfly fashion, and then slaps it down hard on the wooden chopping board. This last step creates a pleasant texture and allows the clam to display its freshness, by contracting when it hits the board. The chef will offer you not only the orange foot but also a long, thin strip of silky flesh, *himo,* that is connected to the gill. *Himo* is prized as a delicacy by sushi lovers.

Because this clam isn't indigenous to American waters, it must be imported, frozen, from Japan, Korea, or China. Strict testing requirements make *akagai* hard to find in the United States.

Clams

Aoyagi, *Hen Clam.* In Japan, this clam has a nickname—*bakagai,* "foolish clam." When the clam encounters danger, it tries to close its shell immediately, and sometimes it ends up biting its own foot. Ouch!

These triangular, smooth-shelled clams thrive in Maine and Canada as well as Japan, where the locals enjoy them in chowder and clam cakes. Best in winter and early spring, *aoyagi* are usually shucked upon harvest in Japan and sold without shells. Shelled Japanese *aoyagi* are also available in the United States. If you buy some, slap the clams with your fingertips; the muscles should retract if the clams are fresh. The feet are blanched a few seconds for sushi, both to clean them and to give them an attractive orange color. The still-raw flesh is tender and sweet, with a fragrance of seaweed. Even more appreciated than the *aoyagi*'s foot are the two tiny adductor muscles, *ko-bashira* ("clam pillars"), which are often used as sushi toppings.

Hokki-gai, *Surf Clam.* One of the sweetest and most delicious clams available at sushi restaurants during the cold months is *hokki-gai,* northern clam, so named because it comes from the cold waters of northern Japan. This clam is also native to the northeastern United States and Canada, where it is one of the most important commercial clam species, adored for chowder and other preparations.

A member of the same family as *aoyagi, hokki-gai* grows much larger, up to 6 inches across. When you open the shell, you find beautiful, dark purplish foot meat. In Japan, the foot meat is removed at harvest and blanched to a reddish pink before being sold for sushi. You may find shelled and blanched *hokki-gai* at large Japanese supermarkets in the United States.

Hotate-gai, *Scallop.* The part of the scallop we usually eat is the adductor, the powerful muscle that opens and closes the shell. The scallop doesn't dig and bury itself in the sand or mud as other clams do; instead, it uses its adductor muscle to eat, to swim by jet propulsion, and to protect itself. For this

Women's Work: Abalone Diving

Thriving in water as deep as 60 feet, *awabi* has traditionally been harvested in Japan by female divers, *ama.* Wearing no diving equipment, they dive and swim as far as 30 feet below the surface, hunt for abalones among the rocks and seaweed, and emerge from the water after as long as ninety seconds with several valuable abalones each. Legend has it that women worked as divers to support their families while their husbands were fishing out at sea for long periods. Women make better divers than men, it is said, because they store more fat under the skin and can therefore stay in cold water longer. Though hard, the work of the *ama* was respected and well paid. Today *ama* are few, both because women can find even better paying jobs and because the numbers of wild abalones have declined.

The Spy Who Studied the Clam

The Siebold abalone is named for Philipp Franz von Siebold, a German native born in the late eighteenth century. After studying in the Netherlands, he worked as a doctor in Japan before the country was opened to the West. Besides introducing Western medicine and technology to Japan, Siebold cataloged Japanese flora and fauna, including the *megai* abalone. On leaving Japan, he did a forbidden thing: he tried to take a map of the country with him. Japanese officials, who searched his possessions, discovered the map. Siebold was arrested and expelled as a spy. Today Siebold's former house in Leiden is home to the Siebold Huis Museum, which houses the wonderful collection of Japanese artifacts that Siebold gathered during his years in Japan.

Texture Terms in Japanese

The Japanese appreciate so many different textures in foods that a whole vocabulary has developed to describe each sensation. Some of the terms are delightfully onomatopoeic; they give an aural description of what your mouth and ears sense. Here is a sampling of Japanese texture terms.

yawarakai	tender
katai	firm
saku saku	crispy like deep-fried foods
shaki shaki	crisp like raw vegetables
pari pari	crispy like rice crackers
tsuru tsuru	slippery
neba neba	slimy
kori kori	firm and resistant, but then giving way, like cartilage and the strip of *akagai* called *himo*
danryoku ga aru	resilient
nameraka	creamy like custard or silky tofu
boso boso	crumbly like corn bread
fuwa fuwa	the texture of cotton candy or whipped egg white
fuk-kura	tender like moist steamed rice or sponge cake
kochi kochi	hard like well-frozen ice cream
neto neto	sticky like peanut butter
nettori	moist, heavy, and sticky like honey
shiko shiko	al dente, firm like cooked Japanese noodles or rice cakes

Gaper clam

reason, its adductor grows very meaty and strong.

If you can get scallops in the shell, select those that close immediately at your touch. They should resist strongly when you open them. After you remove each adductor muscle, try to save the thin, silky string of flesh, *himo,* that surrounds the muscle meat; this *himo* is even better than *akagai*'s as sushi or *sashimi.*

Although wild scallops have become rare in Japan because of overfishing, they are harvested in Maine and Massachusetts from autumn through winter. Most scallops served at sushi restaurants are farmed ones from Japan.

Miru-gai, *Gaper Clam.* An oval clam about 8 inches long, the gaper has a siphon so long that it cannot be fully retracted into the shell; this gives the creature an amusingly grotesque appearance. Burying itself in the sand as deep as 3 feet below the seafloor, *miru-gai* stretches its long siphon up and out of the sand to search for food. The gaper gets its Japanese name from *miru* seaweed, which covers the seabed wherever the clam lives and conceals the top of each siphon.

The gaper—or its siphon, the part we eat—has the sweetest, richest flavor and meatiest texture among clams. Check the freshness by pulling on the siphon; it should feel firm and resilient.

Japanese cockle

thinner, less meaty flesh than other clams, but its flavor is sweet and its fragrance distinctive. *Tori-gai* used in the United States is imported.

Awabi, *Abalone.* During the heat of summer—abalone season—my mother often used this large clam in *mizu-gai,* a *sashimi* dish of fresh-shucked, cubed abalone served with cucumber cubes and wedges of small tomatoes in individual bowls with cold water and ice cubes. This special treat cooled our bodies more effectively than our family's electric fan.

In Japan, two *awabi* varieties are used in the sushi kitchen. For eating raw, we use *kuro awabi,* disk abalone, whose strong, dark green muscle meat enables it to move as far as 160 feet in a single night. For cooking, we use *megai,* Siebold's abalone, whose meat is lighter in color and more tender than that of *kuro awabi.* For the best flavor and texture, we simmer *megai* in *sake* broth for several hours before slicing it for sushi or eating on its own.

In American markets and sushi restaurants, wild *awabi* comes fresh or frozen from Japan. A variety farmed in California, *nagareko,* is available fresh in April and May.

Sushi Shellfish and Other Sushi Seafood

Ebi, *Prawn and Shrimp.* Eight pounds—that's the amount of prawns and shrimp the average Japanese eats each year. *Ebi* appears in sushi, *sashimi, tempura,* quenelles, dumplings, stuffings, and numerous simmered, grilled, stir-fried, and steamed dishes.

***Kuruma* prawn**

More than three thousand varieties of shrimp and prawn swim in the world's waters. Here I describe three sushi favorites.

Kuruma-ebi, Kuruma *Prawn.* With its head on, this prawn is about 6 inches long and has charming large black eyes. When you see *kuruma* prawn alive in the water, the shell looks semicrystalline and transparent, with a brown brushstroke across each section. The prawn bends and curls like a cart wheel, *kuruma.* The raw meat is almost transparent, with a pleasantly resilient texture and a melting, sweet flavor.

Kuruma-ebi thrives in the waters of Japan, Korea, Southeast Asia, and the Indian Ocean. The season is from summer through autumn, but connoisseurs claim that the best prawns are harvested in late autumn. *Kuruma-ebi* is generally unavailable in the United States, where good, less expensive substitutes are also available: black tiger prawn from Southeast Asia and white tiger prawn from South America and Mexico. Both of these can be found fresh or frozen in U.S. markets.

Because they are very perishable, *kuruma* prawns were always served cooked in the past, but today they are also served raw in Japan. Only live prawns, sold swimming in water, are suitable for raw consumption. Unfortu-

Miru-gai's season begins in October and ends in February. During these months, the clam is caught in Japanese inlets from the main island of Honshu to the southern island of Kyushu. In American markets and sushi restaurants, fresh gapers come from Alaska, the Pacific Northwest, and Baja California.

Tori-gai, *Japanese Cockle.* If your sushi chef gives you a small bicolored clam—half white and half velvety, dark purple—this is *tori-gai,* "bird clam." It is said that *tori-gai* is so named because its foot resembles the beak or legs of a bird, *tori,* but you may need to use your imagination to concede this. When I see *tori-gai* sitting on top of a *nigiri-zushi* rice ball, the clam's shape and colors remind me of a black bird with a long white tail stretching down from the top of the rice ball.

The *tori-gai* sold in Japan for sushi is already shucked from its grooved shell, which resembles that of the *akagai.* We choose clams with meat that is thick, firm, and resilient and an intense purple color—all qualities that indicate freshness. The clam is blanched before it is used for sushi, and this brightens the purple color. You must handle *tori-gai* delicately to avoid rubbing away the color.

Harvested from the waters of Honshu, Kyushu, Korea, and China, *tori-gai* has

Northern shrimp

Humpback shrimp

Common flying squid

nately, live prawns are so far unavailable in the United States. Prawns that are not alive at purchase should be used only for cooking.

Choose fresh prawns that are plump, resilient to the touch, and encased in semitransparent, wet shells. If the prawns still have their heads, avoid any that are blackened or loosely attached to the body.

Ama-ebi, *Northern or Pink Shrimp.* This large-headed, small, very red shrimp has been used in the sushi kitchen for only about twenty years. *Ama-ebi* got its name because it is intensely sweet, *amai.* It is always served raw, with or without its eggs.

The shrimp carries its dark green-blue eggs, as tiny as *tobik-ko* (flying fish roe), on its belly for one year. Because all the *ama-ebi* I have eaten carried eggs, I once wondered where all the males were. In fact, every *ama-ebi* is male for two to three years, and then it begins to change into a female. After two to three more years, it is a large female, about 4½ inches long. Only the large females are caught.

This shrimp lives in the cold waters of the northern Pacific and northern Atlantic. *Ama-ebi* in markets and sushi restaurants comes mostly from Russia, Alaska, and Maine, although some are caught in Japanese waters. The season

for this shrimp is winter, but frozen *ama-ebi,* which dominates the world market, is available year-round. Keep thawed *ama-ebi* in the refrigerator no longer than two days.

Botan-ebi, *Humpback Shrimp.* A cousin to *ama-ebi,* this plump, meaty shrimp has a very similar flavor and texture but grows larger, to about 8 inches long. Another sex changer, *botan-ebi* is often eaten with its eggs, which are slightly larger than those of *ama-ebi.* I don't know why this shrimp is named for the peony, *botan;* perhaps it is because when *botan-ebi* is shelled and butterflied, the surface of its flesh displays a beautiful wavy, petal-like appearance. Sushi chefs often serve the head deep-fried—a delicious treat—following a dish of *botan-ebi nigiri-zushi.*

In Japan, *botan-ebi* is caught in winter off Hokkaido and northern Honshu. Because the catch is small, *botan-ebi* is one of the most expensive sushi ingredients. In North America, *botan-ebi* is harvested off California, Alaska, and Canada.

Ika, *Squid.* This is one of those foods that the Japanese enjoy more for its texture than its flavor. There are several species of sushi squid, with slight differences in texture. No matter the species,

squid that are properly selected, handled, and prepared are tender with a slight resilience. If you have been served rubbery squid, try a different restaurant.

We appreciate squid for its flavor and appearance, too. The various species differ subtly but distinctively in flavor. All of them have snow-white, smooth surfaces that look lovely combined with other sushi toppings such as red tuna, pink prawns, caramel conger eel, yellow sea urchin, faintly pink yellowtail, and silver-blue mackerel.

Squid just out of the water has a glossy, dark brown color that rapidly fades to dull brown. Make sure squid is alive or freshly killed by flicking your finger against its body; the pattern or color of the skin should change. Check also that the body is plump and resilient.

Inside the body is a plump intestine. In Japan, we use this intestine, very fresh, in *shio-kara,* a dish of cut-up squid meat fermented in the salted intestine. Many sushi restaurants offer this salty, fishy, *kori kori* (firm and resilient) dish, though it may not be on the menu. Ask for *shio-kara* and enjoy it with *sake.*

Here are three varieties of squid that are sushi kitchen staples.

Surume-ika, *Japanese Common Flying Squid.* About a foot long, *surume-ika* is the best-known squid in the world. Its head, in the center of its

Big-fin reef squid

body, is marked by large, shiny, protruding black eyes. As the squid swims in the water, the petal-like pattern on its body spark-les and shines like stars. When night falls, the squid swims closer to the surface of the water, and that is when *surume-ika* is caught, in summer and autumn, by huge fleets of fishing boats in the Sea of Japan. Each small boat carries between its masts a line of powerful lights, to which the squid is attracted like a moth.

In the past, squid for sushi was always cooked, but today it is served raw. In one popular *sashimi* dish, *surume-ika* is cut into noodlelike strips and served with grated ginger and *shoyu,* soy sauce. Because this dish reminds us of cold *somen* noodles, we call it *ika somen sashimi.*

Most *surume* squid used in American sushi kitchens comes, fresh or frozen, from Japan. Another squid, *yari-ika* (spear squid), which very much resembles *surume-ika,* is caught in the northern waters of the East Coast of the United States and appears in local sushi restaurants.

Aori-ika, *Big-Fin Reef Squid.* A warm-water relative of *surume-ika,* this squid grows larger, to a length of about 16 inches and a weight of 3 to 4 pounds. Instead of a transparent, thin, and flexible "quill" like that of *surume-ika,*

aori-ika's is chalk-white, brittle, wide, and easy to remove. *Aori-ika* is known as the meatiest, sweetest, and best squid for sushi, and since the catch is small, it is an expensive summertime delicacy. In addition to the body, the plump tentacles are used.

Fresh and frozen *aori-ika* for sushi is imported to the United States from Japan and Australia. Japanese *aori-ika* is said to be sweeter and meatier.

Sumi-ika *or* Ko-ika, *Golden Cuttlefish.* Resembling *aori-ika,* this squid has thicker flesh and a different body structure. The central bone is large and white like *aori-ika*'s but rigidly calcified in the squid's plump, round body. To remove the bone, make a long, straight cut from the top to the bottom of the body. Hold the squid with its head and tentacles up, and push down the body until the bone slips out.

The shell-like bone is the source of the name *ko-ika,* "shell squid." The cuttlefish's other name, *sumi-ika,* "char-coal squid," refers to the copious black ink that this creature squirts for defense and camouflage.

For sushi, *sumi-ika* is cut and flattened into a single wide sheet, and then the skin is peeled from both surfaces. To check the freshness of the squid, rub its peeled, cleaned surface. If it is smooth,

(continued on page 182)

Telling a Prawn from a Shrimp

Whereas a prawn's shells overlap slightly from the front to the tail, a shrimp's middle shell overlaps both the front shell and the back one. A female shrimp carries fertilized eggs on her body for a long period (see page 180), but a female prawn sheds her eggs in the water immediately after fertilization. These differences, however, aren't generally known among those who speak English, many of whom call any large shrimp prawns. The Japanese avoid confusion by using one term for both.

A Squid Flask

If you wander around the dried-fish stores in any large food market in Japan, you will spot among the many kinds of fish and seaweed a shriveled, brown flasklike container, its neck squeezed to a narrow opening. Made from *surume* squid, this is a flask for warming *sake* while infusing it with the flavor of squid. *Sake* from a *surume* flask was a special winter treat in the past, though whether this drink is exceptionally delicious or just fishy is up to you to decide. With changes in lifestyles and improvements in the quality of *sake,* my guess is that this culinary tradition may come to an end very soon.

(continued from page 181)

the squid is fresh. If the surface feels rough, the squid is getting old.

Sumi-ika is caught in the waters of southern Japan, southern Korea, and northern Australia from late autumn through winter. It is imported fresh from Japan and Australia to the United States. Like *aori-ika,* *sumi-ika* is an expensive sushi topping.

Ikura, *Salmon Roe.* I was surprised to learn that the word *ikura* is not Japanese. It was borrowed at the beginning of the twentieth century from the Russian *ikra,* meaning "fish roe." In Japan, the best sushi salmon roe is said to come from fish that swim offshore from September through October on their journey back to their home rivers for spawning. At this stage, the roe has a thin and tender skin; when pickled in brine or marinade, it has the perfect bite. Some sushi chefs, however, like to cure more mature roe, with slightly thicker and more durable skin.

Bouncing Salmon Roe

Ken Tominaga, sushi chef at Hana Japanese Restaurant in Sonoma County, California, likes to cure roe when it is more mature than usual—so mature, in fact, that I saw one of his salmon eggs bounce like a rubber ball on the wooden sushi counter. Mr. Tominaga has a good supply of wild roe from nearby Bodega Bay and other Northern California waters, as well as Washington and Canada. Marinated overnight in *sake* and *shoyu,* his roe look like shiny orange pearls. Biting into the firmer skin of such roe was a novel experience for me; after a bit of resistance, the skins broke and juice splashed inside my mouth. No wonder these eggs could bounce!

Pickled salmon roe from Japan is available in Japanese markets. I have also used salmon roe that is salt-pickled in the United States; it is sold in small glass jars at supermarkets and fish stores. But the American roe is saltier than the Japanese, and usually the eggs are partially crushed. When choosing American salmon roe, avoid eggs that have broken skins and have lost their plumpness.

At sushi restaurants, *ikura* is always served *gunkan* (battleship) style (see page 211).

Tako, *Octopus.* True lovers of octopus are still limited to the Japanese, Mexicans, Italians, Spanish, Portuguese, and Greeks. Among these, the Japanese are said to consume two-thirds of the world's catch.

If you have eaten a slice of rubbery, cold octopus with no distinctive flavor or fragrance, I am sure you did not like it, and I don't blame you. But octopus

Octopus

properly cooked on the day it is served has completely different characteristics—a sweet flavor, a distinctive fragrance, and a tender texture with some bite.

In addition to being used in sushi and *sashimi,* octopus is cooked in a broth containing *mirin* (sweet cooking wine), sugar, and *shoyu* (soy sauce). It is a chef's pride to serve this dish, *tako no yawaraka-ni* (tender cooked octopus, page 226), along with sushi when octopus is in season, in summer and autumn.

The octopus used in the sushi kitchen is *ma-dako,* common octopus, which is caught in the warm waters off the coasts of Japan and Africa. At most sushi restaurants in the United States, most chefs use octopus that is imported, already cooked, from Japan.

Uni, *Sea Urchin.* Eaten in Japan since the eighth century, sea urchin became a sushi ingredient only after World War II. Good *uni,* mostly from Hokkaido, is expensive in Japan today. I developed my love for sea urchin as a child; its tonguelike shape, creamy texture, and

Sea urchin

sea-breeze fragrance captivated me. *Uni* does not travel well, so nothing compares to eating it fresh from local waters, as I did during my college years in Hokkaido at an early-morning fish market. The *uni* were lavishly heaped on top of lukewarm sushi rice in a bowl. The dish tasted so good.

Of the several varieties of sea urchins in the world, we use two in the sushi kitchen. Our favorite is the green sea urchin, *bafun uni* ("horse dung sea urchin"). It has short spikes on a deep greenish brown shell that grows to about 3 inches in diameter, and it gets its Japanese name from its dunglike appearance as it rests in groups in shallow water. This sea urchin's gonads— the parts we eat—have an intense orange color and a fragrance and strongly sweet flavor that are the best among sea urchins.

The other *uni* used for sushi is the purple sea urchin, which includes two Japanese species. *Kita murasaki uni,* northern purple sea urchin, comes from Hokkaido and northern Honshu. Its dark purple shell, covered with long spikes, grows to about 4 inches in diameter.

Before World War II and the raw-seafood craze that followed, fishermen hated this creature, because it ate up the kelp that they farmed. *Kita murasaki uni* has a yellow gonad whose flavor is considered a little inferior to that of *bafun uni.*

Murasaki uni, Japanese purple sea urchin, inhabits the waters of southern Japan. Its dark purple shell grows to only about 2 inches across, with strong spikes that are as long as the shell is wide. This *uni* has a very mild flavor.

All *uni* is delicious right out of the shell. Fresh *uni* is bright orange or yellow, firm and plump, and covered with tiny, grainy particles that quickly smooth out as *uni* ages. To keep shelled *uni* from getting soft and runny, most is treated at the factory with brine containing alum. Untreated *uni* is best, of course.

In the United States, green sea urchin comes from Maine, purple sea urchin from California. Although these can be of excellent quality, many sushi chefs buy the expensive Hokkaido *bafun-uni* because they believe it has a more intense, sweet flavor.

Faux Salmon Roe

According to Junji Watanabe, writing in the Japanese culinary magazine *Ryori Hyakka,* the making of artificial salmon roe came about in the early 1970s. A chemical company in Toyama Prefecture was trying to develop a two-component liquid glue that would be easy to use and wouldn't set before it could be applied. A chemist at the company was devising a tiny capsule to hold the glue when a colleague passing by commented, "That looks just like salmon roe—jumbo salmon roe!" This was not a surprising reaction, since seafood plays a major role in the culinary culture in Toyama Prefecture, famous for its salmon trout. Eager for an opportunity to diversify, the company wasted no time in developing faux salmon roe. Several other companies began devising their own versions, and soon machine-made faux salmon roe spread across the country. Advertised as being cholesterol-free, low in calories, shelf-stable, color-stable, hygienic, and inexpensive, faux salmon roe created a sensation among the *ikura*-crazed Japanese population.

With a skin made from alginic sodium extracted from seaweed, an inner liquid flavored with natural salmon oil extract, and an eye made of dyed vegetable oil, a faux salmon egg looks much like the real thing. If you have good taste buds, though, you can easily detect the unpleasant, chemical flavor of faux roe. Even just by looking, you can tell the difference: God's version has eggs of slightly different sizes, whereas the manufactured ones are all exactly the same size. If you drop an egg or two into hot water, the real roe will become whitish, like a boiled hen's egg, whereas the faux roe will remain clear.

Faux roe, labeled as such, is easy to find in Japanese markets. In inexpensive chain sushi restaurants, *ikura* is often the fake kind.

Chapter 11
Filleting and Basic Preparation Techniques for Sushi Fish and Shellfish

This chapter is devoted both to professionals and to amateur cooks who are eager to join in making sushi with raw seafood. You will learn about basic techniques for preparing fish and shellfish, including filleting, curing, blanching, cooking, and simmering. These techniques include those that I learned from sushi chef Suehiko Shimizu. According to him, "There is no absolutely unique and correct way to do all of these tasks." Each chef develops an individual style, learning from superiors and then passing on the knowledge to his or her juniors. It is a continuing cycle of training, experience, and instruction. If you are a sushi chef, you may find that some of the techniques I explain are different from what you have learned. But I believe it is always good to understand how different chefs accomplish the same objectives.

The varieties of fish described and the recipes chosen for this chapter certainly do not exhaust the possibilities for sushi and *sashimi.* I have concentrated primarily on methods that must be mastered by both Japanese and American sushi chefs. These techniques are often applicable to other fish and seafood, and I indicate when such substitutions are viable.

For amateur cooks, some of the varieties introduced here and fish of superb sushi quality may not yet be available at the retail level. Try the ones that are readily available—for example, tuna or a fish you may have caught. I believe that the widespread popularity of sushi will bring more varieties of sushi seafood to your neighborhood markets in the near future.

As you practice these techniques, remember that you are handling fish that is going to be consumed raw or nearly raw. If you plan to do this often, you may wish to purchase two new chopping boards, each for a different use—one for scaling, gutting, and filleting fish and the other (this one is required) for cutting fish into slices for sushi and *sashimi.* Try to work in a cool room and rinse the blood-tainted chopping board frequently with cold soapy water. Keep your fish refrigerated when it is not being handled.

If you have long fingernails, it is better to cut them short to prevent anything's being trapped under your nails. Before handling fish, remove your rings and wristwatch and thoroughly wash your hands and arms with soap. If you have any cuts or open sores on your hands, or you are coughing and/or sneezing, wait until you are well. The *Staphylococcus aureus* bacteria that you transmit can multiply under such conditions and produce toxins in the fish. Also, do not lick your hands or touch other parts of your body or a dirty counter while working.

Another bacterium related to raw-fish and raw-shellfish consumption is *Vibrio parahaemolyticus.* It thrives in salt water, particularly during the summer, but it is almost killed when fish is rinsed thoroughly with cold running tap water. So be sure to do so before scaling, gutting, and filleting.

Finally, work quickly, touching the fish and shellfish as little as possible. Sushi fish and shellfish require care and high standards of hygiene, but if you take these sanitary precautions, you have nothing to fear and only delicious sushi to anticipate.

Tuna
Maguro

I recommend that you purchase sushi tuna, *maguro,* from a Japanese fishmonger or an American fish market that carries sushi tuna, not "sushi-grade tuna" (see page 168). Sushi tuna is usually professionally cut into small rectangular blocks—for example, approximately 2½ inches × 5 inches × 1 inch—for slicing into strips for sushi or *sashimi.* The blocks are packed individually in a sealed Styrofoam container with a sell-by date, and the tuna sits atop a strip of paper that absorbs moisture coming from the fish. If the fish was frozen, it is packed in an airtight plastic bag. The entire cutting and packaging process is done under strict hygienic conditions. Before using such a piece of tuna, quickly and carefully rinse it under cold running tap water and wipe it dry with a paper towel. Do not overrinse, or you will wash away the good flavor of the fish.

These small blocks are made from a whole tuna that is filleted into four very large pieces—two back-side fillets and two belly-side fillets. Each fillet is then cut into three parts: *kami* (the upper section, which is the head end part), *naka* (the middle section), and *shimo* (the tail section). The sections that fetch the highest prices are the *kami* and *naka* sections of the belly fillets and back fillets because of the fatty, valuable *toro* in these cuts. The *shimo* sections, which yield the *akami,* red flesh tuna, are the least expensive. Each section is cut into large blocks and then into small sushi and *sashimi* blocks.

When you get a big chunk of tuna, here is how you cut. Following the illustrations, 1. slice off the thick top part to make an even layer 2½ inches high. 2. Then remove a 1-inch-thick block from the skin with a horizontal slice. The whole breaking process is designed to give you the grain with each slice. These are the white membranes between the muscle layers that run perpendicular to the short side of the block. If the slices are not cut across the grain, the meat would be difficult to chew.

Tuna is said to taste better when it ages somewhat. Seiji Nojiri, a professional tuna dealer at the Tsukiji Fish Market in Tokyo, told me that fresh, unfrozen tuna that weighs more than 400 pounds tastes better with three to four days of maturing after the catch. He cautioned me that this is not a generalization that can be applied to all similar-size fish. "Each tuna is different, like human beings. The health condition, fat content, conditions during the catch, killing, and transportation of the tuna become the decision-making factors for the length of aging. It is my job to figure this out and give a precise recommendation to my customers."

When *nigiri-zushi* first became popular in the nineteenth century, there was, of course, no refrigeration nor even enough ice available to preserve a large fish such as tuna after it was caught. So the technique of curing tuna, *zuke,* was developed. One story has it that when a sushi chef one day found his tuna a bit old, he quickly marinated it in *shoyu* (soy sauce) to mask any unpleasant flavor. He used this fish in his *nigiri-zushi* and sold it to the customers at a low price. It was a big hit. The customers loved the additional flavor and the firmed-up texture. *Shoyu,* which has a high sodium content, lactic acid, and other organic acids, as well as some alcohol from fermentation, acted as both a preservative and a sterilizing agent. For decades, the *zuke* technique has been favored by a few traditional sushi chefs in Japan. Today *zuke* has gained renewed popularity, and chefs in both Japan and America are using this technique, not to preserve the fish but rather to add flavor and texture.

Zuke is yet another of those techniques for which every chef has his or her own secret method. But the basic ingredients of the marinade are *sake* (rice wine), *mirin* (sweet cooking wine), and *shoyu* (soy sauce). Sushi chef Suehiko Shimizu uses *tsuke-joyu* (page 77), which includes *katsuobushi* (bonito fish flakes).

1. Slice off the top to make an even layer 2½ inches high.

2. After slicing a 1-inch-thick block, remove it from the skin with a horizontal cut.

Shoyu and *Mirin* Curing

In this recipe, the tuna is quickly dipped in boiling water before it is placed in the *zuke* marinade. Blanching removes excess liquid from the fish so that the sauce is not diluted; it also firms up the outside texture of tender tuna.

For more information on tuna, see page 172.

ZUKE SAUCE:
¼ cup *sake* (rice wine)
¼ cup *mirin* (sweet cooking wine)
¾ cup *shoyu* (soy sauce)

1 small block sushi or sashimi *maguro, akami* (tuna, red meat), about 7 ounces

Shoyu *and* mirin *curing:* Pour the *sake* and *mirin* into a pot and bring to a simmer over medium heat. Add the *shoyu* and heat until it begins to simmer gently. Turn off the heat, cool the liquid, then store it in a clean bottle in the refrigerator.

Have a bowl of cold water with ice cubes at hand. Pour enough water (to cover the tuna when blanching) into a pot and bring it to a boil. Turn the heat to medium and gently drop the tuna into the boiling water. It will quickly turn from red to a whitish color. (The length of time for blanching is a matter of personal choice. I like flash-blanching so that the very rare flesh is just covered with a very thin white, firmed layer.) Immediately remove the tuna from the pot with a slotted flat spatula and transfer it to the bowl of ice-cold water. Cool thoroughly, then remove it from the water and wipe dry with a paper towel.

Place the tuna in a plastic container and pour in the *zuke* sauce until the fish is barely covered. Let the tuna stand in the sauce for 20 to 30 minutes (the longer the marination, the more color and flavor the fish takes on). Flip the fish over once during marination. Remove the tuna and gently wipe it dry with a paper towel.

Final preparation: Cut the tuna into sushi or *sashimi* slices (pages 200–201 and 218).

Frozen Tuna
Reito maguro

No matter how professionally tuna is frozen and stored, if the defrosting process is not done correctly, the fish turns an unappealing brown color. Tuna, especially bluefin and bigeye tuna, has a bright red color because of the large amount of myoglobin in the muscle. When the tuna is alive, the myoglobin is bluish purple, and when it is frozen at its very freshest stage, the flesh will retain this bluish purple color. Once the myoglobin is exposed to oxidation, it first becomes a beautiful red that is recognized as the very fresh, appetizing color of bluefin and bigeye tuna. As time passes, however, further oxidation transforms the color to an unappetizing brown—and it can happen fairly quickly.

If you defrost the tuna slowly at a temperature of around 18° to 30° F, it faces a long period of oxidation and turns brown. Correct defrosting techniques, as described below, can produce tuna that is almost as good as fresh tuna in terms of texture, nutritional value, water content, and bright color. After tuna is defrosted, its internal temperature should be kept quite cold, around 32° F (the colder part of the refrigerator).

If you purchased frozen tuna that was kept in a professional freezer at a very low temperature, and then you put it in your home freezer (0° F or less), the higher temperature will affect the color and quality of the frozen tuna. So it should be defrosted and consumed as soon as possible, within five days at the most.

Defrosting Techniques
Kaito no shikata

2 tablespoons sea salt per 1 quart water
1 large block (18 ounces) or 1 small block
(7 ounces) sushi and *sashimi* frozen
***maguro* (tuna)**

Pour water (enough to submerge the tuna) at around 95° F into a large bowl and stir in the salt to make a salt solution. Have tap water in the 68° to 95° F range running nearby.

Take the frozen tuna from your freezer and remove the plastic bag. Hold the fish with both hands under the running lukewarm water and clean off the surface. Transfer it to the warm salt water and leave it for 1 minute for the small block or 5 minutes for the large block. Remove the tuna and wipe it thoroughly dry with a paper towel. At this stage, the tuna is still half frozen. Store the tuna wrapped up in a *fukin* cloth (see page 44) or paper towel on a platter in the refrigerator. After 20 minutes for the small block or 60 minutes for the large block, the tuna is ready to be cut into sushi or *sashimi* slices. If you have defrosted more than one piece, spread them on a platter, making sure the pieces do not touch or overlap one another. After the tuna is defrosted, consume it within two days.

Salmon
Sake

Salmon is a naturally oily fish with tender flesh, and the farmed ones are particularly full of fat. I like to cure salmon with salt for a short period to remove excess liquid from the meat, firm up the very tender flesh, and cut some of the oiliness.

See page 175 for more information on salmon, especially with regard to freezing to eliminate common salmon parasites.

Salt Curing
Sake no shio-jime

Sea salt
1 fillet of very fresh, parasite-free sushi
or *sashimi* salmon with skin

Salt curing: Spread enough sea salt to thickly cover the bottom of a large shallow dish. Dredge the salmon in the salt and let it stand with the salt for about 30 minutes. Remove the salmon from the dish and rinse off the salt under cold running tap water. Wipe it dry with a paper towel.

Cutting into blocks for sushi: Place the salmon on a chopping board and remove the belly bones on the belly side (see horse mackerel photo number 9 on page 188). With a pair of tweezers, remove the center bones. Following the illustration, cut the fillet lengthwise into two pieces, making a back fillet and a belly fillet. Skin the salmon from the tail end to the head and reserve the skin for a salmon skin roll (page 115). If the salmon is large, the back-side fillet may be too thick (it should be about 1 inch high) to produce a proper rectangular slice. For cutting, insert your *sashimi* knife horizontally into the flesh 1 inch above the chopping board and cut an even slice of the fillet (see the tuna photos on page 185). You can use this irregularly shaped top part of the fillet for *nigiri-zushi;* it is especially good for being cut into sticks or chopped fine to make fillings for sushi rolls.

Final preparation: Following the illustration, cut the uniform block into sushi (pages 200, 202) or *sashimi* slices (page 218).

Mackerel
Saba

Mackerel, which contains abundant oil, has quite a strong flavor and very tender flesh. So the fish has traditionally been cured with heavy salt and vinegar—a technique called *sujime*. The curing cuts the oiliness, mellows the flavor, and firms the texture.

Because mackerel is quite perishable, it is important to find a very fresh, properly handled fish from a Japanese or other trusted fishmonger. You can learn more about mackerel on page 168.

The same filleting technique can be applied to similarly tender-fleshed fish such as Spanish mackerel, but heavy salt curing and vinegar pickling is unique to the mackerel.

Filleting and Heavy Salt and Vinegar Curing
Saba no oroshi-kata to sujime

Saba (mackerel), about 1⅓-pound size, *ike-jime* slaughtered
Sea salt
Kokumotsu-zu (grain vinegar)

Filleting: Mackerel is very tender, so always hold the fish with two hands, supporting its head with one and its body with the other. Soak the fish in a bucket of cold salt water (1 quart of water with 2 tablespoons of salt) before you begin working on it.

Remove the fish from the salt water and, following the illustrations, **1.** place it on a chopping board. **2.** Insert a *deba* knife (see page 45) behind the pectoral fin, tilting the cutting edge slightly toward the head at an angle, and push down on the knife until you have reached the backbone, then withdraw it. **3.** Turn the fish over and finish cutting off the head with another similar cut. Insert the knife at the anus, slice toward the head to cut open the belly, **4.** then remove and discard the intestines. Carefully open the belly and slice open the thin white membrane covering the center bone. With the tip of the *deba* knife, scrape out the blood from the cavity. Rinse the fish under cold running tap water and clean it, using a toothbrush to remove all blood stuck to the center bone.

Place the fish on the cleaned chopping board, head end to the left, belly side facing you. Rotate the fish 45 degrees counterclockwise. **5.** Insert the knife at the tail, just above the small bones, and cut open the belly side to the anus, reaching as far as the backbone. **6.** Rotate the fish 180 degrees, back side

1. Place the mackerel on the cutting board at an angle, head to the left and back side toward you.

2. Insert the *deba* knife behind the pectoral fin at an angle and make a slanted cut down to the bone.

3. Turn the fish over and finish cutting off the head.

7. Grasping the tail with your left hand, insert the knife at the tail end and run it toward the head to free one fillet.

8. After filleting the other side in the same way, you now have two fillets (*foreground*), separated from the backbone (*background*).

9. Scrape away the bones on the belly side.

to the right. Insert the knife just above the back fin and run it from the head end toward the tail. Push the knife deeper, penetrating as far as the backbone. Rotate the fish back to its original position, then **7.** grab the tail of the fish and slide the knife over the backbone toward the head to free the first fillet. Sever the fillet at the tail end.

8. Turn the fish over and separate the second fillet from the backbone on the side in the same way. **9.** Scrape away the bones on the belly side and discard the backbone. (When curing fish, omit scraping the bones on the belly side at this point.)

Heavy salt and vinegar curing:
Spread a thick layer of sea salt on a sheet pan until the bottom is white with salt. Place the fillets skin side down on the salt and cover them with an additional thick layer of salt until they are almost submerged. Let stand for 2 hours.

The duration of salting depends on the size and oiliness of the fish. Smaller, less oily, fish require less salting time.

Have at hand a large bowl of cold water. Remove the fillets from the salt, discarding the salt; transfer them to the bowl of cold water in the sink. Run cold water into the bowl (but do not allow the running water to strike the fillets directly; although salt-cured fish attains a firmer texture, rough handling destroys the delicate flesh) and rinse off the salt. Remove the fish from the water and wipe it dry with a paper towel.

Prepare a bowl of vinegar water— 3 parts water and 7 parts grain vinegar (you need enough vinegar water so that the fillets are barely submerged). Pour a small quantity of the vinegar water into a bowl and quickly rinse the fillets. Place the fillets skin side down in a container in which they can lie flat without overlapping. Add the remaining vinegar water until they are barely submerged. Place

plastic wrap over the fillets (to ensure that the surface is covered with the vinegar water) and let stand for 1½ hours. This cures the fish to "medium-rare." For lighter "rare" flesh, cure them for 30 minutes.

After removing the fillets from the vinegar water, drain them on a bamboo basket or on a flat strainer and wipe dry with a paper towel. Place the fillets skin side down and cut the bones from the edge of the belly part of each fillet. With tweezers, remove the small center bones along the length of the fillets. Wrap them in plastic wrap and refrigerate. The cured fish tastes best the next day and can be enjoyed for up to two days.

Before using the fish, remove the skin by picking up the end of the skin from the head and peeling it off to the tail.

Final preparation: Cut the fish into sushi (pages 200–201, 202) or *sashimi* slices (page 218), or make *saba-zushi,* pressed mackerel sushi (see page 129).

4. After opening up the belly, cut out the membrane covering the center bone and scrape out the blood.

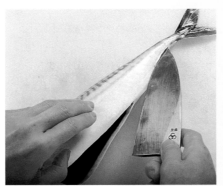
5. Make a cut from the tail (at the anus) through to the center bone.

6. Rotate the fish without turning it over and cut open the back side.

Olive Flounder
Hirame

Flounder is covered in very tiny scales, so scaling this fish requires a different technique, called *kokehiki,* for which I use a very well sharpened *yanagiba* knife (*sashimi* knife). To fillet the fish, I use a *deba* knife. (For a discussion of Japanese knives, see page 44.) You can apply this same scaling technique to similar flatfish and great amberjack.

Scaling is easier when the body of the fish is moist—that is, when it is fresh and bathed in its natural moisture. To keep the skin from drying out, cover the fish with wet newspaper or paper towels before you begin.

You can enjoy flounder in different stages. Its pre–rigor mortis meat has a wonderfully resilient texture. Toward the end of the rigor stage, the texture begins to soften, but the flavor peaks. The fish is also delicious cured in kelp, which results in a uniquely pleasing aroma and texture. The curing technique, *kobu-jime,* was developed as a way of prolonging the edible period of fish long before advanced refrigeration. Other seafood such as sea bass, sea bream, salmon trout, shrimp, and squid are also suited to kelp curing.

You can apply the same filleting techniques to other flatfish such as fluke and sole.

To learn more about *hirame* and other flatfish for sushi, see page 170.

Flatfish Filleting and Kelp Curing
Hirame no oroshi-kata to kobu-jime

Hirame (Japanese flounder), about 3-pound size, *ike-jime* slaughtered
2 sheets *kombu* (kelp), 10- × 2-inch rectangles
Kokumotsu-zu (grain vinegar) or *komezu* (rice vinegar)
Sea salt

Filleting: Rinse the fish thoroughly under cold running tap water and drain. Following the illustrations, 1. place it on a chopping board, head to the left, belly side facing you. With a moist paper towel, wipe the fish to remove any slimy liquid. 2. Insert a *yanagiba* knife into the surface of the fish between the skin and

1. Place the rinsed fish on a chopping board.

2. Run your *yanagiba* knife between the scales and the skin.

3. Using a *deba* knife, cut off the head following the gill line.

7. Remove the fillets on the other side.

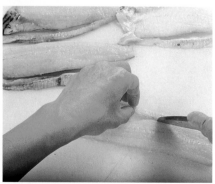

8. Cut off the *engawa* strip from each fillet.

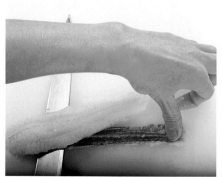

9. Remove the skin.

the scales and, with a gentle sawing motion, run it from tail to head. The scales will come off as though you were peeling off a strip of thin skin. Using this technique, remove all the scales on both sides of the fish.

3. Using a *deba* knife, cut off the head following the gill line. Remove the entrails. 4. Cut off the fins on both sides of the body. Clean the inside of the cavity under cold running tap water. Drain the fish. Rinse the chopping board and wipe it dry with a paper towel.

Return the fish to the chopping board, head to the left, belly side facing you. Rotate the fish 45 degrees clockwise. 5. With a *deba* knife, make a center cut over the backbone from the tail end to the head. 6. Remove the fillet on the belly side. Rotate the fish 180 degrees and remove the back fillet. 7. Turn the fish over and remove both fillets from the other side in the same manner. At

this stage, each of the four fillets has an *engawa*—a thin strip of muscle meat found on the edge of the body of the fish (page 171)—attached to it. 8. Cut off the *engawa* strip from each fillet. Now you have four fillets and four *engawa* strips. Cut off the bones that are attached to the two belly-side fillets (see horse mackerel photo number 9 on page 188). 9. Remove the skin with a *sashimi* knife, working from the tail end to the head end of each fillet and *engawa* strip.

Cut the fish into sushi (pages 200–201, 202) or *sashimi* slices (page 218) or follow the instructions for kelp curing.

Kelp curing: Place the *kombu* between clean, moist kitchen towels for 30 minutes or until the kelp sheets soften and are easily spread open. Mix a tablespoon each of water and vinegar in a cup and, using a paper towel, wipe the softened kelp with the vinegar water.

Sprinkle some salt over the kelp and place the fillet on the sheet of kelp. Sprinkle additional salt over the fillet and cover it with the remaining kelp. Wrap the kelp tightly in plastic wrap and place it in a container. Put a small, flat chopping board or light weight on top of the package and store it in the refrigerator overnight. The fish is wrapped, but putting it in the container makes it free from any contamination/touch from other food items in the refrigerator. You can keep the fish for three days, but it is better to remove it from the kelp the next day (longer curing transfers too strong a kelp flavor to the fish and also dehydrates the fish).

Final preparation: After removing the fish from the kelp, cut it into sushi (pages 200–201, 202) or *sashimi* slices (page 218).

4. Cut off the fins on both sides.

5. Make a center cut over the backbone from the tail end to the head.

6. Remove the fillets on the belly side and the back.

Kuruma Prawn
Kuruma-ebi

Unlike ordinary cooked prawns (see "Telling a Prawn from a Shrimp," page 181), which curl up on cooking, *nigiri-zushi* prawns must be straight so they can lie flat on the sushi rice. A very simple technique—putting a thin bamboo skewer through each prawn before cooking—can force it to maintain a flat profile. Although in this recipe you are cooking the prawns, you should start with very fresh, high-quality prawns, preferably live ones—a sushi chef's choice in Japan. Finding live prawns is impossible for the home cook, so at least choose ones with heads attached that are plump, resilient to the touch, and encased in semitransparent, wet shells. Avoid any whose heads are blackened or loosely attached to the body.

For more information about *kuruma-ebi,* see page 179.

Cooking on a Skewer
Kuruma-ebi no ni-kata

SWEET VINEGAR MARINADE:
½ cup *kokumotsu-zu* (grain vinegar)
2½ tablespoons sugar
⅛ teaspoon salt

10 *kuruma-ebi* (*kuruma* prawns) or similar prawns, heads on, about 6 inches long; preferably alive or very fresh, not frozen
½ teaspoon sea salt
1 tablespoon *kokumotsu-zu* (grain vinegar)

Sweet vinegar marinade: Put all the ingredients in a pot with ½ cup water and bring to a simmer over medium heat. Remove from the heat and cool. Store in a jar in the refrigerator.

Cooking on a skewer: Following the illustration, insert a bamboo skewer into the prawn, starting at the tail end, and run it through its body closer to the belly side. Prepare all the remaining prawns in the same way.

Bring 3 quarts of water in a pot to a boil, add the salt and vinegar, and cook the prawns about 2 to 3 minutes. To check for doneness, remove one prawn from the water and press it between your thumb and index finger. It should feel firm but slightly tender in the center. Do not overcook (overcooking develops a flaky flesh). Remove the prawns from the water, then drain and spread them on a strainer to cool. If you are using frozen prawns, cook them for a full 3 minutes (they need to be cooked through). After removing them from the water, cool them immediately in a bowl of cold water (natural flavor is lost during freezing, so plunging into water to cool does no harm).

Cut off the head and peel each prawn whole, but do not remove the two large, fanned-out parts of the tail. Cut open the prawn from the belly side and butterfly it. Remove the brown vein, if present. Square off the head end of the body. Prepare all the rest of the prawns in the same way. Spread them out on a flat strainer or cookie rack without overlapping, sprinkle a little salt over them, and let them stand for 5 minutes. Rinse the prawns in a bowl of cold water and drain. Toss them in a bowl with the sweet vinegar marinade, then drain and store in a container. Prawns, even when cooked, are very perishable; salting and rinsing them in the vinegar extends the storage period, up to 2 days in the refrigerator.

Final preparation: Use one prepared prawn for each *nigiri-zushi.*

Insert a bamboo skewer into the tail end of the shrimp.

Octopus
Tako

It is important to start with an energetic live octopus. When you pick up the octopus, the legs should curl up, and the strong suckers will stick to you if you let them. This may sound like an unpleasant test, but it is the best way to make sure that your octopus will produce sweet, tender flesh with a pronounced fragrance. If you cannot find a live octopus, purchase one that has been killed but is still very fresh and, preferably, not a frozen one that has been defrosted. After cooking the octopus by the method described below, you can enjoy it in many preparations including *nigiri-zushi;* octopus with salad greens (page 223); octopus, cucumber, and *wakame* salad (page 222); or sauté the boiled, sliced octopus in olive oil with chopped garlic.

For more information on octopus, see page 182.

Cleaning and Cooking
Tako no ni-kata

One 2-pound octopus, live
2 quarts *ban-cha* tea (page 36) infused with ½ cup tea leaves
1 tablespoon sea salt, and additional for cleaning octopus

Cleaning: Holding the head of the octopus, make a swift cut over the eyes. Quickly turn the head inside out and remove the intestines, including the ink sac, being careful not to break it (a real mess if you do!). If the octopus has already been butchered and cleaned, omit this step.

Spread out the octopus in a clean sink, sprinkle one handful of sea salt all over it, and rub to clean it. As you do so, the mixture of salt and body liquid produces a fine white foam. Clean the inside of the suckers as well. Plunge the octopus into a big bowl containing plenty of water with cold tap water still running into it and clean and rinse it until all foam and sliminess disappear.

Cooking with ban-cha *tea:* Pour the *ban-cha* tea along with 1 tablespoon sea salt into a large pot. Add enough water so that the octopus can later be submerged and bring it to a boil. Holding the head of the octopus, gradually lower it into the boiling water, starting with the tips of the legs. After confirming that the tips have curled up, push the octopus little by little farther into the water, and finally submerge the head. Cook the octopus over medium heat about 12 to 15 minutes, skimming off the foam as it surfaces. When you remove the octopus from the water, it will be a beautiful deep reddish purple color that we call *azuki-iro,* or *azuki* bean color. Drain the octopus on a strainer and cool at room temperature.

Final preparation: Cut the cooked octopus into sushi (pages 200–201, 203) or *sashimi* slices (page 218).

Sea Bream
Ma-dai

There are two ways to serve *ma-dai*, red sea bream, as sushi and *sashimi*—without skin and with skin. The purpose of retaining the skin is to enjoy the most delicious part of this fish—the very thin fatty layer of flesh immediately beneath the skin. But the skin of the raw fish is too chewy and unpleasant to bite, and it also tastes fishy. So the *shimofuri* technique is used to treat the skin with boiling water. You can apply these filleting and blanching techniques to all bream, porgy, and snapper family fish.

Learn more about *ma-dai* on page 172.

Snapper and Bream Family Filleting and Blanching
Ma-dai no oroshi-kata to shimofuri

Ma-dai (red sea bream), 4-pound size, *ike-jime* slaughtered
Sea salt

Filleting: Rinse the fish thoroughly under cold running tap water, being careful not to stab your fingers with its very sharply pointed fins. Place the fish in a large clear plastic bag to keep the scales from flying about as you remove them. Working with your hands inside the plastic bag, remove the scales with a fish scaler or the tip of a *deba* knife, scraping it against the flesh, moving from tail to head, working on one small area at a time. Rinse the fish thoroughly under cold tap water.

To fillet this fish, you can follow the same methods as detailed for mackerel (page 188), bearing in mind these key points: Sea bream has a thick, hard backbone, and cutting off the head requires considerable strength. So use the thick part of the *deba* knife near the handle to cut off the head, which will give the knife the most power; also, because of the position of the knife, you avoid cutting the intestines and crushing the fish. Reserve the head. After separating the flesh on the belly side and back side, insert the knife at the tail end perpendicular to the backbone and make a cut to separate the tail end. Lift up the tail end and run the knife over the backbone in a sawing motion toward the head end to free the whole fillet.

You now have four unskinned fillets.

Blanching: Have at hand a kettle of boiling water; a large bowl of cold water with ice cubes in the sink; and a 1-square-foot *fukin* (page 44), piece of muslin, or doubled paper towel. Place the fish skin side up on a chopping board and sprinkle a little sea salt over the fish skin (the salt helps make the cooked skin tender). Cover the fillet with the cotton cloth or paper towels, then tip the chopping board toward the sink and pour the boiling water over the fish until the skin curls and the flesh becomes white. You can see this change through the cloth or paper towel—it happens very quickly, after just a few seconds. Immediately transfer the fillet to the bowl of ice water to stop heat from penetrating the fish. When the fish has cooled (do not leave it in the water too long), quickly remove it, drain, and wipe dry with a paper towel. Repeat the process for the other fillets.

You may want to skin some of the fillets, especially the ones from the back side. If so, place the fillet skin side down on the cutting board. Loosen some skin at the tail end, then place the knife on the skin, holding down the fillet with your other hand. Move the knife with a slight sawing motion toward the head end, pulling off the skin as you go (see flounder photo 9 on page 190).

Final preparation: Cut the blanched skinned or unskinned fish into sushi (pages 200–201, 203) or *sashimi* slices (page 218).

With the reserved *ma-dai* head, you can make a delicious, very easy to prepare simmered dish, *tai no nimono* (page 230).

Horse Mackerel
Aji

Horse mackerel is a small fish, about 8 inches long. Its flesh is medium-firm, and it is one of the easiest fish to fillet.

You can apply the horse mackerel filleting technique to other small fish, such as baby sea bream and Japanese whiting.

In the past, before modern refrigeration, filleted horse mackerel was always cured with salt and vinegar to extend its period of freshness. Today, quickly rinsing the fish in salt and vinegar water is preferred to better maintain its raw texture and flavor. You can also vinegar-rinse Japanese whiting, sardines, or other small oily types of fish.

Read about horse mackerel (page 168) before proceeding.

Small-Fish Filleting and Quick Salt and Vinegar Curing
Ma-aji no oroshi-kata to su-arai

Ma-aji (horse mackerel), about 4- to 7-ounce size, *ike-jime* slaughtered
Sea salt
Kokumotsu-zu (grain vinegar)

Filleting: Rinse the fish thoroughly under running tap water and then put it in a bowl of salt water (1 quart water and 2 tablespoons salt) for about 5 minutes (this preserves the shiny silver-blue color of the fish and makes scaling easier).

Remove the fish, taking care not to rub your fingers on the thorny scales, and reserve the soaking water. Place the fish on a chopping board, head to the left, back side facing you. Insert the *deba* knife at the end of the thorny row of scales (about 2 inches long) closest to the tail, holding the knife parallel to the flesh, and move toward the head, scraping off the scales. After this row is removed, the scales become flatter and more or less invisible toward the gill. Continue to move the knife toward the head over these less prominent scales, being careful not to cut into the skin. Turn the fish over, head still to the left, and remove the scales on the other side as well.

Cut off the head, plunging the knife straight down behind the gills and pectoral fin, and discard it. Gently press the belly part with your thumb until the entrails emerge from the head end. Using the tip of the *deba* knife, remove the entrails and discard them. Clean the fish in the reserved salt water, then rinse it under cold running tap water. Clean the chopping board and wipe it dry with a paper towel.

Place the fish on the chopping board, head end to the right, back side facing you. Cut open the back side, inserting the knife above the back fin and running it over the center bone, reaching as far in as the belly-side skin (be careful not to cut through the belly). Now you have butterflied the fish, with the backbone still in place on one side.

Flip the fish over so the skin side is up, head end to the left. Rotate the fish about 45 degrees counterclockwise. Insert the knife above the back fin on the side containing the bones and make a shallow cut from the tail to the head end. Then run the knife deep from the head end toward the tail to separate the fillet from the bone. When you reach the tail, cut off the backbone by turning the knife perpendicular to the chopping board and bearing down. Discard the backbone. Remove the anal fin.

Flip the fish over again so it is skin side down. Remove the thin bones in the belly area, being careful not to cut too deeply into the flesh. Remove the tail end.

Quick salt and vinegar curing: Have at hand a bowl of water and vinegar mixture—3 parts water and 7 parts grain vinegar—and a fresh bowl of salt water (1 quart water, and 2 tablespoons salt). Rinse the fish in the salt water for 30 seconds, turning it over gently with both hands. It should feel slippery. Remove the fish from the water and lay it flat in a strainer to drain. Fold each fish in half, skin side in, and place the folded pieces in the vinegar water, gently turning them in the water, then remove them (if the fish is in the water too long, the protein begins to cook and the color and texture of the fish change). Drain the fish well, laying it flat in the strainer. Run your index finger along the flesh and remove any remaining center bones with tweezers. Store the fish in a clean container covered with plastic wrap in the refrigerator for up to two days.

Final preparation: Peel off the skin and cut the fish into sushi (pages 200–201, 204) or prepare *tataki sashimi* (page 219).

Great Amberjack
Kampachi

It is always challenging to fillet a medium-size fish such as *kampachi,* which weighs about 6 pounds and is about 2 feet long. The scales resemble those of the flounder, so use the *kokehiki* technique (page 190). The filleting technique is almost the same as for sea bream but requires more care, since *kampachi* is a larger fish and its flesh is tender. You can apply the same filleting techniques to yellowtail and striped jack.

For more information on *kampachi,* see page 170.

Medium-Size Fish Filleting
Kampachi no oroshi-kata

Kampachi (great amberjack), about 6-pound size, *ike-jime* slaughtered

Filleting: Rinse the fish under cold running tap water. Place the fish on a large chopping board, head to the left, belly side facing you. Scale the fish on both sides with a *sashimi* knife or other very sharp straight-bladed knife, using the *kokehiki* technique (page 190). Cut off the head behind the pectoral fin and remove the intestines, discarding the intestines. Cut open the belly side from the anus to the head end. Open the cavity and, with a *deba* knife, make a long slit over the white membrane covering the backbone. Using the tip of the *deba* knife, scrape out any blood (see mackerel photo number 4 on page 189) and, under cold running tap water, rinse the inside cavity and clean it thoroughly with a toothbrush. Drain the fish. Rinse the chopping board and wipe it dry with a paper towel.

Place the fish on the chopping board, head end to the right, belly side facing you. Rotate the fish 45 degrees counterclockwise. Insert the knife at the anus and cut open the belly side toward the tail, running the knife over the fine bones on the upper side of the fish. Move the knife farther toward the backbone to separate the upper belly-side flesh from the bone. Rotate the fish 180 degrees and insert the knife just above the back fin at the tail end and run it toward the head. Insert the knife deeper, penetrating as far as the backbone, and slide the knife over the bone toward the head to separate the upper back-side fillet from the bone. Now cut across the tail to free the end of the upper fillet and run the knife along the backbone to separate the entire upper fillet from the bone. Turn the fish over and remove the fillet from the other side in the same way.

Remove the belly bones on the belly sides of the fillets (see mackerel photo 9 on page 188), being careful not to scrape too much meat from the belly. Cut each fillet in half lengthwise along the line of small bones where the backbone was and remove the fillets on both sides. Discard the thin red strip with the bones. Remove the skin from each of the four fillets: Place the fillets skin side down on the chopping board and insert the knife at the tail, moving it toward the head end. The *kampachi*'s skin is easy to tear, so be careful as you move the knife. Each fillet will have a thin strip of red meat, *chiai-niku,* the part that was nearest the backbone, most of which was removed. This meat is rich in vitamins and iron. In America, according to sushi chefs I know, many people associate red flesh with blood, so the chefs meticulously remove this nourishing, flavorful part of the meat. I urge you to give it a try and appreciate its excellent flavor.

Store the fillets in the refrigerator wrapped in plastic wrap. If the fish is fresh, these fillets (with skin) may be stored for up to 2 days.

Final preparation: Cut the fish into sushi (pages 200–201, 204) or *sashimi* slices (page 218).

Conger Eel
Anago

Chances to fillet *anago,* conger eel, even in Japan, if you are not a chef, are rare. Today, already filleted and frozen *anago* is so readily available that even some chefs in Japan are not familiar with the filleting technique. But now that whole frozen uncooked eel is being imported into the United States, knowing how to fillet this fish is important. The technique is unique and interesting, and at the very least, understanding it will surely add to your pleasure in ordering *anago* the next time you are at a good sushi restaurant.

In order to fillet *anago,* the professional kitchen needs three items—a chopping board that is about 40 inches long, a sharp ice pick–like tool, and a very well sharpened *deba* knife. The filleting technique explained here is the Kanto style (page 169), in which I was trained.

After the fish is filleted, the remaining head and bones are used to make a broth in which the filleted fish is simmered. This broth is used again to cook the following day's batch of *anago.* Finally, that same broth is cooked down to make the velvety brown, rich sweet eel sauce, *tsume* (page 79).

The same filleting and simmering techniques can be applied to freshwater eel, *unagi.*

For more information on *anago,* conger eel or sea eel, see page 169.

Filleting and Sweet-Simmering Conger Eel
Anago no oroshi-kata to ni-kata

4 pounds *anago* (conger eel), preferably *ike-jime* slaughtered
Sea salt
3 1/2 cups plus 2 tablespoons *sake* (rice wine)
2/3 cup plus 2 tablespoons sugar
1 1/4 cups plus 3 tablespoons *shoyu* (soy sauce)
3/4 cup *mirin* (sweet cooking wine)

Filleting: Rinse the fish under cold running tap water, then in cold salted water (1 quart water and 2 tablespoons sea salt). Wipe the fish dry with a paper towel and place it on the chopping board, head to the right, back side facing you. Stab a small ice pick through the head just in back of the eye into the chopping board so that the fish is held securely to the board.

Insert the *deba* knife below the gill just above the dorsal fin and make a cut to the backbone. Run the knife over the backbone until you come to the anus. Then run the knife over the whole upper bone area (do not poke into the belly side) and butterfly the fish. Remove and discard the intestines. Hold the knife upside down (cutting edge facing upward) and run the knife along both edges of the backbone to loosen it (this makes it easy to remove the backbone). Cut the backbone near the head (do not cut through it; the head is still attached to the fillet). Run the knife under the backbone and separate it from the fillet, reserving it. Cut off and dispose of the back fin and center fin, then cut off the head, reserving it.

Sweet simmering: Rinse the fish in a bowl of cold water and drain on a strainer. Pour fresh cold water into the bowl in the sink. Bring a large pot with plenty of water to a boil and blanch the fish 10 seconds or until the skin turns white. Immediately remove the fish from the water and cool it in the bowl of cold water. With a semihard brush—a *tawashi* (page 53) or a potato brush—gently scrub the skin to remove the thin white film produced during blanching. Drain the fish on a strainer.

Cook the fish head and backbone under a broiler or over a grill until lightly char-browned. Place the backbone, the head, and 7 1/2 cups of water in a large pot (in which the fish can fit without much bending). Bring to a boil, then reduce to a simmer and cook for 25 minutes. Strain the stock into a large bowl, discarding the backbone and head. Clean the large pot, pour in the *sake,* and bring to a simmer to cook off the alcohol. Add the strained broth and sugar to the *sake* and bring it to a simmer. Place the fish skin side down in the pot and cook, covered with a drop lid (page 51) or a parchment paper disk, for 15 minutes. Add the *shoyu* and *mirin* and cook, covered with the drop lid, over low heat for 20 minutes. Turn off the heat and let the fish cool in the cooking liquid for 20 minutes. Remove the fish and drain it on a flat strainer with the skin side up, reserving the liquid.

You can enjoy the best natural tenderness and sweet fragrance of the cooked conger eel on the day of preparation without refrigeration. Storing it in the refrigerator firms up the flesh and eliminates the fragrance. However, if you need to store the fish, cover it with plastic wrap, place it in a container, and refrigerate. Before using the stored fish, reheat it.

Final preparation: Cut the conger eel into sushi slices (pages 200–201, 204).

Japanese Common Flying Squid
Surume-ika

Choose the freshest squid, as indicated by its translucent skin. You can apply the same filleting techniques to similar species of squid.

See page 180 for information on *surume-ika* and other squid for sushi and *sashimi*.

Cleaning
Surume-ika no oroshi-kata

Surume-ika (Japanese common flying squid), very fresh
Sea salt

Cleaning: Rinse the squid under cold running tap water. Insert a finger or two into the body cavity and, when you feel the soft bone, detach it and pull it out. Again insert a finger or two into the body cavity around the intestines and pull them out along with the head and the tentacles. Be careful not to break the ink sac. Fold the two triangular fins so they meet and pull them down. As you do so, part of the thin strip of skin will peel away from the body, so continue to pull and remove the fins. Now, with a paper towel, grab the remaining skin and peel it all off.

Place the squid on the chopping board and, with a *sashimi* knife, cut it open along the line where the fins were pulled off, forming a single broad triangular sheet. Rinse the squid sheet in cold tap water and wipe dry with a paper towel. Remove the thin layer of skin from the inside surface of the squid with paper towel. Rinse the squid in a bowl of cold salted water (1 quart water and 2 tablespoons salt). Drain and wipe dry with a paper towel, then store in the refrigerator, wrapped in plastic wrap.

The short, meatier tentacles are excellent for making *nigiri-zushi* or *sashimi* dishes, but they need to be cooked. There are two long, poor-flavored tentacles at each side that should be cut off at the base and discarded before cooking. Also cut off and discard the eyes. Bring a large pot of water to a boil and cook the tentacles about 2 to 3 minutes, or until they are porcelain-white. Drain in a strainer and cool at room temperature.

Final preparation: Cut the squid into sushi (pages 200–201, 205) or *sashimi* slices (page 218).

Gaper Clam
Miru-gai

Storing live *miru-gai,* gaper clams, in salt water keeps them alive for 4 to 5 days. But remember that these clams are not living in their natural environment; they are stressed out and digesting their own stored energy resources. So flavor is impaired with each day of storage. Choose clams with firm, strong, and resilient siphons. Only the long, meaty siphon is used for sushi and sashimi.

See page 178 for more information on the *miru-gai.*

Shucking and Cleaning
Miru-gai no atsukai-kata

Miru-gai (gaper clam), very fresh
Sea salt

Shucking and cleaning: Bring a pot of water to a boil and keep it at a simmer. Hold the clam so that the siphon is up, the hinge away from you. Insert a small knife into the clamshell near the siphon and run it around the inner surface to loosen the clam. Force open the shells and pull out the entire clam along with its siphon. Remove the gill and soft parts from the siphon.

Rub some salt over the siphon, then rinse it thoroughly to remove any trapped sand and drop it in the boiling water for 10 seconds. Remove it from the pot and soak it in a bowl of cold water to cool quickly. Take the siphon from the water and peel off the black skin that has been loosened by the blanching.

Butterfly the siphon by making an incision on the thin side and opening it up. Again, carefully rinse the siphon under running tap water to clean it and remove any remaining sand. Cut away the rough-edged tip of the siphon. To enhance the color, holding the siphon, lower only an inch of its tip into the boiling water for 10 seconds (the blanched part will acquire a subtle pink color).

Final preparation: Cut *miru-gai* into sushi (pages 200–201, 205) or *sashimi* slices (page 218).

Japanese Gizzard Shad
Kohada

Kohada has been used since *nigiri-zushi* was first invented in the mid-nineteenth century. Because of its fundamental place in the sushi tradition, it is important to learn how this fish is prepared.

The quantity of salt and vinegar used and the duration of curing vary from one chef to another. To learn more about *kohada,* see page 172.

You can apply the same treatment to baby sea bream.

Special Filleting and Salt and Vinegar Curing
Kohada no oroshi-kata to su-jime

Kohada (Japanese gizzard shad)
Sea salt
Grain vinegar

Filleting: Rinse the fish under cold running tap water and soak it in a bowl of cold water for 20 minutes. *Kohada* is covered with tiny scales, and scaling is easier when the fish is wet. Remove the fish from the water and put it on the chopping board, head to the left, back side facing you. With a *deba* knife, cut off the back fin and remove all the tiny scales on one side by scraping the tip of the knife across the flesh from the tail end toward the head. Flip the fish over, head to the left, the belly side facing you, and remove the scales on the other side. Then remove the head by cutting straight down behind the pectoral fin.

Rotate the fish 90 degrees counterclockwise, so the head end is toward you and the belly side is to the right. Make a cut from the anus on the right toward the head (about 1½ inches) to remove a triangular piece, which is the small belly. With your thumb, gently push out all the intestines. Rinse the fish in the bowl of cold water. Cut the fish open on the belly side and open it up butterfly fashion. Flip the fish over so it is skin side up, head end toward you. Insert the knife deep into the head end and then run the knife toward the tail to separate the fillet. Flip the fish over so the flesh side is up and the tail end is toward you, and remove the small bones from each side of the belly. Rinse the fish in a large bowl of cold tap water. Change the water and rinse it again. Lay the fish flat on a large strainer to drain.

Salt and vinegar curing: Sprinkle enough salt on a flat bamboo basket or a flat stainless steel strainer (a large fine steaming basket will do) to lightly cover the surface. Place several fish, skin side down, without overlapping, on the salted surface and sprinkle additional salt over them. Then place another layer of fish (skin side down) partially overlapping the first layer and sprinkle additional salt over them. Finish by layering all the fish in the same manner. Let the fish stand 20 minutes. Prepare a bowl of vinegar and water—3 parts water and 7 parts grain vinegar (you need enough vinegar water so that the fish can be completely submerged in it).

Rinse the fish in a large bowl of cold tap water. Lay them flat on a strainer to drain. Pour some of the vinegar water (enough to barely submerge the fish) into a bowl and rinse them in it. Remove the fish quickly from the vinegar water and drain in the strainer. Pour the remaining vinegar water into another bowl and submerge two fish together back-to-back, skin side in. Continue to submerge the rest of the fish this way. Let the fish marinate for 8 to 10 minutes. Remove the fish from the vinegar water, separate the pieces, and place them on the flat strainer, skin side up, spreading them out in a few layers. Refrigerate for 30 minutes. Now transfer them to a container, standing them up vertically, leaning against one another; cover with plastic wrap and store in the refrigerator. Prepared *kohada* tastes best the next day, and you can enjoy it for up to 2 days.

Final preparation: Cut the whole butterflied fish into two fillets, cutting off and discarding the thin strip of fin. Cut each fillet into sushi (pages 200–201, 205) or *sashimi* slices (page 218).

Chapter 12
Making Classic
Nigiri-zushi

Nigiri-zushi (or *nigiri* for short) is like art created by a magician. In about 6 seconds, a chef cuts a slice from a prepared fillet or block of fish, scoops up a small quantity of sushi rice, forms it in his or her hands into a small egg shape, adds a condiment such as *wasabi,* and fuses the topping and rice together into a delicious morsel. It is an amazing performance to observe.

Doing this at home is not as easy as it looks. Here I will show you how to cut seafood for use in *nigiri-zushi,* then how to make a small, warm rice ball that is airy and tender to the bite. To complete the *nigiri-zushi,* you just need to place the sliced seafood on top of your rice ball. Speed is not the issue here, so relax and enjoy making the *nigiri-zushi.* And you will get better and better at it.

Techniques for Slicing Seafood for Sushi

For *nigiri-zushi,* you need to make thin rectangular slices of fish and shellfish (1¼ inches × 2¾ inches) to cover the rice ball. The thickness varies depending on the type of fish: fish with tender flesh, such as tuna, skipjack tuna, yellowtail, and salmon, is cut into ⅕-inch slices, whereas seafood with firm flesh, such as sea bass, flounder, sea bream, great amberjack, and squid, is cut thinner—into ⅐-inch slices.

The finished slice of fish should reveal the thin membranes that separate the layers of muscle. Because you have cut through them, the slice will be more tender.

All the slicing of fish is done with the long-bladed *sashimi* knife, also called a *yanagiba* knife (see the illustration on page 45). A very well sharpened *sashimi* knife cuts into the flesh by its own weight with no additional downward pressure, making a clear, sharp line.

The instructions given here are for right-handed cooks, so if you are left-handed, you should mentally construct a mirror image to translate these instructions. You will also be using a left-handed knife.

Master Recipe for Making *Nigiri-zushi* Slices Tuna, *Maguro*

Here I am using tuna, *maguro*, as it is the most readily available fish for *nigiri-zushi*.

Set your 2½- × 5 × 1-inch block of tuna on the chopping board and first remove a triangular piece from the upper left corner, which will leave a 2¾-inch-long edge (save the irregular piece to make rolls). Now make the first slice, about ⅕ inch thick, following that diagonal line: first place your long *sashimi* knife at an angle so that the end rests on the near edge of the piece of fish, then pull the blade toward you in one swift motion, following the illustration. Continue to make additional cuts.

For the *koba* cut, follow the instructions in the accompanying box.

If you are cutting *toro,* the fatty belly part of the fish, you may cut it a little thinner than the *akami,* red flesh, because it is very rich.

For the Pro: *Koba o tsukeru,* Creating a Thicker Edge

Koba is a technique whereby, instead of cutting the fillet straight down, you cut it decoratively into a rectangular slice in which the far edge of one long side is a little thicker than the rest. This thicker edge is noticeable, because the slice lies flat on the rice ball. It is a bit of tromp l'oeil that makes the slice look more plump and appetizing. It is a very popular practice, one that I prefer over the straight slice. But some chefs do not use it. And it is a little more difficult for the unpracticed cook.

To create the thicker edge, *koba,* 1. after you have sliced almost all the way through at an angle, following the illustrations 2. turn the blade vertical just before the tip goes through the flesh, then continue to pull the blade on through. 3. Now you have created a slice with the lower edge slightly thicker than the rest of the slice.

1. Slice at an angle almost all the way through the fish.

2. Turn the blade vertical just before the tip goes through the flesh and continue to pull the blade toward you.

3. The finished *koba* slice.

Salmon
Sake

Because the back side of this fillet is thick, your slices would be too large unless you trim off some of the top part of the fillet to produce a thinner, 1-inch-thick piece of fish (see page 187). After trimming, place the fish skinned side down on the chopping board, tail end to the left, and following the illustration, cut the fish into ⅕-inch-thick slices.

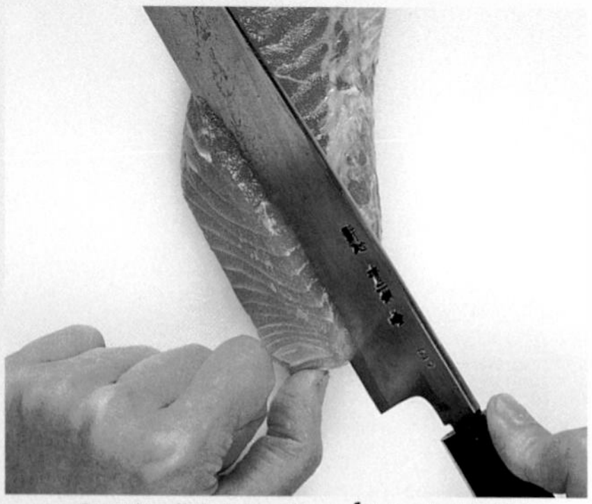

Cut the fish into slices ⅕ inch thick.

For the *koba* cut, follow the instructions on page 201.

Mackerel
Saba

Place the cured fish (from page 188) skin side up on the chopping board. Peel the skin from the wider top head end to the tail. You can do this using the back side of a *sashimi* knife. Then place the fillet skinned side down on the chopping board and, starting at the tail end, cut it into ⅕-inch slices.

For the *koba* cut, follow the instructions on page 201.

Flounder
Hirame

Your initial preparation of the fillets will give you two back-side and two belly-side skinned fillets (from page 190) as well as four *engawa* strips. Following the illustration, place the meaty back-side fillet skinned side down, tail end facing left, on the chopping board. Cut the fish into slices, about ⅐ inch thick, starting at the tail end.

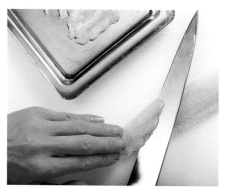

Cut thin slices at an angle.

For the *koba* cut, follow the instructions on page 201.

Cut the belly-side fillets in the same way. Cut the *engawa* into 2¾-inch lengths.

Kuruma Prawn
Kuruma-ebi

After you have prepared the prawn according to the instructions on page 192, there is no further cutting.

Octopus
Tako

After preparing the *tako,* octopus (page 193), cut off and separate the individual legs. Do not cut them directly across the legs but at an angle, leaving a white surface about 2 inches long. Cut off the curled tip of the thin end of the legs. Place one leg, thicker side to the left, on the chopping board with the white cut surface facing up and cut it into slices, about 1/7 inch thick. While cutting through the flesh, rock the knife back and forth in small movements to create a wavy pattern on the cut surfaces. The wavy surface has three benefits: the sliced octopus sits more securely on top of the rice; it is easier to bite into; the sauce clings to the wavy surface more readily. Also, it looks very attractive.

Sea Bream
Ma-dai

After the initial filleting and preparation, you have two back-side skinned fillets and two belly-side fillets with skin attached that have been *shimofuri* treated—that is, blanched (see page 194). Place one of the back-side fillets skinned side down, tail facing left, on the chopping board. Cut the fish into 1/7-inch-thick slices, starting at the tail end.

For the *koba* cut, follow the instructions on page 201.

Cut the back-side fillets in the same way.

Horse Mackerel
Ma-aji

Place the butterflied fish (from page 195) skin side down on the chopping board and cut it into two fillets by removing a strip from the center part where the belly fin is. Turn each fillet over, skin side up, and peel the skin by hand from the head end toward the tail. You can also do this with your *sashimi* knife, which leaves the skinned fillet with a more attractive silvery color. To do so, first peel off some skin at the head end by hand. Flip the fish over. Place the blunt back side of the knife (cutting edge up) on the peeled area, holding the skin with your left hand, and push the knife to the right. As you move the knife along, separate the skin from the flesh.

Place the fillet skinned side down on the chopping board and cut it into 1/5-inch-thick slices.

For the *koba* cut, follow the instructions on page 201.

Flip each cut piece over (skinned side up) and make a decorative crosscut in the center; when this slice is placed on top of the sushi rice ball, the cut opens up and creates a beautiful pattern contrasting the reddish flesh of the fish and the silver skin residue.

After placing the fish slice on top of the rice ball, mound some grated ginger in the center of the cuts that have opened up and garnish with finely julienned chives.

Great Amberjack
Kampachi

After the initial preparation, you have two back-side and two belly-side fillets, skinned. The back-side fillets are thick—usually more than 1 inch thick—and if you cut a slice from one, as with the tuna (see the illustrations on page 185), it will be too broad. So you must slice off some of the top of the fillet to make it about 1 inch thick. To do so, place the fillet on the chopping board skinned side down, insert the knife at the head part parallel to the chopping board, about 1 inch above it, and run the knife to the tail end, maintaining the 1-inch thickness. The sliced-off diagonal piece can be used in sushi. Now position the 1-inch-thick fillet (still skinned side down) with the tail to the left and cut the fish into 1/5-inch-thick slices, starting at the tail end.

For the *koba* cut, follow the instructions on page 201.

Conger Eel
Anago

A whole cooked conger eel (from page 197) is roughly 12 to 13 inches long and makes about three pieces that can be cut for *nigiri-zushi*. For *anago no nigiri-zushi,* we ignore the standard size. The length of the eel topping may vary, and some cuts of eel may be almost one and a half times as long as the sushi rice ball. If you look at the prepared conger eel, placed skin side down, you will notice that the surface of the fish is wavy. The part closer to the head has about a 3- to 3 1/2-inch-long depression (depending on the length of the conger eel) where the gut was encased; then, from the end of the depression to the tail, the surface becomes smoother and slightly mounded.

Place the fish on the chopping board skin side down, tail end to the left, and cut the fish vertically on the bias into three pieces, each approximately 3 to 3 1/2 inches long. The first cut should contain most of the depressed area, and the second cut should divide what remains into two equal lengths. When preparing a *nigiri-zushi* with the head end—the depressed part—place the depressed part on top of the rice ball, skin side up. When using the tail end parts, place the conger eel skin side down on the rice ball. Complete the sushi by basting its top with *tsume* sauce (page 79).

Japanese Common Flying Squid
Surume-ika

Place a whole sheet of squid that has been prepared according to the recipe on page 198 on the chopping board, inner side up, one long edge facing you. Cut a strip of squid 2¾ inches wide, measuring from the edge near you. Cut another strip the same width. The remaining triangular tip can be used in a roll or other sushi.

Now place one strip facing you on the chopping board. Hold the *sashimi* knife tilted down and make ⅕-inch-thick slices, starting from the left as you do for tuna (page 201).

For the *koba* cut, follow the instructions on page 201.

Gaper Clam
Miru-gai

You have prepared the butterflied and blanched gaper clam siphon following the instructions on page 198. If the siphon is small, perhaps only 3 inches long, first cut it into two identical pieces lengthwise, then cut each of those pieces into two lengthwise pieces. If the siphon is long and narrow, instead of cutting it in half, make diagonal slices starting at the bottom. When you have only 3 inches left, cut the remaining piece lengthwise into two thin, broad slices, then cut each of those pieces lengthwise into two thin, broad slices.

Japanese Gizzard Shad
Kohada

Place the butterflied and cured *kohada* (from page 199) skin side down on the chopping board and cut it into two fillets by removing a thin strip from the center part. Each fillet is usually the proper size for making one *nigiri-zushi*. If it is larger, cut it into two pieces. Place one fillet on the chopping board skin side up and make two decorative parallel slits on the skin to expose the meat below the surface.

Master Recipe for Making *Nigiri-zushi* Kuruma Prawn *Nigiri-zushi*, *Ebi no nigiri-zushi*

In this master recipe, I am using only prawns, but try to include one or two more seafood varieties, such as tuna or salmon, to make your *nigiri-zushi* meal more colorful and flavorful.

Although it might be fun to emulate the graceful ballet that the sushi chef performs to make each *nigiri-zushi*, it is undoubtedly simpler for the home cook, who is not yet practiced in this art, simply to prepare, up to 1 hour before serving, as many rice balls as will be needed.

MAKES 28 *NIGIRI-ZUSHI* RICE BALLS, OR 3 TO 4 SERVINGS

3 cups (lightly packed) prepared sushi rice (page 58)
28 pieces prepared prawns (page 192)
Wasabi paste

Set up the working counter with sushi rice, prawns (and fish), *wasabi*, and a bowl of vinegar water.

Dip the tips of the fingers of your right hand in the vinegar water and rub both your hands together to distribute the water over your palms. Remember that too much water makes the sushi rice watery and too little makes it stick to your hands.

Following the illustrations, 1. reach into the sushi rice container with your right hand and pick up a small Ping-Pong-ball-size portion of rice (1/2 to 3/4 ounce). If you are a beginner, I recommend that you weigh the rice on a scale until you can eyeball the right amount to pick up. Without squeezing, quickly

1. Pick up a small Ping-Pong-ball-size portion of rice.

2. Make a depression in the rice with your left thumb.

3. A small depression remains in the center.

7. Place the index and middle fingers of your right hand on top of the rice ball.

8. Rotate the rice ball 180 degrees.

9. The finished rice ball.

roll the rice over several times in the tips of your fingers, palm facing down. Transfer the rice to your left hand, placing it along the base of your four fingers. 2. Hold the rice in place with the thumb and index finger of your right hand as you make a depression on the top of the rice with your left thumb. 3. When you lift your thumb, the small depression remains in the center; it will not be visible when the sushi is completed, but it keeps the rice ball light and airy.

Place the index and middle finger of your right hand on top of the sushi rice ball and 4. roll the rice toward the tips of your fingers (the depression is down). 5. Slide it back to the original

space at the base of the fingers of your left hand. Now you will make two motions simultaneously: 6. Grab the rice ball between the thumb and index finger of your right hand and move your left thumb back and forth across the top of the rice ball, exerting gentle pressure to smooth and flatten it. Do not squeeze the rice or press it down. 7. Continue to shape with the index and middle fingers of your right hand.

8. Pick up the sushi rice ball, rotate it 180 degrees clockwise, and return it to the base of the four fingers of your left hand. Repeat the process of grabbing the sides of the rice ball between the thumb and index finger while smoothing the top with the thumb as in step 6.

Continue to shape as in step 7. 9. Now you have made a perfect rice ball. (See page 208 to judge it.) Repeat until you have used up all the rice. You should have about 28 rice balls.

Now smear a dab of *wasabi* on top of each rice ball, if called for, and 10. then place the prawn on top pressing it into the rice just enough so that it will adhere. Or you can follow the steps illustrated on page 210 that a sushi chef would do, working with the rice and seafood at the same time to more fully integrate them and make for a neater finish. There is nothing difficult about the technique. It just takes a little practice to do it as swiftly and efficiently as your sushi chef does.

4. Roll the rice toward the tips of your fingers.

5. Slide the rice back to the original space at the base of your fingers.

6. Grab the rice ball between the thumb and index finger of your right hand and smooth it gently.

10. Place the prawn on top of the rice ball.

Making Rice Balls Ahead of Time

Line the rice balls up in a clean plastic container, then cover them with a clean damp towel plus a lid to keep them from drying out. Float the container in a bowl of warm water, changing the water as it cools down. Also, up to half an hour before serving, slice the raw, cooked, or cured

seafood you will be using as toppings into the right size. At the last moment, all you have to do is smear a small dab of *wasabi*, if called for, on top of the rice ball and then put the topping on, pressing down slightly to hold it in place. That's it.

The Size of Rice Balls Matters

The size of your *nigiri-zushi*—one-bite size—is very important. The "bigger is better" philosophy does not apply here. The proper sushi rice ball should weigh about ¾ ounce—one-third of a large egg. In Japan, that is a lunchtime *nigiri-zushi* size. In the evening, chefs make the rice ball a little smaller, about ½ ounce, in order to accommodate diners who will be enjoying alcoholic beverages (alcohol is high in calories). The size of the toppings—fish and shellfish—should also be proportional to the size of the sushi rice ball. Supersized slices of seafood destroy the good flavor and texture balance of a delicacy that should be enjoyed in one bite.

Nonstick Hands

In practice, you will find that rice grains stick to your hands. This is nearly unavoidable except by the most experienced chefs, whose red hands (from constant exposure to vinegar) somehow seem to develop a nonstick coating. When you are a beginner, use the proper amount of vinegar water to wet your hands, and keep them free of any stuck rice particles by wiping your hands with a clean, moistened cloth.

Judging Your Rice Ball

Put a finished *nigiri* rice ball in one hand and observe the shape. It should not look squeezed or pressed. Hold it up to a bright light. The light should filter through it, especially through the center, where you made the depression. Now bite into it: the rice ball should fall apart readily. At the same time, it must be made just strong enough to be picked up in your hand. Try to achieve this perfect balance of lightness, strength, and fragility.

When to Use *Wasabi*

You may be surprised to learn that *wasabi* is not always used in making sushi. For example, toppings of omelet and strong-flavored fish are not enhanced by *wasabi*. How much to use depends on each diner's preference. I usually call for a dab in my recipes—less than ⅛ teaspoon. Incidentally, in Japan additional *wasabi* is not usually served with your sushi.

Popular *nigiri-zushi, starting at twelve o'clock:*
three tuna, two shrimp, and two salmon,
and a cucumber cup filled with pickled ginger.

Nigiri-zushi for the Pro—Working with Rice and Seafood Simultaneously

Dip the tips of your fingers into the vinegar water and rub your hands together to distribute the water all over your palms. Reach into the sushi rice container with your right hand and pick up a portion of rice the size of a small Ping

Pong ball (about ½ to ¾ ounce). Without squeezing your right hand, roll the rice several times, following the illustrations on pages 206–207. Pick up the shrimp—or whatever fish you are using—and place it on your left hand at the base of your finger.

Smear a dab of *wasabi* in the center of the fish and quickly place the rice on top. Continue the final shaping by following the illustrated instructions.

1. Smear wasabi in the center of the shrimp.

2. Put the rice ball on top of the shrimp.

3. Make a depression with your thumb in the center of the rice.

4. Roll the rice ball toward the tips of your fingers.

5. Slide the rice ball back to the base of your fingers.

6. Grab the rice ball with your right thumb and index finger and smooth the top gently with your left thumb.

Nigiri-zushi Rice Ball Practice for the Pro

If you are aiming to be a serious chef, you should practice intensively for a month or so making rice balls—about two hundred pieces a day. You need not make a large quantity of sushi rice for this. Just prepare 6 cups of sushi rice (page 58) and make as many rice balls as you can, lining them up on a chopping board where you can inspect and critique your work. When you have finished the first practice round, return all the sushi rice balls to their container, breaking them up, and repeat the practice by making an additional batch. You can do this three times before the rice becomes too mashed for practice. Sorry for the waste, but after three rounds, you must discard the rice.

How to Cut *Tamago* (Omelet) for *Nigiri-zushi*

Cut the omelet into $\frac{1}{2}$-inch pieces crosswise. Prepare a rice ball, smear a little *wasabi* on the rice, if you wish to use it, then top with a slice of omelet. The egg topping may be bound to the rice using a thin strip of *nori*.

Another Style of *Nigiri-zushi, Gunkan*

The creation of the sushi called *gunkan* (battleship) is credited to Hisaji Imada, the owner-chef of Kyubei, one of the most venerable sushi restaurants in Tokyo. In the 1940s, one of his regular customers came in one night with some *uni,* sea urchin, and asked chef Imada to make a *nigiri-zushi* with it. Sea urchin from Hokkaido was a new ingredient to the chef, and since it is tender and loose, he realized that he needed to restructure the traditional *nigiri-zushi* so that it could contain this fragile topping. So he made a *nigiri-zushi* rice ball and wrapped around it a strip of *nori* that was considerably taller. He then spooned the creamy orange sea urchin into the *nori*-walled space above the rice.

It became an instant hit, and other sushi restaurants quickly adopted it. The restaurant did not call this new-style sushi *gunkan,* and why it was eventually given that name seems to have been lost in the mists of the past.

Part Five
Great Sushi Accompaniments

A sushi dinner, especially when you enjoy it at home, can be expanded and made into a more complete and balanced meal by adding several easy-to-prepare dishes consisting of additional seafood or vegetable side dishes and soups.

The traditional way to end your sushi dinner is with some seasonal fresh fruit, but there are other desserts you can explore, and I have included them here. You will find all these light and refreshing Japanese desserts excellent complements to the meal.

Chapter 13
Fish and Shellfish Dishes

Tuna with Grated Yam
Maguro no yamakake

Maguro no yamakake (tuna with grated yam) is one of the most popular tuna *sashimi* dishes in Japan. The bright red cubed tuna is served with snow-white grated yam, *nagaimo* (page 115). The yam has two faces: served as raw cubes or sticks, it is crunchy and crispy; served grated, it has a unique foamy, watery texture.

Tuna and yam complement each other in many ways: tender, red fish has a strong, metallic, and rich flavor, whereas white, crisp yam is rather bland, light, and refreshing. This dish can be quickly assembled using tuna left over from making sushi the same day.

MAKES 4 SIDE DISHES

¼ pound sushi *maguro* (tuna) (for information on shopping for sushi fish, see page 168, and sushi tuna, page 185)

1½ tablespoons *shoyu* (soy sauce)

1 teaspoon toasted sesame oil

¼ to ½ teaspoon *wasabi* paste or *yuzu kosho* (salt-cured green chile spiced *yuzu* paste) (page 227) or ¼ teaspoon roasted, peeled, and minced jalapeño pepper

7 ounces *nagaimo* (yam)

2 tablespoons komezu (rice vinegar)

1½ tablespoons *tsuke-joyu* (sushi dipping sauce) (page 77)

2 tablespoons chives, cut into thin rings

¼ sheet *nori* (laver), cut into needle-thin strips

Cut the tuna into quarters lengthwise, then into ⅔-inch cubes. Mix the soy sauce, sesame oil, and *wasabi* paste in a medium bowl. Add the tuna and toss. Let stand for 15 minutes.

Peel the yam and grate it. The best equipment to use is the Japanese *suribachi* grinding bowl (page 53) (the inside surface of the bowl, a rough comb pattern, does the best job of grating the tender yam) or, alternatively, use the smallest spikes of an ordinary Western box grater. Or cut the yam into julienne strips, 1½ inches long and soak in 3 cups cold water with 2 tablespoons rice vinegar for 20 minutes. Place equal amounts of the grated or sliced yam in the bottom of four small serving bowls. Add 1 teaspoon of the sushi dipping sauce (*tsuke-joyu*) to each bowl. Top each yam portion with one-quarter of the tuna cubes. Sprinkle the top with the chive rings. Just before serving, garnish the top of each bowl with the needle-thin *nori* strips.

To best enjoy the dish, mix the tuna, yam, chives, and *nori* together before eating. Picking up the slippery components of the dish with chopsticks and transferring them to your mouth may be a little challenging, so the best solution is to hold the bowl close to your mouth.

Tuna *Tatsuta-age* with Bright Green Cucumber Dressing

Maguro no tatsuta-age oroshi kyuuri-zoe

The *tatsuta-age* technique was introduced on page 122. In this recipe, tuna is cooked to medium doneness. You can use the tuna you prepared for sushi the same day or purchase sushi-grade fresh tuna (page 185) from your local fishmonger. I serve this dish (see photograph on page 213) with a light, refreshing cucumber dressing. You can also present it in a more Western way with the tuna topped with seasonal salad greens dressed with a *shoyu–yuzu kosho* dressing (page 217).

MAKES 4 DISHES

2 tablespoons *shoyu* (soy sauce)

2 teaspoons freshly squeezed ginger juice from grated ginger

2 garlic cloves, grated on a very fine grater or crushed in a garlic press

2 tablespoons *mirin* (sweet cooking wine)

2/3 pound sushi or sushi-grade *maguro* (tuna), cut into large cubes or into slices 2 inches square × 1/2 inch thick

1/4 cup potato starch

Vegetable oil for frying

CUCUMBER DRESSING:

2 Japanese cucumbers (7 ounces) or 2 Kirby cucumbers

1/2 teaspoon salt

1 small *daikon* radish (3 1/2 ounces)

1 teaspoon *umeboshi* paste (salt-pickled plum) (page 106)

1/2 teaspoon sugar

1 tablespoon *dashi* (fish stock) (page 74)

1/2 teaspoon *komezu* (rice vinegar)

2 teaspoons vegetable oil or olive oil

Mix together the soy sauce, ginger juice, grated garlic, and *mirin* in a bowl. Add the tuna, toss, and let stand for 20 minutes. Remove the tuna, discarding the marinade.

Bring a medium potful of water to a boil. Remove and discard the seedy part of the cucumber, then peel and grate it on a fine grater (you will have about 1/2 cup). Transfer the cucumber to a bowl and toss it with 1/2 teaspoon salt. Peel and grate the *daikon* radish using a fine grater (you will have about 1/2 cup). Toss with the grated cucumber and transfer to a finely woven cotton cloth (*fukin* or muslin; see page 44). Close the top of the cloth with a rubber band and slowly lower the bag into the boiling water. Count to about 30. Remove the bag from the water and cool it under cold running tap water (this blanching removes the strong flavors from the grated *daikon* and cucumber). Squeeze the vegetables gently to get rid of excess water and transfer them to a bowl. Add the salt-pickled plum paste, sugar, fish stock (*dashi*), vinegar, and oil.

Wipe the tuna dry with a paper towel and dredge the pieces in the potato starch. Heat about 1 inch of vegetable oil in a skillet to 340° F. Add the tuna in small batches and cook the pieces over medium heat until the outside is golden, about 1 minute. Drain the tuna on a steel strainer, and while it is hot, serve equal amounts on four plates with the cucumber and *daikon* dressing on the side or over dressed salad greens.

Blanched Tuna with Early Summer Vegetables
Shimofuri maguro no shoka yasai sarada

ere the *shimofuri* blanching technique, which I described on page 194, is applied to bright red tuna, which is then cut into slices or cubes to produce a beautiful color contrast—the thin outside layer of the white cooked flesh against the uncooked bright red inner flesh. I serve this attractive tuna with early summer vegetables.

½ pound sushi *maguro* (tuna) (for information on shopping for sushi fish, see page 168, and sushi tuna, page 185)

SHOYU–YUZU-KOSHO DRESSING:
1 tablespoon *shoyu* (soy sauce)
1 tablespoon *komezu* (rice vinegar)
½ teaspoon Dijon mustard
1 teaspoon honey
¼ teaspoon *yuzu-kosho* (salt-cured green chile spiced *yuzu* paste) (page 227) or ¼ teaspoon roasted, peeled, and minced jalapeño pepper
1 tablespoon olive oil
Sea salt

1 cup shelled fava beans or green peas
8 asparagus spears
2 cups snow peas
2 very small fennel bulbs (about ½ pound), cut into thin slices

Cut the tuna into three 1-inch-square logs. Have a bowlful of cold water with ice cubes nearby. Bring a medium potful of water to a boil. Place the tuna logs on a large flat steel skimmer and lower them into the pot. Cook the tuna until the outside turns white, for only 10 seconds or so. Quickly transfer the tuna pieces to the cold water. Cool quickly, then remove the tuna immediately from the water. Wipe dry with a paper towel and cut into 1-inch cubes.

Mix the soy sauce, rice vinegar, mustard, honey, *yuzu kosho,* and olive oil in a bowl. Add salt to taste. Pour 1 tablespoon of the dressing over the tuna and toss.

Bring another medium potful of lightly salted water to a boil, add the fava beans, and cook for 3 to 4 minutes. Scoop them out, cool them, and remove the thin skins.

Cook the asparagus in the pot for 1 minute. Scoop out the asparagus spears, plunge them into cold water, and drain again. Cut into 1½-inch-long pieces.

Cook the snow peas in the same pot for 10 seconds. Drain, cool in cold water, and drain again. Toss all the vegetables, including the baby fennel, in a bowl with the remaining dressing. Arrange the tuna pieces alongside the vegetables on four appetizer dishes and serve.

Vinegar-Cured Mackerel Sashimi Salad
Shime-saba no sashimi sarada

Home-cured *saba,* mackerel (page 188), is delicious to use in many preparations—*nigiri-zushi, sashimi,* pressed sushi, broiled, or salad dishes. Here it is served with refreshing red cabbage salad that has been pickled overnight.

PICKLED CABBAGE:

¼ small red cabbage (5 ounces), *finely* shredded

¼ medium red onion, cut into paper-thin slices, soaked in water for 5 minutes, then drained

1 small carrot, cut into fine julienne strips, 2 inches long

⅓ cup finely julienned ginger, 1½-inch-long sticks

¾ teaspoon sea salt

1 teaspoon sugar

1 tablespoon vegetable oil

1 tablespoon *komezu* (rice vinegar)

1 fillet (7 ounces) *shime-saba* (vinegar-cured mackerel) (page 129)*

*If you buy already cured mackerel, the average package contains 3½ ounces, so you will need two packages.

Mix the red cabbage, onion, carrot, and ginger together in a bowl. Add the salt and sugar and toss. Stir in the vegetable oil and rice vinegar. Refrigerate the vegetables half a day or preferably overnight.

Cut the mackerel into ⅙-inch-thick slices using the *sogi-zukuri* or *hira-zukuri* technique (see the accompanying box). Place equal amounts of the cabbage salad in four individual serving bowls and arrange the mackerel slices alongside.

Sashimi Cutting Techniques, Presentation, and Garnishes

CUTTING TECHNIQUES

There are several basic *sashimi* cutting techniques: *hira-zukuri, sogi-zukuri, hoso-zukuri,* and *usu-zukuri.* You use the technique that is right for the fish and how you want to present it. You need a *yanagiba* knife, or *sashimi* knife (see page 45), to do the most effective cutting.

Hira-zukuri, the most basic cutting technique, is used for fish with tender flesh such as tuna, skipjack tuna, yellowtail, and salmon. Place a block or fillet of fish in front of you (if cutting fillet, have the thinner side

Cut ¼-inch slices, pulling the knife toward you.

toward you) and, following the illustration, cut down vertically ¼ inch or a little less from the right side of the fish. If you are using a Japanese knife with a sharpened edge on one side only, tilt the blade slightly to the left to make a truly vertical cut. After making each slice, push it to the right side of the chopping board with the tip of the knife.

Sogi-zukuri is used for fish with firm flesh such as sea bream and flounder. Fish and shellfish for *nigiri-zushi* toppings are also cut using this method. Place a fish fillet or block on the cutting board (if cutting fillet, have the thicker side away from you) and slice against the grain, as shown in the illustration on page 202, drawing the knife toward you. You need to tilt your knife slightly toward the right to make a thinner and broader slice, generally ⅙ to ⅕ inch

Horse Mackerel
Tataki-Style
Aji no tataki

In this dish, *aji no tataki,* filleted, peeled *absolutely* fresh horse mackerel (pages 168 and 195) is sliced and briefly chopped with seasonal herbs and spices. Chopping (*tataki*) facilitates the release of the flavor of the herbs and spices. At a sushi restaurant, a chef usually prepares this dish in front of you at the counter upon receiving your order.

To purchase fresh horse mackerel for this dish, visit a Japanese food store and tell the fishmonger what you are planning to make. If the fish is not available, use *sashimi* tuna or yellowtail instead.

In this recipe, I serve this traditional *sashimi* on top of slices of crisp baguette—an elegant hors d'oeuvre.

MAKES 8 HORS D'OEUVRES

1 filleted and boned *ma-aji* (horse mackerel) (page 168) or ¼ pound sushi tuna or yellowtail
1 tablespoon chives, finely sliced
1 tablespoon finely julienned ginger, 1½ inches long, soaked in cold water
1 tablespoon *gari* (sweet pickled ginger) (page 66), minced
10 *shiso* (perilla) leaves, 2 finely julienned and 8 left whole
1 teaspoon white sesame seeds, toasted
Several drops of *usukushi shoyu* (light-colored soy sauce)
Coarse sea salt
1 teaspoon freshly squeezed lime juice
8 thinly sliced medium-size baguettes, crisped in the oven

Remove the skin from the fillet, starting at the head end and working toward the tail. Cut the fillet into thin strips, ¼ inch, crosswise. If you are using tuna or yellowtail, cut it in the same way. Place the chives, the two kinds of ginger, *shiso,* and white sesame seeds on the fish and with a knife chop across the flesh at intervals both vertically and horizontally—about 15 chops in all. Sprinkle drops of *shoyu,* pinches of sea salt, and lime juice to flavor and toss with chopsticks gently and thoroughly. Place a shiso leaf on top of a crisp slice of bread, then scoop up a portion of the fish and serve it on the leaf.

---

thick. While making the cut, place the thumb of your left hand lightly at the edge of the piece you are cutting to support it. After you have made each cut, pick up the slice and set it on the left side of the chopping board.

Hoso-zukuri is used to cut fish or squid with firm flesh into thin strips or sticks, which are easier to bite into. First, cut the fillet crosswise into 3-inch-long pieces. If the flesh is thicker than ⅕ inch, trim off the top of the piece to produce an even sheet about ⅕ inch thick. Then rotate the piece and cut it into strips or sticks about ⅕ inch × ⅕ inch × 3 inches.

Usu-zukuri is used to cut blowfish, *fugu,* and firm-textured whitefish such as flounder into nearly transparent slices. Place a fish fillet skinned side down on the chopping board and cut along the grain starting at the left side of the fillet. You need to slant the knife heavily toward the chopping board so that you can produce a very thin, broad cut.

PRESENTATION AND GARNISHES

The traditional *sashimi* presentation has four elements on a plate: the sliced fish and the subsidiary ingredients, called *ken, tsuma,* and *yakumi.*

Ken, the principal garnish, is usually julienned *daikon* radish, and the fish slices are propped against a mound of it. *Ken* has three functions: it gives a voluminous appearance to the flat slices of fish; it absorbs excess liquid from the sliced fish, so that the fish stays fresh looking; and it refreshes the palate. *Ken* is also made with carrot, cucumber, and Japanese squash.

Tsuma, the secondary garnish, is usually flower buds or baby vegetables or herbs in season. The popular ones are *shiso* (perilla), *myoga* (*mioga* ginger), *kogomi* (a mountain vegetable similar to fiddlehead fern), flowers of baby chrysanthemums or baby cucumbers, or buds of the *shiso* flower.

Yakumi is the spice that complements the fish. It can be freshly grated *wasabi* or ginger.

The *sashimi* dishes presented in this chapter are not traditional, but use them as guidelines, following the rules as to when to use *wasabi* or ginger in a particular dish.

Sushi Salmon Cured in Kelp
Sake no kobu-jime

Kelp curing (see page 191) has become a popular technique among sushi chefs in America. You can easily do the curing in your own kitchen. Traditionally we use white flesh fish, but I tried this preparation with salmon and it was excellent. Use absolutely fresh, parasite-free sushi salmon. The kelp-cured salmon is good for *nigiri-zushi, sashimi,* and other sushi preparations. Here I serve it with a mixture of sprouts and sea vegetable in an attractive salad.

MAKES 4 SIDE DISHES

Kokumotsu-zu (grain vinegar)
One 12- × 3 1/2-inch *kombu* (kelp), after softening (see below)
Sea salt
1/2 pound sushi salmon (for information on sushi salmon, see page 176) or homemade gravlax (page 138)
1 package *kaiware* (*daikon* sprouts) (3 1/2 ounces), roots removed
1/4 package chive sprouts (1/4 cup)
1/4 package alfalfa sprouts (1/4 cup)
1/4 cup dried *wakame* (*wakame* sea vegetable), soaked in cold water for 10 minutes, drained, and squeezed to remove excess water
1 to 2 teaspoons olive oil
1 tablespoon or more *ponzu* sauce (page 78)

Mix 2 tablespoons of water and 2 tablespoons of grain vinegar in a small cup. Dip a paper towel into the vinegar water and wipe the kelp. Wrap the kelp in a clean moistened paper towel and leave it at room temperature for about 30 minutes to make it tender and allow it to expand (it will double in size).

Place the softened kelp on the working counter and sprinkle pinches of salt over half of the kelp. Place the salmon on the salted area and sprinkle additional pinches of salt over the salmon. Cover with the remaining part of the kelp; wrap it tightly in plastic wrap and put it into a shallow stainless steel container. Place a similar-size shallow stainless steel container on top of the fish as a weight and put three rubber bands around the containers at intervals. Refrigerate for 18 hours.

Remove the salmon from the kelp, discarding the kelp, and cut the salmon into thin slices, about 1/5 to 1/6 inch thick, using the *sogi-zukuri* technique (page 218). Toss the sprouts and *wakame* in a bowl with the olive oil, then add 1 tablespoon or so of *ponzu* sauce to flavor. Serve the sliced fish with the sprout salad.

Traditional Flounder *Sashimi* with *Ponzu* Sauce
Hirame no usu-zukuri ponzu-zoe

Using the *usu-zukuri* technique (page 219), the fish is cut so thin that you can see the color of the plate underneath on which the *sashimi* is presented. Creating such slices makes the fish easy to chew and appealing to look at (as if those slices on the large platter resembled the petals of a chrysanthemum; see page 163). Here I serve the sliced fish with traditional *ponzu* sauce (page 78) and *momiji oroshi,* spiced grated *daikon* (page 75).

To prepare this dish, you must have *absolutely* fresh, *properly butchered and filleted* flounder (page 190). You can find such quality fish, whole or already filleted, skinned, and packed at Japanese food stores. If sushi flounder is not available, use boiled octopus (page 193) or freshly shucked scallops instead.

1 back-meat fillet of sushi flounder (for information on shopping for sushi fish, see page 168) or 8 very fresh scallops or 1 large leg of boiled octopus

¼ cup *momiji oroshi* (spiced grated *daikon*) (page 75)

2 tablespoons chives, finely sliced

2 tablespoons or more *ponzu* sauce (page 78)

Cut the fish into very thin slices using the *usu-zukuri* technique (page 219). Arrange the slices on a serving platter, slightly overlapping one another, in concentric rings. You can make a beautiful fan or a flower shape with the slices. Garnish the center of the platter with the *momiji oroshi* and chives. Serve the dish with the *ponzu* sauce.

Flounder with Salsa Sauce
Hirame no sarusa sauce

Here I offer the traditional *usu-zukuri* flounder with a modern sauce. If you cannot find sushi flounder, use freshly shucked scallops, gravlax, or even flounder that you would ordinarily cook.

MAKES 4 SIDE DISHES

40 slices (⅘ pound) sushi flounder (for information on shopping for sushi fish, see page 168), sliced using the *usu-zukuri* technique (page 219) or scallops or flounder for cooking

SALSA SAUCE:

¼ cup ripe tomato, peeled, seeded, and finely diced

¼ cup fennel bulb, finely diced

¼ cup yellow bell pepper, stemmed, seeded, and finely diced

¼ cup green bell pepper, stemmed, seeded, and finely diced

¼ cup red onion, finely diced; soaked in water for 20 minutes and drained

¼ cup avocado, ripe but firm, pit removed, peeled, and finely diced

¼ cup fresh coriander leaves, finely chopped

½ to 1 jalapeño, finely diced

¼ cup lime juice

½ to 1 teaspoon sea salt

1½ teaspoons honey

½ tablespoon *komezu* (rice vinegar)

2 tablespoons or more virgin olive oil

2 tablespoons or more *komezu* (rice vinegar) to brush over the sliced fish

First, cut the fish into thin (about ⅕-inch), broad slices.

Mix the tomato, fennel bulb, yellow and green bell pepper, red onion, avocado, coriander, and jalapeño (adjust the quantity of jalapeño to achieve the level of "heat" you desire) in a bowl with the lime juice, sea salt, honey, and rice vinegar. Refrigerate for 2 hours.

Coat a large plate with a very thin layer of olive oil. Arrange the sushi flounder slices on the plate without overlapping and paint the fish slices with additional olive oil. Then paint with a thin layer of rice vinegar.

Spread equal amounts of the vegetable mixture on four serving plates and arrange the flounder slices on top.

Salmon Roe in Grated *Daikon*
Ikura oroshi

What makes this extremely simple dish—golden orange salmon roe sitting on a bed of snow-white *daikon* radish in a small serving bowl (see page 237)—so special is the use of very good quality salmon roe, *ikura,* and sweet, juicy wintertime *daikon* radish. The *daikon,* which is rich in vitamin C and digestive enzymes, mellows the strong flavor and oiliness of salmon roe.

To eat, just stir the two ingredients with a few drops of *shoyu* (soy sauce) or *tsuke-joyu* (sushi dipping sauce). This is not a chopstick-friendly dish, as you can imagine. So hold the bowl close to your mouth as you pick up portions with your chopsticks. At the end, you may need to shovel the last little bit directly from the bowl into your mouth. Your mother might not approve, but in Japan, it is perfectly acceptable table manners.

MAKES 4 SIDE DISHES

1 cup freshly grated *daikon* from the upper part of the root (page 75)

½ cup *ikura* (cured salmon roe) (page 182), preferably Japanese *ikura*

1 whole *yuzu* citrus fruit or lemon, with the rind cut into julienne strips (reserve the juice)

Tsuke-joyu (sushi dipping sauce) (page 77)

Place equal amounts of the grated *daikon* in four small serving bowls. Mound up equal amounts of the salmon roe in each bowl. Garnish the top with *yuzu* strips and squeeze a little *yuzu* juice over the top. Serve the dish with the *tsuke-joyu,* adding ¼ to ½ teaspoon to the bowl at the table to each diner's taste.

Octopus, Cucumber, and *Wakame* Salad
Tako-su

Tako-su, vinegar-tossed octopus, is a regular feature at Japanese and sushi restaurants in Japan and America. The appeal of this simple combination lies in using very good quality boiled octopus, Japanese cucumber, and properly reconstituted dried *wakame* sea vegetable.

Already boiled octopus is available at most Japanese food stores, or you can cook your own following the instructions on page 193. It is very easy to do, and you can produce the best results. If you prefer, use boiled shrimp, squid, or scallops instead. A combination of these seafoods is even better.

MAKES 4 SIDE DISHES

TAKO-SU DRESSING:

¼ cup *komezu* (rice vinegar)

1½ tablespoons *dashi* (fish stock) (page 74)

2 teaspoons sugar

1 teaspoon *usukuchi shoyu* (light-colored soy sauce) or ordinary *shoyu* (soy sauce)

⅛ teaspoon salt

Sesame oil (optional)

1 Japanese cucumber (6 ounces) or 1 small Kirby cucumber (1 inch in diameter)

½ teaspoon salt

¼ cup dried *wakame* (*wakame* sea vegetable), soaked in cold water for 5 minutes and drained

⅔ pound boiled octopus (page 193)

Put the rice vinegar, *dashi,* sugar, soy sauce, and salt in a small cup and stir well to dissolve the sugar. Add drops of sesame oil if you like.

Cut the cucumber crosswise into paper-thin slices and toss in a bowl with 1/2 teaspoon salt. Let stand for 10 minutes. Drain, then rinse the cucumber in a strainer under cold running water and squeeze firmly to remove excess water. Taste a slice and, if it seems rather salty, rinse further—it should have only a faint saltiness. Toss the cucumber in a bowl with 1 tablespoon of the *tako-su* dressing.

Bring a medium potful of water to a boil and blanch the drained *wakame* for 2 seconds. Drain and cool under cold running water. Squeeze the *wakame* to remove excess water, then toss with 1 tablespoon of the *tako-su* dressing.

Cut the octopus into thin slices using the *usu-zukuri* technique (page 219) or into small cubes, making about 20 slices or pieces. Toss in a bowl with 1 tablespoon of the *tako-su* dressing.

Gently squeeze the *wakame* and mound up equal amounts in four small serving bowls. Gently squeeze the cucumber and place equal amounts alongside the *wakame.* Arrange equal amounts of the octopus on top of the cucumber. Spoon some of the remaining *tako-su* dressing (about 3 tablespoons) equally over each bowl.

Octopus, Salad Greens, and Tomato with *Tosazu* Dressing
Tako no tosazu sarada

This is another delightful dish you can make using the octopus that you have cooked for your *nigiri-zushi* dinner. Here I serve thinly sliced octopus with frisée (salad greens whose leaves are finely spiked, so that they hold the dressing effectively) drizzled with a *tosazu* dressing. *Tosazu* is a rice vinegar dressing with *katsuobushi* fish flakes added for a robust flavor. Choose an onion that has a mild, sweet flavor, such as Vidalia.

***TOSAZU* DRESSING:**
3 tablespoons *komezu* (rice vinegar)
3 tablespoons *usukuchi shoyu* (light-colored soy sauce)
1/4 cup sugar
1 cup *dashi* (fish stock) (page 74)
1/2 cup *katsuobushi* (dried bonito flakes)

2/3 pound prepared octopus (page 193)
1/4 head frisée or other salad leaves, separated
4 leaves radicchio, cut into thick strips
1 small ripe tomato, cut into small cubes
2 tablespoons olive oil
Sea salt

Pour the rice vinegar, soy sauce, sugar, and *dashi* into a small saucepan and bring to a boil, stirring to dissolve the sugar. Add the bonito flakes (*katsuobushi*), turn off the heat, and cool. Strain the liquid and discard the fish flakes.

Cut the prepared octopus into paper-thin slices using the *usu-zukuri* technique (page 219). Arrange equal amounts of the salad greens in four salad bowls. Place equal amounts of the sliced octopus on top of the vegetables and garnish with tomato cubes. With a spoon, drizzle the olive oil and *tosazu* dressing over the salad leaves and octopus, then sprinkle with sea salt to taste.

Crisp
Sea Bream Chips
Tai no usugiri
tatsuta-age

ish chips! Here I coat fish that has been pounded into a very thin sheet with ample potato starch and fry it crisp in oil (see page 251). The potato starch gives a unique texture to the fish chips—crisp with a slight chewiness. You can prepare this with leftover fish from your sushi making. Shrimp, pork, and chicken breast are also good done this way. Serve as snacks with a glass of cold beer.

MAKES 4 SIDE DISHES

MARINADE:

2 teaspoons ginger juice (page 122)
2 garlic cloves, finely grated
1½ tablespoons *shoyu* (soy sauce)
1 tablespoon *mirin* (sweet cooking wine)

5 ounces sea bream or other whitefish
   fillet, cut into 10 to 12 thin slices
½ cup potato starch
Vegetable oil for frying
Sea salt
½ cup raw cashew nuts
1 lemon, cut into 4 wedges

Mix the ginger juice, grated garlic, soy sauce, and *mirin* in a bowl, add the fish slices, and let stand for 15 minutes. Remove the fish slices, discarding the liquid, and wipe with a paper towel.

Spread about 1½ feet of plastic wrap on the working counter with one short side facing you. Spread 2 tablespoons of potato starch in the center of the upper half of the plastic wrap (the starch layer needs to accommodate two slices of fish). Place two fish slices on the potato starch with space between them. Spoon an additional 2 tablespoons of potato starch over the fish slices. Fold the lower half of the plastic wrap over the fish. With a rolling pin, roll the fish slices to make them thinner and triple their surface area. Spoon additional potato starch over the fish slices, if necessary, so the fish slices don't stick to the plastic. Unfold the plastic wrap, remove the fish slices, and spread them out on a large platter. Finish coating and thinning the remaining fish slices.

Heat 3 inches of vegetable oil in a skillet to 320° F. Add the fish slices in small batches and fry them over low heat until they are crisp and lightly golden, about 2 to 3 minutes. Drain the fish on a paper towel and sprinkle some sea salt over it. Finish cooking all the fish slices. Add the cashew nuts to the heated oil and cook until lightly golden. Drain the nuts on a paper towel and sprinkle some sea salt over them. Serve the fish slices on a large serving platter, piled on top of one another like a pancake stack, with cashews and lemon wedges alongside.

Simmered
Sea Bream Roe
Tai no ko nimono

n early spring in Japan, simmered sea bream roe, which is cooked in a broth of *sake* (rice wine), *mirin* (sweet cooking wine), and *dashi* (fish stock) with some fresh ginger slices, appears at every dining table, both at home and in restaurants. I could never find sea bream roe in New York, but one day in early summer, I encountered some beautiful fish roe at a nearby fishmonger. I was told that it was from shad, a fish I had never heard of, and that it was a seasonal delicacy in the northeastern United States. I took some home and sautéed it American-style with some olive oil and butter in a skillet, and it was so good that now I cannot wait to enjoy this treat every year in early spring. I even tried cooking the shad roe the way we would do it in Japan. It was delicious.

MAKES 2 SIDE DISHES

1 pair sea bream roe or shad roe (about
   7 ounces)
½ cup *sake* (rice wine)
¼ cup *mirin* (sweet cooking wine)
1½ cups *dashi* (fish stock) (page 74)
1 thumb-sized piece of ginger, peeled,
   half of it sliced thin and the other half
   finely julienned
¼ teaspoon sea salt
1½ tablespoons *usukuchi shoyu* (light-
   colored soy sauce) or ordinary *shoyu*
   (soy sauce)
10 shelled fava beans

Remove any veins from the roe. Cut the pair into its two sacs, then slice each sac lengthwise and butterfly it. Now cut each piece in half crosswise. Bring a medium potful of slightly salted water to a boil. Blanch the roe until it has turned pale on the outside, about 30 seconds (this cleans the roe and prepares it for further cooking). Remove the roe from the water and drain.

Pour the *sake* and *mirin* into a medium pot and bring it to a simmer. Add the *dashi* and, when it comes to a simmer, drop in the roe and ginger slices. Cook over medium-low heat, covered with a drop lid (page 51) or parchment paper, for 10 minutes. Add the sea salt and light-colored soy sauce and cook 5 more minutes. Turn off the heat and let the roe cool in the cooking liquid.

Bring a medium pot of lightly salted water to a boil and cook the fava beans for 3 to 4 minutes. Drain, cool in a bowl of cold water, and remove the thin skins.

Serve equal amounts of the roe with fava beans in two small serving bowls with some strained cooking broth. Garnish the top of the roe with the julienned ginger.

Oysters with *Ponzu*
Su-gaki

In Japan, the popular oyster is the *magaki,* or giant Pacific oyster. It is two or three times the size of North American and European varieties. *Magaki* is one of the creamiest and most richly flavored of all oysters. We enjoy them in the simplest way—shelled and served with a little *ponzu* sauce garnished with grated spiced *daikon* radish, *momiji oroshi.* The slightly metallic taste, the sea-breeze aroma, and the creamy texture burst in your mouth.

MAKES 2 SERVINGS

3-inch-long *daikon* radish disk, peeled
24 giant Pacific oysters or your favorite oysters
1 1/2 cups *ponzu* sauce (page 78)
1/3 cup *momiji oroshi* (spiced grated *daikon* radish) (page 75)

Grate the *daikon* radish into a bowl. Open the oysters and reserve the shells. Let the oysters drop into the bowl with the grated *daikon.* With both hands, gently turn the oysters over with the grated *daikon* until the pulp and juice acquire a grayish color. Transfer the oysters to a strainer, discarding the grated *daikon,* and rinse them under running cold tap water. Do this quickly to preserve the good flavor of the oysters. Drain.

Clean the reserved shells and return the oysters to them. Arrange half a dozen on two serving plates. Pour 1/2 to 1 teaspoon of the *ponzu* sauce over each oyster and garnish each with 1/4 teaspoon spiced grated *daikon* (*momiji oroshi*).

Tip for Cleaning Oysters

After shucking the oysters, rinse them in grated *daikon* radish, as described in the Oysters with *Ponzu* recipe. Enjoy your favorite oysters in the Japanese way.

Eel and Cucumber Roll
Ana-kyuu maki

Ana-kyuu, a contraction of the words anago (conger eel) and *kyuuri* (cucumber), is an eel and cucumber roll made without sushi rice. The sweet and tender conger eel, refreshing and crunchy cucumber, along with the crisp *nori* sheet offer a marvelous combination of tastes and textures. You can easily enjoy this at home with already prepared, purchased eel, *unagi no kabayaki.*

MAKES 7 ROLLS

½ pound whole simmered conger eel (page 197) or 1 package (6 ounces) *unagi no kabayaki* (prepared eel)

4 sheets *nori* (laver), cut into halves crosswise; choose crisp sheets

1 Japanese cucumber (about 3½ ounces) or 2 small Kirby cucumbers, cut into thin 2½-inch-long strips

2 tablespoons toasted white sesame seeds

Anago no tsume (eel sauce) (page 79) or homemade *tsume* (quick rich brown *shoyu* sauce) (page 79) (optional)

Reheat the eel following the instructions on page 99 and cut it into five pieces crosswise, each about 2½ inches long. Cut each piece into ½-inch-thick strips. Pick up one half-sheet of *nori* and place it on your left hand with one long side facing you. Place one-seventh portion of the eel and cucumber on the left edge of the *nori.* Sprinkle some white sesame seeds on top and spoon a little *tsume* sauce over, if desired. Make a cone-shaped hand roll following the instructions on page 120.

Japanese Mustard

Japanese mustard has a dark yellow color and a pleasant bitter flavor. It is sold in powdered form in a small can or in paste in a plastic tube. To use the powder, mix it with an equal amount of lukewarm water and stir with chopsticks or a spoon until it develops a sharp spiciness. If you cannot find Japanese mustard, use Colman's English mustard.

Tender Cooked Octopus
Tako no yawaraka-ni

Tender cooked, flavored octopus, served as a side dish at sushi restaurants in both Japan and America, reminds me of a Spanish octopus dish, *pulpo a la gallega,* because it is so melting tender. But the taste of the Spanish version of sliced octopus bathed in olive oil and laced with paprika in no way resembles the Japanese preparation, in which no fragrant oil is used, so you can better enjoy the subtle but excellent sweet flavor and aroma of the octopus.

To ensure that the octopus is tender, I pound each leg with an empty glass bottle before cooking it in carbonated water, to which *azuki* beans and *ban-cha* tea leaves are added. The carbonated water helps to tenderize the meat, the *azuki* beans preserve the bright, attractive purple color of the octopus, and the tea prevents the skin from breaking off during cooking. This is an easy recipe to master and is well worth the effort. Try to find octopus that has not been frozen.

MAKES 10 SIDE DISHES

⅓ cup *ban-cha* tea or other green tea leaves

3- × 6-inch *kombu* (kelp)

1 cup *azuki* beans, cooked in 2 cups water for 30 minutes

2 pounds raw octopus legs, rubbed with salt and rinsed

2 cups *sake* (rice wine)

2 cups carbonated water

1½ cups *mirin* (sweet cooking wine)

½ cup plus 3 tablespoons sugar

¼ cup plus 2 tablespoons *shoyu* (soy sauce)

¼ cup *tamari shoyu* (*tamari* soy sauce)

THE CONDIMENT: hot mustard paste (see the accompanying box)

Bring 10 cups of water in a pot to a boil, add the *ban-cha* tea or other green tea leaves, then turn off the heat and steep, uncovered, for 2 minutes. Strain the infused tea, discarding the tea leaves.

Place the kelp (*kombu*) on the bottom of the pot, spread the firmly cooked *azuki* beans over, and place the octopus legs on top. Add the tea, *sake*, and carbonated water and cook, covered with a drop lid (page 51) or parchment paper on top, for 2 hours. Add the *mirin*, sugar, and soy sauce and continue to cook over low heat for 1 hour. Add the *tamari* soy sauce and cook for another 20 minutes. Cool at room temperature.

Cut the legs into bite-size pieces, about 1 inch. Arrange equal amounts of the octopus in ten small serving bowls. Spoon some of the leftover cooking liquid without beans over the octopus and garnish the top of each bowl with a dab of hot mustard paste.

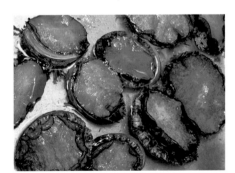

Braised Abalone
Awabi no yawaraka-ni

In past years, my students have often asked me how to tenderize abalone, which can be as tough as a rubber tire. Here is the answer. I cook the abalone in *sake* broth in a steamer for about 1 hour until the flesh becomes quite tender. *Daikon* radish, which I add to the cooking broth, also helps to tenderize it.

In Japan, we use *megai,* Siebold's abalone. But an abalone called nagareko, which is similar to *megai* and is farmed in the waters of Southern California, is good for this dish. Its flesh is lighter in color, and the muscle meat is more tender. Ask your fishmonger if he or she can get it for you.

MAKES 4 SIDE DISHES

One *megai* (Siebold's abalone) or nagareko abalone, shelled (about 4 ounces)
1/4 pound *daikon* (*daikon* radish), cut into 4 pieces
1/2 cup *sake* (rice wine)
1 tablespoon *mirin* (sweet cooking wine)
1 cup *dashi* (fish stock) (page 74)
1/2 tablespoon *usukuchi shoyu* (light-colored soy sauce) or ordinary soy sauce
1/2 teaspoon salt
1 small Kirby cucumber, cut into paper-thin slices

Yuzu-kosho (salt-cured green chile spiced *yuzu* paste) (see the accompanying box)

Sprinkle salt over the muscle side of the abalone and scrub with a hard brush. Continue to scrub under cold running tap water. Use a flat broad metal tool to remove the abalone from the shell. Remove the intestines and cut off the frilly flesh surrounding the body.

Set a steamer over high heat. Put the abalone and *daikon* pieces in a medium bowl. Pour the *sake* and *mirin* into a medium pot, set it over medium heat, and bring it to a simmer. Add the *dashi*, light-colored soy sauce, and salt and bring it to a simmer, then pour it over the abalone and *daikon.* Cover the bowl with plastic wrap and set it inside the hot steamer. Cook the abalone for 40 to 50 minutes. Keep a simmering kettle of water nearby to replenish the water in the steamer as needed.

Remove the bowl from the steamer and let the abalone cool in the cooking liquid. Cut off the protruding top round disk of the abalone and cut it into slices using the *sogi-zukuri* technique (page 218). Then cut the remaining larger portion into 1/6-inch-thick slices. Arrange equal amounts of the sliced cucumber in four serving bowls and place the sliced abalone over them. Garnish each top with a little dab of *yuzu-kosho.*

Yuzu-kosho
Salt-Cured Green Chile Spiced *Yuzu* Paste

Yuzu-kosho is a spicy and salty condiment with the fragrance of *yuzu* citron. To make *yuzu-kosho,* the rind of *yuzu* is pickled with green or red chile pepper along with salt for nearly one year. Both green and red have similar flavor characteristics. So choose green or red according to how you want your final dish to look. It is available at Japanese food stores.

Salmon Roe, Persimmon, and *Daikon* Salad
Ikura Kobachi

When bright orange persimmons (*kaki*) appear at fruit stands in the cold weather, *daikon* radishes are at their sweetest, too. In this dish, these two perfect mates make a light and refreshing side dish. When persimmons are not available, use dried apricots.

MAKES 4 SIDE DISHES

¼ cup *komezu* (rice vinegar)
¼ cup *dashi* (fish stock) (page 74)
2 tablespoons sugar
1 tablespoon plus ¼ teaspoon salt
7-ounce head part of *daikon,* cut into ¼-inch cubes (about 2 cups)
1 medium persimmon, ripe but not too soft, or 4 to 6 dried apricots, cut into ¼-inch cubes (about 1 cup)
¼ cup *ikura* (salmon roe)
½ *yuzu* citron or lemon rind, julienned

Mix the rice vinegar, *dashi,* sugar, and ¼ teaspoon of the salt in a medium bowl and let stand for 30 minutes.

Place the *daikon* and the remaining 1 tablespoon of salt in a bowl, toss, and let stand for 10 minutes. Transfer the *daikon* to a colander and rinse under cold running tap water. Drain and squeeze it tightly to remove excess water. Toss the *daikon* and persimmon with the dressing and refrigerate, covered, for as long as 6 hours. Arrange equal amounts of the *daikon* and persimmon in four small serving bowls, top each with equal amounts of salmon roe, and sprinkle the julienned *yuzu* or lemon rind over them.

Namban Monkfish
Namban anko

Namban means "southern barbarian," the name given to the tall, fair-skinned, redheaded Portuguese who landed in Japan in the sixteenth century, sailing up from Southeast Asia. The preparation uses techniques and ingredients adopted from the Portuguese—deep frying, vinegar marination, and dried red chile pepper. Here I quickly deep-fry the fish and marinate it in vinegar that has been spiced with dried red chile pepper and sweetened. The dish is usually prepared and served cold during the hot summer months. The vinegar gives a lift to our appetite and energy level.

MAKES 4 SERVINGS

***NAMBAN* MARINADE:**
½ cup *komezu* (rice vinegar)
½ cup *dashi* (fish stock) (page 74)
¼ cup sugar
2 tablespoons *shoyu* (soy sauce)
1 teaspoon sea salt
2 *akatogarashi* (Japanese red chile peppers) or other small dried red chile peppers

1 small American eggplant
Vegetable oil for frying
4 small cauliflower florets, about 1½ inches in diameter
10 ounces monkfish fillet, boned and skinned, or other whitefish fillet
½ cup all-purpose flour

Put the rice vinegar, *dashi,* sugar, soy sauce, and salt into a medium pot and bring it to a simmer, stirring. Pour the marinade into a bowl and add the chile peppers.

Cut the eggplant in half and make a shallow crosscut on the skin side of each piece. Cut each half eggplant into six pieces.

Heat 2 inches of the vegetable oil in a skillet to 340° F. Add the eggplant in batches and fry over medium-low heat for 1 minute or so, or until the outside is lightly golden. Remove the pieces from the oil, drain well, and toss into the marinade. Finish frying and marinating all the eggplant. Add the cauliflower florets to the heated oil and cook over medium heat for 1 to 2 minutes, until the outside is lightly golden. Remove them from the oil, drain well, and transfer to the marinade.

Cut the monkfish into 12 pieces. Dredge each piece in the flour, add to the skillet in small batches, and fry the pieces until they are lightly golden, about 2 minutes. Remove the fish from the oil and transfer it to the marinade with the vegetables. Cover the bowl and refrigerate at least 2 hours to overnight.

Arrange equal portions of the fish, eggplant, and cauliflower in four serving bowls and spoon 1 tablespoon of the remaining marinade over each bowl. Cut the softened red chile pepper in the marinade into thin rings and garnish each bowl with some of the rings.

Fish Carpaccio
Sakana no karupaccho

Carpaccio is an Italian dish consisting of very thin slices of raw beef served cold with a creamy vinaigrette. It was natural for innovative chefs to create a seafood version of this. To make it, I use sushi salmon that I have cured in kelp. If sushi-quality salmon is not available, use homemade gravlax (page 138) or sushi tuna or flounder.

1 pound sushi salmon (for information on shopping for sushi fish, see page 168, and sushi salmon, page 176) or homemade gravlax cured in kelp (for information on curing in kelp, see page 190) or sushi tuna
Olive oil
Freshly ground black pepper

SHOYU DRESSING:
2 tablespoons olive oil
2 tablespoons freshly squeezed lemon juice
1/2 teaspoon Dijon smooth mustard
1 1/2 tablespoons *shoyu* (soy sauce)
1/2 to 1 teaspoon finely grated garlic

2 cups thinly sliced radicchio or endive
2 cups frisée or other salad leaves
2 tablespoons chopped coriander leaves
2 scallions, finely sliced

Cut the salmon into 28 to 30 thin, broad slices, using the *sogi-zukuri* technique (page 218). Lightly grease a large platter with olive oil and sprinkle on pepper, then arrange the fish slices on top, without overlapping. Brush the surface of the fish with additional oil and sprinkle on additional pepper. Cover the platter with plastic wrap and refrigerate.

Whisk the olive oil, lemon juice, mustard, soy sauce, and garlic in a bowl. About 15 minutes before serving time, arrange equal amounts of the fish on four serving plates and drizzle each plate with 1 tablespoon of *shoyu* dressing. Toss the salad greens in a bowl with 1 tablespoon of *shoyu* dressing. Decorate the center of each plate with the salad greens. Serve immediately.

Sea Bream, Simmered
Tai no nimono

I was raised by a mother who knows which fish and which part of each fish tastes the best, and she imparted that knowledge and appreciation to her children. When my mother would simmer or grill a whole, large sea bream, I had to fight with my siblings over who got the cheeks, the succulent meat behind the neck, and the eyeballs—not the white eyeballs but the gelatinous part surrounding them. And I am not alone in my love of these foods.

In the sushi kitchen, after filleting the sea bream, chefs make *kabuto-ni* (simmered fish head) by cooking the meaty head in a broth of *sake*, *shoyu*, and *mirin*. Since that is not to everyone's liking, I make this delightful dish that uses whole sea bream (or porgy is also good).

MAKES 2 TO 3 SIDE DISHES

1 sea bream or porgy (about 2 pounds)
Sea salt
1½ cups *sake* (rice wine)
2 ounces ginger, half julienned and the
    other half cut in thin slices
¼ cup *mirin* (sweet cooking wine)
2 to 2½ tablespoons *shoyu* (soy sauce)
¼ cup scallion, finely sliced

Scale the fish with a fish scaler or a sturdy knife using a pointed tip. Remove the gills and entrails. Cut off the thin white film that lines the gut cavity and rinse the blood clotted on the backbone (see page 189). Cut off the head behind the pectoral fin and remove the gills. The head has two small, meaty collarbones behind the gill slits. Separate these from the head and cut the head in half lengthwise. Cut the body of the fish crosswise into thirds. Now you have two halves of the head, two collarbones, and three pieces of the body. (If you prefer, ask your fishmonger to do this for you.) All bones and skin are left in place, as they add flavor. Make slits on both sides of the three body pieces and put them in a pan. Salt the fish pieces on both sides and refrigerate for 30 minutes.

Rinse the fish under cold running tap water and drain. Bring a medium pot of water to a boil and, using a large slotted spoon, lower the fish pieces one or two at a time into the boiling water and blanch until the outside is white, about 30 seconds. Remove to a bowl of cold water set under cold running water. Carefully and thoroughly clean the fish, making sure to remove any debris or remaining scales. Drain the fish pieces.

Pour the *sake* into a medium shallow pot and bring it to a simmer to cook off the alcohol. Add 1½ cups of water and bring to a simmer. Add the fish pieces, including the head halves and collarbones, and sliced ginger and cook over medium-low heat, covered with a drop lid (page 51) or parchment paper. At the beginning, skim off any foam until it has all been removed. Pour the *mirin* into a small saucepan and bring it to a simmer to cook off the alcohol. Add the *mirin* to the pot with the fish and bring to a simmer. After it has cooked for 5 minutes, add the *shoyu* and cook another 3 minutes, occasionally scooping up some of the cooking liquid and pouring it over the fish. Blanch the julienned ginger in a small pot of boiling water for 30 seconds. Drain and cool in cold water. Drain again.

Serve the fish in two or three individual small bowls with some of the cooking broth. Garnish with the blanched ginger and scallion rings. Watch for bones. And please do try the delicious head meat.

Steamed Monkfish Liver with *Ponzu*
An'kimo no ponzu-zoe

If you love foie gras, you should certainly try this monkfish liver, which in Japan inspires the same kind of affection and respect as foie gras in Europe and America. Monkfish liver is cooked by steaming it to a creamy tenderness and is served with *ponzu* sauce and *momiji oroshi,* spiced grated *daikon* radish. The prepared fish liver has a slightly firmer texture than foie gras and a much lower fat content.

At our neighborhood farmers' (and fishermen's) market in New York City, two fishmongers sell this delicacy caught in local waters during the cold winter months. I seem not to be the only buyer of this still largely undiscovered treat. To my surprise, if I come to the market late, the livers may be gone. I always wonder who bought them and how he or she prepares them. When purchasing, choose those that are meaty, plump, and light pink color. Avoid any with bloodstains.

1 pound monkfish livers (about 2 pieces; size varies)
Sea salt
About ¼ cup *momiji oroshi* (spiced grated *daikon* radish) (page 75)
About 2 tablespoons chives, cut into thin rings
About ½ cup *ponzu* sauce (page 78)

Rinse the livers under cold running tap water. Remove the clear stringlike veins. Cut around any clotted blood and squeeze to remove it. Remove as much blood as possible, as blood gives an off taste and a stained appearance.

Drain the livers and wipe well with a paper towel. Spread a layer of salt ⅙ inch deep on a large plate on which the livers will fit, place the livers on top, and cover with an additional thick layer of salt, about ⅙ inch. Refrigerate for 30 minutes. Remove the livers from the salt and rinse well in a bowl of cold water.

Set a steamer over high heat. Wipe the livers with a paper towel and cut them into two logs, each 2 inches in diameter, then wrap in plastic. Choose a durable wrap which can stand for 2 hours steaming without tearing. Roll each log in a bamboo rolling mat and put three rubber bands around each to secure. Transfer the livers to the steamer and steam for 2 hours.

Take the livers out of the steamer and cool at room temperature. Remove the livers from the rolling mat and plastic wrap and cut each log into ½-inch-thick disks. Arrange equal amounts in ten small serving bowls, garnish with the spiced grated *daikon* radish (*momiji oroshi*), and sprinkle chive disks on top. Pour a tablespoon or so of *ponzu* sauce over each bowl.

Scallops in Sea Urchin Sauce
Hotate no uni sosu

In this dish, I quickly sear large, meaty scallops in a skillet and serve them with my favorite sea urchin sauce—a rich dish, so a small portion is fully satisfying.

SEA URCHIN SAUCE:
½ wooden tray *uni* (sea urchin) (page 139) (about 2 ounces) or 10 to 12 fresh sea urchins, shelled
2 tablespoons heavy cream
1 egg yolk from large or medium egg
Shoyu (soy sauce), *komezu* (rice vinegar), and salt

2 small Kirby cucumbers, 1 inch in diameter
8 very fresh large scallops, preferably not chemically treated, cut in 2 thin disks
Olive oil
4 teaspoons or more *tsuke-joyu* (sushi dipping sauce) (page 77)
1 to 2 tablespoons *wasabi* paste
¼ sheet *nori* (laver), cut into needle-thin julienne strips

Steam the sea urchin in a bowl placed in a steamer over boiling water for 8 minutes. If using a metal steamer, make sure to wrap a towel around the inside of the lid to prevent condensed moisture from dripping onto the sea urchin. Remove the sea urchin from the steamer and press it through a fine sieve into a small bowl (you will get about ¼ cup). Mix in the heavy cream and egg yolk and place the bowl over a pan of boiling water. While stirring with a small plastic spatula, cook the sea urchin and egg yolk for 10 minutes. Add the soy sauce, a little vinegar, and salt to taste. Cool the sauce by setting the bowl in a large bowl of ice-cold water. You should have about ⅓ cup.

Cut the cucumber into paper-thin slices, salt lightly, toss, and let it sit for 5 minutes. Transfer the cucumber to a strainer and rinse off the salt under cold running tap water. Drain and squeeze the cucumber between your hands to remove excess water.

Lightly salt the scallop pieces and let them stand for 5 minutes. Wipe them with a paper towel to remove excess moisture. Heat a large heavy-bottomed skillet and add a little olive oil. When the skillet is hot, cook the scallop slices without overlapping over medium-low heat until both sides are golden, a total of 2 minutes.

Place equal amounts of the sea urchin sauce in four individual serving bowls. Arrange the cucumber slices on top and then the cooked scallops. Pour about 1 teaspoon of the sushi dipping sauce (*tsuke-joyu*) into each bowl and garnish the top with a dab of *wasabi* and julienned *nori.*

Chapter 14
Vegetable Dishes

Garlic Chives with *Ponzu* Dressing
Nira no ponzu-ae

If possible, try to keep homemade *ponzu* sauce (page 78) in your refrigerator, so that you can prepare delicious, quick vegetable dishes like this in a flash. Here I cook very fresh garlic chives and then serve them with homemade *ponzu*. That's it! Simple is the best for good, fresh vegetables. Try the same with spinach, scallions, broccoli, asparagus, mustard greens, eggplant, or bell peppers: cook scallions, spinach, broccoli, and mustard greens in water; broil asparagus, eggplant, and bell peppers.

MAKES 4 SIDE DISHES

7 ounces garlic chives or scallions, whole
¼ cup homemade *ponzu* sauce (page 78) or purchased *ponzu*
1 package *ito-katsuo* (julienned bonito fish flakes) (page 104)

Bring plenty of water in a large pot to a boil. Cook the garlic chives for 2 minutes. Drain and cool the chives under cold running tap water. Squeeze tightly to remove excess water and cut each piece into 2-inch lengths (when using other vegetables, cut them into the same 2-inch pieces).

Place equal amounts of the garlic chives in a neat disk shape in individual small serving bowls. Pour the *ponzu* sauce over and garnish the top with the julienned bonito fish flakes.

Kon'nyaku Yuzu Miso Dressing

Kon'nyaku no yuzu-miso-zoe

Kon'nyaku is a humble-looking, gelatin-like cake, made from a plant in the taro family called *kon'nyaku imo.* It has a resilient texture, and although it has no distinctive flavor and no calories, it is rich in dietary fiber. At the store, you will find two varieties of *kon'nyaku*—one for cooking and one for consuming raw. The one for cooking simply needs to be put into a hot bath over medium heat for almost 1 hour. The raw edible type, called *sashimi kon'nyaku,* is cut into *sashimi*-like thin slices. Both the hot and cold types are served with a *yuzu miso* sauce (page 81); the former is a winter preparation, and the latter is a summer dish.

WINTER PREPARATION

MAKES 4 SIDE DISHES

2 cakes *kon'nyaku* (taro gelatin) for cooking (9 ounces each), cut into quarters crosswise
¼ cup sweet white *miso*-based *yuzu miso* sauce (page 81)
Yuzu (*yuzu* citron) or lemon rind, grated (optional)

Bring a medium potful of water to a boil. Thread each piece of *kon'nyaku* onto a bamboo skewer. Lower the *kon'nyaku* pieces into the pot and cook, over low heat, for 1 hour.

Remove the *kon'nyaku* from the water, drain, and serve on the bamboo skewers topped with 1 tablespoon *yuzu miso* sauce per skewer. If you like, garnish with a dab of grated *yuzu* or lemon rind.

SUMMER PREPARATION

MAKES 4 SIDE DISHES

1 cake *sashimi kon'nyaku* (taro gelatin for *sashimi*), (7 ounces)
¼ cup brown *miso*-based *yuzu miso* sauce (page 81)
2 tablespoons dried *wakame* (*wakame* sea vegetable), reconstituted in cold water for 15 minutes and drained
½ cup chive sprouts or other seed sprouts
½ teaspoon *shoyu* (soy sauce)
½ teaspoon toasted sesame oil

Cut the *kon'nyaku* into paper-thin slices, using the *sogi-zukuri* technique (page 218), to make a total of 20 slices. Arrange equal amounts of the *kon'nyaku* slices on four serving plates, with the slices slightly overlapping. Place a tiny drop of the *yuzu miso* sauce on each slice.

Toss the *wakame* and chive sprouts in a bowl, add the soy sauce and sesame oil, and mix thoroughly. Garnish the plates with equal amounts of the *wakame* and chive sprouts.

Fava Beans and Green Peas with Black Sesame Dressing
Soramame to grinpisu no kurogoma-ae

Black sesame seeds, which are richer in flavor and more fragrant than the white variety, make a wonderful dressing. In early summer, I dress fava beans and green peas this way. The bright green vegetables will have an interesting smudged appearance (see page 237)—and they taste so good. Cooked spinach, asparagus, broccoli, broiled and peeled eggplant, fresh green *edamame* soybeans, or string beans are all good done this way.

1½ cups shelled fava beans, from 1¼ pounds unshelled beans

Salt

1 cup fresh green peas, shelled

SESAME DRESSING:

¼ cup plus 1 tablespoon black sesame seeds

1 tablespoon *shoyu* (soy sauce)

3 tablespoons *dashi* (fish stock) (page 74)

1 teaspoon sugar

Bring a medium potful of lightly salted water to a boil. Add the fava beans and cook for 3 minutes. Drain and cool the beans in a bowl of cold water. Drain again, then peel off the skins.

Fill the pot with water again and bring to a boil, add some salt, and cook the green peas for 1 minute. Drain and drop them into a bowl of lukewarm water (to prevent the peas from wrinkling).

Heat a skillet over medium-low heat. When hot, toss in the sesame seeds and toast them until plump, about 1 to 2 minutes. Transfer them to a Japanese *suribachi* mortar (page 53) or to a food processor and process while hot until the seeds turn to paste and begin to exude some oil. If your food processor cannot do this job thoroughly, after processing for some time, transfer the seeds to a porcelain mortar and grind them. Add the *shoyu,* 2 tablespoons *dashi,* and sugar and grind well. Add the remaining *dashi* and mix well.

Drain the green peas and wipe them dry with a paper towel. Toss them with the fava beans and dressing. Place equal amounts of the salad in four small serving bowls.

Red Onion and Bonito Flakes with *Ponzu* Dressing
Murasaki tamanegi to katsuobushi no ponzu-ae

This superquick onion salad is great to add to your daily menu. The story about the slaves who built the Egyptian pyramids being fed with onions and garlic is well known. Modern research has also confirmed that onions contribute to our health in many ways. They increase HDL ("good") cholesterol, inhibit the formation of blood clots, help regulate blood sugar, increase the flexibility of blood vessels, fight asthma, increase appetite, and build up energy. Red onions taste best in this very pristine and simple Japanese preparation.

MAKES 4 SERVINGS

1 large red onion (about 7 ounces)
2 tablespoons *wakame* (*wakame* sea vegetable), soaked in water for 15 minutes
¼ cup *ponzu* sauce (page 78)
¼ cup shelled pistachio nuts or pine nuts, toasted and chopped
¼ cup *ito-katsuo* (julienned bonito flakes)

Peel the red onion and cut it crosswise into *paper*-thin slices. Soak the onion slices in a bowl of cold water for 30 minutes, changing the water several times. Drain the onion slices and put them in a salad spinner to dry. Drain the reconstituted *wakame* and squeeze to remove excess water.

Arrange equal portions of the *wakame* in mounds in four serving bowls. Place equal amounts of the onion slices on top and pour 2 tablespoons *ponzu* sauce over each bowl. Garnish with the pistachio nuts and bonito flakes.

Eggplant with *Yuzu Miso* Sauce
Nasu no dengaku

When cooked in oil, eggplant tends to absorb quite a bit of the oil, but the excellent flavor compensates for the few extra calories. Here I shallow-fry eggplant for a short period and top it with *yuzu miso* sauce. The sauce cuts some of the oiliness and allows the creamy texture of the eggplant to come through.

MAKES 4 SIDE DISHES

4 Japanese eggplants or 1 medium American eggplant
Vegetable oil for frying
½ cup brown *miso*-based *yuzu miso* sauce (page 81)
2 tablespoons white or black poppy seeds

Remove the stems of the eggplants and cut each in half lengthwise. With a small pointed knife, make several shallow cuts in a checkerboard pattern on the cut surfaces of each eggplant. If using the larger American eggplant, cut it into four disks crosswise and make several shallow checkerboard cuts on both cut surfaces.

Heat 1 inch of vegetable oil in a skillet and cook the eggplant over medium heat until the cut surface is golden. Turn the eggplant over and cook it through, about 3 minutes over medium-low heat. Drain the eggplant on a paper towel.

Serve equal amounts of the eggplant on four serving plates, with the *yuzu miso* sauce spread over the surface and topped with the poppy seeds in the center.

On the platter, left, Salmon Roe in Grated *Daikon* (page 222);
right, Eggplant with *Yuzo Miso* Sauce (page 236);
in back, Fava Beans and Green Peas with Black Sesame Dressing (page 235).

Kinpira Lotus Root
Kinpira renkon

Kinpira is a popular preparation: thinly sliced or julienned ingredients are quickly stir-fried in sesame oil; flavored with sugar, *shoyu* (soy sauce), and *shichimi togarashi* (seven-spice powder); and served, after resting, at room temperature. *Renkon,* lotus root, is a vegetable frequently used in this recipe, since it gives a pleasant crunchiness to the finished dish. If lotus root is not available, try using burdock, fennel bulbs, parsnip, carrot, or jicama.

½ pound *renkon* (lotus root), sliced (about 2 ¼ cups)
2 tablespoons grain vinegar, rice vinegar, or lemon juice
1½ tablespoons vegetable oil
2 tablespoons *sake* (rice wine)
1 tablespoon *mirin* (sweet cooking wine)
1 to 2 teaspoons sugar
1 tablespoon *shoyu* (soy sauce)
Tamari (*tamari* soy sauce)
2 tablespoons white sesame seeds
½ to 1 teaspoon *shichimi togarashi* (seven-spice powder) or chile pepper flakes

Peel the lotus root and cut it into paper-thin slices. Put 2 tablespoons vinegar and 1 quart cold water in a bowl and soak the lotus root for 20 minutes. Drain.

Heat the vegetable oil in a wok or large skillet over high heat, scatter in the lotus root, and cook, stirring, for 1 to 2 minutes. Add 3 tablespoons water and the *sake, mirin,* and sugar and cook until the liquid is absorbed. Add the soy sauce and cook until it is absorbed, stirring continuously. Season the mixture to taste with *tamari.* Toss in the sesame seeds and seven-spice powder and give several large stirs. Total cooking time in the wok or skillet is no more than about 3 to 4 minutes (overcooking damages the lotus root's crispiness and appearance).

This dish tastes better when it has rested (prepare it half a day in advance) and is served at room temperature. Arrange equal mounds of the lotus root in four to six small serving bowls.

Fresh Vegetable Sticks with Spicy *Miso* Dip
Nama yasai to karamiso sosu

Cucumber, carrot, celery, cabbage, endive, scallion, bell peppers—they are all excellent to eat fresh and raw. In this dish (see page 213), I serve the vegetable sticks with a *miso*-based dip that I always make rather spicy. Remember that *miso* is high in sodium, so do not eat too much of the sauce no matter how tasty it is.

SPICY *MISO* DIP:

9 ounces pork belly meat or ground pork, fatty part

1 tablespoon sesame oil

2 tablespoons minced ginger

2 tablespoons minced garlic

1 tablespoon *toban jiang* (Chinese chile bean sauce)

5 tablespoons sugar

1/2 cup *akamiso* (brown *miso*)

1 tablespoon *sake* (rice wine)

2 tablespoons *mirin* (sweet cooking wine)

1/3 cup chopped walnuts or peanuts

1/3 cup minced parsley

1/2 small cabbage, cut into quarters

2 Kirby cucumbers (6 inches long), partially peeled, leaving some strips of skin along the cucumber, and cut into halves

1 small green bell pepper, stemmed, seeded, and cut into 8 strips

1 small red bell pepper, stemmed, seeded, and cut into 8 strips

1 medium carrot, peeled, cut into 1/2-inch-square sticks, about 5 to 6 inches long

Chop the pork belly fine. Heat the sesame oil in a skillet until hot. Add the ginger, garlic, and *toban jiang* and stir with a wooden spatula until fragrant, about 20 seconds. Add the pork and cook until it is white, stirring continuously. Add the sugar and cook until it melts and caramelizes. Add the *miso, sake,* and *mirin* and cook until it is no longer watery. Add the nuts and parsley and give several large stirs.

Arrange the vegetables on a platter and serve with the spicy *miso* dip in a cup on the side.

Grilled Eggplant with *Yuzu-kosho* Dressing
Yaki nasu

During the summer and autumn, I love to serve eggplant in this way. I cook the eggplant directly on a gas flame until the flesh is tender and creamy and the outside develops a smokiness. Then I remove the skin, cut up the flesh into bite-size pieces, and serve it with home-made *ponzu* sauce spiced with a little *yuzu-kosho* (salt-cured green chile spiced *yuzu* paste). The dish is quite simple, but it does require flavorful freshly picked eggplants, preferably from your local area.

2 medium American eggplants (each about 5 to 6 ounces)

1/3 cup *ponzu* sauce (page 78)

2 teaspoons vegetable oil

Yuzu-kosho (salt-cured green chile spiced *yuzu* paste) (page 227)

2 tablespoons scallion rings or coriander leaves, chopped

Remove the frill around the stem of each eggplant and then make a very shallow cut through the skin where the frill was located. Make 4 to 5 more very shallow cuts along the length of the eggplant (these cuts make peeling the skin easier). Place the eggplant on a steel grill and set it directly over a gas flame. Cook the eggplant over medium heat, rotating it from time to time, until the whole surface is lightly charred and the flesh is cooked through and tender (poke with a small knife to check). Transfer the eggplant to the sink and peel it—but do not rinse with water. Cut each eggplant in half lengthwise, then each half into thirds lengthwise. Now cut the eggplant strips into thirds crosswise. Mound up equal amounts of the eggplant in four small serving bowls and refrigerate until eggplants are cold.

Whisk the *ponzu,* vegetable oil, and green chile paste, *yuzu kosho* (to taste), in a bowl. Spoon the dressing over the eggplant. Garnish the top of the eggplant with scallion rings before serving.

Vegetables in *Namban* Dressing
Yasai no namban-zuke

I introduced you to the preparation of *namban* in the preceding chapter (page 228). Any fresh vegetables taste wonderful done this way—asparagus, eggplant, bell peppers, endives, radicchio, fennel bulbs, zucchini flowers, mushrooms. Use your own imagination and what is available. Everything must be very fresh and in season, so that the cooking time is short, preserving the full flavor, aroma, and color of each vegetable. The prepared dish tastes better after it has been refrigerated overnight.

NAMBAN MARINADE:

2/3 cup *komezu* (rice vinegar)
1/3 cup *dashi* (fish stock) (page 74)
1/4 cup sugar
2 tablespoons *shoyu* (soy sauce)
1 teaspoon salt
2 *akatogarashi* (Japanese dried red chile peppers) or other small dried red chile peppers

Vegetable oil for deep-frying
2 baby fennel bulbs, about 3 ounces each, cut in half
1 medium red bell pepper (about 5 1/2 ounces), stemmed, seeded, and cut into 2- × 1-inch rectangles
2 red onions (about 5 1/2 ounces each), cut into 1/2-inch-thick rings
2 endives, about 3 ounces each, cut in half lengthwise

Bring the vinegar, *dashi,* sugar, soy sauce, and salt to a simmer in a medium pot, stirring. Transfer the marinade to a medium-size flat-bottomed container and add the chile peppers.

Wipe all the vegetables with a paper towel to remove as much water as possible so they won't spatter excessively in the hot oil. Heat 1 1/2 inches of vegetable oil to 330° F in a deep-bottomed skillet, scatter the fennel bulbs in, and cook over medium-low heat until they are lightly golden, or for 2 minutes. With a slotted spoon, take out the fennel bulbs, drain, shake to remove as much oil as possible, and transfer to the marinade. Cook and marinate the red bell pepper, onion, and endive in the same way, one variety at a time.

Arrange equal amounts of the vegetables on four small salad plates and spoon some of the remaining marinade over the vegetables.

Spinach *Ohitashi* Dressing
Horenso no ohitashi

*O*hitashi is a dish that consists of quickly blanched spinach, chrysanthemum leaves, or other green leafy vegetables served in *ohitashi* dressing—a mixture of *dashi* (fish stock), *shoyu* (soy sauce), and *mirin* (sweet cooking wine). Because the dressing uses no oil, this preparation highlights the purest and cleanest flavor of the vegetable.

And here is a special treat. Early every spring, we in New York and the surrounding regions are blessed with the appearance of scallionlike ramps in the market. This is a delightful wild vegetable, which is available in my locale for only a few weeks each year. It has a *very* strong garlic flavor that is moderated (but not eliminated) by cooking. I have found that ramps are wonderful prepared in this *ohitashi* style.

Here I use spinach and fresh, grilled *shiitake* mushrooms for added flavor. You can prepare it with any green leafy vegetable.

OHITASHI DRESSING:
1/2 cup *dashi* (fish stock) (page 74)
1 teaspoon *usukuchi shoyu* (light-colored soy sauce) or ordinary *shoyu* (soy sauce)
1 teaspoon *shoyu* (soy sauce)
2 tablespoons *mirin* (sweet cooking wine)
1/4 teaspoon salt

1 pound spinach, with roots attached, well washed
6 fresh *shiitake* mushrooms (2 1/2 ounces), preferably *donko* (the meaty, plump, thick variety), or brown mushrooms
1 *yuzu* citrus fruit or lemon

Pour the *dashi,* soy sauce, *mirin,* and salt into a small saucepan and bring to a simmer. Transfer the *dashi* mixture to a small cup and cool to room temperature.

Bring a large potful of lightly salted water to a boil, add the spinach, and cook for 1 minute. Drain and rinse under cold running water. Squeeze the spinach firmly to remove excess water. Cut off and discard the roots of the spinach, then chop the leaves and stems into 2-inch lengths.

Cook the *shiitake* mushrooms on a steel mesh grill over low heat on top of a gas stove until they are lightly brown. If you don't have a mesh grill, cook under the broiler about 1 minute each side. Remove from the heat and cut them into thin slices.

Toss the spinach and mushrooms in a bowl with 2 tablespoons of the *ohitashi* dressing. Let stand for 5 minutes. Gently squeeze the vegetables to remove the dressing, discarding the dressing. Return the vegetables to the bowl and toss them again with a new round of the remaining *ohitashi* dressing, about 2 tablespoons. Squeeze juice of the small *yuzu* or lemon to taste into the bowl.

Mound up equal amounts of the salad in four small serving bowls and garnish with julienned *yuzu* or lemon rind.

Okra Salad
Okura no sarada

When midsummer comes, light green okra, one of my favorite vegetables, appears in many dishes in Japan. If you have never cooked okra before, try this dish for a start. It is a simple, quick recipe that does not encourage the okra to produce its distinctive sliminess but rather helps it maintain a pleasantly firm texture. If okra is not available, use other vegetables such as string beans, bell peppers, or asparagus.

30 pods *okura* (okra), about 10 ounces
1/2 teaspoon sea salt
1 tablespoon vegetable oil
1/2 tablespoon butter
1 teaspoon *shoyu* (soy sauce)

Cut off the stems of the okra pods. Bring plenty of water in a medium pot to a boil, add a little salt and the okra, and cook for 10 seconds. Drain the okra and cool in a bowl of cold water with ice cubes for 30 seconds or so. Drain again and wipe dry with a paper towel. Cut each okra pod in half diagonally.

Heat a heavy-bottomed skillet, add the vegetable oil, and when hot, toss in the okra and cook over medium-high heat until the cut surfaces are lightly golden, stirring from time to time. Stir in the butter and quickly toss. Remove from the heat and add the *shoyu* (soy sauce can easily burn and become bitter), then set the skillet back on the heat briefly and give several tosses.

Spoon equal amounts of the okra into four small serving bowls.

Fried Leek in Piping Hot *Tempura* Broth
Age-dashi riiku

Slow-braised leeks American-style is one of my favorite wintertime vegetable dishes. Here I treat the leek in the Japanese way: boiled, fried, and served in a hot *tempura* broth. The broth removes the oiliness, at the same time adding wonderful flavor to the sweet leek. Grated *daikon* radish is an essential accompaniment to this dish.

MAKES 4 SERVINGS

TEMPURA BROTH:

1⅓ tablespoons *mirin* (sweet cooking wine)

1 cup *dashi* (fish stock) (page 74)

2½ tablespoons *usukuchi shoyu* (light-colored soy sauce) or ordinary *shoyu* (soy sauce)

¾ tablespoon *shoyu* (soy sauce)

¾ tablespoon sugar

4 leeks, cleaned and cut into 2-inch-long pieces, discarding the green tops

4 strips of bacon, cut in half lengthwise

¼ cup potato starch

Vegetable oil for frying

¼ cup *daikon oroshi* (grated *daikon* radish) (page 75)

1 tablespoon grated ginger

Put all the *tempura* broth ingredients in a saucepan and bring to a boil. Remove from the heat. You can store the broth for one week, covered and refrigerated.

Bring plenty of water in a medium pot to a boil, add the leeks, and cook for 3 minutes. Drain the leeks and gently squeeze to remove excess water. Cut the pieces of leek in half crosswise, then in half lengthwise. In order to hold the layers together, wrap each piece with a strip of bacon and insert a toothpick to secure the end. Wipe the leek pieces with paper towel and dredge them in the potato starch.

Heat 2 inches of vegetable oil in a deep skillet to 340° F. Fry the leek pieces in batches until the outsides are lightly golden, about 30 seconds to 1 minute. Drain them on a steel rack and remove the toothpicks. Finish cooking all the leek pieces. Have the *tempura* broth in a saucepan simmering over low heat.

Cut the bacon-strip-rolled leeks into bite-size pieces and put equal amounts in four serving bowls. Pour ¼ cup hot *tempura* broth into each bowl and garnish the top with the grated *daikon* radish and ginger.

Quick Stir-Fried Cabbage
Kyabetsu no itame-mono

Cabbage is good for our health, but it is bulky and hard to eat raw. So I quickly stir-fry it with brown *miso.* Cooking intensifies the sweetness of the cabbage, which is balanced with the salty *miso.* It is a simple and hearty dish. You can add carrots, bean sprouts, Chinese chives, or scallions for extra color, flavor, and texture.

MAKES 4 SERVINGS

1 tablespoon sesame oil and $1/2$ tablespoon vegetable oil
$1/4$ small cabbage ($1/2$ pound), cut into $11/2$-inch cubes
2 to 3 large garlic cloves, sliced
$1/2$ teaspoon *toban jiang* (Chinese chile bean sauce)
1 tablespoon *akamiso* (brown *miso*)
Freshly ground white pepper powder
Shoyu (soy sauce)

Heat a wok or a large skillet, then add the sesame and vegetable oils. When it is hot, add the cabbage and cook over medium heat, stirring and turning over the leaves, until the cabbage begins to wilt. Push the cabbage to one side, add the garlic and *toban jiang,* and cook until fragrant, about 20 seconds, stirring. Add the brown *miso* and mix with the garlic and *toban jiang.* Push the cabbage back into the center and toss, coating the leaves with the *miso* sauce. Sprinkle on white pepper, then taste, adding a little soy sauce, if needed. The whole stir-frying process should be done in about 2 to 3 minutes, so the cabbage stays crisp.

Place equal amounts of the cabbage on four small plates.

Stir-Fried Carrot and Parsnip
Ninjin to pasunippu no itame-mono

I had never tasted parsnips until I moved to America and quickly fell in love with this carrot-shaped winter vegetable. It tastes particularly great cooked in the Japanese style. Here I stir-fry it—not a quick stir-fry but a slow one.

MAKES 4 SERVINGS

1 tablespoon sesame oil and $1/2$ tablespoon vegetable oil
$1/2$ pound parsnips, peeled and julienned, 3 inches long (about $21/2$ cups)
1 medium carrot (about $31/2$ ounces), peeled and julienned, 3 inches long (about 1 cup)
2 tablespoons *sake* (rice wine)
1 tablespoon *mirin* (sweet cooking wine)
Pinch sugar
1 tablespoon *shoyu* (soy sauce)
$1/3$ cup pine nuts or sliced almonds

Heat the sesame and vegetable oils in a wok or large skillet over high heat. Add the parsnip and carrot and cook, turning the heat to medium-low, stirring occasionally, until they are lightly golden. Turn the heat to high, add the *sake, mirin,* and pinch of sugar and cook, stirring, until almost all the liquid is absorbed. Add the soy sauce and cook for 30 seconds. Toss in the pine nuts and give several large stirs.

Place equal amounts of the vegetables in four small serving bowls.

Chapter 15

Soups

Miso Soup with Clams
Kai no miso-shiru

My favorite *miso* soup is made with clams, and the clam of choice in this country is a short-neck clam. Because the water in which the clams are cooked becomes richly flavored, *dashi* (fish stock) is not used as a base for the soup, but do not forget to add a piece of *kombu* (kelp) to the cooking water. Clams contain abundant vitamin B$_{12}$ and iron, so a cup of clam *miso* soup is good for you as well as being a delicious soup course.

MAKES 6 SERVINGS

12 ounces short-neck clams or other small hard-shell clams
Sea salt
One 3-inch-square *kombu* (kelp)
1 tablespoon *sake* (rice wine)
3 tablespoons to ¼ cup *shiromiso* (white *miso*)
½ cup thinly sliced scallion

Put the clams in a colander, set it in a large bowl of salted cold water (1 tablespoon salt to 1 quart water), and let stand for 2 to 3 hours to expel any sand the clams have ingested. Remove the clams from the water and scrub and rinse them under cold running water.

Put 5 cups water, the clams, and the kelp in a medium pot and bring to a simmer over medium heat, skimming off any foam that rises. Reduce the heat, add the *sake,* and cook, covered, until all the clams are open, 3 to 4 minutes.

Discard any unopened clams and the kelp. Strain the soup through a sieve lined with a double layer of paper towels. Return the broth and the clams in their shells to the pot and blend in the *miso* with a whisk.

Add the scallion rings, ladle the soup and clams into six small soup bowls, and serve immediately.

Clear Clam Soup
Kai no ushio-jiru

This is another version of clam soup. It is flavored only with *kombu* (kelp), sea salt, and some drops of *usukuchi shoyu* (light-colored soy sauce). Use a larger variety of hard clam such as cherrystone clams. Cooking them in water with a piece of good-quality *kombu* produces a rich, hearty broth that has real body. Spending a little more for the good *kombu* is a must.

MAKES 4 SERVINGS

10 *hamaguri* (hard-shell clams) (about 1½ pounds) or cherrystone clams
Sea salt
½ ounce *kombu* (kelp), 3 × 5 inches, soaked in 5 cups water for 1 hour
2 tablespoons *sake* (rice wine)
½ teaspoon *usukuchi shoyu* (light-colored soy sauce), preferably, or ordinary *shoyu* (soy sauce)
½ cup *kaiware* (*daikon* sprouts)
Rind of half *yuzu* or lemon, cut into thin strips

Put the clams in a colander, set it in a large bowl of salted cold water (1 tablespoon salt to 1 quart water), and let stand for 2 to 3 hours to expel any sand the clams have ingested. Scrub the shells with a brush and rinse under cold running water.

Put the kelp with its soaking water and the clams in a pot. Bring to a simmer and cook over medium heat, skimming off any foam that rises until the clams are all open. Remove the kelp and the clams from the pot, discarding any clams that do not open. Scrape each clam from its shell into a bowl and reserve along with four whole shells. Strain the clam broth into a bowl through a sieve lined with a double sheet of paper towels. Clean the pot, return the clam broth to it, and bring to a simmer. Add the *sake* and soy sauce to the broth. After the broth comes to a simmer again, turn the heat to very low and return the clams along with the four shells.

Bring a small saucepan of water to a boil. Tie the bottoms of the stems of all the *daikon* sprouts together with cooking thread or a rubber band. Drop them into the boiling water and cook for 2 seconds. Remove and cut off the bottoms of the lower stems, including the cooking thread or rubber band.

To serve, place 1 clamshell containing 2 clams in each of four soup bowls and ladle in equal portions of the soup. Add the *daikon* sprouts and garnish the top with *yuzu* or lemon rind strips.

Miso Soup with Crab
Kani no miso-shiru

For this soup, choose any small crab, such as blue crab or Shanghai crab, to make a richly flavored soup. The crabs give their all to the soup, so there will not be much crabmeat to enjoy. The choice of very fresh (not frozen) crabs, live if possible, is the key to success for this dish. Here I flavor the soup with *shiromiso,* white *miso,* which is less strong than *akamiso,* brown *miso,* and is not as sweet as *Saikyo shiromiso,* sweet white *miso.*

MAKES 6 SERVINGS

3 small blue crabs
5 cups *dashi* (fish stock) (page 74)
3 tablespoons to 1/4 cup *shiromiso* (white *miso*)
1/2 cup *kaiware* (*daikon* sprouts) or watercress leaves
Freshly ground black peppercorns

Bring a medium potful of water to a boil. Add the crabs and cook about 30 seconds. Remove them from the boiling water and rinse them under cold running water. Tear off the apron from each crab, separate the shell from the leg part, and remove the gills, discarding the apron, shell, and gills. Cut each crab into quarters.

Put the cold *dashi* and the crab pieces into a fresh pot, set it over medium heat, and cook for 10 minutes. Add the *miso,* whisking until it is dissolved.

Serve equal portions of the soup in six soup bowls with the crab pieces garnished with the *kaiware.* Grind some black pepper over the top. Serve immediately.

Seafood *Miso* Soup
Kaisen miso-shiru

For this soup, I include salmon and shrimp along with diced vegetables to make a full-meal dish. You can create similar flavorful soups using leftover seafood from your sushi preparation.

MAKES 4 SERVINGS

Sea salt

20 medium shrimp (31 to 35 count per pound), in shells

¼ pound boned salmon, cut into 1-inch cubes

1 tablespoon vegetable oil

½ cup carrot, cut into ¼-inch cubes

½ cup celery root, cut into ¼-inch cubes

½ cup potato, cut into ¼-inch cubes

½ cup onion, cut into ¼-inch cubes

4 cups *dashi* (fish stock) (page 74)

¼ cup *Saikyo shiromiso* (sweet white *miso*)

1 tablespoon *akamiso* (brown *miso*)

1 teaspoon *toban jiang* (chile bean sauce)

Freshly ground black pepper

Bring a medium potful of lightly salted water to a boil, add the shrimp, and cook for 30 seconds. Drain and peel off the shells. Blanch the salmon in the same way and drain.

Heat the vegetable oil in a medium pot, add all the cubed vegetables, and cook over medium-low heat for 1 minute, stirring. Add the *dashi* and cook, covered, until the vegetables are soft, about 15 minutes. Add the salmon and shrimp and cook for 3 minutes. Add the *miso* and *toban jiang,* whisking until it is dissolved.

Serve equal portions of the soup in four soup bowls. Grind some black pepper over the top.

Ginger-Spiced *Kabocha* Squash Soup
Kabocha no miso-shiru

This modern *kabocha* soup is especially good during cold winter months. *Kabocha* squash is a turban-shaped dark green squash that originally came from South America but today is largely known as a Japanese vegetable. Its bright orange flesh becomes smooth, creamy, and very sweet when it is cooked. Adding ginger juice to this soup will drive away the winter chill.

MAKES 4 SERVINGS

10 ounces peeled and seeded *kabocha,* cut into large pieces

1 medium peeled carrot (3 ½ ounces), cut into large pieces

½ ounce *kombu* (kelp), about 3 × 4 inches

3 to 4 tablespoons *Saikyo shiromiso* (sweet white *miso*)

¼ teaspoon salt

1 tablespoon freshly squeezed ginger juice (page 122)

1 tablespoon scallion rings

Put the *kabocha* squash, carrot, and kelp in a medium pot along with water to cover. Set it over medium heat and cook for 10 minutes. Discard the kelp and continue cooking the vegetables until tender, another 10 to 15 minutes. Remove from the heat and let cool.

When cool, purée the vegetables and the liquid in a food processor. Add the *miso* and salt and process until the *miso* is dissolved.

Return the puréed vegetables to the pot and add as much water as needed to make 4 cups. Heat the soup and add the ginger juice.

Serve equal portions of the soup in four soup bowls, garnished with scallion rings.

Sliced Pork and Root Vegetable *Miso* Soup
Ton'jiru

My mother frequently made this very hearty, body-warming rustic *miso* soup during the winter. In this recipe, I use potato, carrot, *gobo* (burdock), *daikon* radish, and *kon'nyaku* (taro gelatin). If any one of these vegetables is not available, substitute root vegetables from your local market.

MAKES 4 SERVINGS

1 tablespoon vegetable oil
5 ounces pork belly, cut into paper-thin 1- × 2½-inch rectangles*
1 medium potato, peeled, cut into 1- × ½-inch cubes, soaked in cold water for 15 minutes
½ medium carrot (3 ounces), cut into 1- × ½-inch cubes
½ *gobo* (burdock), cut into 1- × ½-inch cubes and soaked in cold water
5 ounces *daikon* (*daikon* radish), cut into 1- × 1½-inch cubes
1 cake *kon'nyaku* (taro gelatin), cut into 1- × 1½-inch cubes
¼ cup *akamiso* (brown *miso*)
¼ cup finely sliced scallion or chopped coriander leaves

*For a less fatty soup, use pork chops without bone.

Heat the vegetable oil in a medium pot over medium heat. When hot, add the sliced pork and cook, stirring, until the meat turns white. Add all the vegetables except the scallion and cook, stirring, until they are coated with the oil. Pour in 6 cups water and cook over medium heat, covered, for 20 minutes. Whisk in the *miso* until dissolved and cook another 30 seconds.

Serve the soup piping hot in four soup bowls, garnished with the scallion rings.

Chilled *Edamame* Soup
Hiyashi edamame-jiru

In addition to the summertime enjoyment of eating boiled *edamame* (green soybeans) accompanied by a cold beer, you can make a delicious and attractive *edamame* soup. This is the kind of soup that cools your body and offers good nutrients when your appetite is down during the hot, humid summer. I add a dash of crème fraîche, which gives the soup an attractive contrasting appearance—stark white against the deep green.

MAKES 4 SERVINGS

14 ounces shelled *edamame* (green soybeans), fresh or frozen
4 cups *kombu dashi* (kelp stock) (page 74)
2 teaspoons sea salt
¼ cup crème fraîche or heavy cream
Coarse sea salt

Put the *edamame* and kelp stock in a pot and bring it to a simmer. Cook the beans until tender, about 6 minutes. Purée the beans with the cooking liquid in a food processor with the sea salt. Press the puréed bean soup through a fine sieve into a jar. If you wish, you can omit this step, but the sieved soup has a smoother, creamier texture. Add the sea salt and refrigerate for half a day.

Serve the soup in four small soup bowls with a dollop of crème fraîche in the center of each bowl. Sprinkle some additional coarse sea salt over to taste.

Pouring the strained egg mixture into cups

Traditional Egg Custard Soup
Chawan-mushi

*C*hawan-mushi, egg custard soup, is so popular in Japan that there are porcelain cups with lids made specifically for preparing this soup dish. *Chawan-mushi* may resemble a Western sweet custard dessert in appearance, but this soup is much more tender, looser in texture, and savory with fragrant *dashi* (fish stock) flavor. It also contains small morsels of fillings, such as fish, chicken, shrimp, or vegetables—the choice is up to you and the season. If Japanese *chawan-mushi* cups are not available, use 1-cup-size ramekins. Ramekins are actually quite thick, though, so the cooking time must be extended. Steaming produces the best results, but you can also cook this dish in the oven. I include instructions for both ways.

MAKES 4 SERVINGS

1 thin chicken breast fillet, cut into eight ½-inch slices crosswise, 1½ inches long
4 medium shrimp (41 to 50 count per pound), heads removed, peeled, and deveined
2 fresh *shiitake* mushrooms (preferably the plump and meaty *donko* variety) or brown mushrooms

CUSTARD BASE:
3 large eggs
1½ cups *dashi* (fish stock) (page 74)
1½ teaspoons *usukuchi shoyu* (light-colored soy sauce), preferably, or ordinary *shoyu* (soy sauce)
1½ teaspoons *mirin* (sweet cooking wine)
Sea salt

2 *mitsuba* (trefoil) stalks, cut into 1-inch lengths, or ½ cup baby spinach
Rind of ½ *yuzu* citron or lemon, finely grated

Set a steamer over high heat. If you are using the oven, preheat it to 320° F.

Bring a small saucepan of water to a boil and blanch the chicken pieces until the outsides turn white, about 5 seconds. Remove them from the water and rinse under cold running water. Drain the chicken and wipe dry with a paper towel. Do the same quick blanching for the shrimp. Cut each *shiitake* mushroom in half. Spoon equal portions of the chicken, shrimp, and mushroom into four *chawan-mushi* cups or ramekins or 1-cup-size Pyrex dishes.

Break the eggs into a bowl and beat gently with a pair of chopsticks. Add the *dashi,* soy sauce, *mirin,* and salt (to taste) and stir to mix thoroughly. Strain the egg mixture through a sieve into a measuring cup, then pour equal amounts into each cup or ramekin. Transfer the cups to a heated steamer and cook for 15 minutes. For the first 1 to 2 minutes, have the heat high, then reduce it to medium and cook the custard an additional 13 minutes. Maintaining the temperature this way ensures that the texture of the soup custard is silky smooth. If the trapped steam reaches a temperature of 190° F inside the steamer, the egg protein coagulates quickly, leaving many tiny air pockets in the custard, and the resulting custard will have a rough appearance and texture.

To cook the custard in the oven, place the filled ramekins or Pyrex dishes in a deep oven pan. Pull out the oven rack, set the pan on it, and pour 1 inch of hot water into the pan. Bake for 40 to 50 minutes. The time varies depending on the thickness of the cups that you are using.

Two minutes before the custard is supposed to be removed from the steamer or oven, check for doneness by inserting a wooden skewer in the center. Clear liquid should run out of the custard soup when it is done. If not, cook a few minutes longer. Place equal amounts of the *mitsuba* on top of each custard soup and cook 1 minute more.

Remove the custard from the steamer or oven and decorate the top with the grated *yuzu* rind. Cover each cup with a lid or saucer and serve hot with small teaspoons.

Sea Urchin Egg Custard Soup
Uni chawan-mushi

This is a special-occasion egg custard soup made with *uni* (sea urchin). The flavor is rich, so I make it in small espresso cups (ovenproof) and serve it as one part of an appetizer course. If you cannot obtain good-quality sea urchin or if you believe your guests might prefer a different ingredient, use good-quality crabmeat. Cook either in a steamer or in a pan of boiling water in the oven.

4 ounces *uni* (sea urchin) (pages 139 and 182) or 2 ounces good-quality crabmeat

CUSTARD BASE:

3 large eggs

1½ cups *kombu dashi* (kelp stock) (page 74)

¾ teaspoon *sake* (rice wine)

¾ teaspoon *mirin* (sweet cooking wine)

¾ teaspoon *usukuchi shoyu* (light-colored soy sauce), preferably, or ordinary *shoyu* (soy sauce)

2 tablespoons heavy cream

Sea salt

½ cup *sake* (rice wine)

9 rock shrimp, cut in half

1 large scallop, cut in half crosswise and then into cubes of the same size as the rock shrimp

1 tablespoon *wasabi* paste

4 teaspoons *tsuke-joyu* (sushi dipping sauce) (page 77)

Press 2 ounces of the sea urchin through a fine sieve into a paste and set the remaining whole sea urchins aside to use for decoration. You will have about 2 tablespoons of sieved sea urchin paste.

Heat the oven to 325° F. Have a large pot of boiling water at hand. Break the eggs into a bowl and lightly beat with chopsticks or a whisk. Add the kelp stock, sea urchin paste, ¾ teaspoon *sake, mirin,* soy sauce, cream, and salt to taste.

Pour ½ cup *sake* into a small skillet and bring it to a simmer. Add the rock shrimp and cook until the outsides turn white, about 30 seconds. Scoop out the rock shrimp with a slotted spoon and cook the scallop pieces in the same way. Drain the seafood and wipe with a paper towel. Place equal amounts of the seafood (except the whole sea urchins reserved for decoration) in nine espresso cups. If using crabmeat, distribute it among the cups now.

Strain the egg mixture through a fine sieve and pour into each espresso cup. With a paper towel, remove any bubbles floating on top of the egg liquid. Put the espresso cups in a pan about 2 inches deep and pull out the oven rack. Carefully pour 1 inch of boiling water into the pan and cook for 30 minutes. To check for doneness, insert a wooden skewer into the center. Clear liquid should run out of the custard when it is done. If the liquid is not clear, cook a few minutes longer.

Garnish the top of each cup with a piece of whole sea urchin and place a tiny dab of *wasabi* paste on top. Pour 1 teaspoon warmed *tsuke-joyu* into each cup. Serve immediately.

Crisp Sea Bream Chips (page 224) and bowls of Sea Urchin Egg Custard Soup (page 250)

Kabosu Sherbet with Green Tea Cookies
Kabosu shabetto to ocha no kukki

Like *yuzu, kabosu* is one of the small citrus fruits of Japan that is used only for its very strong and fragrant juice. The juice makes a wonderful, refreshing ice dessert. Small bottles of the plain juice are sold in Japanese food stores and other large markets.

I got the idea of serving green tea cookies with this dessert both because I like biting into a cookie that gives respite from the cold sensation of sherbet in the mouth and because I wanted to use up the two egg yolks left over from making the sherbet. The bittersweet green tea of the cookies complements the sweet and sour *kabosu* flavor very nicely.

KABOSU SHERBET

MAKES 12 SERVINGS

1 teaspoon unflavored gelatin powder (about 1 package)
½ cup plus 2 tablespoons sugar
2 tablespoons brandy
¼ cup *kabosu* juice or a mixture of lemon and lime juice
2 whites from large eggs (reserve the egg yolks for the cookies)
⅛ teaspoon salt

Dump plenty of ice cubes in a large bowl with some water. Pour 2 tablespoons of water into a small cup and sprinkle in the gelatin powder. Pour 2 cups of water into a medium pot with ½ cup sugar and set it over medium heat. Cook, stirring with a spoon, until the sugar is dissolved. Add the brandy, *kabosu* juice, and gelatin and continue to cook until the gelatin is dissolved. Transfer the liquid to a stainless steel bowl and set it in the large bowl with ice cubes. When it is cold, put the bowl in the freezer.

Bring a large pot of water to a simmer. Pour the egg whites, salt, and remaining 2 tablespoons sugar into a medium stainless steel bowl and whisk over the pot of simmering water until firm peaks are formed, about 10 minutes. Transfer the bowl to a bowl of cold water with some ice cubes. Continue to whisk until the egg white cools off.

Remove the bowl of *kabosu* juice (it will have just started to freeze) from the freezer, add the egg whites, and mix thoroughly with a whisk. Return the bowl to the freezer and freeze for 4 hours, stirring once every hour.

GREEN TEA COOKIES

MAKES 24 COOKIES

3 ounces butter, softened at room temperature
¼ cup sugar
2 yolks from large eggs (reserved from the sherbet recipe)
¾ cup cake flour
2 teaspoons *matcha* green tea powder, sifted (page 37)
¼ cup *sen-cha* green tea (page 36)
Pinch salt

Preheat the oven to 375° F.

Put the softened butter in a bowl and whisk until creamy. Add the sugar in three batches, whisking each time until the mixture is fluffy. Add the egg yolks, one at a time, and continue mixing. Add ¼ cup of the flour, *matcha* tea powder, *sen-cha* tea leaves, and a pinch of salt and continue to mix well with the whisk. Add the remaining flour and mix with a wooden spatula.

Place the dough in a pastry bag with a ½-inch-diameter tip and squeeze the dough out into 24 small balls onto a parchment-lined or nonstick oven cookie sheet with 2 inches of space between. With slightly moistened fingertips, lightly press the center of each dough ball to make it into a flat 1½-inch disk. Put the pan in the preheated oven and bake for 18 minutes. Remove the cookies to a steel rack and let them cool.

Clockwise, starting top right:
Kabosu Sherbet with Green Tea Cookies (page 252);
Chilled *Azuki* Gelatin Squares in a bamboo leaf (page 256);
Chilled Sesame Pudding with strawberries (page 254)

Chilled Sesame Pudding
Goma kuzu yose

This dessert uses arrowroot starch, *kuzu,* a popular sweets ingredient in Japan. Arrowroot starch, among all other starches, produces the clearest and stickiest mixture when cooked. As a small child, whenever I began to catch cold or was running a temperature, my mother would make me a home remedy of slightly sweetened arrowroot starch soup. It always seemed to help me get well quickly.

In this recipe, arrowroot starch, nutty-sweet white sesame paste, milk, and cream are bound together into a silky, firm pudding (see page 253). Serve it with molasses syrup.

MOLASSES SYRUP:
1/2 cup brown sugar
1/4 cup granulated sugar

2 cups whole milk
1/4 cup heavy cream
1/2 cup Japanese white sesame paste
    or tahini (3 ounces)
2 tablespoons *kuzu* (arrowroot starch)
    (1 ounce)
2 cups small strawberries

Make the molasses syrup first. Put the brown sugar and granulated sugar into a medium pot with 1 1/4 cups of water and set over medium heat, stirring. When the sugar is dissolved, turn the heat to low and cook until the liquid is slightly thickened.

Mix together in a bowl the milk, cream, and sesame paste, stirring with a whisk until the sesame paste is all dissolved. Do not beat. Strain the milk mixture through a finely woven steel sieve, using a wooden spoon to press the lumpy parts of the sesame paste through. Add the arrowroot starch and mix thoroughly.

Transfer the mixture to a medium shallow pot, set it over medium heat, and stir continuously with a wooden spatula. It will become sticky in 2 to 3 minutes. Turn the heat to low and cook, stirring continuously, for 15 minutes.

Have at hand a large bowl of cold water with plenty of ice cubes. Line eight teacups with strong plastic wrap (thin wrap may break from the heat). Pour equal portions of the sesame mixture into the teacups. Pick up the edges of the plastic wrap, squeeze to remove air, and secure the neck tightly with a bag tie. Put the plastic-wrapped ball in the ice water to cool quickly. Repeat with the remaining seven packages. Chill the sesame puddings in their plastic wrappers in the refrigerator.

Just before serving, remove the plastic wrap and serve the sesame pudding with strawberries in individual glass dessert bowls with molasses syrup poured over them.

How Arrowroot Came to America

The *kuzu* plant, *Pueraria lobata,* has been cited in many poems since the eighth century in Japan. Its beautiful reddish purple flower, which blooms from summer through early autumn, made a vivid impression on our ancestors. The plant belongs to the pulse family, and its vines can grow up to 60 feet long.

Unfortunately, the plant today has a horrible reputation in the United States, where it is known as kudzu. It was imported from Japan in 1876 as part of a display by the Japanese government at the U.S. Centennial Exposition held in Philadelphia. It immediately attracted attention for its lovely leaves and blossoms and quickly became an ornamental plant. By the 1920s, it was being sold by a Florida nursery as nutritious animal forage, and in the 1930s, recognizing kudzu's ability to control soil erosion, the U.S. government actually paid farmers to plant it. But then things got out of hand. With no natural enemies and an ideal growing climate in the southeastern United States, more than 7 million acres were swamped with kudzu, and by the 1970s, the U.S. government declared it a "weed." The plant continues to proliferate despite attempts at control and eradication. It is a classic story of the unintended consequences of introducing nonnative animal and plant species into the environment.

Chilled Arrowroot Noodles in Molasses Syrup
Kuzukiri

Semitransparent chilled arrowroot noodles dipped in molasses syrup are a favorite sweet during the summertime. The dish resembles a stream of flowing water, and it brings a feeling of coolness to all who partake. Commercially made arrowroot starch noodles, ready to cook, are available at Japanese food stores. But making the noodles from scratch, as I do here, is very easy and fun.

3 1/2 ounces *kuzu* (arrowroot starch) (about 1/2 cup)
1 large white or yellow peach, pitted and cut into thin wedges
1 cup blueberries and raspberries mixed
Molasses syrup (page 254)

Mix the arrowroot starch in a bowl with 1 1/2 cups water. Make sure that the starch is completely dissolved. Strain through a fine sieve into a bowl.

Have at hand a large bowl of water with lots of ice cubes. You will also need a metal pan, about 8 inches square and 1 1/2 inches deep, and a large pot, about 4 inches deep, into which the square metal pan can fit comfortably. Bring plenty of water (about 2 1/2 inches deep) in the large pot to a boil and keep it simmering over medium heat. Scoop part of the arrowroot mixture up with a ladle and spread it evenly in a 1/8-inch-thick layer in the metal pan. Lower the pan into the simmering water and let it float on top. Cook until the arrowroot starch liquid becomes half translucent and set. Now carefully submerge the pan in the boiling water, allowing the water to seep into the pan. The arrowroot layer will quickly turn transparent. Remove the pan from the water, pouring off the water in the pan, and quickly transfer it to the bowl of ice-cold water. When the arrowroot has cooled, peel it from the pan in a single sheet and place it on a chopping board. Cut the sheet into 8-inch-long noodles about 1/6 inch wide. Repeat the process until the arrowroot water is all used.

Serve the arrowroot noodles in four small glass bowls barely submerged in ice water with ice cubes, garnished with equal portions of the peach slices and berries. Serve the molasses syrup in individual small cups on the side. Pick up some noodles or fruit, dip them into the molasses syrup, and enjoy a cooling Japanese summer treat.

Japanese White Sesame Paste

The Japanese version is different from other white sesame pastes—tahini or Chinese sesame paste. It is sweet with no bitterness and has a silky smooth texture and fragrance. Avoid the Chinese sesame paste, which contains additives such as other oil or sugar.

Chilled *Azuki* Gelatin Squares
Mizu yokan

½ stick *bo-kanten* (agar-agar), broken
  into 1-inch-long pieces
1 envelope unflavored gelatin powder
3½ ounces *koshi-an* (sweet *azuki* bean
  powder)
1 cup sugar

Wherever you go across Japan—from large cities to tiny country towns—you will find fine artisan sweetshops. Chilled *azuki* bean gelatin squares, *mizu yokan,* are a delicacy that can be bought at any of these Japanese sweetshops in summer. However, the flavor and texture of *mizu yokan* differ considerably from one store to another, because of the choice of *azuki* beans, the quality and volume of sugar used, and, of course, the skill of the artisan. I miss the wonderful *mizu yokan* from my local Tokyo shop, which was always wrapped in fresh, bright green cherry leaves. But since I am too far away from my source today, I make my own and am very proud of them (see illustration on page 253).

You need a 6- × 6-inch metal mold, or use a similar-size baking pan or Pyrex dish.

Soak the agar-agar pieces in a bowl of cold water for 30 minutes. Pour ¼ cup of water into a small bowl and dissolve the gelatin in it, about 5 minutes. Drain the agar-agar in a strainer, pressing hard to remove excess water. Put the agar-agar with 1¼ cups of water into a medium pot and cook over medium heat, stirring with a wooden spoon, until all lumps disappear. Remove the pot from the heat.

Place the *azuki* bean powder with 1 cup of water and the sugar in another medium pot, set it over medium-low heat, and cook for 2 minutes, stirring continuously with a wooden spatula. Remove from the heat.

Return the pot with the agar-agar liquid to medium heat and mix in the *azuki* paste. When all the ingredients are well mixed, add the dissolved gelatin and cook, stirring, until it dissolves. You should now have about 2⅔ cups of the *azuki* mixture. Let it stand for 5 minutes.

Wet a square pan with cold water, pour in the warm *azuki* mixture, leveling the surface by shaking the mold right and left, and cool to room temperature. Cover the mold with plastic wrap and refrigerate overnight.

Remove the *azuki* gelatin from the mold, cut it into squares, and serve in individual small cups.

Oven-Steamed Chocolate Cake with *Sake* Apple
Chokoreto keki to ni ringo

When I worked with Kristin Eycle-shymer, a pastry chef, at one of my book events, she suggested that we prepare my steamed chocolate cake recipe in the oven rather than in a bamboo steamer. The slow rate of steam production in the oven turned my usually light and spongy cake into a pleasantly moist and dense one. Since then, I have been using the oven cooking method.

The sauce served with this chocolate cake is made from apples cooked with *sake*. For apples, I have been using Pink Ladies, a sweet yet tart local variety. For the best results, find an apple that has a balanced acidity and sweetness.

MAKES 8 SERVINGS

1 cup cake flour
½ cup *joshinko* (rice flour)
¾ teaspoon salt
12 ounces bittersweet chocolate, broken into rough pieces
¼ cup bitter orange marmalade, smooth
¼ cup orange liqueur
6 large eggs, separated
⅓ cup sugar

SAKE APPLE SAUCE:
6 large tart/sweet-flavored apples, peeled, cored, and cut into small pieces
2 star anise
6 cloves
1 cinnamon stick
3 cups *sake* (rice wine)
1 cup sugar
Juice from 1 lemon

Preheat the oven to 350° F. Have at hand a kettle full of boiling water. You will also need a square oven pan, about 2½ inches deep, into which you can put your cake mold. Butter an 8-inch cake mold, dust lightly with flour, and refrigerate.

Sift together into a medium bowl the cake flour, rice flour, and ½ teaspoon salt. Place the chocolate in a bowl with ¼ cup cold water and put it in a pot of simmering water. Let the chocolate melt, stirring from time to time. Remove the chocolate from the heat and add the marmalade and orange liqueur. Add the egg yolks one at a time, stirring.

Beat the egg whites in a bowl with ¼ teaspoon salt and ⅓ cup sugar until soft peaks form. Stir one-quarter of the egg whites into the chocolate mixture and mix with a whisk. With a wooden spatula, fold in the remaining egg whites gently but thoroughly. Fold in the flour mixture. Pour the batter into the baking mold and set it in the deep pan. Place the pan containing the baking mold on the oven rack and carefully pour boiling water into the pan until the water level reaches half the height of the mold. Bake the cake for 40 to 50 minutes. To check for doneness, insert a bamboo skewer in the center. When it comes out dry, the cake is done. Let cake cool in the mold.

Meanwhile, make the *sake* apple sauce. Put the apples, star anise, cloves, and cinnamon stick in a large pot and pour the *sake* over them. Add cold water until the apple pieces are barely submerged. Cook the apples, covered, over medium-low heat until tender, about one hour. Add the sugar and lemon juice and continue to cook, uncovered, until the liquid is cooked away and the apples are almost mashed, an additional 30 minutes. Transfer the cooked apples to a bowl and remove the cloves, cinnamon stick, and star anise, discarding them. Cool the *sake* apple sauce, then cover the bowl and refrigerate until used.

Cut the cake into bite-size wedges and serve on plates with chilled *sake* apple sauce on the side.

Kiwi and Egg White Gelatin
Kiui no hosetsu-kan

Hosetsu literally means "light snow." This is a stunning-looking double-decker, two-colored—green and snow-white—chilled dessert. The upper snow-white layer is composed of egg white that has been beaten to a fluffy foam and jellied with agar-agar. When you bite into this part, tiny bubbles of egg white foam burst and quickly disappear in your mouth. The lower green layer is made from kiwi and jellied with agar-agar and Western-style gelatin.

You need an 8- × 8-inch metal or plastic mold or cake pan. Before using the mold, rinse it with cold water so you can easily remove the set agar-agar jelly.

LOWER KIWI LAYER:

½ stick *bo-kanten* (agar-agar), broken into 1-inch pieces, soaked in cold water 30 minutes
¼ cup plus 2 tablespoons sugar
1 tablespoon brandy
1 envelope unflavored gelatin powder, soaked in 2 tablespoons water
5½ kiwis, 4 puréed and 1½ cut into 16 thin disks

UPPER EGG WHITE LAYER:

1 stick *bo-kanten* (agar-agar), broken into 1-inch pieces, soaked in cold water 30 minutes
¼ cup plus 2 tablespoons sugar
1 tablespoon lemon juice
2 small egg whites mixed with ⅛ teaspoon salt and 2 tablespoons sugar

Mint leaves

To make the kiwi layer: Drain the soaked agar-agar in a strainer and press to remove excess water. Put the agar-agar with 2 cups water in a medium pot, set it over medium heat, and bring to a boil. Reduce to a simmer and cook, stirring occasionally, until the agar-agar fibers are dissolved. Add the sugar and brandy, and cook, stirring, until the sugar is dissolved. Continue to cook over medium-low heat for another 10 minutes. Add the gelatin and cook until dissolved. You should now have about 1⅔ cups.

Have at hand a pan of ice-cold water with plenty of ice cubes. Transfer the agar-agar liquid to a bowl and add the puréed kiwi. Place the bowl in the large pan of cold water and stir with a spatula to cool it off briefly. Run the cake mold under cold water, drain, and pour the kiwi mixture into it, leveling the surface with a plastic spatula. It will begin to jell quite quickly. Let the mold rest in the large pan of cold water with ice cubes.

To make the egg white layer: Drain the agar-agar and press in a strainer to remove excess water. Place the agar-agar with 2 cups water in a medium pot, set it over medium heat, and bring it to a boil. Reduce to a simmer and cook, stirring, until the agar-agar fibers are all dissolved. Add the sugar and cook until the sugar is dissolved. Continue to cook over medium-low heat another 10 minutes. Stir in the lemon juice. Transfer the agar-agar liquid to a large bowl.

Put the egg whites, salt, and sugar in a stainless steel bowl and whisk over a pot of simmering water until firm peaks are formed. Remove from the simmering water and set the bowl over a large bowl of cold water. Whisk the egg whites until they cool. Add ⅓ of the cooled egg white to the agar-agar liquid, whisking continuously. Then add the remaining egg white, whisking continuously. Again, put the bowl into the larger bowl of cold water with ice cubes and continue whisking until the egg white and agar-agar liquid cools and doubles in size. Immediately pour the egg white liquid over the kiwi layer in the mold, smooth the surface with a plastic spatula, cover with plastic wrap, and refrigerate for 3 hours.

Remove the gelatin cake from the mold and cut into sixteen squares. Decorate the top of each square with a slice of kiwi and mint leaves.

Sources for
Japanese
Food Products

Sources for
Japanese
Kitchen Equipment

Bibliography

Index

Sources for Japanese Food Products

ARIZONA

FUJIYA MARKET
1335 W. University Dr., No. 5
Tempe
AZ 85281
480-968-1890

NEW TOKYO FOOD MARKET
3435 W. Northern Ave.
Phoenix
AZ 85051
602-841-0255

99 RANCH MARKET
668 N. 44th St.
Phoenix
AZ 85008
602-225-2288

CALIFORNIA

EBISU SUPERMARKET
18930–40 Brookhurst St.
Fountain Valley
CA 92708
714-962-2108

MITSUWA MARKETPLACE
665 Paularino Ave.
Costa Mesa
CA 92626
714-557-6699

333 S. Alameda St.
Los Angeles
CA 90013
213-687-6699

3760 Centinela Ave.
Los Angeles
CA 90066
310-398-2113

4240 Kearney Mesa Rd., No. 119
San Diego
CA 92111
858-569-6699

515 W. Las Tunas Dr.
San Gabriel
CA 91776
626-457-2899

675 Saratoga Ave.
San Jose
CA 95129
408-255-6699

21515 Western Ave.
Torrance
CA 90501
310-782-0335

99 RANCH MARKET
651 N. Euclid St.
Anaheim
CA 92801
714-776-8899

15333 Culver Dr., No. 800
Irvine
CA 92604
949-651-8899

5402 Walnut Ave.
Irvine
CA 92604
949-651-8888

250 Skyline Plaza
Daly City
CA 94015
650-992-8899

SAKAI K. UOKI COMPANY
1656 Post St.
San Francisco
CA 94115
415-921-0514

SURUKI SUPERMARKET
71 E. Fourth Ave.
San Mateo
CA 94401
650-347-5288

CONNECTICUT

FUJI MART CORPORATION GREENWICH
1212 E. Putnum Ave.
Old Greenwich
CT 06878
203-698-2107

FLORIDA

ISEYA ORIENTAL MARKET
5623 SW 107th Ave.
Miami
FL 33173
305-274-7284

JAPANESE MARKET
1412 79th St. Causeway
N. Bay Village
FL 33141
305-861-0143

NOBUKO'S FAR EASTERN BAZAAR
73 Sailfish Dr.
Atlantic Beach
FL 32233
904-241-4758

GEORGIA

FOOD MART INOUE
6253 Peachtree Industrial Blvd.
Doraville
GA 30360
770-454-9234

99 RANCH MARKET
5150 Buford Hwy.
Doraville
GA 30340
770-458-8899

TOMATO JAPANESE GROCERY
2086 Cobb Pkwy.
Smyrna
GA 30080
770-933-0108

7124 Peachtree Industrial Blvd.
Norcross
GA 30071
770-263-7838

HAWAII

99 RANCH MARKET
1151 Mapunapuna St.
Honolulu
HI 96819
808-833-8899

ILLINOIS

MITSUWA MARKETPLACE
100 E. Algonquin Rd.
Arlington Heights
IL 60005
847-956-6699

KENTUCKY

SMITH'S ORIENTAL FOOD STORE
1587 N. Dixie Blvd.
Radcliffe
KY 40160
270-351-9588

MARYLAND

DARUMA
6931 Arlington Rd., Ste. E
Bethesda
MD 20814
301-654-8832

HAN AH REUM ASIAN MART
800 North Rolling Rd.
Catonsville, MD 21228
443-612-9020

12015 Georgia Ave.
Wheaton, MD 20902
301-942-5071

MASSACHUSETTS

CHERRY MART
349 Newbury St. #B
Boston
MA 02115
617-437-1939

KOTOBUKIYA
1815 Massachusetts Ave.
The Porter Exchange Bldg.
Cambridge
MA 02140
617-354-6914

MIRIM ORIENTAL GROCERIES
152 Harvard Ave.
Allston
MA 02134
617-783-2626

YOSHINOYA
36 Prospect St.
Cambridge
MA 02139
617-491-8221

NEVADA

99 RANCH MARKET
4701 S. Cameron St., No. F
Las Vegas
NV 89103
702-252-0666

4155 W. Spring Mountain Road
Las Vegas
NV 89102
702-364-8899

NEW JERSEY

DAIDO MART
1385 16th St.
Fort Lee
NJ 07024
201-944-0020

HAN AH REUM ASIAN MART
1720 Rt. 70 E.
Cherry Hill
NJ 08003
856-489-4611

25 Lafayette Ave.
Englewood
NJ 07631
201-871-8822

260 Bergen Tpk.
Little Ferry
NJ 07643
201-814-0400

321 Broad Ave.
Ridgefield
NJ 07657
201-943-9600

MITSUWA MARKETPLACE
595 River Rd.
Edgewater
NJ 07020
201-941-9113

NY Mutual Trading Inc.
(restaurant supply)
25 Knickerbocker Rd.
Moonachie
NJ 07074
201-933-9555

NEW MEXICO

A-1 ORIENTAL MARKET
1410 Wyoming Blvd. NE
Albuquerque
NM 87112
505-275-9021

NEW YORK

DAIDO
522 Mamaroneck Ave.
White Plains
NY 10605
914-683-6735

FISH-ONE SEAFOOD CENTER
71-45 Yellowstone Blvd.
Forest Hills
NY 11375
718-544-0942

FUJI MART SCARSDALE
816 White Plains Rd.
Scarsdale
NY 10583
914-472-1468

HAN AH REUM ASIAN MART
29-02 Union St.
Flushing
NY 11354
718-445-5656

141-40 Northern Blvd.
Flushing
NY 11354
718-358-0700

400 Hillside Ave.
Williston Park
NY 11596
516-699-0270

KATAGIRI
224 E. 59th St.
New York
NY 10022
212-755-3566

SUNRISE MART
4 Stuyvesant St., 2nd Fl.
New York
NY 10003
212-598-3040

494 Broom St.
New York
NY 10013
212-219-0033

NORTH CAROLINA

HATOYA MARKET
605 E. North Polk St.
Pineville
NC 28134
704-889-6600

LOTTE ORIENTAL STORE
4211 South Blvd.
Charlotte
NC 28209
704-527-8949

TOYO SHOKUHIN
748 E. Chatham St., Ste. L
Cary
NC 27511
919-319-1620

OREGON

PACIFIC FARM (*WASABI*)
P.O. Box 51505
Eugene
OR 97439
800-927-2248 Ext. 313
www.freshwasabi.com

SUNRISE ASIAN MARKET
70 W. 29th Ave.
Eugene
OR 97405
541-343-3295

UWAJIMAYA
10500 SW Beaverton-Hillsdale Hwy.
Beaverton
OR 97005
503-643-4512

PENNSYLVANIA

HAN AH REUM ASIAN MART
1138 Bristol Oxford Valley Rd.
Levittown
PA 19057
215-949-1003

7320 Old York Rd.
Elkins Park
PA 19027
215-782-1801

7050 Terminal Square
Upper Darby
PA 19082
610-734-1001

MIDORI MART
2034 Chestnut St.
Philadelphia
PA 19103
215-569-1200

TOKYO JAPANESE FOOD STORE
5853 Ellsworth Ave.
Pittsburgh
PA 15232
412-661-3777

SOUTH CAROLINA

ORIENTAL IMPORTS
1305 Laurens Rd.
Greenville
SC 29607
864-235-6089

TENNESSEE

ORIENTAL BEST MARKET
3588 Ridgeway Rd.
Memphis
TN 38115
901-366-1570

TEXAS

NIPPAN DAIDO
11146 Westheimer Rd.
Houston
TX 77042
713-785-0815

VIRGINIA

HAN AH REUM ASIAN MART
10780 Lee Hwy.
Fairfax
VA 22030
800-427-9870

8103 Lee Hwy.
Falls Church
VA 22042
703-573-6300

NANIWA FOODS
6730 Curran St.
McLean
VA 22101
703-893-7209

WASHINGTON

ASIA ORIENTAL MARKET
2408 Meridian St.
Bellingham
WA 98225
360-671-0446

MARUTA SHOTEN
1024 S. Bailey St.
Seattle
WA 98108
206-767-5002

UWAJIMAYA BELLEVUE
15555 NE 24th St. & Bel Red Rd.
Bellevue
WA 98007
425-747-9012

UWAJIMAYA SEATTLE
600 5th Ave. S.
Seattle
WA 98104
206-624-6248

ONLINE VENDORS

ESAKÉ, WWW.ESAKE.COM (*SAKE*)

WWW.VINECONNECTIONS.COM

WWW.WASABIFARM.COM

WWW.FRESHWASABI.COM

WWW.ASIANFOODGROCER.COM

WWW.ETHNICFOODSCO.COM

WWW.SHOPPING.COM

Sources for Japanese Kitchen Equipment

KATAGIRI
224 E. 59th St.
New York
NY 10022
212-755-3566

KORIN
57 Warren St.
New York
NY 10007
800-626-2172 (toll-free)
212-587-7021

MITSUWA MARKETPLACE
See under California in
Sources for Japanese
Food Products

NY MUTUAL TRADING, INC.
(restaurant supply)
25 Knickerbocker Rd.
Moonachie
NJ 07074
201-933-9555

SOKO HARDWARE
1698 Post St.
San Francisco
CA 94115
415-931-5510

WWW.EKITRON.COM

WWW.ITKITCHENKNIFE.COM

WWW.KITCHENKNIVES.COM
800-338-6799

Bibliography

Foods Bio Technology Jiten (Foods Bio Technology Encyclopedia). Tokyo: Sangyo Chosakai Jiten Shuppan Center.

Hideaki Ohta, Takeo Shiina, K. Sasaki. *Shokuhin Sendo Tabegoro Jiten* (Food Freshness Encyclopedia). Tokyo: Science Forum, 2002.

Hiroko, Shimbo. *The Japanese Kitchen: 250 Recipes in a Traditional Spirit.* Boston: Harvard Common Press, 2000.

Hirotaka, Matsumoto. *New York Takezushi Monogatari* (New York Takezushi Story). Tokyo: Asahi Shimbunsha, 1995.

Hisao, Nagayama. *Tabemono Edoshi* (Edo Period Food History). Tokyo: Shin-jin'butsu Oraisha, 1976.

Japan Tea Industry Central Committee. *Shintei: Ryokucha no Jiten* (New Edition: Green Tea Encyclopedia). Tokyo: Shibata Shoten, 2002.

Junji, Watanabe. *Ryori Hyakka Tokushu: Sushi—Jinzo Ikura no Fushigi* (Miracle of Imitation Salmon Roe). Tokyo: Shibata Shoten, 1997.

K., Higuchi. *Shinpan Nihon Shokumotsu-shi* (New Edition: Japan Food History). Tokyo: Shibata Shoten, 1959.

Makoto, Fukue. *Sushi no Rekishi* (Sushi History). Tokyo: Tokyo Sushi Academy, 2004.

Masa-aki Takeuchi, Takeo Fujii, Masakatsu Yamazawa. *Suisan Shokuhin no Jiten* (Fishery Products Encyclopedia). Tokyo: Asakura Shoten, 2000.

Masao Fujimaki, Hiroshi Miura, Ken'ichi Ohtsuka, Shunji Kawabata, Susumu Kimura. *Shokuhin Kogo* (Industrial Food). Tokyo: Kosei-sha Koseikaku, 1985.

Masuo, Yoshino. *Sushi, Sushi, Sushi Sushi no Jiten* (Sushi Encyclopedia). Tokyo: Asahiya Shuppan, 1990.

Mitsutoshi, Hibino. *Sushi Gurume no Rekishi-gaku* (Sushi Gourmet History). Gifu: Gifu City History Museum, 1992.

Nihon Chori Kagaku Gakkai-ron. *Sogo Chori Kagaku Jiten* (Integrated Cooking Science Encyclopedia). Tokyo: Koseikan, 1997.

Nihon Fuzokushi Gakkai-ron. *Zusetsu Edo-jidai Shokuseikatsu* (Illustrated Edo Period Food and Life Encyclopedia). Tokyo: Yuzankaku, 1978.

Nori Omoshiro Yomihon (Nori Story). Saga: Shin Umai Saganori Tsukuri Undo Suishin Honbu, 2002.

Ryori to Shoku Shirizu (Cooking and Food Series—Sushi). Tokyo: Asahiya Shuppan, 1998.

Sadao, Maneyama. *Edomae-zushi ni Ikiru* (Devoted to Preserve Edomae-zushi Tradition). Tokyo: Asashi Shuppan, 2003.

Shinya, Iwasaki. *Sekai ni Hirogaru Nihon no Su no Bunka* (Japanese Rice Vinegar Culture Spread Worldwide). Tokyo: Mizkan Group, 2003.

Shinzo, Satomi. *Sukiyabashi Jiro Shun o Nigiru* (Sukiyabashi Jiro: Nigiri-zushi in Season). Tokyo: Bungei Shinju, 1997.

Shio no Hon (The Salt Book). Tokyo: Shibata Shoten, 1998.

Shoji, Konosu. *Sakana no Kagaku Shirizu* (Fish Science Series: Food Science). Tokyo: Asakura Shoten, 1994.

Shokuhin Sogo Kenkyujo Henshu. *Shokuhin Daihyakka Jiten* (Food Encyclopedia). Tokyo: Asakura Shoten, 2001.

Shokuzai Zuten: Food's Food (Illustrated Food Ingredients Encyclopedia: Food's Food). Tokyo: Shogakukan, 1995.

Takashi, Ichikawa. *Seikoho no Chakuso* (Business Tactics and Japanese Food History in America). Tokyo: Sangokan, 1996.

Takeo, Fujii. *Dento Shokuhin no Chie* (Wisdom in Traditional Food). Tokyo: Shibata Shoten, 1993.

Tomomi, Kawano. *Sakana I & II: Shin Shokuhin Jiten* (Fish I & II: New Edition—Food Encyclopedia). Tokyo: Shinju Shoin, 1991.

Yukiko, Honda. *Sushi Neta Zukan* (Illustrated Sushi Topping Encyclopedia). Tokyo: Shogakukan, 1997.

Yukio, Moro-oka. *Kanda Tsuruhachi Sushi Banashi* (Kanda Tsuruhachi Sushi Story). Tokyo: Soshisha, 1986.

Index

Page numbers in *italics* refer to illustrations.

ILLUSTRATION CREDITS

The illustrations on the following pages
are provided with the permission and
courtesy of the following:

Hiroko Shimbo: x, xiii, 4–5, 12, 15, 26, 28, 32, 47,
63, 139, 164, 167, 169–176, 178–183, 203, 205

Seikado Bunko Art Museum: x

Tokyo National Museum: xiv–1, 2, 6, 76

Takahiro Arakawa: 4, 5

Iris Weinstein: 27, 34, 38, 39

Ryoichi Matsushita, Mizkan Group: 62

Holly McNeely: 117

All other photographs are by Jim Smith.

A NOTE ON THE TYPE

This book was typeset in a font named
Gotham, designed by Tobias Frere-Jones at
Hoefler Type Foundry in New York.

Frere-Jones wanted Gotham to exhibit the
"mathematical reasoning of a draftsman"
rather than the instincts of a type designer.

In 2000, Tobias Frere-Jones undertook a
study of building lettering in New York,
inspiring the design of Gotham. It is an honest
and straightforward font that is neutral
without being clinical, authoritative without
being impersonal, and friendly
without being folksy.

COMPOSED BY
North Market Street Graphics,
Lancaster, Pennsylvania

PRINTED AND BOUND BY
Tien Wah Press,
Singapore

DESIGNED BY
Iris Weinstein